MODERNITY AND THE REINVENTION OF TRADITION

The idea of tradition seems a timeless one, but our modern understanding of the term was actually shaped by the Victorian revival of tradition as a cornerstone of religion, art and culture. Stephen Prickett traces how the word 'tradition' fell out of use in English by the middle of the eighteenth century and how it returned in the nineteenth having radically changed and gained in meaning. Prickett analyses the work of authors who, like Burke, perhaps unexpectedly, avoid use of the concept, as well as those who, like Coleridge, Keble and Newman, who, variously influenced by German Romantics, explored it in detail, and disagreed profoundly with each other as to its implications. An important contribution to literature, history and theology, this sweeping work shows how people manufacture their own idea of truth, customs, or ancient wisdom to make sense of the past in terms of a problematic present.

STEPHEN PRICKETT is Regius Professor Emeritus of English at the University of Glasgow. His many publications include *Origins of Narrative: The Romantic Appropriation of the Bible* (Cambridge University Press, 1996) and *Narrative, Religion and Science: Fundamentalism versus Irony, 1700–1999* (Cambridge University Press, 2002).

MODERNITY AND THE REINVENTION OF TRADITION

Backing into the Future

BY

STEPHEN PRICKETT

CAMBRIDGE UNIVERSITY PRESS

CAMBRIDGE UNIVERSITY PRESS

Cambridge, New York, Melbourne, Madrid, Cape Town, Singapore, São Paulo, Delhi

Cambridge University Press
The Edinburgh Building, Cambridge CB2 8RU, UK

Published in the United States of America by Cambridge University Press, New York

www.cambridge.org
Information on this title: www.cambridge.org/9780521517461

© Stephen Prickett 2009

First published 2009

Printed in the United Kingdom at the University Press, Cambridge

A catalogue record for this publication is available from the British Library

Library of Congress Cataloguing in Publication data
Prickett, Stephen.
Modernity and the reinvention of tradition : backing into the future / Stephen Prickett.
p.   cm.
Includes bibliographical references.
ISBN 978-0-521-51746-1 (hardback)
1. Tradition (Philosophy)–History.   2. Tradition (Theology)–History of doctrines.
3. Literature, Modern–19th century–History and criticism.
4. Literature, Modern–18th century–History and criticism.   I. Title.
B105.T7P75 2009
148–dc22   2009004698

ISBN 978-0-521-51746-1 hardback

Contents

Acknowledgements

The idea that tradition, as both word and concept, fell so far out of use during the seventeenth and eighteenth centuries, and underwent such a dramatic revival in the nineteenth and twentieth centuries is not in itself an inherently improbable discovery. What is improbable is that this decline and revival seems hitherto to have passed virtually unnoticed. None of the few books that discuss the history of the word and its meanings even suggest massive historical fluctuations in its fortunes. My first acknowledgement must therefore be to the anonymous referee at Oxford University Press who, on reading the manuscript of an article on 'Robert Lowth and the Idea of Tradition' (an early draft of Chapter 2 of this book) noted in an Olympian manner that Prickett's thesis, though he seemed to have found some circumstantial evidence for it, was 'inherently improbable'. It was this comment which convinced me that it was worth assembling what turned out to be an overwhelming mass of evidence – mostly, as we shall see, direct rather than circumstantial.

To name all of my friends and colleagues who have contributed in one form or another to this book would be impossible, but should mention professors Adina Ciugureanu, Miriam Elior, Jan Gorak, and Michaela Irimia, all of whom have helped or enlightened me on vital points. I must also record the invaluable assistance of the late Paul Jeffries-Powell, of the Glasgow University Department of Humanity, who made for me what I believe is the first, and probably only translation of Keble's 1839 Crewian Oration. I owe a vast debt to Bob Tennant, of the English Pulpit Project, who has amply confirmed my initial hunches with massive statistical evidence of the word's virtual absence in eighteenth-century religious polemics. I am also greatly indebted to Daniel Weidner, of the Berlin *Zentrum für Literatur-und Kulturforschung* who first gave me the opportunity to present my tentative theories on Herder to a German audience, corrected my German, and introduced me to some of his circle of fellow Herderians – in particular, Ernest

Menze. Finally I am deeply grateful to James Pereiro, who shared with me his essay on 'Tractarians and the Oxford Movement' – later to be included in his book *'Ethos' and the Oxford Movement* (Oxford University Press, 2008).

Behind these lie my Baylor University research assistants, Dana White and Jamie Crouse, who patiently combed swathes of eighteenth- and nineteenth-century literature, much of it unavailable in electronic form, in search of references to, and, more often, paraphrases of the concept. Without them this book simply would not exist. I can only hope that their unusual knowledge of specialist debates of the period stands them in good stead throughout their future academic careers. Finally, my heartfelt thanks to Christi Klempnauer and Scott Myers for producing a scan of the Bewick Jachet picture in the nick of time.

As mentioned above, part of Chapter 2 has appeared in *Sacred Conjectures: The Context and Legacy of Robert Lowth and Jean Astruc*, edited by John Jarrick (T & T Clark, 2007) and parts of Chapters 6 and 7 will appear in 'Translating the Spirit of Hebrew Poetry' in Daniel Weidner (ed.), *Urpoesie und Morgenland. J.G. Herders 'Vom Geist der Ebräischen Poesie'* (Kadmos Verlag, 2008).

Ancient & modern: the braid of Cassiodorus

Sometime in the year 580 the late Roman scholar, Cassiodorus, then in his ninety-second year, sat down to write a primer on spelling. During his lifetime he had been a senator, an eminent statesman and diplomat, a scholar, and, finally, a monk. In 535 he had laid plans with the most learned Pope of the age, Agapetus, to create a Christian university in Rome 'to match the flourishing state of secular studies with a corresponding institution for sacred letters'.[1] Nearly thirty years later, around 562, he still had sufficient hopes for the survival of classical learning to begin his great work, *Institutiones divinarum et saecularium litterarum*, with the aim of accommodating the Greek and Latin classics to an organized programme of Christian education.

A mere eighteen years later, he had to acknowledge that the monks in the monastery he had founded on his estate in southern Italy were functionally illiterate. 'When I was working on my *Complexiones* of the Apostles, monks suddenly began to clamour, "What use is it to us to know the thoughts of the ancients, or even your own, if we have no idea [*omnimodis ignoremus*] how to write them down? Neither can we read aloud things written in indecipherable script." '[2] In the changed circumstances

---

[1] A scheme which had collapsed with the untimely death of the Pope the following year, and Cassiodorus's subsequent exile in Byzantium. See R.A. Markus, *The End of Ancient Christianity* (Cambridge University Press, 1990), p. 217–18; James O'Donnell, *Cassiodorus* (University of California Press, 1979); Cassiodorus, *An Introduction to Divine and Human Readings by Cassiodorus Senator*, intro. and trs. L. W. Jones (Octagon 1966); and Stephen Prickett, *Reading the Text: Biblical Criticism and Literary Theory* (Blackwell, 1991), p. 6.

[2] Cassiodorus, *De orthographia* 143.1–6. See James O'Donnell:

'The very need for the textbook clearly shows us something of the state of affairs inside the Vivarium around 580. For comparison, we should first recall that Cassiodorus had already had something to say about the subject of correct spelling, in the *Institutiones*; in the chapter on copying manuscripts, after the careful instructions to observe the idioms of scripture, there follows about a page of orthographic instructions (*Inst.* i.15). The instructions are simple and very much to the point; they enjoin, for example, careful observation of the use of b and v, n and m, and -e and -ae endings. Some of what he advised was exotic as well, as his insistence that *narratio* be spelled with one r out of deference

Cassiodorus clearly had to cut his coat to suit the cloth. 'My purpose,' he writes in his introduction, 'is to plait together into one braid what ancient tradition has made available for proper use by modern custom, and to make it quickly and easily accessible. It is right to omit in this enterprise what is of merely antiquarian interest, so as to avoid requiring unnecessary and anachronistic labour, useless in the present age.'[3]

If before he had been in denial, Cassiodorus had now finally come to terms with the fact that the traditions and learning of the classical age, in which he had been brought up and played such a distinguished part, had finally passed away – and with it all dreams of institutions of scholarship, of higher education or the reading of the literature of the past. All that could now be hoped for was a basic literacy which might preserve the study of the Christian scriptures:

Farewell, brethren, and please remember me in your prayers. I have taught you, among other things, in a summary manner, the importance of correct spelling and punctuation, universally acknowledged to be a precious thing; I have prepared a full course of reading to assist you in the understanding of the holy scripture.[4]

To describe the new world of diminishing expectations and reduced resources in which he found himself at the end of his long life, Cassiodorus coined a new word: 'modern' (*modernus*).[5] Formed from *modo*, meaning 'just now', Cassiodorus takes as his analogy the word *hodiernus*, from the word *hodie* (today), meaning 'that is of today' (the origin of our English word 'diurnal'). In his new word we can, perhaps, detect a wistful hope that the conditions 'just now' prevailing were an aberration which would prove as temporary as it was regrettable. If so, it was to take between three

---

to its derivation (and he has his etymology right for once) from *gnarus* – not even the manuscripts of that particular passage obey him on that point. But in general at that stage, Cassiodorus was addressing serious problems faced by the best scribes of the period; his advice reflects not any local weakness of scribes but a general difficulty in the contemporary Latin culture. If we date that state of affairs to around 560, we can see how much things had changed by the time Cassiodorus came to write the *De orthographia*. We see first that the idea for the work came from someone else (as Cassiodorus always claimed except, significantly, for the *Institutiones*). The picture conjured up is striking and sufficiently unflattering to Cassiodorus and his enterprise to make us think there is truth in it. Consider the situation: Cassiodorus, in his tenth decade of life, the most senior and most revered member of the community, even if loved as much for his knowledge as for his sanctity, is approached by his monks to set down on paper a last volume of ideas for their benefit: a spelling book.'

Cassiodorus, Ch. 7.

[3] *De orthographia Praef.* (PL 70. 1241 D). Cited by Markus, *End of Ancient Christianity*, pp. 219–20.

[4] Ibid., *Concl.* (ibid., 1270B). Markus, *End of Ancient Christianity*, p. 220.

[5] See O'Donnell, *Cassiodorus*, p. 235; Markus, *End of Ancient Christianity*, p. 219.

hundred and a thousand years, depending on where you place the revival of learning, for that 'temporary' situation to disappear.[6] Meanwhile, what he had sadly termed 'modernity', has not gone away.

Given the poignancy of the occasion, it is unlikely to have been of great comfort to the elderly monk to realize that the 'ancient tradition' that was being so sadly reduced and attenuated by 'modern custom' was not quite the thousand-year riches of Greek and Roman literature that it might have seemed, but was itself little more than a century-and-a-half old. As we shall see, like all traditions, it had been created and projected into the past as an act of deliberate cultural appropriation.

What had been at stake from the fourth-century Church onwards was nothing less than its own identity. It had needed to demonstrate in ways both visible and symbolic its continuity with the persecuted Church of earlier centuries. Before the political success of the Catholics under Constantine, the many competing Christian sects had all been perse-cuted – some, the Donatists in North Africa, or the Nicene opposition under Arianising emperors, even more vigorously and savagely than the Catholics themselves. The Church that had finally emerged victorious had had to wrest the legacy of the persecuted saints and martyrs of the past from other possible claimants.[7] To this end Eusebius's great *Ecclesiastical History*, written in the first half of the fourth century, laid the greatest pos-sible stress on the traditions of the Church as constant, enduring and con-tinuous.[8] The rope or braid of hallowed tradition invoked by Cassiodorus had to be composed of as many separate strands as possible to be strong enough to bear the full weight of that heroic period to which the now-dominant Christians paid tribute and claimed as their heritage.

Thus this was not just a matter of history-writing. What had to be appropriated was nothing less than the Roman Empire itself. In R.A. Markus's words:

the territory of the Roman Empire was the spatial projection of an ancient cul-ture and alien religions with their own pasts. To appropriate its space, Christians needed to take imaginative possession of it: to annex its space as they had to annex their own past. But whereas that past had been their own, the topography of the Roman Empire was not. Their past they had to make their own like exiles returning to their homeland; the territory of the empire had to be colonised like a foreign land not long conquered. Like so many white settlers in Africa, they

[6] For many it would come with the twelfth-century rediscovery of Aristotle, and the creation of 'theology' as a distinct academic discipline by Abelard, thus allowing a world of secular logic and learning again to flourish in such universities as Paris.
[7] See Markus, *End of Ancient Christianity*, p. 85.　　[8] Ibid., pp. 91–2.

had to impose their own religious topography on a territory which they read as a blank surface, ignoring its previous religious landmarks and divisions. [9]

After the fall of Jerusalem and the destruction of the Jewish Temple in 70 CE, Christians had initially been quick to emphasize that *theirs* was a temple not made with hands. Irenaeus, at the end of the second century, roundly condemned the Ebionites, a surviving Jewish Christian sect, for still continuing to revere Jerusalem 'as if it were the house of God'. Similarly Augustine had been initially indifferent to the idea that one specific place might be more sacred than another. But increasingly by the fourth century, churches which had just come through persecution were defining what it meant to be a Christian in terms of martyrdom.[10] Church buildings were becoming repositories of the bones of the martyrs – places where saints (especially their local saints) could be venerated. Ambrose's new church in Milan, the *basilica Ambrosiana*, could not be consecrated without appropriate (and locally discovered) holy relics. The congregation wanted to be the spiritual descendants not merely of martyrs in general, but of their *own* local Milanese martyrs.[11]

For Ambrose's younger, North African contemporary, Augustine, the appropriation of the past had to include not merely the territory of the Roman Empire, but its culture as well. It was a world with less and less room for the purely secular,[12] and the justification of all values had to be clearly traceable to biblical roots. Just as the message of Philip to the Ethiopian in Acts 8, that the Jewish Scriptures had found their fulfilment in Christianity, allowed the Christians to appropriate – and re-arrange – the Jewish Scriptures to form their own Bible,[13] so, by the fourth century they claimed for themselves much of the writings of the former pagan world as well. Augustine's desire for a Christian culture supported by an educational programme emerged from a direct ideological confrontation with pagan claims of sole rights over a heritage to which Christians could only be seen as alien interlopers. Rejecting this claim, Augustine asserted Christian rights to borrow and to integrate whatever was valuable in the old classical culture into a new synthesis, now firmly based on a scriptural foundation.[14]

---

[9] Ibid., p. 142.

[10] See, for instance, Rowan Williams, *Why Study the Past? The Quest for the Historical Church*, Eerdmans, 2005, pp. 34–8.

[11] Markus, *End of Ancient Christianity* pp. 143–4.   [12] Ibid., p.15

[13] See Stephen Prickett, *Origins of Narrative: the Romantic Appropriation of the Bible* (Cambridge University Press, 1996), Part I.

[14] Markus, *End of Ancient Christianity*, p. 221.

Indeed, Cassiodorus himself, like his contemporary, Boethius, had joined in just such a programme of cultural appropriation with his *Institutiones* thirty years before. His first book had begun with a syllabus of sacred reading; the second with a course of study in the seven liberal arts, a knowledge of which he believed not merely helpful but essential for a proper understanding of Christian texts. This (to us) somewhat dubious affirmation was only the latest manifestation of the concerted and ongoing attempt to appropriate for Christ the whole of the literature of the pagan world.[15] Though Tertullian (b. c160?) had famously resisted this melding of classical and Jewish traditions, demanding 'What has Athens to do with Jerusalem?',[16] he was swimming against a powerful and strengthening tide. As early as Justin Martyr (d. 165), Socrates had been hailed as 'a Christian before Christ' – in the Middle Ages he was sometimes known as 'Saint Socrates'. Such claims were given greater substance around 200, when Clement of Alexandria helped to establish a school of Christian philosophy (the *Didascalia*) where Platonist theology, Aristotelian logic and Stoic ethics were melded into the biblical tradition with the historical claim that Plato and his fellow-philosophers had themselves studied the works of Moses and the Hebrew prophets. For numerous commentators, Virgil's Fourth *Eclogue*, with its prophecy of a child born under the sign of the Virgin who will be a great ruler, and bring peace and harmony even to predatory nature, was an unmistakable parallel to Isaiah 44, and a prophecy of the coming of Christ.[17] But what had begun as a series of isolated raids on classical literature had become with Augustine and his successors a full-scale occupation and settlement of once-undisputed pagan terrain. The tradition which Cassiodorus saw as being lost to the narrowness and illiteracy of modernity was one in which Christianity claimed to be the rightful inheritor of a thousand years of Jewish and classical traditions alike but, despite the implication that it was part of the natural order of things, it was, in effect, less than two centuries old.

---

[15] See the 'Epilogue' by P.G. Walsh to G.J. Kenney (eds.), *The Cambridge History of Classical Literature*, Vol. ii, part 5: *The Later Principate* (Cambridge University Press, 1982), pp. 107–8.

[16] *De Praescriptione Haereticorum*, 7

[17] See, for example, lines 22–5:

> *ipsae lacte domum referent distenta capellae*
> *ubera nec magnos metuent armenta leones;*
> *occident et serpens et fallax herba veneni*
> *occident.*

'The she-goats will bring home of their own accord their udders filled with milk, and the flocks will have no fear of great lions; the snake will be no more, no more too the deceptive poison plant.' (Translated by Professor Alden Smith, Baylor University, Texas.)

Moreover, both the older traditions so appropriated had been themselves, of course, equally retrospective and appropriative in their turn. The Talmudic tradition of interpretation and comment on the Hebrew scriptures, even then one of the oldest continuous traditions in the world, had also provided the ideology behind the arrangement of the actual books of the Hebrew Bible. This had originally been a matter of open choice, since before the invention of the codex, or single bound volume, each 'book' was a separate scroll that could be read in any order the reader chose. But though it offered a markedly different arrangement from the no less ideologically driven Christian Old Testament, the codex of the Hebrew Bible represented a 'tradition' that was in reality no older than the Christian version, since the work of creating the Hebrew canon only really began after the destruction of Jerusalem in 70 CE – by which time some of the New Testament books (Paul's letters, for instance) were certainly in existence.[18]

This Christian attempt to try and integrate the Jewish and Classical traditions was not the first time it had been attempted. The answer to Tertullian's question 'What has Athens to do with Jerusalem?' has been the subject of some debate. Edward Shils cites A.D. Momigliano to the effect that there was little cross-cultural exchange between the Jews and Greeks in the Hellenistic period.[19] Yet in fact, if we look at the Hellenistic period, Momigliano's own study shows considerable evidence of repeated attempts from the third century BCE onwards to claim a shared cultural lineage with the Greek world. There was at least a brief period around 300 BCE when Greek authorities were prepared to represent the Jews as philosophers, legislators and wise men.[20] More important, from the Jewish side, was the tradition attributed by both Josephus and Eusebius to the otherwise unknown second-century writer, Cleodemus Malchus, that among Abraham's many children were three sons who joined with Heracles in his war against the Libyan giant Antaeus. After his victory, the Greek hero had supposedly married the daughter of one of these sons of Abraham, whose name, Africa, was then given to the whole continent.[21] Presumably in reference to this same legend, 1 Maccabees 12. 20–23 has a correspondence between the Jews and Arius I, King of the Spartans, in which the

---

[18] See Stephen Prickett and Robert Carroll, Introduction to World's Classics Bible (Oxford University Press, 1997), p. xii.

[19] Edward Shils, *Tradition* (University of Chicago Press, 1981), p. 241; A.D. Momigliano, *Alien Wisdom: The Limits of Hellenization* (Cambridge University Press, 1975), pp. 97–132.

[20] Ibid., p. 92.

[21] Josephus, *Antiquities of the Jews*, trs William Whiston, 4 vols. (Glasgow 1818), Vol. 1, pp. 40–1. Eusebius, *Prophetric Extracts*, 9.20. 2–4.

latter acknowledge their kinship with the Jews, both being 'of Abraham's blood'. The story is again taken up by Josephus and, however doubtful the original legend, current scholarship seems inclined to think that at least the Spartan response is genuine enough.[22]

About 200 BCE, the biographer Hermippus accepted without difficulty the notion that Pythagoras had been a pupil of Jews and Thracians. The first Jewish embassy to Rome under Judas Maccabaeus in 161 BCE appears to have included the historian Eupolemus, whose Greek language history of the Jews had maintained that the Phoenicians, and consequently the Greeks, had learnt the art of writing from Moses.[23] Hermippus also records an exchange of letters between the twelve-year-old Solomon and his client kings Vaphes of Egypt and Suron of Tyre.[24] Aristobulus of Paneas allegorized Hebrew tradition in a dialogue in which Ptolemy VI, whose reign, 181–145 BCE, coincides with much of the translation of the Septuagint, asked questions about the Bible.

Commenting on such legends, Erich Gruen dismisses what might look like the obvious idea that these Jewish stories should be interpreted as an attempt at 'a ticket of admission to the Hellenic club'.[25] On the contrary, he argues, the naming of Abraham as the common forefather makes it plain that the Jews were trying rather to appropriate the Greeks to their *own* traditions rather than subordinating themselves to Hellenism.[26] The logical corollary of Hebrew monotheism was that just as in the Exodus stories, where Yahweh's power over the Egyptians had to be demonstrated, the new dominant Mediterranean force of Hellenism had to be seen also to acknowledge the only true God. In short, the claim was not so much a gesture towards Greek culture as yet another affirmation of the uncompromising nature of Judaism.

So far from being an exception, such examples are actually typical of the formation of the books of Hebrew scripture. Intensive investigation reveals not an Ur-text, but only layer upon layer of appropriation from older and yet older sources. Modern archaeology and comparative scholarship have shown something of the degree to which the Hebrew Bible had absorbed and appropriated earlier stories and beliefs from many surrounding cultures – Aramaic, Mesopotamian, Canaanite, and Egyptian.[27] Nor were

---

[22] Ibid., p. 10 (1 Macc. 12. 20–23; Josephus, *Antiquities*, 12.225–227).

[23] 1 Macc. 8.17.   [24] Eusebius, *Prophetic Extracts*, 9.31–4.

[25] As claimed by E.J. Bickerman, *The Jews in the Greek Age* (Harvard University Press), 1988. p. 184.

[26] Erich S. Green, 'Cultural Fictions and Cultural Identity' (University of California), *Transactions of the American Philological Society*, Vol. 123 (1993), pp. 11–12.

[27] Parts of the Book of Daniel were written in Aramaic, the language of the Persian Empire. Resemblances between Genesis stories and the Mesopotamian *Atrahasis Epic* and the *Epic of*

these earlier cultures themselves free from retrospectively inventing yet earlier traditions on which to build their own. In the first half of the second millennium BCE priests of the temple of Shamash, in Sippar, in southern Mesopotamia, erected a monument covered with inscriptions on all twelve sides dealing with the temple's renovations and an increase in royal revenue. But instead of dating it to their own time, they carefully attributed it to the reign of King Manishtushu of Akkad (c2276–2261 BCE), thereby *back-dating* their new-found funding to a remote era of the past, and giving them (as they hoped) a head-start in seniority over all other competing temples. The inscriptions conclude with the defiant assertion: 'This is not a lie, it is indeed the truth.'[28]

Similarly, what by Augustine's time might have looked like a homogenous classical tradition in reality had been created by the Latin appropriation of the Greek world – itself composed of many strands of dramatic, literary, medical, and philosophic schools and texts. Virgil's *Aeneid*, though it purports to show the founding of Rome by Aeneas the Trojan, fleeing from the sack of his native city by the victorious Greeks, is of course similarly legitimated by its appropriation of Homer.[29]

Gilgamesh have led some critics to argue for the existence of a genre of creation-to-flood epics in the ancient Near East. Many biblical terms for household items, including clothing, furniture, and perfumes, are demonstrably Ugaritic in origin. There are clear parallels in the use of metaphors: where Psalm 137 ('By the waters of Babylon') reads, 'If I forget thee, O Jerusalem, let my right hand forget her cunning', an earlier Ugaritic text has 'If I forget thee, O Jerusalem, let my right hand wither.' There are also strong Egyptian influences on parts of the Old Testament. Psalm 104, for example, bears a striking similarity to the 'Hymn to Aten', reputedly written by the heretical monotheistic Pharaoh, Akhenaten, in about 1345 BCE. Similarly the story of Joseph and Potiphar's wife (Genesis 39) first occurs in an Egyptian story called the 'Tale of Two Brothers' dating from at least 1200 BCE. Some stories seem to bear the marks of at least two external sources. Thus, although the name 'Moses' is an authentic Egyptian one, the story of the baby in a floating reed basket caulked with pitch is also told of King Sargon, who, by the Bible's own dating, lived more than a thousand years earlier than Moses around 2500 BCE. Pitch, moreover, does not occur in Egypt, but was a common material in Sargon's Mesopotamia. See Prickett, *Origins of Narrative*, pp. 53–4.

[28] Mark Jones (ed.), *Fake? The Art of Deception* (University of California Press, 1990). Cited by Alberto Manguel, *A History of Reading* (HarperCollins, 1996), p. 180.

[29] It enabled Rome to associate itself with the rich and complex fabric of Hellenic tradition, thus to enter that wider cultural world, just as it had entered the wider political world. But at the same time it announced Rome's distinctiveness from the dominant element in that world . . . The celebrated Trojan past lay in remote antiquity, its people no longer extant, the city but a shell of its former self. Troy, unlike Greece, persisted as a symbol, not a current reality. So Rome ran no risk of identification with any contemporary folk whose defects would be all too evident – and all too embarrassing. The Romans could mold the ancient Trojans to suit their own ends. As in so much else, they astutely converted Hellenic traditions to meet their own political and cultural purposes. The Greeks imposed the Trojan legend upon the west as a form of Hellenic cultural imperialism, only to see it appropriated by the westerner as a means to define and convey a Roman cultural identity.

See Gruen, 'Cultural Fictions and Cultural Identity', pp. 11–12; and Prickett, *Origins of Narrative*, pp. 36–9.

Nor was classical Greece – so often seen by others as a source of traditional authentication – above seeking similar roots in other, older, traditions. Perhaps one of the most famous examples of this is in Plato's *Timaeus*, where Critias relates the story of Solon, the Athenian poet and philosopher, who goes to Sais in the Nile delta of Egypt and hears the story of Atlantis from an ancient priest of the temple. But before beginning his story, the Egyptian priest berates the Solon and his fellow Athenians for their lack of traditions:

you Hellenes are never anything but children, and there is not an old man among you. Solon in return asked him what he meant. I mean to say, he replied, that in mind you are all young; there is no old opinion handed down among you by ancient tradition, nor any science which is hoary with age . . .

As for those genealogies of yours which you just now recounted to us, Solon, they are no better than the tales of children. In the first place you remember a single deluge only, but there were many previous ones; in the next place, you do not know that there formerly dwelt in your land the fairest and noblest race of men which ever lived, and that you and your whole city are descended from a small seed or remnant of them which survived. And this was unknown to you, because, for many generations, the survivors of that destruction died, leaving no written word. For there was a time, Solon, before the great deluge of all, when the city which now is Athens was first in war and in every way the best governed of all cities, is said to have performed the noblest deeds and to have had the fairest constitution of any of which tradition tells, under the face of heaven.[30]

Here, then, is a handing down of ancient wisdom that outlasts the written word, and is now used to confound (in the usual Socratic fashion) the conventional assumptions of the assembled company. Whether the story is not a mere legend, but an actual fact, as Socrates says, depends upon one's reading of Socratic irony – not to mention the underlying assumptions of Benjamin Jowett's translation used here – but the point is that 'tradition' in this context is to be taken seriously for itself, whether it is literally true, or a story composed for a symbolic purpose.

But behind this appropriation and re-appropriation of ancient texts there lurks a further irony, for the original, pre-Christian meaning of 'tradition' was concerned not with the legitimation of texts at all, but specifically with oral transmission – and in particular with the kind of debate that challenged conventional thinking. Plato's word for this process, the Greek term *paradosis*, described a kind of knowledge that could *only* be transmitted by word of mouth. It reflects, in short, the form of teaching ideally practised

---

[30] Plato, *Timaeus*, trs. Benjamin Jowett, 2nd edn (Clarendon Press, 1875), Ch.1.

in Plato's Academy: not so much a matter of facts, but of the 'dialectic' – a relationship between teacher and pupil that could only be created by face-to-face contact. '*Paradosis*' was immediate, local, and specific. It was essentially first-hand rather than second-hand. The verb form, like its Latin equivalent, *tradere*, often has to be translated as 'inform' or 'tell' rather than 'hand down'. It meant 'deliver' not so much in the sense of delivering a package but in the sense of 'delivering' an address, homily, or sermon.[31] As we shall see, its other association of 'betray' conveys the idea that what is handed down is not necessarily beneficial to the recipient.

If, later on, *paradosis* was extended to include the handing down of ideas by means of written texts, it never lost touch with its oral roots. In particular, it was to retain the Platonic flavour of surprise – challenging the obvious, the conventional and the superficial assumptions of society. As James Moffatt puts it:

> 'tradition' had to be a disturbing force: it was critical because it sought to be progressive . . . The real paradox for us, as we look back into the Hellenistic age immediately prior to Christianity, is that men found it quite natural to use a term like 'tradition' for the method as well as for the content of any philosophy which challenged traditional opinions and practices, including the superstitions of popular religion.[32]

Thus, as so often, Christianity's mixed inheritance from Hellenistic and Jewish roots contained an unresolved tension between two radically different attitudes towards the wisdom of the past. The tension was not, however, simply *between* Greek and Jewish modes of thought, but also to some extent *inside* both. It is always difficult to maintain challenging or potentially disruptive ways thinking beyond the first generation. Even before the Christian era the idea of *paradosis* was increasingly nuanced with the authority of the past, and had acquired many of the connotations of 'handing down' associated with the more strictly legal Latin word *tradere*. Moreover, by New Testament times, *paradosis* had passed from its philosophical and Platonic context to become part of the vocabulary of the various mystery cults against whose 'traditions' Paul warns in Colossians.[33]

It is perhaps hardly surprising, therefore, that the noun *paradosis* is rarely used in the Jewish Greek of the Septuagint. On the few times when it is used, it invariably comes as a literal term for surrendering a town or delivering a prisoner to punishment, rather than with any Platonic

---

[31] See James Moffatt, *The Thrill of Tradition* (Macmillan, 1944), pp. 5–7.
[32] Ibid., p. 11.   [33] See, for example, Colossians 2.8ff.

metaphorical implications. 'The noun is equally rare in the apologists of the second century,' writes Moffatt, 'and strangely enough it has no Christian associations there; Justin once mentions rabbinic traditions, and Tatian alludes to Greek traditions, but that is all. Elsewhere and later, however, the word is as dominant as its Latin equivalent 'tradition'.[34]

There is, however, one striking counter-example to this reticence over *paradosis* – and it involves the use not of the noun form, but of the verb. In Matthew 6.27, Jesus says (in Moffatt's own translation): 'All things have been delivered to me by my Father, and no one knows the Son except the Father, neither does anyone know the Father except the Son, and any-one to whom the Son chooses to reveal him.' There is nothing unusual in this Hebrew conception of revelation as truth imparted by God, but the word for 'delivered' is here the verbal (as distinct from the noun) form of *paradosis*. According to Moffatt, 'deliver' in this metaphorical sense never occurs at all in the Greek Old Testament, where, as in nearly all the New Testament, it means literally surrender, yield, betray, or hand over. Moffatt draws no conclusion from what he calls 'this singular point' beyond noting the obvious fact that it is easily missed by anyone simply reading Matthew in English.[35] Yet the fact that Jesus is cited as endorsing *paradosis* not in its pejorative or legal sense, but in its older Platonic sense is surely very significant. Not merely does it suggest direct face-to-face personal delivery from God, with the further implication that this might challenge the conventional wisdom of the time, but it also might support what some have always speculated, that Jesus (or the author of Matthew's Gospel) was well aware of Plato.

Though the Old Testament prophetic tradition had always had a chal-lenging and disruptive element, Jewish oral tradition had generally fol-lowed the principle that if a practice or belief had a good pedigree, this gave it substantive legitimacy. 'Long descent,' writes Moffatt, 'invested it with authority and placed it above questioning.'[36] Though it clearly played a *de facto* role in the Christian appropriation of the Hebrew Bible, the conscious articulation of progressive revelation as a historical process had to wait for German romantics such as Lessing, Herder and Schiller, whence it would pass to nineteenth-century Catholic apologists, such as Chateaubriand, Newman, and even G.K. Chesterton.[37]

---

[34] Moffatt, *Thrill of Tradition*, p. 57.   [35] Ibid., p. 47   [36] Ibid., p. 20.

[37] See, for example, G.E. Lessing, *On the Education of the Human Race*, 1778; J. G. Herder, *The Spirit of Hebrew Poetry*, 1783; F.C. Schiller, *On the Aesthetic Education of Man*, 1794. Chateaubriand, *The Genius of Christianity*, 1802; J.H. Newman, *The Development of Christian Doctrine*, 1845; G.K. Chesterton, *The Ball and the Cross*, 1910.

Once again, in the case of all these writers, the clue to understanding the present is sought by an attempt to find in the past an explanatory tradition – a way of reading history. As we shall see in the first chapter of this book, what exactly constitutes 'tradition' (with or without definite or indefinite articles) has always been a controversial topic, and the word has carried many different connotations for different people and periods. Yet though – like most important ideas – the idea of tradition may lack exact definition, it has represented, at least at some epochs, a powerful cultural and psychological need. Yet how is it to be separated out from the total cultural freight delivered by any educational system based on book-learning rather than rote? As Cassiodorus found, even the successful transmission of literacy itself constitutes a tradition of considerable complexity (not to mention anxiety) – the more so if one takes into account the variety of tacit cultural assumptions embodied in any particular literary tradition. If we tend to find historically that invocations of tradition usually involve tactical definitions, distinguishing it for the purposes of that debate from some other quality within the culture, what remains constant is that tradition has *always* been retrospective: claiming the past in order to try and influence the future.

Tradition, in other words, is an immensely complicated polyvalent system of reference. If it has been the glue that holds most – if not all – societies together, this particular glue has always had an ambiguous value. Such is its importance in human affairs that we speak confidently of 'traditional societies', and, in those societies that equally confidently think of themselves as being non-traditional, we find elaborate and controversial theories of tradition being developed as a way of sticking things back together again. Seventeenth-century Spain, for instance, was a time and place where tradition mattered intensely. In Velázquez's painting of the official ceremony of *La Tela Real*, we find tradition at its most powerful, and – because there is in reality little else *beside* tradition in the example – possibly at its most absurd (see Appendix). Glue, by itself, can only stick to itself. Paradoxically, as we shall see, within a century of Velázquez large parts of Europe, including the English-speaking world, had almost ceased to use the word at all – and it was precisely in those societies where new metaphors, new concepts, new ideas of tradition had to be developed. It was to take a variety of factors, ranging from external German, French and even American influences, to those, like the Oxford Movement, peculiar to the British scene, to restore the word to general use in English. What follows is a brief sketch of the story of the decline, fall, and eventual revival of a word – and of the complex of often contradictory ideas that such a problematic word can imply.

For reasons of space – not to mention scholarship – to offer an adequate survey of the changing meaning of tradition even from the time of Velázquez, let alone Cassiodorus, would be an almost impossible task. To understand seventeenth-century Spain, one would need not merely Spanish history, but that of the Reformation as well. Moreover, for obvious reasons, most discussions of tradition have always been concerned with defending or re-stating entrenched ideological positions. Such polemical exhortations may or may not have achieved their purpose in their original contexts – readings of the French Revolution, for instance, are still controversial – but they are rarely of value in understanding the evolution of the word or of the accompanying concept. This study will more modestly confine itself mostly to how the idea has helped to shape our own times – and thus with the changing fortunes of the word over the last 300 years together with its extraordinary relationship to what we have now come to mean by 'modernity'. In particular we shall be inevitably concentrating on those places where we can see significant alterations, deliberate or perhaps even unconscious, in the way in which the word is being used. If the general disappearance of the word in the eighteenth century will be perhaps the most surprising aspect of this history to many readers, the story of its eventual restoration and ever-rising popularity thereafter is no less fascinating.

At the same time, we shall be trying to understand how a word whose original meaning was largely confined to law and religion, and only later, by extension, to politics, came to be a vital part of that quality of historical imagination that we take for granted in the modern self-understanding. Today nostalgia for 'traditional beliefs' has merged seamlessly into the conservative politician's cry for 'traditional values', and morphed finally into the advertisers' dream world of 'traditional Christmases', 'traditional' recipes, country fare (or more likely 'fayre'), 'traditional' hospitality, 'traditional' ice-creams, architecture, furniture, or more vaguely, 'traditional' styles, in the ephemeral world of fashion itself. We shall, in short, be looking at how the idea of tradition has become an essential ingredient in modernity.

CHAPTER I

Tradition, literacy and change

EPISTEMOLOGICAL CRISES, SPURIOUS NARRATIVES, AND INVENTED TRADITIONS

Few recent accounts of tradition have room for the idea that it was itself an evolving concept. Nor was its essentially retrospective quality easy to see from the first comprehensive general study of the concept, Edward Shils's ground-breaking book, *Tradition*, published in 1981. His concern was more with taxonomy than analysis, and the exhaustive summary of all possible variations of meaning for tradition allows only limited place for the conditions of its creation.[1] Not so a collection of essays edited by Eric Hobsbawm in 1983 entitled *The Invention of Tradition*. For him, 'tradition' is to be distinguished from both 'custom' (the way so-called 'traditional societies' are commonly organized) and 'convention' (the regular way of doing things that has no ritual or symbolic function) by its formal and self-conscious nature.[2] An entirely functional convention can, of course, be transformed into 'tradition' by even a small shift in social context. Thus, for Hobsbawm, 'a hard hat for a soldier or bike-rider is functional; in conjunction with hunting pink, it has a different significance'.[3] An 'invented tradition' is 'a set of practices, normally governed by overtly or tacitly accepted rules and of a ritual or symbolic nature, which seek to inculcate certain values and norms of behaviour by repetition, which automatically implies continuity with the past . . . where possible . . . a suitably historic past'.[4] While admitting that 'the actual process of creating such ritual and symbolic complexes has not been adequately studied by historians',[5] – he was either unaware of Shils, or (more likely) did not see a sociologist as a serious 'historian' – Hobsbawm makes the point that

---

[1] Edward Shils, *Tradition* (University of Chicago Press, 1981), p. v.
[2] *The Invention of Tradition*, ed. Eric Hobsbawm and Terence Ranger (Cambridge University Press, 1983), pp. 2–4.
[3] Ibid., p. 3.   [4] Ibid., p. 1.   [5] Ibid., p. 4.

traditions are 'most often invented when a rapid transformation of society weakens or destroys the social patterns for which "old" traditions had been designed, producing new ones to which they were not applicable, or when such old traditions and their institutional carriers and promulgators no longer prove sufficiently adaptable and flexible'. These conditions, he assumes, were peculiarly likely to have occurred in that last 200 years.[6] The essays in the rest of the volume are all concerned with such recently invented 'traditions' as Scottish clans and tartans, the rituals of the British monarchy, and various forms of nationalism and nation-building in Asia and Africa. All these were indeed carefully crafted and invented. Yet the tacit implication that accompanies these examples, that there is thereby something fake or illegitimate about their origins, may be premature. As the metaphor of *intention* suggested by his phrase about 'the social patterns for which "old" traditions had been *designed*' might have suggested, had he paused over it, the notion that 'old' traditions were somehow more 'natural' or 'spontaneous' than recent ones looks, on the available evidence, to be highly questionable.

It will, on the contrary, be the initial thesis of this book that *all* traditions – if not in Shils's all-embracing taxonomy, then at least in the fairly narrow sense in which Hobsbawm defines the word – are the product of some degree of self-conscious creation, and that so far from being handed down from an unquestioned past, they *always* represent, to a greater or less degree, an attempt to appropriate a past which was ambiguous, dangerous, or even capable of interpretations subversive to the ideology of the creators of that tradition. If the appropriation of the pagan classical world by Augustine and his early fourth-century contemporaries seems a very glaring example of such an invented tradition, we shall see on closer inspection, that other seemingly more spontaneous traditions have similar roots, and spring from essentially similar ideological needs.

In *Why Study the Past?*, his Salisbury lectures on the quest for the historical Church, Rowan Williams aptly notes that:

When people set out to prove that nothing has changed, you can normally be sure that something quite serious has. The very fact of feeling you need to show that things are the same implies that there has been an unsettlement of what was once taken for granted. When there is no awareness of things changing, certain questions are not asked; what exists seems obvious, natural. If you have to *prove* that it's natural, you may succeed or you may not, but there has been a sort of loss

---

[6] Ibid., pp. 4–5.

of innocence. It has become plain that you can no longer take for granted that everyone really knows what is obvious or natural.[7]

In an important coda, Williams adds that 'when you sense that you cannot take for granted that things are the same, you begin to write history, to organise the collective memory so that breaches may be mended and identities displayed.'[8] Citing the French historian, Michel de Certeau, that 'History (in the modern sense of the word) and revolution are born together', he suggests how, read 'with imagination, the New Testament can be seen as a great attempt to write history in just the sense that our French philosopher intended – as a consequence of revolution'.[9] While we need to recognize that 'revolution' has a somewhat stronger (and more positive) meaning in French than in English, the real key to that sentence – and one that we shall return to – is 'read with imagination'. 'Imagination', it turns out, is a word that naturally occurs in conjunction with any close examination of tradition.

Though it is well put, however, Williams' point is in itself hardly a new one. Alasdair MacIntyre in his 1988 book, *Whose Justice? Which Rationality?*, sees traditions arising specifically from ideological interpretations of what he calls 'epistemological crises'. These occur when established traditions have become sterile and are seen to lead intellectually to a dead end; when the use of hitherto accepted ways of thought 'begins to have the effect of increasingly disclosing new inadequacies, hitherto unrecognised incoherencies, and new problems for the solution of which there seem to be insufficient or no resources within the established fabric of belief'. Such crises, he argues, are resolved by the adoption of 'new and conceptually enriched' schemes, which can simultaneously deal with the problems raised by their predecessors, account for the previous difficulty in doing so, and carry out these tasks 'in a way which exhibits some fundamental continuity of the new conceptual and theoretical structures with the shared beliefs in terms of which the tradition of enquiry had been defined up to that point'.[10]

This description certainly fits the crisis of the fourth-century Church we saw in the Introduction, but readers of Thomas Kuhn's *The Structure of Scientific Revolutions* (1962) will also notice a striking similarity between such a process and what he calls 'paradigm shifts' in the history of science – when an older system of explanation for certain phenomena is replaced by

---

[7] Rowan Williams, *Why Study the Past? The Quest for the Historical Church* (Eerdmans, 2005), p. 4.
[8] Ibid., p. 5.   [9] Ibid., pp. 5–6; 8.
[10] Alasdair MacIntyre: *Whose Justice? Which Rationality?* (University of Notre Dame Press, 1988), p. 362.

a newer system that makes better sense not merely of the original phenomena, but also has greater predictive value.[11] In each case, what has to be invented is a *new* tradition: a new narrative of origins, a new way of reading, understanding, and coming to terms with the past.

The analogy with Kuhn is strengthened by the fact that in looking for the roots of tradition in epistemological crises, MacIntyre is returning to the theme of another essay of his, published eleven years earlier, specifically on the philosophy of science. 'One of the signs that a [scientific] tradition is in crisis', he writes, echoing Kuhn, 'is that its accustomed ways for relating seems and is beginning to break down':

> Inherited modes of ordering experience reveal too many rival possibilities of interpretation. It is no accident that there are a multiplicity of rival interpretations of both the thought and the lives of such figures as Luther and Machiavelli in a way that there are not for the equally rich and complex figures as Abelard and Aquinas.[12]

Significantly, MacIntyre's next example, that of Galileo, is also one that was central to Kuhn's argument, but MacIntyre introduces a new factor into his description. Whereas Kuhn writes of the scientific tradition largely in terms of 'paradigms', MacIntyre prefers to see it in the more universal shape of 'narratives', which permits him to incorporate interpretations of historical thinkers – Luther, Machiavelli, Abelard and Aquinas – and interpretations of cosmological problems, such as the orbit of Mars, within a single umbrella form.[13] In doing so, he seems to be addressing a problem in the history of science that Kuhn also recognizes, but sees more in terms of an objection to be overcome than an inherent constituent of the material itself.

For Kuhn, the history of science does not seem to involve a steady progression of knowledge, but has proceeded by a series of 'revolutions' in which the definition of what constitutes 'knowledge' itself changes radically.[14] Yet, he continues, unless we actually read the 'pre-revolutionary' documents themselves, such revolutions are almost invisible to those who

---

[11] Thomas Kuhn, *The Structure of Scientific Revolutions [International Encyclopedia of Unified Science*, Vol. II, no. 2, 1962] (University of Chicago Press, 1962).

[12] Alasdair MacIntyre, 'Epistemological Crises, Dramatic Narrative and the Philosophy of Science', *The Monist*, Vol. 60, no. 4, October 1977, p. 458. The degree to which rigid disciplinary boundaries have inhibited the study of so broad a phenomenon as tradition is illustrated by the fact that Shils, a sociologist, seems to have been unaware of MacIntyre's philosophic work in the field, and Hobsbawm, a historian, makes no mention of either.

[13] Ibid., p. 460.

[14] For a wider discussion of this point see Stephen Prickett, *Narrative, Religion and Science* (Cambridge University Press, 2002), pp. 62–71.

come after. This is because of the way in which both scientists and laymen alike acquire their knowledge. Unlike our knowledge of, say, the literature of the past, which we gain by reading the books themselves, the main sources of scientific information about either the present or the past are textbooks, popularizations, and works on the philosophy of science. All three 'record the stable *outcome* of past revolutions and thus display the bases of the current normal-scientific tradition'.[15]

Unless he has personally experienced a revolution in his own lifetime, the historical sense either of the working scientist or of the lay reader of textbook literature extends only to the outcome of the most recent revolutions in the field . . . From such references both students and professionals come to feel like participants in a long-standing historical tradition. Yet their textbook-derived tradition in which scientists come to sense their participation is one that, in fact, never existed . . . The depreciation of historical fact is deeply, and probably functionally, ingrained in the ideology of the scientific profession.[16]

The invisibility of each previous paradigm, once the new paradigm has been firmly established, gives a quite unhistorical illusion of continuity to the development of science.

MacIntyre's argument looks at first sight as if it is following Kuhn closely. But a second glance suggests that he is, in effect, not so much echoing Kuhn as standing his argument on its head. Whereas Kuhn is primarily interested in the concealed discontinuities of scientific history, MacIntyre is more concerned with what *caused* us to ignore those discontinuities in the first place – the fact that we are, as it were, *programmed* wherever possible to read science as a continuous narrative, even where a closer examination of the facts reveals obvious fractures and breaks. In part this may indeed be, as Kuhn complains, due to faults in the way in which the history of science is taught. But it is clear that MacIntyre also sees a more complicated psychological factor at work. In short, where Kuhn sees an 'ingrained' 'depreciation of historical fact' as a kind of intellectual failure, MacIntyre discovers something much more positive – an ingrained human preference for narrative – and thus for tradition. MacIntyre writes:

The criterion of a successful theory is that it enables us to understand its predecessors in a newly intelligible way. It, at one and the same time, enables us to understand precisely why its predecessors have to be rejected or modified and also why,

---

[15] Kuhn, *Structure of Scientific Revolutions*, pp. 135–6.
[16] Ibid., pp. 136–7.

without and before its illumination, past theory could have remained credible. It introduces new standards for evaluating the past. It recasts the narrative which constitutes the continuous reconstruction of the scientific tradition.

The connection between narrative and tradition has hitherto gone almost unnoticed, perhaps because tradition has usually been taken seriously only by conservative social theorists. Yet those features of tradition which emerge as important when the connection between tradition and narrative is understood are ones which conservative theorists are unlikely to attend to. For what constitutes a tradition is a conflict of interpretation of that tradition, a conflict which itself has a history of rival interpretations.[17]

MacIntyre's dialectical use of the word 'tradition' looks at first sight a far cry from the apparent certainties of Hobsbawm – as if it would blur rather than clarify his careful distinctions between tradition, custom, and convention. Yet that is not necessarily so. For Hobsbawm an 'invented tradition' is essentially an oxymoron – a description of a bogus and artificial creation. Whereas, for him, both 'custom' and 'convention' are natural, unselfconscious and pragmatic ways of proceeding, 'tradition' is in contrast nothing if not self-conscious. An 'invented tradition' is like Frankenstein's monster – an imitation of true organic life composed of stolen dead parts. Yet the 'rules of a ritual or symbolic nature' implying an ersatz 'continuity with the past' which, for Hobsbawm, are characteristic of 'invented traditions', do not have to refer merely to the wearing of Scottish clan tartans, or the coronation ceremonies of the British monarch. They apply equally well, for instance, to the actions of an Anglican or Roman Catholic priest at the Eucharist, which is hardly an 'invented tradition' in Hobsbawm's restrictive sense – though a prime example of it in MacIntyre's sense. Though it links the actions of a twenty-first-century priest in Waco, Texas, Canberra, Australia, or Singapore, with those of the early Church in the Near East or Europe 1,700 years earlier, the words and actions of the Mass were themselves quite consciously designed at that time (or earlier) to echo those of the Last Supper in the Gospels, and before that, of the Jewish Passover ritual, and so forge a temporal link to the events of Jesus's life and death.

Yet few traditions have been sources of greater – or more lasting – conflict of interpretation. We speak without hesitation of 'the Catholic tradition', 'the Reformed tradition', or, even more specifically, 'the Anglican' or 'Presbyterian' traditions. Each constitutes, in effect, a constructed narrative that reads the past in relation to the present. Even where the confused

---

[17] MacIntyre, 'Epistemological Crises', p. 460.

and often polyvalent historical evidence is acknowledged, each must in the end explain how the current state of affairs was reached in terms of linear narrative. As we shall see, for the Tractarians the Anglican *via media* had to be defended in terms of historical tradition, just as Newman's decision to leave that tradition and 'pervert'[18] to that of the Roman Church in 1845 was accompanied by a book, *Essay on the Development of Christian Doctrine*, which was, yet again, a re-interpretation of the disputed territory of the past.

But even something as apparently ill-defined or amorphous as a 'literary tradition' similarly involves the rituals of particular verse-forms not to mention invocations of muses or patrons as inspiration. We can speak quite properly of the 'traditional sonnet form' – self-consciously taken into sixteenth-century English from the Italian of Petrarch, and intended to assert a continuity with what was then seen as an older established and therefore 'superior' cultural tradition. Though we might hesitate to describe anything so utterly original as the *Divine Comedy* as 'ritualized', in fact few creations of the human mind are as densely symbolic or owe as much to an idea of the past. While the Christian theme, and even the Christian calendar (by which the action moves from Good Friday to Easter Day) are omnipresent, the fact that Dante, the character, is accompanied by Virgil through Hell and Purgatory is symbolic (among other things) of his claim to write in the tradition of both the *Aeneid* and, through that, of the *Iliad* and the *Odyssey* – thus carefully re-asserting Augustine's claim to the Christian appropriation of the pagan classics. Even Chaucer, later described by Victorian critics as 'the father of English literature', was at pains to display 'traditional' credentials – and even where these sometimes amount to a tongue-in-cheek invocation of unspecified 'olde bookes', the exact degree of whose seriousness or irony is almost impossible for the modern reader to guess, there is no doubt at all about the *self-consciousness* of the enterprise.

Nor, I think, should we be over-hesitant in seeing behind the creation of such traditions shadows of the 'epistemological crises' described by MacIntyre. We have already seen how such a term might make sense of the actions of the fourth-century Church. The term would equally well apply to both fourteenth-century Italy and to Dante's own life in exile when he began the *Commedia*. Crises of both of legitimation and epistemology similarly underlie the development of new literary forms. Not for

---

[18] The Victorian term for conversion from the Church of England – especially to Roman Catholicism.

nothing does Sterne begin his ground-breaking and profoundly original *Sentimental Journey* with the (quite deliberately false) claim, "'They do these things better in France!" I said.' Even that final piece of reported speech represents a pseudo-appeal to the authority of a past moment.

Indeed, the more we look at such crises, and the accompanying creation of new traditions, the more it becomes apparent that we cannot see events of this kind in terms of a single medium, whether religious, literary, or scientific. Cassiodorus' metaphor of plaiting together into 'one braid' the many strands of what he believes is 'ancient tradition' is in fact peculiarly appropriate. Despite the attempts of specialized historians to tell stories of particular disciplines in isolation, the reality is that science, religion, and the arts are all contributory strands to an overall cultural nexus.

The fact that the biblical was universally accepted as a 'religious' tradition, while the classical was seen as either 'secular' or 'pagan' (according to the taste of the commentator), is from a socio-historical viewpoint of little importance. Like the cultures it had assimilated, the fourth-century Christianity of Ambrose and Augustine was essentially a synthetic construct – what Clifford Geertz has described as 'an historically transmitted pattern of meanings embodied in symbols, a system of inherited conceptions expressed in symbolic forms by which men communicate, perpetuate, and develop their knowledge about and attitude towards life'.[19] Even if such dry functionalist analyses of religion do not allow for what has been called the 'interiority' of religious experiences, they at least suggest something of the powerful social value of religious tradition. In the broadest sense of the word, traditions have always been part of the glue holding all human societies together; in a narrower sense, they have seamlessly bound religion and culture together to preserve what was most distinctive and valuable within those societies. But the breadth of Geertz's view of religion should also remind us of the universality as well as the sheer complexity of this cultural nexus of tradition, society, and the arts.

This is a point supported by a more recent observation on tradition – the more effective for the fact that it is looking at culture from a slightly unusual viewpoint:

What we call *culture* takes its place where tradition and innovation intersect. Tradition is made up of knowledge, techniques, values which were handed down to us. Innovation exists inasmuch as this knowledge, these techniques, these

---

[19] Clifford Geertz, 'Religion as a Cultural System', in *The Interpretation of Cultures* (Basic Books, 1973), p. 89.

values modify the place of man in the environmental context, rendering him able to experience a new reality. *A very successful innovation*: that is how we could define tradition. *Culture* is the interface between these two perspectives.[20]

What is remarkable about this definition of tradition from Massimo Montanari is not just that he sees it in terms of innovation (a point to which we shall return repeatedly in this study) but its context: a book called *Food is Culture*, a volume in a series entitled *Arts and Traditions of the Table: Perspectives on Culinary History*. The failure of tradition that so depressed Cassiodorus towards the end of his life, was not simply a loss of literacy, it was also the collapse of a culture that included food as much as philosophy.

Indeed, the sadness and frustration of Cassiodorus, no longer even able to describe to his monks what they had lost, is part of a tragedy at least dimly familiar to every teacher who has failed to awaken in students a sense of the complexity and energizing power of their great traditions. Few of us, however, can really imagine what it must have been like to recognize that such a loss was happening throughout an entire society. Like an old-fashioned negative – part of an already almost obsolete technology in the twenty-first century – it will provide us with an enduring image of absence throughout the following pages.

ORALITY AND LITERACY

First, however, we need to think a little more about the history of tradition, and how it came to be such an inflammatory and controversial topic. In his ground-breaking book, *Orality and Literacy* (1992), the Japanese–American Jesuit, Walter J. Ong, makes a number of distinctions between oral and literate cultures crucial to any understanding of the nature of tradition.

Oral cultures, he argues, are essentially *static*. This does not mean, of course, that they do not change at all – every literate culture was once oral, after all. What it means is that oral cultures find it very difficult to *conceptualize* change. When change comes it is either so gradual as to be unnoticeable over living memory, or unplanned, contingent, and bewildering – often with randomly Darwinian consequences, that can involve the decimation or extinction of the village, group, or tribe. The primary task in such a society is not innovation but remembering. Bruce Chatwin's

---

[20] Massimo Montanari, *Food is Culture*, trs. Albert Sonnenfeld (Columbia University Press, 2004), p. 7.

book, *The Songlines* (1987), vividly portrays the way in which Australian aboriginal peoples must learn their tribal songs in order to survive in the harsh desert conditions of the Outback. Encoded in the songs for each area is vital information concerning the location of water-holes, food, or possible dangers. If you have to travel over the territory of another tribe, it is not just a matter of courtesy but of survival to learn their songs first. In other areas of the world specific elders are charged with the task of acting as the tribal memory-bank, recalling vital genealogies, medicines, emergency diets in times of famine, etc. In West Africa the collective knowledge of the tribe can be stored not so much in songs as in proverbs. To be a respected elder means to know the proverbs of the village, clan, or tribe.[21] In such cases the whole structure and syntax of the language can be essentially proverbial. Among the Mende of Sierra Leone, the English words 'I'm hungry' are translated by a whole metaphor: 'An empty sack cannot stand by itself.' Moreover, the phrase 'I have eaten' refers only to the staple diet of rice and palm-oil. Someone who tells you he has 'not eaten for three days' may (or may not) have been eating something else. Rather than being poetic, such proverbial linguistic structures are, by definition, time-tested and functional, but they do not necessarily facilitate accurate dietary discussions.

In such a context the idea of 'tradition' is profoundly different from that of a Western Judeo-Christian culture. Where oral tradition represents the collected wisdom of all time – the equivalent, in effect, of all the contents of all our libraries combined – the idea of 'change' makes no sense at all. Indeed, it could be suicidally dangerous. A mistake in the songlines could kill. Accuracy of repetition is absolutely paramount. This concept of tradition can, of course, persist even in semi-literate societies, and for very similar reasons: one thinks of Koranic schools in the Near East where students are obliged to learn by heart written passages of the seventh-century Arabic of the Koran. Rabbinic schools teaching Hebrew to Jews who may speak anything from first-century Aramaic to modern American, or the mediaeval memorizing of the Vulgate by peoples who had never spoken Latin, present very similar concepts of tradition as blind repetition.[22] Alongside such activities, however, a very different concept of tradition

---

[21] In many traditional societies, including some in Eastern Europe (such as Romania) there is a tendency for older or conservative people to use proverbs not simply as illustrations of knowledge – what one might call *gnomic* wisdom – but as assertions of personal prestige.

[22] Other writers have noted the *resistance* to writing down certain types of information in societies where written records exist alongside oral tradition – often in deference to sacred information or meanings. See, for instance, André Hurst, *Education and the Knowledge Society* (Springer, 2005).

has existed for thousands of years, where 'midrash', or an ongoing tradition of exegesis and comment, has always accompanied the teaching of the sacred texts. 'What is the Torah?' runs one Jewish catechism, with its answer, 'It is midrash Torah' – it is the Law *and* its associated tradition.[23] The Law, sacred as it is, is incomplete without its related tradition of comment and discussion. Here, of course, is the origin of what T.S. Eliot was to see as the distinctive quality of the great European literary tradition: its capacity for innovation and change. For him, only the new could truly be traditional.[24] But such a notion of tradition as change presupposes a firm grasp on what is being changed. A commentary on the Jewish dietary prescriptions – even the progressive rejections of it in the New Testament by Jesus, Peter and Paul – would be without meaning or use if we did not have the original texts themselves. Such a record of debate and change is only possible in a literate and textually based society.

Associated with this new meaning of tradition made possible by writing are two other key innovations. The first is the movement from 'outer' to 'inner'. Reading was once quite as noisy a process as consulting the tribal memory-man. To read, was to *read aloud*. In some early English manuscripts the injunction to the reader to 'rede' can mean either to read for one's own personal edification, or to give a recitation for the benefit of all present. The difference between the two interpretations was not so much one of vocalization as of volume. Both involved movement of the lips and tongue. At what point people started reading silently, to themselves, and therefore, in that sense at least, 'internalizing' what they were reading is unclear. Julius Caesar's ability to read silently was a source of wonder to his contemporaries. Four hundred years later it had become proof of extraordinary holiness. St Augustine records his astonishment as a young man when, on paying an unexpected visit to St Ambrose studying in his cell, he found the holy Bishop of Milan poring over a book *without moving his lips*. The fact that Augustine, who had moved in literate and educated circles all his life had never seen such a phenomenon before tells us much – as does his immediate conviction that this was a product of the most advanced spirituality.[25] At what point such internalizing became the norm is difficult to determine, but we have sufficient historical descriptions

[23] See Michael Wadsworth, 'Making and Interpreting Scripture', *Ways of Reading the Bible*, ed. Michael Wadsworth (Harvester Press, 1981), p. 8.

[24] T.S. Eliot, 'Tradition and the Individual Talent', *Selected Essays* (Faber and Faber, 1932).

[25] 'When he read, his eyes scanned the page and his heart sought out the meaning, but his voice was silent and his tongue was still. Anyone could approach him freely and guests were not commonly announced, so that often, when we came to visit him, we found him reading like this in silence,

of the noise created by 'hard-working' school classes to suggest that in some English-speaking areas at least it persisted well into the eighteenth century. In part this was actually a product of the teaching method itself. Children in country schools, where there might be all ages and abilities in one classroom pursuing different courses of study alongside one another, were specifically ordered to read out loud so that the single teacher in the room could know what they were all doing. We have ample records of such so-called 'blab schools' in the United States in the early nineteenth century: Abraham Lincoln, for instance, is said to have attended one.

In the meantime, a second source of internalization had transformed both author and readership: the invention of the movable-type printing-press. Protestantism was the product of advanced technology: it is no co-incidence that the first book published by Gutenberg in Mainz was a Bible. Whilst one should not exaggerate the spread of either printing or literacy across Europe (Gutenberg went bankrupt), within 200 years – by the middle of the seventeenth century – it was possible to assume that the Protestant faithful could, and did, read the Bible in the privacy of their own homes even if, as so often, they read virtually nothing else. By becoming a commercial artifact, the Bible had passed for ever beyond the institutional control of the Church – whether Catholic, or one of a grow-ing number of Protestant sects, increasingly to be distinguished from one another by their biblical interpretations. Moreover, just as these new read-ers were free to interpret the Bible directly in terms of their own contexts and circumstances, so too were they free, and even encouraged, to intern-alize its message as speaking directly to them.

Both these developments contributed to corresponding changes not merely in the meaning of words, but in the way in which words them-selves were understood to function. With the invention of writing, history passed from legend and dream-time to the story of a past that could be written down and studied, debated, compared and – often – disputed. Thus the form and development of Christianity was shaped by its essentially literary origins. Not merely was it centred upon a particular book – the Bible – but it was created by and for literate people who had just such a power of re-reading and re-interpreting existing texts. Jesus him-self was certainly literate – indeed, very possibly quadri-lingual[26] – and

for he never read aloud.' [*Confessions*, trs. E.B. Pusey, Everyman, 1907, VI.3.] See also Alberto Manguel, *A History of Reading* (HarperCollins 1996), p. 42.

[26] Aramaic, the language of the Persian Empire, and the spoken language of the Jews of first-century Palestine; Greek, the language of the Septuagint, and of educated people of the day; Hebrew, the

though he (notoriously) never wrote anything himself, others did. Four accounts of his life and death – the Gospels – are central to the New Testament.

The consequences of this were of incalculable importance both for the nature of the new Christian religion, and for the subsequent development of the societies and civilizations that evolved from it. From the outset, the teachings of Jesus are presented within an *existing* written tradition: the familiar phrases 'It is written . . . but I say unto you' or 'this day have the scriptures been fulfilled' immediately place them in dialogue with a *written* past. Within the first century this dialogue was aided by a second invention almost as momentous as the invention of writing itself – the codex, or bound book, in which pages follow a pre-set order. As we have mentioned, until this invention, each book of Hebrew scriptures was written on a separate scroll, and kept in a wooden chest or cupboard. Stored like this, of course, they could be read in any order the reader desired. With the coming of the book, the Hebrew scriptures were gathered by Christians into what now became the Old Testament,[27] specifically arranged in an order designed to illustrate that dialogue, and leading forward to the grand narrative of the New Testament: the coming of Jesus and the spread of Christianity through the known world.

Insofar as the new religion involved a controversial re-reading of a written past, moreover, it also highlighted the way in which not just texts, but the *words* of which those texts were composed, were equally open to re-interpretation and the discovery of new meanings. In a fascinating and seminal article, 'The Meaning of *Literal*', Owen Barfield has pointed out that most of our words for inward and especially moral qualities were originally derived, as metaphors, from material things. Thus, for instance, the word 'scruple' is a metaphor from the Latin *scrupulus*, a small sharp stone that might get into your sandal and so prevent you walking uprightly and evenly. 'Noble' was originally a coin of high value; we now speak of 'feelings' almost exclusively in terms of emotions – and so on.[28]

Such internalized meanings are thus products of long evolutionary processes. But some words have evolved by an almost diametrically opposite

language of his own Jewish scriptural tradition; and Latin, the language of the Roman occupiers, and (possibly) the language in which Jesus spoke to Pilate.

[27] This was not, of course, a 're-arrangement' as is sometimes claimed. The arrangement of the Hebrew Bible, like that of the Old Testament, dates from after the fall of Jerusalem in 70 CE and is thus more or less contemporaneous with the Christian Bible. See Introduction above, p. 6.

[28] Owen Barfield, 'The Meaning of Literal', Basil Cottle and L.C. Knights (eds.), *Metaphor and Symbol* (Butterfield, 1960); reprinted in *The Rediscovery of Meaning* (Wesleyan University Press, 1977).

process. For instance, since the root words from which our modern idea of 'spirit' evolved, the Hebrew *ruach*, the Greek *pneumos*, or the Latin *spiritus*, all originally referred to wind, it would be easy to conclude that the word 'spirit' was similarly originally a metaphorical construction of this kind. However, Barfield argues, to say that 'spirit' is a metaphor in this sense would imply that there was already an idea of what it meant already present in the language, and this, of course, is not so. We have, therefore, to think of the wind as *always* having had a ghostly, numinous, and magical quality about it, and it was only when the notions of wind and spirit had finally been separated that the literal (and scientific) meaning of 'wind' could finally emerge sometime around the seventeenth century. Similarly, it was only then that the idea of the 'spirit' as a purely abstract, moral, and inward phenomenon, purged of all material associations could finally make its appearance – which coincides with the coming into use of derivative terms such as 'spirituality'.[29]

Whether in this process of what Coleridge called 'desynonymy'[30] other qualities may have been lost is beside the point – though if we were to have clear evidence that this was so, there would be nothing to stop those who wished to retrieve such a lost meaning coining (or desynonymizing) yet another term that would cover it.[31] What is clear is that such an evolution of meaning was only possible in a literate and textually orientated society. Desynonymy doubtless occurred thousands of times in oral societies, and, incidentally, we also know a little of some oral societies where the reverse seems to have happened, and a once-rich and complex language 'degenerated' into a much cruder and more simplistic one.[32] There is no law of inevitable linguistic progress. My point is rather that except in very rare (and usually highly debatable) instances there is, by definition, no record of the process, and therefore no sense of it as constituting an ongoing and dynamic tradition. It is in this power to hold past and present in

[29] For precisely this reason, French does not distinguish between 'soul' and 'spirit', but rather uses *esprit* for both. The same is true of other Romance languages like Italian, Spanish and Portuguese – but not Romanian, which is more under Greek influence.

[30] S.T. Coleridge, *Lectures 1818–1819 On the History of Philosophy*, ed. J.R. de J. Jackson, Bollingen Series (Princeton University Press/Routledge, 2000), lecture v, pp. 173–4.

[31] The revival of 'ponder' in Luke 2.19 may be such an example. See David Norton, *History of the Bible as Literature*, 2 vols. (Cambridge University Press, 1993), p. 82.

[32] The Mayan language and mathematical notation, a written system that was unknown to the later people living in the area, who may, or may not be their descendents, has been cited as one example; another possible example has been the loss of vocabulary and technology among the Tasmanians prior to white settlement who had apparently lost the art of both navigation and fishing which archaeology confirms they once possessed.

simultaneous focus that a literate society possesses, at least potentially, a sense of unfolding tradition almost impossible for an oral one. Tradition, in other words, is a product not merely of literacy, but of the recognition of the possibility of change.

Nevertheless, a record of historical etymology such as the Oxford English Dictionary suggests that at first sight there has actually been remarkably little change in the meaning of the word 'tradition' itself from the time when Tertullian and the Church Fathers took the Latin *traditio*, in its legal meaning of 'handing over' or 'delivery', and wrote by analogy of the *Traditio evangelica* – or *Catholica*. This standard ecclesiastical definition, that of 'bequeathing any Doctrine to posterity from age to age' remained more or less unaffected by its translation into English and the Reformation. Nor should we lose its connection with another Latin legal term: 'testament', a 'bearing witness' handed down into English in both the making of wills – the 'last will and testament' – and, of course, the two 'Testaments' of the Bible. Yet there was another meaning of the Latin distinctly less user-friendly. The idea of 'handing over' could (and did) equally well lend itself to 'surrender' or even 'betrayal'. In a more specialist sense it was even applied in Church history to 'the surrender of sacred books in time of persecution'. Certainly there is nothing in its origins wholly inimical to the wholesale acts of appropriation, theft, or surrender of valuable property that has often followed the word's actual history. Nor does the history of the word give much support to what one might call the 'romantic' view of tradition: that it is simply the handing on of the received wisdom of past ages.

What that history does illustrate, however, is that this apparently innocent and transparent noun is actually a concealed *metaphor*. MacIntyre's insistence that tradition is essentially a narrative form is crucial. Tradition stands for a particular way of telling a story. What is conveyed, or handed on by a theory of tradition, is not a physical object, nor even a particular idea, but something that encapsulates an entire *theory* of conveyance – delivering not merely contents, but, just as significantly, predicating the way in which ideas *should* be passed on from one generation to another. Like all metaphors, its meaning is not immediately self-evident, but requires elucidation, explanation, and unpacking. If the different nuances of the word listed above were already not clear enough evidence, the need for such mediation is also a tacit admission of the inherent ambiguity of tradition. Since at least the time of Cassiodorus, it has constituted, variously, a self-justifying authority, a useful guide, a description of something primitive, a story of doubtful veracity, and a source of unjustifiable tyranny. All of these will figure at different points in our narrative.

Such inherent ambiguity of metaphors reminds us of the degree to which this handing on of received wisdom, however bequeathed or created, is not always a blessing, guide, or crutch, but could be a coercive or even dead weight on its society. Terry Eagleton has taken the twentieth-century philosopher, Hans-Georg Gadamer, to task for making precisely such a normative assumption about the nature of tradition:

> It might be as well to ask Gadamer whose and what 'tradition' he has in mind. For his theory holds only on the enormous assumption that there is indeed a single 'mainstream' tradition: that all 'valid' works participate in it; that history forms an unbroken continuum, free of decisive rupture, conflict, and contradiction; and that the prejudices which 'we' (who?) have inherited from the 'tradition' are to be cherished. It assumes, in other words, that history is a place where 'we' can always and everywhere be at home: that the work of the past will always deepen – rather than, say decimate – our present self-understanding; and that the alien is always secretly familiar. It is, in short, a grossly complacent theory of history, the projection on to the world at large of a viewpoint for which 'art' means chiefly the classical monuments of the high German tradition. It has little conception of history and tradition as oppressive as well as liberating forces, areas rent by conflict and domination. History for Gadamer is not a place for struggle, discontinuity and exclusion but a continuing 'chain', an ever-flowing river, almost, one might say, a club of the like-minded.[33]

Though, as we shall see, the metaphor of 'an ever-flowing river' has more resonance with the past than Eagleton seems to recognize, his complaint is, of course, nothing new. Since at least the late Middle Ages there have been those for whom tradition was little more than the unquestioned tyranny of the past. Indeed, as Sanford Budick has pointed out,[34] for many sixteenth- and seventeenth-century reformers, what Milton called 'the sour leaven of human Traditions mixed in one putrefied Mass with the poisonous dregs of hypocrisy' was, as we shall see, to make the word 'tradition' itself suspect at best, or, at worst, anathema[35] – so much so that for an earlier generation of Renaissance scholars even something as apparently neutral as the activity of reading had itself become a form of oppression.

---

[33] Terry Eagleton, *Literary Theory: An Introduction* (Blackwell, 1983), pp. 72–3.
[34] Sanford Budick, *The Western Theory of Tradition: Terms and Paradigms of the Cultural Sublime* (Yale University Press, 2000), p. xv.
[35] John Milton, 'Of Reformation and Church Discipline', *Milton's Prose*, ed. Malcolm W. Wallace (Oxford University Press, 1959), p. 44.

In his fascinating and eclectic *History of Reading*, Alberto Manguel reminds us just what the process of reading had become in the centuries following Cassiodorus' bleak vision of modernity:

Following the scholastic method, students were taught to read through orthodox commentaries that were the equivalent of our potted lecture notes. The original texts – whether those of the Church Fathers or, to a far lesser extent, those of ancient pagan writers – were not to be apprehended directly by the student but to be reached through a series of pre-ordained steps. First came the *lectio*, a grammatical analysis in which the syntactic elements of each sentence would be identified; this would lead to the *littera* or literal sense of the text. Through the *littera* the student acquired the *sensus*, the meaning of the text according to different established interpretations. The process ended with an exegesis – the *sententia* – in which the opinions of approved commentators were discussed. The merit of such a reading lay not in discovering a private significance in the text but in being able to recite and compare the interpretations of acknowledged authorities, and thus becoming 'a better man'.[36]

Not until this 'tradition' had been obliterated by the epistemological crisis that we now call (loosely enough) the Renaissance, could a different tradition of reading be created, yet again, by a deliberate and highly self-conscious re-construction of the past, and the *invention* of a tradition reaching back, significantly, to Augustine. The creator – or inventor – of this tradition was none other than the poet, Petrarch, who sought to define his idea of reading by entering into imaginary conversations with the venerable saint, whose word, had, of course, been hitherto taken as wholly authoritative and incontrovertible:

What Augustine (in Petrarch's imagining) suggests is a new manner of reading: neither using the book as a prop for thought, nor trusting it as one would trust the authority of a sage, but taking from it an idea, a phrase, an image, linking it to another culled from a different text preserved in memory, tying the whole together with reflections of one's own – producing, in fact, a new text authored by the reader . . . To his readers in the fourteenth century, Petrarch's claim was astonishing, since the authority of a text was self-established and the reader's task that of an outside observer; a couple of centuries later, Petrarch's personal, re-creative, interpretative, collating form of reading would become the common method of scholarship throughout Europe.[37]

In his letters Petrarch describes geographical wanderings about Europe that very patently mirror an inner quest. It has similarly been suggested that such travels, like his parallel archaeological interests, were part of a

[36] Alberto Manguel, *A History of Reading* (HarperCollins, 1996), p. 77.   [37] Ibid., pp. 64–5.

much larger search not merely for a vanished Roman Empire, but also to recover something of its cultural authority[38] – a quest that the ghost of Cassiodorus could reasonably have interpreted as bringing to an end the catastrophic reign of 'modernity'.

Ironically, this is a view that finds wholly co-incidental support from Gerald Bruns in his history of hermeneutics, who makes no reference to the origins of the word, and uses it in its contemporary – and ideological – sense. For Bruns, Terry Eagleton is the perfect example of the 'modernist', who like his theoretical relative, the 'postmodernist', constitutes one pole of what amounts to a re-run of 'the old quarrel between ancients and moderns, which is essentially a quarrel about which way history moves':

The Modernist takes it that everything comes down to us from the future and recedes into the past, often taking its own sweet time; in fact much of what is *vergangen*, or over and done with, gets left behind and accumulates so that we never have enough museums or junkyards. For the Modernist the museum or cultural prison is the prototype of the institution. Its function is to objectify or reify the past, maintain possession of it, or hold it in place so that it won't disappear or grow disruptive; which is to say its function is also exclusionary. The university is a type of museum, and so in an analogous way is the state.[39]

The modernist, by this definition, has no interest in tradition at all. Its narratives belong to the junk-yard of history. Attempts to re-construct the ideas and values of the past are as relevant (if less entertaining) as the antics of a *bricoleur*, or junk-yard sculptor. The besetting anxiety of modernism is thus the haunting fear that despite all attempts to break free from the oppression of constraining systems, there *is* in the end no freedom from history. Bruns continues:

The lesson of Petrarch would be that tradition is not an empire of the dead whose ruins litter the contemporary landscape; not the *bricoleur's* debris. It is not something that requires to be disinterred and reinstituted in a museum or on a throne. It is not *vergangen*, or gone for good. Petrarch's letter in defence of quotations gives us the model of the hermeneutical concept of tradition as an ongoing conversation from which modernity (by definition) excludes itself.[40]

Apparently achieving the semantically impossible, in the period since Cassiodorus the idea of 'modernity' – the state of the ephemeral

---

[38] Thomas Greene, 'Petrarch and the Humanist Hermeneutic', *In the Light of Troy: Imitation and Discovery in Renaissance Poetry* (Yale University Press, 1982), p. 92.

[39] Gerald R. Bruns, 'What is Tradition?', *Hermeneutics Ancient and Modern* (Yale University Press, 1992), p. 196.

[40] Ibid., p. 199.

moment – had achieved permanent, if dynamic, status, now to be always in conflict with its opposite, tradition.

Despite an appearance of stability, therefore, the word 'tradition' was inevitably also undergoing a no-less-momentous change of meaning in that it was becoming progressively *internalized*. Meaning was less a matter of authority than of personal apprehension. Petrarch's idea that a wholly personal and *internal* appropriation of meaning was not merely possible, but even a *necessary* part of the reading process and of the tradition of letters, was to have profound consequences for the subsequent development of Western thought. That it might itself be seen to constitute a tradition – its apparent opposite – was not clear to anyone for several hundred years.

What was eventually to intervene, and give new life and emphasis to Petrarch's stress on the personal nature of knowledge, was the Europe-wide phenomenon we call (again, mostly in retrospect) romanticism. Almost everything about romanticism – including its very existence[41] – has been the subject of intense academic controversy, not worth rehearsing here, but there is one basic contemporary epistemological condition that has received less attention than perhaps it should. Sometime between the middle of the seventeenth and eighteenth centuries there was a profound, if scarcely perceptible, shift in the way people thought about knowledge itself. For people in pre-Civil War England, for instance, truth was assumed to be absolute. If Protestants were right, then Catholics were wrong – or vice versa. The breakdown of this relatively straightforward world-view has been plausibly attributed by Peter Harrison to the century of political and religious turmoil begun in the sixteenth century with the English Reformation and concluding with the Civil War, Commonwealth, and the subsequent restoration of Charles II, where in the course of just over a century England, unlike any other country in Europe, had experienced every form of state-sanctioned religion, from Roman Catholicism to extreme iconoclastic Puritanism. 'If the time of the appearance of this new interpretative framework was the late seventeenth and early eighteenth centuries,' writes Harrison, 'then the place was England'.[42] As Locke had put it, in one of his more deadpan moments, the kings and queens of post-Reformation England had been 'of such different minds in point of religion, and enjoined thereupon such different things', that no 'sincere and upright worshipper of God could, with

---

[41] A trend taken to its logical conclusion in the title of a recent anthology by Anne Mellor and Richard Matlak which omits the word 'romanticism' altogether in its period title: *British Literature, 1780–1830* (Harcourt Brace, 1996).

[42] Peter Harrison, *'Religion' and the Religions of the English Enlightenment* (Cambridge University Press, 1990), pp. 3; 84.

a safe conscience, obey their several decrees'.[43] The Vicar of Bray was a real person, responding with a certain logic, if not integrity, to a real dilemma.

If the idea of the relativity and personal nature of knowledge had found its origins in the theological and political disputes of the post-Reformation era, it was, of course, massively re-enforced by the scientific revolution and the philosophy of the Enlightenment. Philosophers from Descartes to Locke, Berkeley and Hume and eventually Kant were all to struggle with the seemingly intractable limitations of the human mind and possibilities of knowledge. In such a maze of argument and debate the old certainties were no longer tenable. For Friedrich Schleiermacher and his successors there had to be a science of understanding, for which he took the word, 'hermeneutics' from Alexander Gottlieb Baumgarten (1714–1762). This held that all knowledge was inseparable from the mind of the knower. The Romantic critic as much as the Old Testament prophet, was a part of his age, and belonged inescapably to a particular social and historical context and mind-set.

For us, perhaps the only way to give an intelligible shape to the history of such an all-pervasive notion as tradition, is to look *not* at the places where (as frequently happened) traditions were extolled – or abused – from set polemical positions, but rather to look at those rarer moments when we can see the idea of tradition itself undergoing real and significant changes. The chapters that follow will, for the most part, be looking at such moments when, even if those involved could not see or understand the larger changes going on around them, we, in retrospect, can detect the beginnings of a much greater shifting of the foundations. In particular, as we shall see, respect for tradition in any form has gone through huge fluctuations over the past 300 years. For most Enlightenment thinkers, for instance, the possibility that the kind of knowledge offered by tradition – that is, *any* form of knowledge transmitted from the past – was of sufficient value to command allegiance in itself had to seem remote in the extreme. Tradition, in short, had been what they were fighting against. When the Romantics and their successors – Chateaubriand, Coleridge and Schleiermacher, or Keble, Newman and Eliot – returned to the idea of tradition, it was to create from it something very different from what Augustine, Eusebius, or Cassiodorus would have understood by the word. But whether they knew it or not, what the new idea of tradition had in common with its predecessor was its retrospective construction.

---

[43] John Locke, *A Letter Concerning Toleration*, in *Treatise of Civil Government and A Letter Concerning Toleration*, ed. Charles L. Sherman (Appleton-Century-Crofts, 1965), p. 191.

CHAPTER 2

Church versus Scripture: the idea of Biblical tradition

TRENT AND ITS CONSEQUENCES

If, in terms of its dictionary definition, neither translation nor the Reformation and its theological battles were substantially to alter the original Latin meaning of tradition, that was patently *not* true of the word's connotations. One of the prime objectives of the Council of Trent (begun in 1546) had been to prevent scripture from carrying more weight than tradition but, as so often, the eventual Tridentine formula secured this by perpetuating another ambiguity, the question of whether traditions of the Catholic Church were doctrines not contained in Scriptures, or expansions of what scripture somehow already contained.[1]

Nor was this initially strategic obfuscation helped by Cardinal Bellarmine's elaborate defence of the Tridentine restatement of mediaeval Catholicism at the end of the sixteenth century, *De Controversiis Christianae Fidei, adversus huius temporis haereticos*.[2] However theoretical might be the arguments, moreover, this debate had an immediate and practical application over the question of whether to include or exclude from the Bible the deutero-canonical texts – the Protestant Apocrypha. As far back as the third century these had been regarded as historically dubious on good scholarly grounds and Jerome's exclusion of them from the authentic canon had long been taken as definitive – so much so, that as recently as 1532 Cardinal Cajetan had insisted that Jerome's judgement should constitute a ruling for the Church. Now Bellarmine countered that 'tradition' with another. How could such 'semi-Christians' as

---

[1] See James Moffatt, *The Thrill of Tradition* (Macmillan, 1944), p. 87. See also Philippe Labbe (ed.), *Traditiones sine scripto authoritatis: de Traditionibus quae observantur in Ecclesia, et quanto sint usui*, in *Tridentini Concilii: Canones et Decreta* (Ex Lovaniensi Anni MDLXVII), 26 C and D; 1058, B etc.

[2] Ingolstadt, 3 vols.: 1586; 1588; 1593. Bellarmine's arguments were not universally accepted, even within Catholicism – but not for Protestant reasons. Sixtus V would have placed the first volume on the Index, and was prevented only by his death from doing so.

Erasmus seek to exclude the Book of Susanna from canonical scripture, or regard it as merely a pious fiction, when, by tradition, it was read annually in Lent? 'Tradition' was not just any tradition – even that sanctioned by Jerome – it was what the Church ruled it to be. Tradition might rank equally with scripture, but both alike were subject to the authority of Rome. The unspoken corollary was that scholarly debate over the authenticity of doubtful or apocryphal books of scripture – let alone other forms of biblical criticism – was henceforth going to be well-nigh impossible.

This particular debate over the apocryphal texts, however, was not one that was going to go away. Early in the eighteenth century, Leibniz was to return to the question of the Tridentine decision to include the apocryphal books in the Old Testament canon in his friendly and prolonged correspondence with the French Cardinal Bossuet, Bishop of Meaux, whose prose works, notably the *Exposition de la doctrine catholique*, had made him the natural successor to Bellarmine as defender of the Tridentine formulae. Unlike his Italian predecessor, however, his style gave him a much wider cultural authority. In a letter of 30 April 1700, followed up by further communications on 14 and 24 May, Leibniz argued that the decision to defend the canonicity of the Apocrypha was a spiteful error, made for purely controversial purposes. This was, he wrote, nothing but 'a modern innovation made by your party', made in defiance of Jerome, whose judgement had been widely followed by the early and later Church. Bossuet, by then a tired old man, was driven to reply simply that the Trent decisions were binding: no concessions were possible 'on points of defined doctrine, especially such as had been defined by the council'.[3]

Even though Protestants had initially been invited to the Council,[4] there was, in effect, to be no real debate about the role of tradition. The authority of the Church was to be both paramount and self-evident. If scripture could not be separated from tradition, and the Church alone possessed the clue to the meaning of both, then 'tradition' in the sense in which it had hitherto been understood, as a guide through epistemological crises, had, paradoxically, almost ceased to exit. It was simply an extension of dogma. Indeed, it might be said that so far from tradition being a response to epistemological crises, this was an epistemological crisis specifically *about* tradition. Understanding what was going on at this period, argues Rowan Williams, requires a de-familiarizing of the conventional Catholic/Protestant disputes: 'the Reformation debate,' he writes, 'was not one between self-designated Catholics and Protestants; it was a

---

[3] Moffatt, *Thrill of Tradition*, p. 93.   [4] They refused.

debate about where the Catholic Church was to be found. "Is the Pope a Catholic?" was not a joke in the sixteenth century.'[5]

Nor was it necessarily a joke in the seventeenth century. John Evelyn records in his diary for 10 March 1687 a sermon preached to a crowded congregation at Whitehall by Dr Ken, Bishop of Bath and Wells, on 'the blasphemies, perfidy, wrestling of scripture, preference of tradition before it, spirit of persecution, superstition, legends and fables of the scribes and Pharisees, so that all the auditory understood his meaning of a parallel between them and the new Trent religion. He exhorted his audience to adhere to the written Word, and to persevere in the faith taught in the Church of England, whose doctrines for catholic soundness he preferred to all the communities and churches of Christians in the world'[6] The claim for a natural opposition between 'tradition' and true 'catholicism' could hardly have been put more clearly.

What is surprising, however, is that the events of the following year, the so-called 'Glorious Revolution' of 1688, when the Catholic James II was expelled from the throne and the Protestant William III installed, did *not* lead to any increase in anti-Catholic propaganda from the pulpit. There was, in fact, a marked and uncharacteristic drop in published sermons of all kinds in 1687–88. The restoration of Charles II in 1660 had been greeted with a rush of celebratory sermons (some 150 in all). By comparison, only four sermons were published celebrating the 1688 Revolution. This relative silence is the more remarkable when we consider that the sermon was still by far the commonest form of political and social comment of the period – the total number published annually far exceeding the number of all other publications put together.[7]

But by this time the battle was not merely between two versions of 'catholicism'. Some fifty years before, beginning in 1628, after he had moved to the relative intellectual freedom and safety of Holland, René Descartes had begun his life-long exploration of the very bases of mathematical and theological certainty. His aim was quite simply to distinguish what was actually knowable from that which was founded on hearsay or blind obedience to past authorities. The dictum, *Je pense, donc je suis* of the *Discours de la méthode* became the forerunner of the more famous *Cogito, ergo sum*: laying the foundations of all knowledge within the

---

[5] Rowan Williams, *Why Study the Past? The Quest for the Historical Church* (Eerdmans, 2005), p. 63.
[6] Moffatt, *Thrill of Tradition*, p. 82.
[7] See the discussion in Bob Tennant's 'John Tillotson and the Voice of Anglicanism', *Religion in the Age of Reason: A Transatlantic Study of the Long Eighteenth Century*, ed. Kathryn Duncan (AMS Press, 2007).

questioning individual mind. For Descartes this began with a rejection of history, ancient languages (which, of course, did not include Latin – still very much the *lingua franca* of science), as well as the entire scholastic tradition of his Church. As recent scholarship has stressed, Descartes was no crypto-agnostic or religious sceptic, but neither had the so-called 'father of modern philosophy' any desire to be a religious reformer or to join the Protestants.[8] But it is hardly surprising that in the context of seventeenth-century debates over authority, such a rejection of all previous and second-hand thinking should have contributed to an implicit questioning of the idea of tradition within the Roman Catholic world almost as much as in the Protestant, and contributed to the general suspicion of all forms of tradition that was to characterize Enlightenment assumptions on both sides of the Channel.

This very real crisis of meaning might also help to explain some of the more curious uses of the word during this period. Consider, for instance, the claim by one William Watson in 1601 that 'A priest is made by the tradition of the Chalice, Patten and Host into his hands.'[9] Watson was, admittedly, a curious figure – an underground Roman Catholic priest and plotter against James I, who nevertheless published vehemently anti-Jesuit books, and who was (perhaps not surprisingly) eventually betrayed by the Jesuits and executed in 1603. We may understand (we think) what is being meant by 'the tradition of the Chalice', but despite the overtly theological subject, the context suggests something more technical than simply an older use of the word. This suspicion is, of course, justified when we turn to the primary meaning of the English word, which is essentially legal, and concerns the conveyancing or 'handing over' of something from one person or body to another. That 'something', moreover, was usually property. Nor is this a curiosity of the early seventeenth century. As late as 1773 the *Oxford English Dictionary* cites the Scottish Judge, Lord Erskine, who pronounced that 'Tradition, which may be defined, the delivery of the possession of a subject by the proprietor, with an intention to transfer the property of it to a receiver.' It reminds us, too, of the close historical connections between legal and ecclesiastical terminology both in English, and in the *lingua franca* of Latin before that.

Indeed, despite the New Testament distinctions between the 'law' and the 'spirit', the concepts of legal and religious traditions have always been closely tied, even if, like the poles of a magnet, they have sometimes

[8] See Hans Kung, *Does God Exist?*, trs. Edward Quinn (Collins, 1980), pp. 8–16.
[9] William Watson, *A Sparing Discoverie of Our English Jesuits* (1601), p. 13.

represented opposite aspects of that historical transmission. Not least of the ties that bind these odd partners is a deeply ambiguous attitude to the past. Take, again, the case of law. On the one hand it seeks to claim an inherited body of wisdom – to embody stability, order, and eternal values, such as truth, fair play, and justice. The costumes and rituals of the courtroom are visual symbols of the history, continuity, and dignity of its administration. Yet, on the other hand, at the same time, we are all aware that it is in fact in a continual process of change, by both case-law and legislation, as it attempts (usually belatedly) to address new needs and new situations. Indeed, the concept of English common law *depends* not on its immutability, but on just such a process of continual modification and adaptation.

The case of the Church is strangely parallel. On the one hand, as John Keble was to argue,[10] it has the strongest of all claims to be charged with an inherited body of unchanging wisdom and truth – that provided by divine revelation itself. On the other, it has continually found itself called to speak prophetically to the contemporary scene, to interpret the words of scripture to its own day, and to draw from them a meaning appropriate to very different cultural contexts. Reverence for the past has sometimes gone hand-in-hand with radical judgements on the present. Even where such radicalism was notably absent – and the Established Church in the 1740s was scarcely a hotbed of prophetic fervour – there was always a perceived gap between the world of the New Testament (let alone the Old) and the English Church of the period that needed some kind of explanation – and a great deal of religious apologetic, direct or more often oblique, was devoted to explaining the difference between the apparent words of scripture and the interpretations placed on them by later authorities. This is not so much a matter of the absence of the kind of hermeneutics to be pioneered by Schleiermacher in the wake of the Higher Criticism half-a-century later, but at a much more obvious level, such things as the difference between the poverty, simplicity, and peasant life portrayed by the New Testament and the wealthy hierarchies of established European Churches, Catholic and Protestant alike, or the conflict between the Commandment 'Thou shalt not kill' and the practice of war. It is a cliché of scriptural commentary that reading the Bible has *always* been a hermeneutic as well as a textual activity.

But if the concepts of both the law and the Church have been under internal stress from paradoxes both of, and with regard to their history,

---

[10] See Chapter 8, below.

their close involvement over many centuries represents yet another, perhaps deeper, paradox. For an organization whose experience over its first few centuries had only re-enforced its claim to be alien to the political system in which it found itself, the (relatively) sudden accession of political power after Constantine's victory at the Milvian bridge constituted an existential crisis of major proportions. Not merely had a new, 'official' Church to be regulated by what came to be known as 'Canon law', in a world of narrowing secularity, the secular legal system itself rapidly came to need a basis in what had to be demonstrated as God's order. Church and law were in lockstep dance that lasted across Christendom for a thousand years,[11] and which still formally persists wherever there is a state church.

Moreover, the past now had to be *imagined* in a quite new kind of way. As Rowan Williams has noted, after Constantine the Church's previous experiences had left it with 'an agenda, a set of questions about the relation of the *ekklesia* to the changing forms of political life. It left itself, we might say, with a rationale for thinking about history.'[12] He could well have added that it meant a quite new rationale also for the *uses* of history – for imagining its origins. The conditions of the Church's formation – including the appropriation of the Hebrew Scriptures, the Jewish tradition, a sense of both its difference from and continuity with the world and the Roman Empire – also left with what one might call an agenda with regard to tradition. If the Church was indeed, as it claimed, a divinely sanctioned organization, it was also nonetheless one firmly rooted in history.

THE ANGLICAN SETTLEMENT: WESLEY TO WARBURTON

Perhaps not surprisingly, in England the ambiguous sub-text of 'betrayal' that had always lain dormant in the historical idea of tradition, so far from disappearing, was to remain like a virus in the system, flaring into sudden outbreaks of iconoclastic violence against almost every aspect of traditional Catholic forms. Though the Anglicanism of Donne, Hooker, or Ken stressed the new Church's seamless continuity with the apostolic heritage, the wholesale destruction of mediaeval English religious art, including architecture, sculpture, stained glass, and manuscripts witnesses not

---

[11] For the close historical interaction of law and religion see Harold J. Berman, *Law and Revolution: the Formation of the Western Legal Tradition* (Harvard University Press, 1983); and *Law and Revolution II: The Impact of the Protestant Reformers on the Western Legal Tradition* (Belknap Press of Harvard University Press, 2003).

[12] Williams, *Why Study the Past?*, p. 48.

merely to puritan fervour, but to an *anger* against the past that it is scarcely possible for us to comprehend today.

As so often, the unthinking cliché that 'history is written by the victors' is here a fallacy. The truth is, from the Hebrew histories of the Old Testament to the English (or American) Civil Wars, the history we remember is more often that written by the *losers* – and while we have had several centuries of debate over the moral justification of Henry VIII's Reformation, or of the relative corruptness or energy of English Catholicism in the early sixteenth century,[13] we have scarcely any accounts of the fury of the victorious iconoclasts themselves. Few of the earlier generation of sixteenth-century image-breakers kept journals like that of the so-called 'iconoclast general' of East Anglia, William Dowsing, appointed by the Earl of Manchester in Cromwell's time to oversee the destruction of images and glass throughout the region – and, even in his case, the 'journal' itself is lost, and can only be reconstructed from eighteenth-century transcriptions.[14] For him, and for the thousands we must assume he represented over a period of more than a century, the idea of tradition was nothing short of anathema. It not merely represented the dead hand of the past, as Milton said, it stank of privilege and corruption.[15] Even 100 years after the English Reformation there was nothing controversial about Raphael's view of 'traditions' in Book XII of *Paradise Lost*:

> Wolves shall succeed for teachers, grievous wolves,
> Who all the sacred mysteries of Heaven
> To their own vile advantage shall turn,
> Of lucre and ambition; and the truth,
> With superstitions and traditions taint;
> Left only in those written records pure . . .
>
> *[ll. 508–513]*

What had been handed down as the deposit of faith had been almost immediately contaminated by 'superstitions and traditions' of ecclesiastical ceremonies. For most Protestants 'tradition' meant primarily the system of indulgences and penance against which Martin Luther had thundered as compromising the truth of the gospel. It is not surprising that in John Bunyan's *The Holy War*, the three over-optimistic young volunteers to

---

[13] For a sympathetic Roman Catholic view of this, see David Knowles, *Bare Ruined Choirs: The Dissolution of the English Monasteries* (Cambridge University Press, 1976).

[14] See Trevor Cooper, *The Journal of William Dowsing* (Boydell & Brewer, 2001); Margaret Aston, *England's Iconoclasts* (Oxford University Press, 1988).

[15] See p. 29 above.

defend the cause of God were called 'Mr Tradition, Mr Human Wisdom, and Mr Human-Invention.'[16]

Though Milton and Bunyan were non-conformists, with no reason to like Elizabeth's Anglican settlement, and many good reasons to distrust it, even that visceral hatred of what was seen in the sixteenth and seventeenth centuries as the imposition of hypocrisy, superstition, and priestcraft is probably not in itself sufficient to explain the continued low status of the word in the post-1688 Anglican settlement and into the eighteenth century. If at one level, the seventeenth-century Church of England was anxious to distance itself from all association with the Romanism that had played such a part in the downfall of James II and the Stuarts, at another, the idea of the Apostolic succession had, of course, always played a significant part in the rhetoric of Anglicanism. Whether the Church of Rome was viewed as that of the Antichrist, as a corrupted and withered branch of the true vine, or merely as a thriving but parallel stem, it was repeatedly emphasized that the Church of England, at any rate, was a legitimate historical descendant of the original Apostolic Church. The first Primates of the British Church, it was pointed out, had been appointed not by the Bishop of Rome, whose authority was not then universally recognized, but by the Patriarchs of Jerusalem. Unlike those non-conformist Protestants who sought authority solely from the Bible, the inner light, or even from direct divine inspiration, the idea of tradition seemingly lay at the very heart of the eighteenth-century Anglican claim to legitimacy and authority.

Nevertheless, for obvious reasons, the word tradition is rarely used, if at all, by even the most devoutly catholic Anglicans in the eighteenth century. Addison, more commonly accused of Deism than of any remotely catholic leanings, does in fact make some use of the word in *The Spectator* (1711–12). His near-contemporary, Swift, scarcely uses it at all. Comparison with later Anglican writers of the period shows precisely the same assumption that tradition, so far from being a living concept or a guide to the present, refers only to the beliefs and stories of the remote past – legendary and even mythical. John Wesley (far more 'catholic' than ever Addison was) uses all forms of the word very sparingly in his sermons. He does, however, draw a distinction between 'traditions' and 'traditional'. Though all but two of his nine usages of the latter word occur in one work, his *Letter to Conyers Middleton*, all refer to what may be considered

---

[16] John Bunyan, *The Holy War, made by Shaddai upon Diabolus, for the regaining of the metropolis of the world, or, The losing and taking again of the town of Mansoul* (printed for Dorman Newman and Benjamin Alsop, 1682).

sound and approved Anglican practices.[17] The noun 'tradition', however, is *always* pejorative for Wesley – though sometimes weakly so, as in folk stories (five references) or heathen beliefs (six references), including Jewish superstitions (six references), and Muslim (one reference). By far the greatest weight of condemnation, however, falls on the superstition and corruption of Roman Catholic traditions, which get nineteen condemnatory references in all.

This negative association of tradition with the primitive beliefs, corruption, and superstition associated with Romanism is, by and large, typical of the period. Thus William Warburton, writing mid-century in his massive *Divine Legation of Moses Demonstrated* brings the whole problem of oral tradition versus scriptural injunction right to the fore. In volume IV he attacks those who hypocritically pretend:

> that Moses did not indeed propagate the Doctrine of a future state of rewards and punishments in *writing*, but that he delivered it to TRADITION, which conveyed it safely down through all the ages of the Jewish Dispensation, from one end of it to the other. For we see, he was so far from teaching it, that he studiously contrived to keep it out of sight; nay provided for the want of it: and the people were so far from being influenced by it, that they had not even the idea of it. Yet the writers of the Church of Rome have taken advantage of this silence in the Law of Moses concerning the future state, to advance the honour of TRADITION: For, not seeing the doctrine in the WRITTEN LAW, and fancying they saw a necessity that the Jews should have it, they concluded (to save the credit of the Jewish Church and to advance the credit of their own) that Moses had carefully inculcated it, in the TRADITIONAL.[18]

For Warburton, at least, the adjective fares no better than the noun. Both alike can only be sources of error – and failure to see this has led even good-hearted and learned Protestants into giving succour to his Roman opponents:

> A very worthy protestant Bishop does as much honour to *Tradition*, in his way. In some *Miscellanies* of the Bishop of Cloyne, published in 1752, we find these words – 'Moses, indeed, *doth not insist on a future state*, THE COMMON BASIS OF ALL POLITICAL INSTITUTIONS. – The belief of a future state (which it is manifest the Jews were possessed of *long before the coming of Christ*) seems to have obtained

---

[17] John Wesley, *Letter to Conyers Middleton occasioned by his late 'Free Enquiry'* (1748–9). I owe this reference to Dr Bob Tennant.

[18] The weakness of this line of argument, he adds, is shown by the fact that Richard Simon (father of the French Higher Criticism) had to resort to the book of Maccabees, in the Apocrypha, containing books already rejected by Protestants, for evidence. William Warburton, *The Divine Legation of Moses Demonstrated*, Vol. IV, reprinted from the 4th edn, 1765 (Garland, 1978), p. 359.

amongst the Hebrews from primæval TRADITION, which might render it unnecessary for Moses to insist on that article.' Though the Bishop has not the merit of saying this with a professed design, like Father Simon, *pour appuyer la Tradition*, yet the Church of Rome has not the less obligation to him for assigning so much virtue to this their powerful assistant, which has conveyed to them all they want; and indeed most of what they have. But if the *traditional* doctrine of a future state prevailed amongst the Jews, in the time of Moses, and that he would trust to the same conveyance, for the safe delivery of it down to the times of Christ, how came it to pass that he did his best to weaken the efficacy, by studiously contriving to draw men off, as it were, from the Doctrine, and always representing it under the impenetrable cover of temporal rewards and punishments?[19]

So there we have it: George Berkeley, Bishop of Cloyne, like Shakespeare's Brutus, is no doubt an honourable man, but even with the best will in the world too great a belief in 'tradition' sells the pass to Rome. In the end it is the Roman Church's most 'powerful assistant'.

ROBERT LOWTH AND THE IDEA OF SCRIPTURAL TRADITION

It is, therefore, perhaps not as remarkable as it might seem that the work of the man who, more than any other, was responsible for reviving a contextual understanding of the Hebrew world of the Old Testament, and its poetic traditions, should have had such an equivocal response if not to the concept, then to the word itself. Certainly a first reading of Robert Lowth's *Lectures on the Sacred Poetry of the Hebrews* (1787) and, more significantly, his *New Translation* of Isaiah (1778) would suggest that both were written and intended to be understood within this sense of an ongoing apostolic tradition reaching back to the early Church, and through that to the prophetic tradition of the Old Testament.

The history of the previous two centuries alone would help to explain why the word 'tradition' is so frequently absent from the very seventeenth- and eighteenth-century debates where we would most expect to find it – and certainly 'tradition' is *not* a word that occurs often in Robert Lowth's vocabulary. Indeed, given the nature of his subject, without some knowledge of the previous history of the word, it would be little short of astonishing how *absent* the term is from either the *Lectures*, or from *Isaiah*. A careful count reveals only *one* use of the word in the former, and *two* in the latter.[20] Moreover, the sole use in the *Lectures* is both adjectival and – by implication – negative. Citing the authority of Tacitus, he comments

[19] Ibid., pp. 360–1.   [20] I owe this labour to my research assistant, Dana White.

that the Germans 'had no records or annals but the traditional poems, in which they celebrated the heroic exploits of their ancestors'.[21] Not surprisingly, one feels at times that Lowth actually goes out of his way to avoid the word and its associations altogether, preferring to write in purely technical terms of the texts and their 'transmission' 'down to the present time'. 'All writings transmitted to us,' he writes in the Preliminary Dissertation to Isaiah:

> from early times, the original copies of which have long ago perished, have suffered in their passage to us by the mistakes of many transcribers, through whose hands we have received them; errors continually accumulating in proportion to the number of the transcripts, and the stream generally becoming more impure, the more distant it is from its source.[22]

This watery metaphor of a stream, once pure at its source, and becoming progressively more polluted by time and distance from its original spring, is one that explicitly or implicitly dominates Lowth's whole principle of translation in *Isaiah*. It is the role of the translator to filter or purify the corruptions of time, and so *restore* it to its original quality.[23] Though this nominally retains the legal and ecclesiastical notion of 'handing down' a precious legacy, the implications of this are, of course, the very opposite of the accepted ecclesiastical tradition on which the 1688 Anglican settlement was as much dependent as its Catholic rival, and is far closer to the assumptions of the more radical Protestant reformers of the sixteenth and seventeenth centuries, who had wished to 'restore' the structures of a now-lost primitive Church.

Given this rhetorical and polemical context of the 1740s and 1750s it would hardly be surprising if Lowth, too, felt that the word 'tradition', with its associations of an ongoing body of hermeneutic commentary and practice in the interpretation of scripture was potentially too ideologically charged for comfort, and might be seen (like the hapless Berkeley) as selling the pass to Rome. But not merely is there absolutely no evidence of such ideological nervousness on Lowth's part, there is

---

[21] Robert Lowth, *Lectures on the Sacred Poetry of the Hebrews*, trs. G. Gregory (1787), Vol. 1, pp. 84–6.

[22] Robert Lowth, *Isaiah: A New Translation* (1778) (reprinted Routledge/Thoemmes Press, 1995), p. lvii.

[23] Ever the classical scholar, Lowth seems to be here echoing Kallimachos's *Hymn to Apollo*, where the god spurns epic poetry in these words: 'The Assyrian river's stream [i.e. the Euphrates] is great, but it carries a great deal of mud and rubbish along with its waters. The Melissa [priestesses of Deo – i.e. Demeter] do not bring Deo water from just anywhere, but only from the little stream that springs forth, pure and undefiled, from a holy spring, the finest and the best.' (Translated by Amy Vail.)

overwhelming evidence of his interest in consulting *all* possible rival
traditions in the interests of textual accuracy. In *Isaiah*, the primacy
of the Vulgate, and even its old Latin predecessor, is dismissed not on
polemical grounds but simply as being already too far from the source –
'being for the most part the Translation of Jerom, made in the Fourth
Century, [it] is of service . . . in proportion to its antiquity'.[24] Instead he
is happy to invoke authorities from whatever traditions may be appropriate, ranging from the scholarly conjectures of the sixteenth-century
Mantuan Jewish authority, Rabbi Azarias,[25] to the 'learned Mr Woide',
a Coptic scholar, and Chaldean, Syriac, and three early Greek texts,
besides that of the Septuagint. Particular acknowledgement is made to
Benjamin Kennicott's magisterial variorum edition of the Hebrew Bible,
the *Dissertatio Generalis*, which was in preparation at the same time that
Lowth was at work on his own translation.

It is, therefore, revealing that the first time in Lowth's *Isaiah* where the
word 'tradition' *is* used it is in the context of a doubtful authority at the
beginning of the Notes – which are, incidentally, more extensive than
the entire Preliminary Dissertation and the actual text of Isaiah combined. Lowth writes:

Isaiah exercised the Prophetical Office during a long period of time, if he lived
to the reign of Manasseh; for the lowest computation, beginning from the year
in which Uzziah died, when some suppose him to have received his first appoint-
ment to that office, brings it to 61 years. But the Tradition of the Jews, that he was
put to death by Manasseh, is very uncertain; and one of their principal Rabbins
(Aben Ezra . . .) seems rather to think, that he died before Hezekiah, which is
indeed more probable.[26]

In other words, for Lowth, 'Tradition' is *inherently* suspect not on ideological grounds, as one might expect, but on scholarly ones – it consists
of an oral sequence of transmission for which, unlike written texts, one
only has the latest version. Even where this may not be strictly true (one
suspects in this case that this has been for some time a written rather than
an oral tradition) it is still to be contrasted with the more reliable opinions
of specific scholarly authorities, such as, in this case, Aben Ezra. Another
use of the word, at the end of the Notes to Chapter 1, occurs in the gloss
to verse 30, where the 'revolters and sinners' shall be 'as a garden, wherein
is no water'. Here, we are told, 'there never was a more stupendous work of
this kind, than the reservoir of Saba, or Merab, in Arabia Felix. According

---

[24] Lowth, *Isaiah*, p. lxix.   [25] Ibid., pp. xli–xlviii.   [26] Ibid., Notes, p.1.

to the tradition of the country, it was the work of Balkis, that queen of Sheba, who visited Solomon':

It was a vast lake formed by the collection of the waters of a torrent in a valley, where, at a narrow pass between two mountains, a very high mole, or dam, was built. The water of the lake so formed had near twenty fathom depth; and there were three sluices at different heighths, by which, at whatever height the lake flood, the plain below might be watered. By conduits and canals from these sluices the water was constantly distributed in due proportion to the several lands; so that the whole country for many miles became a perfect paradise. The city of Saba, or Merab, was situated immediately below the great dam; a great flood came, and raised the lake above its usual heighth: the dam gave way in the middle of the night; the waters burst forth at once, and overwhelmed the whole city, with the neighbouring towns, and people. The remains of the eight tribes were forced to abandon their dwelling, and the beautiful valley became a morass and a desert. This fatal catastrophe happened long before the time of Mohammed, who mentions it in the Koran, Chap. xxxiv. [27]

Apart from the fact that Lowth is prepared to cite the Koran, what is interesting about this passage is its sheer irrelevance to the text under discussion. No English reader, even from the soggiest bit of fenland around Oxford's greatest rival, was really going to have trouble with the image of a garden without water. Nevertheless, in a piece of almost unequalled overkill, Lowth insists 'That the reader may have a clear notion of this matter, it will be necessary to give some account of the management of their gardens in this respect' – and follows it with no less than three-and-a-half pages on the irrigation of Near Eastern gardens, beginning with that of Eden. [28] Even by Lowthian standards of scholarship this is excessive.

While this may be simply an example of an academic never letting a good footnote get away, a literary critic might also observe that this fascination with hydraulics in the Notes is entirely of a piece with the water imagery running throughout the Preliminary Dissertation. The river of life, beginning with the rivers in the Garden of Eden, is a constant precious flow through the text – and, for us, down to the present. As Lowth is at pains to stress, it is the lifeblood, the artery, that nourishes all civilization, all life. Under proper control, it makes all else possible; without it, without the dam and sluices that deliver and hand on the water supply, the land is dead and barren – made worse, in Isaiah's imagery, because it was once a green and fertile garden.

[27] Ibid., p. 20.   [28] Ibid., pp. 17–20.

Whether or not such a train – or should one say 'flow'? – of imagery was in any way conscious in Lowth's mind, it may also go some way to clarify his own attitude to the biblical tradition he was attempting to expound:

The first and principal business of a Translator is to give us the plain literal and grammatical sense of his author; the obvious meaning of his words, phrases, and sentences, and to express them in the language into which he translates, as far as may be, in equivalent words, phrases, and sentences . . . This is peculiarly so in subjects of high importance such as the Holy Scriptures, in which so much depends on the phrase and expression; and particularly in the Prophetical books of scripture; where from the letter are often deduced deep and recondite senses, which must all owe their weight and solidity to the just and accurate interpretation of the words of the Prophecy. For whatever senses are supposed to be included in the Prophet's words, Spiritual, Mystical, Allegorical, Anagogical, or the like, they must all entirely depend on the Literal Sense.[29]

Now it is possible to hear in such declarations the voice of proto-modernity, of the new-style textual scholar paying ironic lip-service to the flummery of typological and allegorical readings even while secretly dismissing them to the scrap-heap of history. But I believe this to be a profound misreading of Lowth. Firstly, this is evidently such an important point that he repeats it again, almost verbatim, at the conclusion of the Preliminary Dissertation.[30] Secondly, he himself is quite clearly drawn, over and over again, towards the very 'deep and recondite senses' that he modestly assigns to others. If we look only as far as Isaiah 1. 29 – the verse before the 'garden, wherein is no water' – we find this:

For ye shall be ashamed of the ilexes, which ye have desired; and ye shall blush for the gardens, which ye have chosen: when ye shall be as an ilex, whose leaves are blasted . . .

This draws from Lowth over a page-and-a-half of notes concerning the exact tree intended by Isaiah – and the accuracy of the King James Bible's translation of 'oak'. Some of this does indeed concern the precise meaning of the Hebrew, which most commentators have interpreted as Terebinth, but Lowth rejects this not on textual, but on overtly symbolic grounds.

. . .I think neither the Oak, nor the Terebinth, will do in this place of Isaiah . . . [because of] their being deciduous; where the Prophet's design seems to me to require an ever-green: otherwise the casting of its leaves would be nothing out of the common established course of nature, and no proper image of extreme distress, and total desolation; parallel to that of a garden without water, that is, wholly burnt up and destroyed . . . Upon the whole, I have chosen to make it the

---

[29] Ibid., p. lii.   [30] Ibid., pp. lxxiii–lxxiv.

Ilex; which word Voffius . . . derives from the [same Hebrew word]; that, whether
the word itself be rightly rendered or not, I might at least preserve the propriety
of the poetical image.[31]

In other words, where there is any doubt, the 'poetical' takes precedence
over the literal mechanics of textual scholarship. Nor, in practice, does
Lowth neglect the allegorical. Here, for instance, is his note to Isaiah 52.13
which he translates as 'Behold, my servant shall prosper; he shall be raised
aloft, and magnified, and very highly exalted':

The subject of Isaiah's Prophecy, from the Fortieth Chapter inclusive, has hitherto
been, in general, the Deliverance of the people of God. This includes in it three
distinct parts; which, however, have a close connection with one another: that is,
the deliverance of the Jews from the captivity of Babylon; the deliverance of the
Gentiles from their miserable state of ignorance and idolatry; and the deliverance
of Mankind from the captivity of sin and death. These three subjects are subor-
dinate to one another; and the latter two are shadowed out under the image of
the former. They are covered by it as by a vail; which however is transparent, and
suffers them to appear through it . . . Now these three subjects having a very near
relation to one another; for, as the agent, who was to effect the two later deliverances, that is, the Messiah, was to be born a Jew, with particular limitations of
time, family, and other circumstances; the first deliverance was necessary in the
order of Providence, and according to the determinate counsel of God, to the
accomplishment of the two latter deliverances; and the second deliverance was
necessary to the third, or rather, was involved in it, and made an essential part of
it: this being the case, Isaiah has not treated the three subjects as quite distinct
and separate in a methodical and orderly manner, like a philosopher or a logician,
but has taken them in their connective view; he has handled them as a prophet
and poet; he hath allegorised the former, and under the image of it has shadowed
out the two latter; he has thrown them all together, has mixed one with another,
has passed from this to that with rapid transitions, and has painted the whole
with the strongest and boldest imagery.

Perhaps sensing at this point that he has allowed himself to be carried
away by the awe-inspiring reach of the allegorical meaning of this relatively straightforward-seeming verse, Lowth suddenly reverts to his plain
man just-clearing-the-ground style:

This seems to me to be the nature and the true design of this part of Isaiah's
Prophecies; and this view of them seems to afford the best method of resolv-
ing difficulties, in which Expositors are frequently engaged, being much divided
between what is called the Literal, and the Mystical sense, not very properly; for
the mystical or spiritual sense is very often the most literal sense of all.

---

[31] Ibid., p. 17.

Nevertheless, the cat is out of the bag. For all the 'modernism' of his poly-glot scholarship and his careful respect for the text, Lowth is very much a man of his time in his belief in the Mosaic authorship of the Pentateuch, the inspiration of the Holy Spirit, and in the possibility of multi-layered allegorical and typological readings. Perhaps we should look again at the huge commentary constructed around the 'garden, wherein is no water' (Isaiah I. 30). Here too is, in effect, an allegorical structure as elaborate as anything in Augustine or any of the Church Fathers. The difference, of course, is that it is superficially composed of scholarly references (as we have seen, even drawing on the Koran) rather than other biblical texts. In that respect, however, it is not so very different from other, contempo-rary, eighteenth-century biblical commentaries which, even before Lowth, were an increasingly eclectic patchwork of previous authorities. The real difference is that even as Lowth attempts to set his material in its literary and historical context, his imagery is reaching out to create a much more poetic and symbolic frame of reference.

And here, of course, however we may construe Lowth's seeming reluc-tance to use the *word* 'tradition', he is actually being at his most trad-itional. Whatever may have been the Latin legal meaning of tradition, for the *Hebrew* world tradition was not only a 'handing on', it was midrash, an ongoing debate and commentary on what was being conveyed. The law is incomplete without the associated tradition of reflection and discussion by which it was acclimatized and absorbed by each Jewish community, wherever it was to be found. Nor was this only a post-biblical phenom-enon. As David Jeffrey has pointed out:

Isaiah, as a book of prophecy, is itself a powerful 'reading' of another book, the Torah, and . . . its unity comes from the established shape of the canonical trans-mission of Hebrew Scripture and history – the implied as well as explicit rhet-orical patterning of its foundational texts. And this, then, is essential perspective for reading Hebrew prophetic literature: one is required to read it with one eye on the first five books of the Bible. [32]

This may also be one reason, at least, for the seemingly vast weight of notes and commentary in which Lowth had embedded his 'new translation'. If we see it *simply* as a new translation, separated from the Preliminary Dissertation which, together with the 283 pages of Notes, makes up the bulk of the 1778 volume, we miss what is, in effect, the grand midrashic

---

[32] David Lyle Jeffrey, *The People of the Book: Christian Identity and Literary Culture* (Eerdmans, 1996), p. 35.

design of the whole. Lowth's *Isaiah* is in many ways as much a commentary as it is a translation. The Preliminary Dissertation not merely summarizes the insights of the earlier *Lectures on the Sacred Poetry of the Hebrews*, but adds twenty-five years of reflection and research since their publication in Latin in 1753, revealing that he himself had been profoundly influenced by the Higher Criticism that he had earlier helped to create. By 1778 he is, if anything, even more alive to the problems presented by corrupt texts than he was in the 1750s. In addition to a vastly increased list of primary sources, he also cites, with respect, the ideas of the pioneer German biblical scholar Johann David Michaelis who had republished his *Lectures* in the original Latin in Göttingen in 1758, with extensive further notes in German.[33] It was Michaelis who was one of Lowth's principal sources for the notes on the waterworks of Arabia Felix.[34] At the same time, Lowth is, as we have observed, noticeably *more* aware of the poetic possibilities – not to mention those 'deep and recondite meanings' – that can co-exist in a single passage of scripture. Alongside the rediscovery of the Bible within a historical context runs the no less important rediscovery of the Hebrew prophets *as poetry*. Unlike his German contemporaries, Eichhorn or Reimarus, there is in Lowth, as we have seen, no sense that historical criticism diminishes or displaces poetic sensibility.

Lowth's *Isaiah* is, therefore, a deeply traditional work in the Hebrew and biblical sense. But time does not stand still. If, in the sense in which I have been outlining, Lowth's work can be seen as an eighteenth-century continuation of the 'literary' and midrashic tradition of the Hebrew Bible, there are other senses in which, notwithstanding, it also *has* to be seen as a quite different kind of work. To begin with the obvious, it is a *Christian*, not a Jewish work. Lowth's *Isaiah* is most certainly a Hebrew document, but for him, however much it must be read within the context of the Hebrew Bible, it is always also part of the Old Testament. Structurally it may well look backward to a reading of the Torah, but, equally, its prophecies look forward to the coming of Christ and the salvation of all humanity. Similarly, the mystical and recondite layers of interpretation belong to a specifically Christian tradition of hermeneutics by which the Hebrew Bible was appropriated and re-structured to point beyond itself to a fulfilment in the New Testament. Typological and allegorical readings, though

---

[33] See Stephen Prickett, *Words and the Word: Language, Poetics and Biblical Interpretation* (Cambridge University Press, 1986), pp. 49–50; 111–13.

[34] He also had the unusual distinction of translating Richardson's *Clarissa* – then the longest English novel – into German.

not entirely absent from the Hebrew Scriptures, belong more to the Hellenistic world, leading back to Augustine and to the Church Fathers, not to the world of the Hebrew prophets.

But no less importantly, Lowth is always aware that his work is of its time and place: eighteenth-century England. This is not merely a matter of the vastly increased range of the scholarly tools then becoming available – of which the Kennicott Bible was but one. Nor is it simply that of the new horizons opened up by the Enlightenment – essential though these also were. What was also unique to Lowth's England was that it was the world's first *pluralistic* society. We have already cited Peter Harrison's argument that it was only in the late seventeenth century, after the Reformation, Civil War, and the Restoration of 1668, that people became fully aware of 'religion' as a word encompassing radically different possibilities – in short, as a word with a plural form.[35] What had changed, however, with the coming of pluralism, was not merely a new meaning to 'religion', but with it, a whole clutch of words whose meanings had to modify and change in response. One such word was 'tradition' itself.

I began by citing the *Oxford English Dictionary* to the effect that there has been no substantial change in the meaning of the word 'tradition' over the past 300 years, and in lexicographical terms this is certainly true. But religious pluralism not merely brought a plural form to 'religion', it also gave one to 'tradition'. A single religious grand narrative had little or no need for different or competing 'traditions'. Even the violent polemics of the Reformation (together with its no less violent actions) did not necessarily portend competing traditions. For those not prepared to overthrow the established Episcopal structures, the battle was for *possession* of the one true Apostolic tradition, not over how to divide it up. There might be fierce debate as to who best represented that tradition, but no one suggested there might be different Apostolic traditions. As we have noted, Lowth rarely uses the word 'tradition', but he *never* uses the word in its plural form at all.

Yet between 1753 and 1778 other changes were occurring that made the plural form meaningful for perhaps the first time. If the Church of England and the Church of Rome could fight over possession of the Christian Apostolic tradition, could it be said that the Lutherans (whom Lowth was now much more aware of than in 1753) must fight the Anglicans over the same territory ? With a sovereign who was head of the Anglican Church

[35] Peter Harrison, *'Religion' and Religions in the English Enlightenment* (Cambridge University Press, 1990).

south of the border, but a Presbyterian if ever he was to enter Scotland (which none did until the Prince Regent made his famous visit in 1822), in what sense did two such different churches *share* a tradition ? Unlike the 1753 *Lectures*, which had been prepared in a great hurry, Lowth had had twenty-five years – in effect, a life's work – to study Catholic, Coptic, Orthodox, and old Syriac, not to mention Jewish and Muslim sources for his understanding of Isaiah. All had long and scholarly traditions. If, in the past, the concept of tradition had been a matter for dispute between religious polemicists and the evidence of historical scholars, by the late eighteenth century that very evidence was making it increasingly clear that there could be, in effect, *many* traditions, and more than one way of understanding and conveying the wisdom, rituals, and spiritual experience of the former ages down to the present day. Small wonder that Lowth so carefully confined his use of the word to the singular, and then only to the distant past – to Josephus or the writings of pre-Islamic Arabs.

Finally, and perhaps most importantly, a new meaning to the word 'tradition' had been, in effect, created by Lowth himself twenty-five years before with the publication of the *Lectures*. The revolutionary identification of prophecy with poetry in the Hebrew Scriptures had, as we know, set in motion a new critical aesthetics that was to find its culmination in the romantic movement – in England, Blake, Wordsworth, Coleridge, and Shelley; in Germany, Herder, Lessing, Novalis, Schiller, Schleiermacher and the Schlegels – both groups, in this respect, as I have elsewhere called them, 'the children of Lowth'.[36] In the growth of the new concept we can see at work Coleridge's process of 'desynonymy', whereby what was originally thought of as a single concept is divided into two separate, if related, notions – which require the coinage of new words to describe the separation.[37]

The new word here is, of course, 'aesthetics', first used in its modern sense of 'criticism of taste' in Germany in the second half of the eighteenth century, and, despite Kant's opposition,[38] rapidly taken up by the German Romantics. Only a few years later it had passed into regular currency in less theoretical Britain because of a similar need.[39] It is difficult for the

---

[36] See Prickett, *Words and the Word*, Ch. 3.
[37] Samuel Taylor Coleridge, *Philosophical Lectures* (1818–1819), ed. K. Coburn (Routledge, 1949).
[38] First used by Baumgarten in his *Aesthetica* (1750–8). Kant, however, applied it in what he believed was its 'correct' sense of 'the science which treats of the conditions of sensuous perception' in the *Critique of Pure Reason* (1781) and thereafter in his *Critique of Judgement* (1790).
[39] See Coleridge: 'I wish I could find a more familiar word than aesthetic, for works of taste and criticism', *Blackwood's Magazine*, Vol. x, (1821), p. 254.

modern reader, thoroughly secularized and acclimatized to the academic division between literary and biblical studies to recapture the mental set in which the two disciplines could not yet be experienced as requiring separate ways of thinking. Yet if we look at the criticism of the eighteenth century – Dennis, Jacob, Trapp, not to mention Watts, or even Burke – poetry is taken for granted as 'the natural language of religion'.[40] The very idea of poetic sublimity was inconceivable without reference to religious awe. The idea of an aesthetic tradition entirely separable from its religious roots was almost impossible to contemplate, and at first sight Lowth seems no different from his fellow-critics in the 1740s and 1750s. But simply by emphasizing the central role of poetic technique – parallelism, etc. – in the creation of prophecy, Lowth had turned poetry from being the handmaid of religion to its partner. Form influenced content, and *vice versa*. If, on the one hand, Lowth's *Lectures* had re-awakened poets to their prophetic role, he had also paved the way for the idea of a secular aesthetics. Shelley's *Defence of Poetry*, with its blurring of the distinction between poetry and prose, and stress on poets as 'the unacknowledged legislators of mankind', is, in this sense, simply a linear development of Lowthian principles.[41] But, as in this case, the separation of aesthetics from religion, so far from being a clean divorce, has meant that each has returned to haunt the other. If aesthetics has suffered from what I have elsewhere called an 'ache in its missing limb',[42] theology without aesthetics has, as Kierkegaard recognized,[43] become a bumbling, blundering thing, blind to awe and wonder, confused by the poetic, baffled and irritated by irony.

Lowth's *Isaiah* is, in effect, the greatest monument of traditional biblical scholarship of his century, and with it he was to blow wide open the very meaning of the word 'tradition' itself. It is, for him, almost the word that dare not speak its name; the dog that did not bark. From 1778 onwards the debate has raged not so much over who has, or has not, the biblical or Apostolic tradition, it is over the *meaning* of the word itself, of the relationship between religion and aesthetics, and how that can be understood

---

[40] John Dennis, *The Grounds of Criticism in Poetry* (1704); Giles Jacob, *An Historical Account of the Lives and Writings of our most Considerable English Poets* (1720); Joseph Trapp, *Lectures on Poetry*, trs. William Bowyes (1742); Isaac Watts, 'Preface' to *Horae Lyricae* (1709); Edmund Burke, *A Philosophical Enquiry into our Ideas of the Sublime and the Beautiful* (1757).

[41] Percy Bysshe Shelley, *A Defence of Poetry* (1840).

[42] See Stephen Prickett, *Narrative, Religion and Science: Fundamentalism versus Irony 1700–1999* (Cambridge University Press, 2002), Ch. 5.

[43] Hence the savage irony of Kierkegaard's doctoral thesis *The Concept of Irony, with Continual Reference to Socrates* (1841), trs. and ed. Howard V. Hong and Edna H. Hong (Princeton University Press, 1989).

(if at all) in an increasingly pluralistic society. That was the issue as much for Coleridge as for Julius Hare in the 1820s, that was to be the question that was to divide the University of Oxford in the wake of Keble's Assize Sermon of 1833, that was the problem with which Newman was to wrestle in the 1840s, and was to be explored over and over again in his works from the 1845 *Essay on the Development of Christian Doctrine*, to his *Letter Addressed to the Duke of Norfolk* thirty years later. It was the stumbling-block to Keble's godson, Matthew Arnold. It was to give new inspiration to F.D. Maurice, the Unitarian convert to Anglicanism and author of *The Kingdom of Christ*. It was the cause of George Tyrrell's agonies over his Catholic faith in *Through Scylla and Charybdis* (1907). By the twentieth century, still as much a literary as a theological problem, it was to be as central to T.S. Eliot's aesthetics as it was to his theology – and to read his 1919 essay, 'Tradition and the Individual Talent', without an awareness of how its arguments were to affect his conversion to Christianity seven years later, is also to miss how central the idea of tradition is to *Ash Wednesday* and the *Four Quartets*.

What this meant was that, for the generation following Lowth's own, the word had, in effect, to be re-invented. But before that there had first to occur the further epistemological crisis that we call 'romanticism' – and its most shocking material concomitant, the French Revolution.

CHAPTER 3

Revolution and tradition

THE STRANGE AGREEMENT OF BURKE AND PAINE

There could hardly be a better illustration of the low status of the idea of tradition at the end of the eighteenth century than the virtual absence of the word from the most important debate of the age – that over the French Revolution. Burke's *Reflections on the Revolution in France* (1790) are often taken to articulate and even epitomize the eighteenth-century sense of tradition in the face of incipient revolution – by implication in England as much as France. It was certainly to articulate the conservative agenda for much of the next 200 years.[1] Nevertheless, astonishingly for those not already familiar with the sentiment and rhetoric of the period, he actually uses the word 'tradition' only *twice* in the whole work – and then, both times, in parentheses in the same rather convoluted sentence. The form of the word, 'traditionary', as well as its context, make it clear that he is invoking what is an essentially *antique*, even obsolete, concept, enshrined in fittingly antique language:

In the clause which follows, for preventing questions, by reason of any pretended titles to the crown, they declare (observing also in this the traditionary language, along with the traditionary policy of the nation, and repeating as from a rubric the language of the preceding acts of Elizabeth and James), that on the preserving 'a certainty in the SUCCESSION thereof, the unity, peace, and tranquillity of this nation doth, under God, wholly depend'.

His point, of course, is that not merely had the English *never* had an elective monarchy, but that the 'Glorious Revolution' of 1688 had made it clear that in accordance with ancient and well-established tradition, 'the English

---

[1] The reasons for Burke's astonishing successful predictions of the outcome of the French Revolution have been much debated – one the most plausible being Iain McCalman's suggestion that he had been deeply frightened by the Gordon riots ten years before. See 'Mad Lord George and Madame La Motte: Riot and Sexuality in the Genesis of Burke's "Reflections on the Revolution in France"', *Journal of British Studies*, July (1996), pp. 343–67.

nation did at that time most solemnly renounce and abdicate it, for them-selves and for all their posterity for ever.'[2] Implicit in this argument is the assumption that only in a *pre-1688* context does the idea of 'tradition' have any force. Indeed, as a number of critics have pointed out, a close reading of Burke's argument shows that behind such conservative genuflections, the *status quo* that he wishes to preserve is not that of any Tudor or Stuart Divine Right of Kings – the world of earlier tradition – but the essen-tially bourgeois contract established in 1688.[3] In short, in this sense Burke's *Reflections* is not so much a debate about either the monarchy (English or French varieties) or (despite the flourishes over Marie Antoinette) even the recent events in France, but over the nature and meaning of the English Revolution of 1688 – and, significantly, this is *not* something in which the word 'tradition' apparently plays any part.

The immediate target of this polemic was Richard Price, the fiery Welsh non-conformist minister who, in November 1789, had delivered (and sub-sequently published) a *Discourse on the Love of our Country* to the Society for Commemorating the Revolution in Great Britain.[4] For Price, the French ideals of *liberté*, *égalité*, and *fraternité* could immediately be trans-lated into his own deeply-held belief in the peaceful evolution of human society under conditions of personal liberty, democracy and freedom of speech – which had been, for him, the true goals of the 1688 Revolution, but which had so far been best fulfilled by the emerging American democ-racy across the Atlantic. Though in tracing what we would now consider the mainstream tradition of liberal ideas he is quick to invoke the names of Milton, Locke, Sidney, and Hoadley in England, or Montesquieu, Marmontel, and Turgot in France, the word 'tradition' was no more a part of Price's vocabulary than of Burke's. It is a word which, even if it came to mind, would have been irremediably tarnished by defenders of the *ancien régime*. Instead, Price selects freely from organic images of nat-ural growth, rather than from its assumed antithesis, the dead hand of 'tradition' and the past: 'They sowed a seed which has taken root, and is now growing up to a glorious harvest. To the information they con-veyed by their writings we owe those revolutions in which every friend to mankind is now exulting. – What an encouragement is this to us all in

---

[2] Edmund Burke, *Reflections on the French Revolution* (London: Dent, 1940), p. 17.
[3] See, for instance, the Introduction by Conor Cruise O'Brien to the Penguin edition of *Reflections* (Pelican Books, 1968).
[4] For a brief account of Price's sermon see Stephen Prickett, *England and the French Revolution* (Macmillan, 1989), pp. 31–42.

our endeavours to enlighten the world?[5] To twenty-first-century eyes, not the least extraordinary thing is that, in what is essentially a debate about the nature of the 1688 Revolution, and the meaning and implications of the subsequent political settlement, the word 'tradition' is invoked by *neither* side. It is the more extraordinary, in that the debate itself conforms with uncanny accuracy to the conditions and ground rules suggested by MacIntyre for the construction of 'tradition'. The 1688 'Revolution' did indeed constitute an epistemological crisis of monstrous proportions. It had been essentially a compromise hammered out between a large number of individuals and groups – some of whom had learned their skills in not dissimilar negotiations over the Restoration of Charles II in 1660. But on the subsequent interpretation of what had been created effectively by an *ad hoc* alliance of diverse interests for limited ends hung the whole future of the so-called (unwritten) English constitution – and, by extension, that of the United Kingdom after the Act of Union with Scotland in 1707.

Nevertheless, by carefully relegating the word 'tradition' itself to a pre-Stuart world of Divine Right, Burke was, of course, like all good traditionalists, claiming from it a particular interpretation of history and line of descent. But if, like Price, he was laying claim to what we (at any rate) would understand as a particular tradition of interpretation, that interpretation also stemmed from a crisis far deeper than simply one over the nature of political liberty in the late eighteenth century – vitally important as that was. This was a crisis over legitimacy itself. Like the English Reformation, which had preceded the political turmoil of the seventeenth century by more than 100 years, the debate over legitimacy affected not merely its active partisans of both sides, but also a 'silent majority' who could only view events (whatever their outcome) with a deep unease. We have already commented on the deafening silence from the pulpit that greeted the 1688 Revolution. Hence the fact that though (in retrospect) the various Jacobite risings of 1698, 1714, and, most serious of all, the '45', may have seemed doomed to failure, Jacobite sentiment was never far from the surface of British politics for much of the eighteenth century. Dr Johnson's equivocal sympathies have been much discussed[6] – and were more typical than the Whig interpretation of history would have had us suppose.[7] As with the earlier question of the legitimacy of the Anglican Church, no

[5] Richard Price, *A Discourse on the Love of our Country* (1789), p. 14.
[6] See Kevin Hart's summary of this debate in *Samuel Johnson and the Culture of Property* (Cambridge University Press, 1999).
[7] Herbert Butterfield, *The Whig Interpretation of History* (Bell, 1931; reprinted, 1963).

amount of rational polemic could easily disperse the uneasy suspicion that what had been displaced was somehow more than a question of political expediency or even principle, but a divinely ordered structure. Thus any description of the 1688 settlement in terms of 'existential crisis' needs to highlight the fact that it was much more than a change of political regime. It involved profound metaphysical upheavals, creating doubt, anxiety, and residual guilt even among those most ostensibly committed to the new political terms of reference.[8] Conversely, in such circumstances, any notion of 'tradition' was bound to carry with it not merely political and social implications, but also a profound and not wholly welcome metaphysical freight. Small wonder, perhaps, that as we have already seen in the case of Lowth, the word was so seldom deployed in the eighteenth century, and when it was, as in the Burke quotation above, it was handled with all the care normally given to highly explosive material.

What Burke calls 'the traditionary language, along with the traditionary policy of the nation' is linked with such openly ecclesiastical and faintly contemptuous phrases as 'a rubric' of the preceding acts of Elizabeth and James to ensure 'a certainty in the succession' and 'the unity, peace, and tranquillity of this nation'. That it has at least all the appearance of having been handed down from antiquity may give it added *cachet*, but tradition, for Burke, is less a purely human construct than a marker of the confluence of political and divine orders – and, precisely for that reason, perhaps, to be invoked obliquely or by implication only rather than by name. Certainly it is not a word to be raised either in defence of the *ancien régime* in France or the Glorious Revolution of 1688.

It was, of course, precisely the suggestion of even latent divine authority hallowing the existence of accepted traditions that was to so infuriate Tom Paine. His answer to Burke, *The Rights of Man*, was published in two parts in 1791 and 1792. Part I engages Burke over the course and meaning of the French Revolution in familiar enough terms, but more important for our purposes is the much better-selling Part II, which was concerned less with the Revolution than with what a genuinely egalitarian society in general might look like. Though the imbalance in sales seems to have been primarily the result of canny commercial pricing – Part I had originally been sold in 1791 at 3 shillings, whereas when Part II was published the following year both parts were sold at sixpence each, thus increasing sales tenfold – the effect was to shift the debate away from the immediate

---

[8] A point well made by J.C.D. Clark, in *English Society 1688–1832* (Cambridge University Press, 1985).

rights and wrongs of the rapidly changing situation in France towards the political situation in Britain. Much of the rhetorical brilliance of Paine's writing lies in his capacity to de-familiarize what hitherto had seemed to be unquestionable and part of the given make-up of things, and so allow their implications to be scrutinized in the cold light of reason. Here he is, for instance, ostensibly on the French monarchy:

When extraordinary power and extraordinary pay are allotted to any individual in a government, he becomes the centre around which every type of corruption generates and forms. Give any man a million a year, and add thereto the power of creating and disposing of places [i.e. government funded jobs], at the expense of a country, and the liberties of that country are no longer secure. What is called the splendour of the throne is no other than the corruption of the state. It is made up of a band of parasites, living in luxurious indolence, out of public taxes.[9]

Such movements from the particular to the general, from individual cases to underlying principles, immediately lift the discussion from the French context and (as Paine intended it should) bring it nearer home. 'What is called monarchy,' he continues, 'always appeared to me a silly contemptible thing.'[10] It is hardly surprising that after the publication of Part II Paine had to flee to France to avoid arrest. There he was welcomed as a champion of liberty, and, in tune with the still internationalist tenor of this stage of the Revolution, in August 1792 he was made an honorary French citizen, and, the following month, elected to the National Assembly.

It was here, in France, that he embarked on a much more serious challenge to the accepted notions of tradition, in that his new book, *The Age of Reason*, was specifically addressed not so much to the political trappings of the *ancien régimes* as to their metaphysical underpinnings in religion itself. Paine now attacked Christianity. Inevitably it caused immediate controversy when the first volume was published in 1793 – losing him in Britain almost all the popular goodwill that had been created by his earlier *Rights of Man*. True 'revelation' Paine claimed, resided not in the Bible, but in God's genuine creation, the Book of Nature.[11] Following this Deistic principle, the rest of the volume is devoted to natural religion, and to denigrating all forms of revealed religion.

---

[9] Thomas Paine, *Rights of Man. Writings of Thomas Paine*, ed. Moncure Daniel Conway, 4 vols. (A.M.S. Press, 1967), Vol. II, p. 448.
[10] The word 'silly' of course still carried the idea of 'small' – see, for instance, the line about 'the silly buckets on the deck' in Coleridge's *Ancient Mariner* (1798), Part V, stanza 2.
[11] Thomas Paine, *The Age of Reason* [1793–1795], *The Theological Works of Tom Paine* (London, 1827), p. 22.

As to the account of the Creation, with which the book of Genesis opens, it has all the appearance of being a tradition which the Israelites had among them before they came into Egypt; and after their departure from that country, they put it at the head of their history, without telling (as is most probable) that they did not know how they came by it. The manner in which the account opens, shews it to be traditionary. It begins abruptly: it is nobody that speaks; it is nobody that hears; it is addressed to nobody; it has neither first, second or third person; it has every criterion of being a tradition; it has no voucher.[12]

Tradition 'has no voucher'. Here Paine turns specifically on what had hitherto usually been seen as the strength of tradition – the implication of being hallowed by time and custom rather than the result of someone's particular invention. But for Paine, roots lost in the mists of time were not roots at all – and certainly gave neither sap nor sustenance; they are only another form of imposture. From the start he dismisses the 'three principal means that have been employed in all ages, and perhaps in all countries, to impose upon mankind'. These 'are Mystery, Miracle, and Prophecy. The two first are incompatible with true religion, and the third ought always to be suspected.'[13] Then follows a well-informed discussion of the meaning of 'prophecy' – its phraseology so closely echoing Lowth's *Lectures on Sacred Poetry of the Hebrews*, which had been published in English shortly before, in 1787, that one assumes he had been reading it. Any attempts to find the fulfilment of biblical prophecy in contemporary events were, Paine suggests, completely futile.[14] Tradition, he implies, is the principal means by which these 'impostures' have been foisted on the unsuspecting masses. It is, in short, the habitual vehicle of lies and deception.

WATSON VERSUS PAINE: NUMBERS 31

To what extent was this derogatory use of the *word* 'tradition' by both sides in the debate a genuine rejection of all that it stood for? And to what extent is it simply the case that though the word itself had fallen out of fashion, the ideas for which it stood were just being paraphrased in other ways? Clearly it is much too easy to label Burke a 'traditionalist'

---

[12] Ibid., Part I, pp. 12–13.   [13] Ibid., p. 45.
[14] [I]t is owing to this change in the meaning of the words, that the flights and metaphors of the Jewish poets, and phrases and expressions now rendered obscure, by our not being acquainted with the local circumstances to which they applied at the time they were used, have been erected into prophecies, and made to bend to explanations, at the will and whimsical conceits of sectaries, expounders, and commentators. Every thing unintelligible was prophetical, and everything insignificant was typical.

Ibid., p. 50.

in the normal sense, though it can certainly be convincingly argued – as Conor Cruise O'Brien has done[15] – that in *our* sense of the word he is, like other purveyors of tradition, attempting to *create* a particular interpretation of the past that has little to do with that past, and everything to do with the present. Similarly, following MacIntyre, it should be noticed that Paine's rejection of the need for tradition in every form, however thoroughgoing, is in itself at least a consistent interpretation of a past that undoubtedly *required* interpretation. Even a negative sense of tradition is a sense of tradition of a kind. Much stranger, and from the point of view of understanding the fate of tradition at this period, perhaps more significant, is Paine's subsequent theological clash with Bishop Richard Watson.

The second volume of Paine's *Age of Reason* is a very different kind of work from the first. It was largely written in a French prison from December 1793 to November 1794, while Paine, who had been made a Deputy and a French citizen in 1792, during the first flush of revolutionary internationalist enthusiasm, was awaiting trial, and almost certainly the guillotine, for his opposition to the execution of Louis XVI during the Reign of Terror. As he explains in his introduction to the work in 1795, apologizing for the lack of the usual references, both he, and his book, had only survived because the American minister, James Monroe, had put pressure on the French government for his release.

No doubt because of the circumstances of its composition, this volume shows nothing like the earlier range of reference, but consists simply of readings from the Bible with Paine's own comments. These are trenchant enough. Numbers 31. 9–18, for instance, describes what a Hebrew raiding-party had done with their Midianite prisoners:

And the children of Israel took all the women of Midian captive, and all their little ones, and took the spoil of all their cattle, and all their flocks, and all their goods. And they burnt all their cities wherein they dwelt, and all their goodly castles with fire . . .

And they brought the captives and the prey, and the spoil, unto Moses and Eleazar the priest, and all the princes of the congregation of the children of Israel, unto the camp at the plains of Moab, which are by Jordan near Jericho.

And Moses and Eleazar the priest, and all the princes of the congregation went forth to meet them without the camp.

And Moses was wroth with the officers of the host, with the captains over thousands, and captains over hundreds, which came from the battle.

---

[15] See n. 3 above.

And Moses said unto them, Have ye saved all the women alive? Behold these caused the children of Israel, through the counsel of Baalam, to commit trespass against the Lord in the matter of Peor, and there was a plague among the congregation of the Lord. Now therefore kill every male among the little ones, and kill every woman that hath known man by lying with him. But all the women children, that have not known a man by lying with him, keep alive for yourselves. (Numbers 31. 9–10; 12–18)

Paine's comments are uncompromising, and to post-twentieth-century ears, entirely reasonable. 'Among the detestable villains that in any period of the world have disgraced the name of man, it is impossible to find a greater than Moses, if this account be true. Here is an order to butcher the boys, to massacre the mothers, and debauch the daughters.'[16] After a review of similar atrocities, textual contradictions, and improbable events, Paine concludes:

Of all the systems of religion that were ever invented, there is none more derogatory to the Almighty, more unedifying to man, more repugnant to reason, and more contradictory in itself than this thing called Christianity. Too absurd for belief, too impossible to convince, and too inconsistent for practice, it renders the heart torpid, or produces only atheists and fanatics. As an engine of power, it serves only the purpose of despotism; as a means of wealth, the avarice of priests; but so far as it respects the good of man in general, it leads to nothing here or hereafter.[17]

In Britain of the 1790s, under threat of French invasion, and in what amounted, under Pitt, to a police state, such views were unlikely to go unchallenged, even though Paine himself, after his release from prison, had very sensibly fled to America.

By chance or design, it fell to Bishop Watson to lead the charge against Paine. His reply to Paine appeared in 1798 in the form of *An Apology for the Bible in a Series of Letters addressed to Thomas Paine*. Richard Watson would have been an unusual figure, to say the least, at any time – and certainly a most unusual Bishop. An able scientist, he had become Professor of Chemistry at Cambridge at the early age of twenty-seven, and was made a Fellow of the Royal Society only five years later. He had played an important part in the invention of the black-bulb thermometer and had made improvements in the manufacture of gunpowder which were estimated to have saved the British Government more than £100,000 per year (many millions in today's terms) and so contributed later towards British victories in the Napoleonic Wars. With a flexibility perhaps only possible

---

[16] *Age of Reason*, Part II, p. 12.   [17] Ibid., p. 86.

to an eighteenth-century polymath he resigned his Chair of Chemistry in 1771 to become Regius Professor of Divinity at Cambridge. In 1782 he left Cambridge to become Bishop of Llandaff, in Wales. At a period when the Anglican Church was commonly described as 'the Tory Party at prayer', Watson was a Whig, with strongly liberal sympathies. Alone among senior Anglican clergy, he had showed some sympathy for the French Revolution in its early days, and as late as 1795 he had made a speech in the House of Lords opposing war with France, and predicting that:

this abandonment of all religion in France will be followed in due time . . . by the establishment of a purer system of Christianity than has ever taken place in that country, or perhaps any country, since the age of the Apostles. Voltaire, Rousseau, Diderot, and the rest of the philosophers in France, and perhaps I may say, many in our own country, have mistaken the corruptions of Christianity for Christianity itself, and in spurning the yoke of superstition, have overthrown religion. They are in the condition of men described by Plutarch; they have fled from superstition; have leapt over religion, and sunk into Atheism. They will be followed by future Newtons and by future Lockes, who will rebuild . . . the altars which the others have polluted and thrown down; for they will found them on the pure and unadorned rock of Christian verity.[18]

Such bold dismissal of any notion of ecclesiastical tradition, however much it may have been in line with mainstream Enlightenment sentiment, goes far beyond Lowth, and was doubly astonishing for a bishop in the wake of Burke's denunciation of the Revolution and what appeared to be his vindication in the Reign of Terror and the hardly less oppressive rule of the Directory from 1793 onwards.

Doubtless because of the unfulfilled hopes of the more radical writers and poets, when it became clear that at home he was as conservative as his fellow peers, Watson was subjected to a unique torrent of abuse. In 1793 Wordsworth had written, but never sent, a sarcastic Letter to the Bishop of Llandaff, congratulating him, among other things, for his 'enthusiastic fondness for the judicial proceedings of this country' as well as for his belief that in England 'the science of civil government has received all the perfection of which it is capable'.[19] Blake's unpublished annotations to Watson's *Apology* reflect a mixture of rage and despair which, though probably felt more strongly by him than most contemporaries, reflects a much more widespread disillusion.

---

[18] *Parliamentary History*, Vol. 31, p. 267.
[19] William Wordsworth, *Prose Works*, eds W.J.B. Owen and J.W. Smyser, 2 vols. (Clarendon Press, 1974), Vol. 1, pp. 43–4.

Watson's defence of Moses' orders for the massacre and rape of non-combatants in Numbers 31 may be taken as typical of his whole strategy against Paine. He turns for his reply to the very Book of Nature that Paine had seen as the source of true revelation in Part 1:

You profess yourself to be a deist, and to believe that there is a God, who created the universe, and established the laws of nature, by which it is sustained in existence. You profess that from the contemplation of the works of God, you derive a knowledge of his attributes; and you reject the Bible, because it ascribes to God things inconsistent (as you suppose) with the attributes which you have discovered to belong to him; in particular, you think it repugnant to his moral justice, that he should doom to destruction the crying or smiling infants of the Canaanites. – Why do you not maintain it to be repugnant to his moral justice, that he should suffer crying or smiling infants to be swallowed up by an earthquake, drowned by an inundation, consumed by a fire, starved by famine or destroyed by a pestilence? The Word of God is in perfect harmony with his work; crying or smiling infants are subjected to death in both.[20]

Though as Watson says, there is nothing particularly new about this analogy with Nature to defend the atrocities of the Pentateuch – it had been used by such apologists as Morgan, Tyndale, and Bolingbroke earlier in the century – this was, nevertheless, as shrewd a polemical blow against Paine's use of nature to disparage revelation as it was disconcerting to those who, like Blake, thought that Christ's teachings might imply a different code of conduct. 'Watson,' Blake wrote, 'has defended Antichrist.'[21]

Certainly from a theological point of view what is utterly extraordinary about this debate – always one of the most difficult in any Christian apologetic – is the way both Paine and Watson totally disregard centuries of traditional Christian teaching by seeming to accept the same naturalistic premise: that nature reveals an undistorted picture of its creator. Not for a moment does Watson suggest that the teachings of the New

---

[20] Richard Watson, *An Apology for the Bible in a Series of Letters Addressed to Thomas Paine* (Hilliard and Brown, 1828), pp. 4–5.
[21] On the back of the title-page in his copy of Watson Blake had scribbled:

To defend the Bible in this year 1798 would cost a man his life.
The Beast and the Whore rule without control.
It is an easy matter for a Bishop to triumph over Paine's attack, but it is not so easy for one who loves the Bible.
The Perversions of Christ's words & acts are attack'd by Paine & also the perversions of the Bible; Who dare defend either the Acts of Christ or the Bible Unperverted?

For Blake, Watson's 'defence' is simply 'perversion'; his arguments mere casuistry: 'Paine has not attacked Christianity. Watson has defended Antichrist.' William Blake, *Complete Writings*, ed. Geoffrey Keynes (Oxford University Press, 1966), pp. 386–7.

Testament might cancel those of the Old, or raise the Pauline doctrine of the Fall – that all nature 'groans in travail' under the bondage of sin. The paradox of eighteenth-century 'Natural Theology', based on a reasoned rejection of original sin and the fallen nature of the universe, is that, as here, it presents not a God of love and redemption, but one of arbitrary violence, caprice, and murderous injustice. However outlandish its language, Blake's horror at Watson's argument is, ironically, a stand in favour of the centuries of traditional Christian theology that Watson has inexplicably abandoned. By Vincentian standards, Blake is orthodox, Watson heretical.

Something of the curious effect of this attempt to argue from a common base of reason rather than tradition can be seen in the reactions of the young William Hone (1780–1842), a radical publisher, bookseller, and pamphleteer. Born in London during the Gordon Riots of 1780, he was brought up in a poor but literate household, learning to read from the Bible and *Pilgrim's Progress*. His encounter with Watson and Paine is related in an autobiographical fragment:

Bishop Watson's 'Apology for the Bible', in answer to Paine's 'Age of Reason' was given to my father, and he gave it to me. I only knew the 'Age of Reason' existed by his conversing with a friend upon it as a mischievous work; its nature I soon understood from the Bishop's book. Until the 'Apology' informed me, I never conceived the Bible had been, or could be, doubted or disbelieved, and, strange to say, although I thought Bishop Watson proved the untruth of much that Paine had written, yet the Bishop's work alone created doubt in me who had never before doubted.[22]

COLERIDGE: THE VOCABULARY OF A VOUCHER

Ever since John Stuart Mill's famous essay on him (1840),[23] Samuel Taylor Coleridge is often seen as Burke's natural successor as a conservative theorist. Yet both as a political and social thinker and as a poet, his use of the word 'tradition' – especially in his early writings – is entirely in keeping with what we have just seen in other eighteenth-century debates over the values of the past. In other words, he hardly uses it at all. Though he has little else in common with Watson or Paine, at least in terms of

[22] Cited by Frederick William Hackwood, *William Hone: His Life and Times* (T.F. Unwin, 1912), p. 45.
[23] John Stuart Mill, *Bentham and Coleridge*, ed. F.R. Leavis (Chatto, 1950).

vocabulary, Coleridge (unusually for him) is here a man of his time: not so much an innovator as a bell-wether. Moreover, on the relatively rare occasions where Coleridge *does* use the word 'tradition', it is entirely within the accepted eighteenth-century range of meaning. That is to say, it is *never* used for current debates about how to relate to the past, but only for historical ones of no immediate value and doubtful veracity. Typical of this usage is the description of Thales in the *Philosophical Lectures*, who, 'by the admission of all antiquity, was the first who, even in physics, even in natural philosophy, instead of resting with traditions, asked himself what could have been the origin of things'.[24]

Contrarywise, though the conditions of MacIntyre's 'epistemological crises' are everywhere present in the first years of the nineteenth century, and, as in Burke, Coleridge's writings contain no lack of inherently controversial ideological interpretations of the past, those historical judgements are never framed overtly in terms of tradition.

Thus in Coleridge's 1795 Bristol Lectures *On Politics and Religion*, where one might expect the idea of tradition to play an important part, there are actually only two uses of the word, one asserting that the Jewish people were 'superstitiously jealous of their Traditions & Ceremonies',[25] the other, a similar, if hypothetical, description of how the Christian tradition *might* have been handed down by word of mouth if none of its early writings had survived.[26]

Later writings on social, political, and religious topics which deal extensively with the kind of material we would now all cover with the name 'tradition', confirm this singular lack – even avoidance – of the word. Thus in the *Statesman's Manual* of 1816, and the *Lay Sermon* of 1817 the word occurs three times – twice in the former (one of them wholly derogatory), and once in the latter.[27] In all three cases it covers the transmission of ideas either brazenly false or otherwise unverifiable.

---

[24] S.T. Coleridge, *Lectures 1818–1819 On the History of Philosophy*, ed. J.R. de J. Jackson, Bollingen Series (Princeton University Press/Routledge, 2000), Vol. 1. pp. 61–2.

[25] S.T. Coleridge, *Lectures 1795 On Politics and Religion*, ed. Lewis Patton and Peter Mann, Bollingen Series (Princeton University Press/Routledge, 1971), p. 118.

[26] Ibid., p. 174.

[27] The first is a reference to 'men who from their unwillingness to sacrifice their vain *traditions*, gainful hypocrisy, and pride both of heart and of demeanor, demanded a miracle for the confirmation of moral truths…'; the second, to 'a *traditionary* wisdom that had its origin in inspiration', '*Statesman's Manual*', *Lay Sermons*, ed. R.J. White, Bollingen Series (Princeton University Press/Routledge, 1972), Appendix B, p. 58 and Appendix C, p. 95. In the 1817 *Lay Sermon*, the sole reference is to 'this indispensable act, or influence, or impregnation, of which, as of a divine *tradition*, the eldest philosophy is not silent'. Ibid., p. 188.

The 1818 edition of *The Friend* begins with what looks like a much more significant use of 'tradition' – even printed with a capital 'T': 'Antecedent to all History, and long glimmering through it as a holy Tradition, there presents itself to our imagination an indefinite period, dateless as Eternity, a State rather than a Time. For even the sense of succession is lost in the uniformity of the stream.'[28]

But in fact this usage conforms completely with earlier examples. The capitalization affects all major nouns in the sentence, and the period in question is part of a literary myth of a Golden Age where the narrator is hailed by a prophetic figure much along the lines of the Genius that guided Volney in his vision of the origins of religion. Such 'Tradition' has vaguely divine rather than human origins, and offers no effective or practical wisdom to the present.

Throughout the following 500 pages the word only makes five appearances. In its place are what sound to the modern ear like countless paraphrases, and substitutions. A number of Enlightenment thinkers are roundly castigated for their belief in their intellectual self-sufficiency. They had been 'led astray' by disregarding the wisdom of their 'forefathers' and despising everything that had come down from antiquity. Here, for instance, is Coleridge's comment on Rousseau:

> Rousseau, on the contrary, in the inauspicious spirit of his age and birthplace, had slipped the cable of his faith, and steered by the compass of unaided reason, ignorant of the hidden currents that were bearing him out of his course, and too proud to consult the faithful charts prized and held sacred by his forefathers.[29]

By contrast, argues Coleridge, the true (British) Patriot will show an understanding for the interconnectedness of individual, society, and history:

> He will reverence not only whatever tends to make the component individuals more happy, and more worthy of happiness: but likewise whatever tends to bind them more closely together as a people; that as a multitude of parts and functions make up one human body, so the whole multitude of his countrymen may, by the visible and invisible influences of religion, language, laws, customs, and the reciprocal dependence and re-action of trade and agriculture, be organized into one body politic.[30]

---

[28] Samuel Taylor Coleridge, *The Friend*, ed. Barbara E. Rooke, 2 vols., Bollingen Series (Princeton University Press/Routledge, 1969), Vol. I, p. 7.
[29] Ibid., Vol. I, pp. 133–4.   [30] Ibid., pp. 298–9.

How this 'body politic' is to be organized is made much clearer in his essay *On the Constitution of Church and State* (1830)[31] – a work that was to exert an influence on nineteenth-century political thought far beyond its original context of Catholic Emancipation. Here Coleridge expounds his idea of the 'Clerisy', a nation-wide network of clergy, teachers, and other cultural leaders who would ideally 'be distributed throughout the country, so as not to leave even the smallest integral part or division without a resident guide, guardian, and instructor' and whose function would be to:

> preserve the stores, to guard the treasures, of past civilization, and thus to bind the present with the past; to perfect and add to the same, and thus to connect the present with the future; but especially to diffuse through the whole community, and to every native entitled to its laws and rights, that quantity and quality of knowledge which was indispensable both for the understanding of those rights, and for the performance of the duties correspondent.[32]

Such arrangements for preserving and inculcating the inherited wisdom and culture of the past stands in clear contrast to Coleridge's narrow historical use of the word 'tradition' which is never permitted to become a guide to present ritual, educational practice, or political policy. That these 'rights and duties' constitute a tactical rather than an undiscriminating definition of the values of 'past civilization', however, is abundantly clear. The details of Coleridge's arguments in both *The Friend* and *Church and State* illustrate that this is a highly selective reading of history in a time of national crisis – and therefore, in MacIntyre's sense, what one might call a concept of tradition.

Certainly in no way does this 'true' sense of the inherited wisdom of the past give blanket justification for accepting the ideas and practices of the past as a whole. Indeed, Coleridge's unspoken sense of tradition is to be contrasted with what he sees as the errors of those who allow themselves to be blindly dominated by the practices of the past to the point where they must justify every abuse and corruption. Despite a number of favourable references to Burke,[33] Coleridge denounces his followers who would

---

[31] The first two editions were dated 1830, even though the first of these actually appeared in December 1829. *On the Constitution of Church and State*, ed. John Colmer, Bollingen Series (Princeton University Press/Routledge, 1976), p. xiii.

[32] Ibid. pp. 43–4. For a more extended discussion of this idea, see Stephen Prickett, 'Coleridge and the Idea of the Clerisy', *Reading Coleridge: Approaches and Appreciations*, ed. Walter. B. Crawford (Cornell University Press, 1979), pp. 252–73.

[33] 'The extravagantly false and flattering picture, which Burke gave of the French Nobility and Hierarchy, has always appeared to me the greatest defect of his, in so many respects, invaluable Work.' *The Friend*, p. 215.

justify not merely the abuses of the *ancien régime*, but even the Spanish Inquisition on the same grounds.

While they lamented with tragic outcries the injured Monarch and the exiled Noble [sic], they displayed the most disgusting insensibility to the privations, sufferings, and manifold oppressions of the great mass of the Continental population, and a blindness or callousness still more offensive to the crimes and unutterable abominations of their oppressors. Not only was the Bastile [sic] justified, but the Spanish Inquisition itself – and this in a pamphlet passionately extolled and industriously circulated by the adherents of the then ministry. Thus, and by their infatuated panegyrics on the former state of France, they played into the hands of their worst and most dangerous antagonists. In confounding the conditions of the English and French peasantry, and in quoting the authorities of Milton, Sidney, and their immortal compeers, as applicable to the present times, and the existing government, the Demagogues appeared to talk only the same language as the Anti-jacobins themselves employed.[34]

For Coleridge, as for Burke, Paine, Blake, Watson and a host of other thinkers in both France and Germany, it was becoming increasingly necessary to distinguish between finding guidance from the wisdom of the past and a blind reverence for all its malpractices and abuses.

A survey of the later philosophical and religious works reveals much the same pattern. Though Coleridge's emphasis is increasingly on the wisdom of the ancients and the values of old customs, there is little or no change in the actual use of the word 'tradition' itself in his later works. Not surprisingly it occurs most frequently in the *Philosophical Lectures* of 1818–1819 where the word itself is used over fifty times. Perhaps more surprisingly, it plays little part in either *Aids to Reflection* (1825) which has eleven uses of the word, or *Church and State* which has only two, despite the concern in both works with topics where the *idea* of tradition plays an increasingly significant role in Coleridge's thought.

Denotation, however, is not the same as connotation. A word does not have to change meaning to change its field of reference. Tom Paine sums up the problem succinctly when he wrote: 'Tradition has no voucher'. In the early nineteenth century it was not so much that 'tradition' had begun to change its meaning, as that attitudes towards what that meaning might imply themselves began to change. In short, the question of whether or not tradition *had* a voucher was becoming increasingly important – and complex. As so often, imperceptible shifts in attitudes required not merely new vocabularies but new ways of thinking about older vocabularies as well.

---

[34] Ibid.

CHAPTER 4

Re-envisioning the past: metaphors and symbols of tradition

RELIGIOUS LIGHT AND THE BEDIMMING INFLUENCES OF CUSTOM

From a later perspective, what is extraordinary about the whole French Revolution debate over freedom and oppression, political legitimacy, divine inspiration, and the nature of the scriptures, is the way in which its participants steadfastly declined to engage with the language and metaphors by which common notions of tradition had previously been expressed.

Here, I think, we are justified in repeating the obvious question: what does it matter if one metaphor – the Latin legal one of 'tradition' – is replaced by other, no less metaphorical, descriptions for the handing on of received ideas or notions of procedure? There are several replies to this. The first, and probably the most significant, is that it is 'untraditional'. That is to say that, for by far the greater part of the last 2,000 years the word used for the historical conveyance of received notions has been 'tradition', and, as anyone who opens a newspaper or a magazine anywhere in the world of the major European languages today knows well, the word is back in widespread currency in the twenty-first century. In other words, this is not a case of a word falling into disuse to be replaced by another at a different historical phase of a culture, but a case of a word going, or being sent, into abeyance, and then being sharply revived again – with the clear inference, that it conveyed an important, indeed irreplaceable, concept for which no other metaphor proved adequate. In the history of the idea of tradition, the eighteenth century was an aberration.

This is not, of course, the first time that a word has almost disappeared from English, and then made a triumphant return. The word 'host' has a not dissimilar history.[1] David Norton in his magisterial *History of the Bible*

---

[1] See Stephen Prickett, *Origins of Narrative: The Romantic Appropriation of the Bible* (Cambridge University Press, 1996), pp. 89–90.

as Literature gives a number of examples of such words, including 'ate', 'discomfiture', 'eschewed', 'laden', 'nurture', 'ponder' and 'unwittingly' that were current or familiar archaisms in the sixteenth century but which had dropped out of use by the eighteenth century, and were later taken back into common speech in the nineteenth century.[2] Many, though not all of these can be shown to have made their comeback with the increasing popularity of the Authorized Version. The word 'ponder', for instance, seems to have survived on the strength of one famous verse, taken by the Authorized Version straight from Tyndale, Luke 2.19: 'but Mary kept all these things and pondered them in her heart'. By the mid-eighteenth century it is listed as being obsolete, and its revived sense reflects all the solemnity of Luke's Annunciation.

The difference is that tradition had such a central place in the history of the British political system, the monarchy and the law, not to mention the Church – Protestant as much as Roman Catholic – that its replacement had an urgency that none of these other words possessed. 'Tradition' is a word so central to everything that the British came to identify with in the course of the nineteenth century that if the existing equivalent of the 'wheel' had become unmentionable, then it was necessary immediately to *re-invent* the wheel in some guise. In this case, the metaphors that tend to replace those earlier legal ones of authorized transmission, testaments, and entailments tell their own story, and in so doing reveal ambiguities always inherent in the original. Whereas what had hitherto been expressed as the 'handing over' or transfer of documents and 'deeds' – even that word is revealing in its double meaning – suggestive of control *by* the past, the new images were clearly intended point rather towards growth and development in the future.

Though converts to conservatism like Burke, Watson, and the later Coleridge might suspect that the excesses of the French Revolution were not unconnected with the sweeping iconoclasm of the Enlightenment, neither they, nor their age, were in general terms anything like finished with what has more recently been called the 'enlightenment project'. Not surprisingly therefore Coleridge's thought about the nature of what he was unable to bring himself to call 'tradition' is dominated above all by optics: images of light, illumination, and vision. Even the title of *Aids to Reflection* is a play on the way in which mental states are explored in terms of visual metaphors. That this is always a highly selective *vision* of the past is clear

---

[2] David Norton, *History of the Bible as Literature*, 2 vols. (Cambridge University Press, 1993), Vol. II, pp. 80–5.

from his call to 'emancipate ourselves from the *bedimming* influences of custom'.[3] In contrast, we are called to 'pursue the records of history with a reflecting spirit, or look round the world with an observant eye'.[4] So far from being an individual or solitary observation, however, we must be guided in this quest by the collective wisdom of the ages. For instance, we owe to the Press in the years between the Reformation and the Civil War 'such a diffusion of religious light as first redeemed and afterwards saved this nation from the spiritual and moral death of Popery'. Moreover, this same 'religious light' was to prove a force not of revolution but political stability – later to be responsible for 'the gradual ascendancy of those wise political maxims', which cast 'philosophic truth in the moulds of national laws, customs, and existing orders of society'.[5]

Indeed, in the *Aids to Reflection* it is unclear how far the 'religious light' of Protestantism differs from the universal light of reason itself, to which all people, whatever their education, will be naturally receptive – unless, that is, their eyes are overly 'bedimmed' by custom or blinded by false teachings. Education merely provides telescopes to view stars that are visible to everyone who cares to look:

Meanwhile the people, not goaded into doubt by the lessons and examples of their teachers and superiors; not drawn away from the fixed stars of heaven – the form and magnitude of which are the same for the naked eye of the shepherd as for the telescope of the sage – from the immediate truths, I mean of reason and conscience . . . the people will need no arguments to receive a doctrine confirmed by their own experience from within and from without, and intimately blended with the most venerable traditions common to all races, and the traces of which linger in the latest twilight of civilization.[6]

Thus the plain truths of reason were as available to the ancient Greeks as they are to ourselves:

Those great men, Pythagoras, Plato, and Aristotle, men the most consummate in politics, who founded states, or instructed princes, or wrote most accurately on public government, were at the same time the most acute at all abstracted and sublime speculations: the clearest light being ever necessary to guide the most important actions.[7]

---

[3] Samuel Taylor Coleridge, *The Friend*, ed. Barbara E. Rooke, Bollingen Series (Princeton University Press/Routledge, 1993), p. 106.
[4] Samuel Taylor Coleridge, *Aids to Reflection*, ed. James Marsh (1829) (Kennikat Press, 1971), p. 178.
[5] *The Friend*, pp. 80–1.
[6] *Aids to Reflection*, pp. 270–1. There is here an almost certainly deliberate echo of Ovid, from the beginning of the *Metamorphoses*, where the essential characteristic of humanity is the ability to look up at the stars.
[7] *The Friend*, p. 113.

What is clear, is that Coleridge sees in history itself what might be described by later figures as a 'great tradition' of *enlightenment* in the literal sense of 'illumination' – a metaphor of an ever-widening pool of light, at once spiritual and intellectual, in which 'tradition', in Coleridge's sense of the darkness of an unverifiable and primitive past of myth and fable, is slowly and fitfully pushed back by the twin lanterns of knowledge and divine revelation:

Thus in the most ancient books of the Brahmins . . . the doctrines grounded on obscure traditions of the promised remedy, are seen struggling, and now gleaming, now flashing, through the mist of Pantheism, and producing the incongruities and gross contradictions of the Brahmin Mythology.[8]

A similar contrast between 'tradition' and enlightenment can be found in Greek mythology, for Coleridge the difference being that such stories as that of Prometheus, who stole fire and light from the gods of Olympus, are held to foreshadow the coming of Christ:

Here, again, and in the usual form of a historic solution, we find the same fact, and as characteristic of the human race, stated in that earliest and most venerable mythus (or symbolic parable) of Prometheus – that truly wonderful fable, in which the characters of the rebellious Spirit and of the Divine Friend of mankind are united in the same person; and thus in the most striking manner noting the forced amalgamation of the Patriarchal tradition with the incongruous scheme of Pantheism.[9]

Here, however, 'tradition' is given a greater force in that it is attached to the biblical Patriarchs rather than Greek myths. This progressive enlightenment takes a decisive (but not final) turn with the coming of Christianity and the initiation of its members into the light of divine grace: 'This sacrament of Baptism, the ancients do particularly express by light, – Yet are they both nothing but darkness to us, till the same light shine in our hearts; for till then we are nothing but darkness ourselves, and therefore the most luminous things are so to us.'[10] The essential interaction of penitence and grace, learning and insight, reason and conscience, is well illustrated by two quotations from the seventeenth-century Cambridge Platonist Henry More: 'the light within me, that is, my reason and conscience, does assure me, that the ancient and Apostolic faith according to the historical meaning thereof, and in the literal sense of the Creed, is solid and true'.[11] But for More – as for Coleridge – no amount of inner light can overwhelm the far greater illumination already provided by the

---

[8] *Aids to Reflection*, pp. 259–60. [9] Ibid., p. 260. [10] Ibid., p. 317. [11] Ibid., pp. 159–60.

great works of the past: 'Tell me, ye high-flown perfectionists, ye boasters of the light within you, could the highest perfection of your inward light ever show to you the history of past ages, the state of world at present, the knowledge of arts and tongues, without books or teachers?'[12] By 1825 it is clear that 'traditions' for Coleridge no longer imply falsehood. They may be obscure, they may provide only the most fitful gleams from the obscurity of paganism and superstition – but they may, equally, be a vehicle to guide future generations (properly able to understand the movement of history) towards true enlightenment. In such a context, tradition itself will no longer carry the kind of automatic opprobrium that was inherent in the eighteenth-century word.

WHERE STREAMS OF LIVING WATERS FLOW

All thing have their Genesis in Water, and into Water all things resolved – here distinguish this from the traditionary Chaos which is merely historical.[13]

Whereas Lowth's dominant image of tradition is one of progressive deterioration – that of a stream or river, changed and increasingly polluted as it gets further from its source – for his successors, like Coleridge, the metaphor of a river held very different connotations.

We have already noted the link between tradition and flowing water in the first paragraph of the 1818 *The Friend*. Part of what Coleridge in his notebooks was to call his satiric 'Fable of the madning Rain',[14] it was in itself, we observed, an entirely conventional use of the word tradition – referring to a period supposedly long past (in this case even mythical) and certainly lacking 'voucher' in Paine's devastating charge: 'Antecedent to all History, and long glimmering through it as a holy Tradition, there presents itself to our imagination an indefinite period, dateless as Eternity, a State rather than a Time. For even the sense of succession is lost in the uniformity of the stream.'[15] Yet this is not the polluted stream of Lowth, but rather one that purifies itself over time and distance (as partially polluted streams were sometimes claimed to do). It is akin to the biblical metaphor of the river of life which, if, like time, 'bears all

[12] Ibid., pp. 162–3.
[13] *Lectures 1818–1819 On the History of Philosophy*, ed. J.R. de J. Jackson, Bollingen Series (Princeton University Press/Routledge, 2000), draft manuscript of lecture 1, p. 26.
[14] Borrowed, and improved, he tells us with some glee, from Michael Drayton's poem *The Moon-Calf*. Samuel Taylor Coleridge, *Collected Notebooks*, 4 vols., ed. Kathleen Coburn, vol. II: 1804–1818 (Routledge, 1962), paragraph 2626.
[15] *The Friend*, p. 7.

its sons away', nonetheless provides at least a metaphorical link at once with the Golden Age of an Edenic past, and even if not here, by implication, with a Paradisal future. Blake, we recall, had made such a drawing of the 'River of Life' around 1805.[16] It is part of a huge nexus of imagery taken from pure or polluted water-sources that runs throughout the early part of the nineteenth century, which took much of its force and urgency from parallel campaigns for better water-supply, sanitation, and drainage in England – especially in London – affecting such figures as diverse as John Martin, J.W.M. Turner, and Charles Kingsley. Even Shelley's vicious reference to the family of George III as: 'the dregs of their dull race, who flow / Through public scorn – mud from a muddy spring'[17] taps (if one may use the term) the same source of imagery. In Coleridge's *Aids to Reflection*, so short on overt references to tradition and so long on metaphorical explorations of it, much of the paraphrase is taken up with watery images: 'The stream of custom and our profession bring us to the preaching of the Word, and we sit out our hour under the sound; but how few consider and prize it as the great ordinance of God for the salvation of souls, the beginner and the sustainer of the divine life of grace within us!'[18] Here the word 'custom' seems to occupy almost exactly the semantic space of 'tradition', in a way that Hobsbawm could only applaud, and its conjoining with 'stream' as 'stream of custom' creates a phrase almost synonymous with the standard use of 'tradition'. Certainly here is custom of power and continuity which, though it may not have a 'voucher' for one who, like Paine, did not give scripture any authority, would certainly provide voucher enough for Burke and Coleridge alike. The difference between this and 'tradition', of course, is that the stream in question – the custom and practices of the Church – flows down to his own time, and Coleridge, like Burke and even Blake, cannot quite make that leap from past beliefs to their continuity in present actions.

Even closer to Lowth's other model – that of irrigation – is this discursive account of the meaning of the word 'origin', which seems, yet again, to flirt with the unspoken presence of qualities to be enfolded in all but the most antiquarian senses of tradition:

This sense of the word is implied even in its metaphorical or figurative use. Thus we may say of a river that it originates in such or such a fountain; but the water of a canal is derived from such or such a river; the power which we call nature, may be

---

[16] Now in the Tate Gallery, London.
[17] Percy Bysshe Shelley, 'England in 1819' (1819), ll. 2–3.
[18] *Aids to Reflection*, p. 128.

thus defined: A power subject to the law of continuity (*lex continui; nam in natura non datur saltus*) which law the human understanding, by a necessity arising out of its own constitution can conceive only under the form of cause and effect. [19]

Other examples draw out the metaphor in almost every conceivable form. Here, for instance, Coleridge develops an attempt to define nature and natural things in distinction from those of the spirit.

And as no man who admits a will at all, (for we may safely presume, that no man not meaning to speak figuratively, would call the shifting current of a stream the will of the river), will suppose it below nature, we may safely add, that it is super-natural; and this without the least pretence to any positive notion or insight. [20]

In such a flood of metaphors, even the most mundane images, which by themselves would be almost invisible, seem to be part of the mainstream flow: 'Seek not altogether to dry up the stream of sorrow, but to bound it and keep it within its banks. Religion doth not destroy the life of nature, but adds to it a life more excellent; yea, it doth not only permit but requires some feeling of afflictions.'[21] What such streams have in common with the previous metaphors of 'illumination' is that both provide a continuity between the present and the past.[22] 'Seeing' is not something that occurs spontaneously. We must learn, we need instruction from the light of the past in order to understand what we are looking at today – which means, of course, that we are constructing, or selecting, a past by which the present can be illuminated. Similarly, if the past is a river that flows down to us, we seek from it inspiration, legitimacy, and continuity – choosing, as we do so, one tributary rather than another as our source.

THE HOUSES THAT JACK BUILT: GARDENS, ARCHITECTURE, AND THE STATE

Richard Price, like his lake-poet contemporaries, Wordsworth and Coleridge, tended to favour metaphors of progress – of organic growth and development by which small beginnings grow over time into vast and, with luck and even divine guidance, happy results. As befitted a Welsh non-conformist preacher, behind such an image is a huge biblical hinter-land: the parable of the mustard-seed, Christ as the true vine, or his Easter Day appearance to Mary as the 'gardener'.

---

[19] Ibid., p. 246n.   [20] Ibid., pp. 110–11.   [21] Ibid., p. 123.
[22] Coleridge may well also have known the Cabbalistic connections between the Hebrew 'light' (Nehara) and a 'river' (Nahar). I owe this interesting suggestion to Professor Rachel Elior, of the Hebrew University of Jerusalem.

However much Burke may have disagreed with Price over their application, he too makes frequent use of such images: though for him nature is a garden rather than wild and uncontrolled – and, as for many of his contemporaries, landscape gardening is in the end a sub-section of architecture. In 1726 John Dyer had published an immensely popular poem, *Grongar Hill*, celebrating the natural beauties of his native Towey valley in south-west Wales. In a series of somewhat mixed images, a ruined castle on its summit is first seen as a 'crown' and then as moralized metaphor first of political and then social decay:

> Deep are his feet in Towy's flood
> His sides are cloath'd with waving wood,
> And ancient towers crown his brow,
> That cast an aweful look below;
> Whose ragged walls the ivy creeps,
> And with her arms from falling keeps;
> So both a safety from the wind
> On mutual dependence find.
> 'Tis now the raven's bleak abode;
> 'Tis now the apartment of the toad;
> And there the fox securely feeds;
> And there the poisonous adder breeds
> Conceal'd in ruins, moss and weeds;
> While ever and anon there falls
> Huge heaps of hoary moulder'd walls,
> Yet time has seen, that lifts the low,
> And level lays the lofty brow,
> Has seen this broken pile compleat,
> Big with the vanity of state;
> But transient is the smile of fate!
> A little rule, a little sway,
> A sun beam on a winter's day,
> Is all the proud and mighty have
> Between the cradle and the grave.
> (lines 69–82)

This was not a new image even then, but henceforth the English landscape, with its many picturesque ruins, was constantly invoked as a literary trope of human transience.[23] But for Dyer, a clergyman, such change and decay was not so much a nascent sense of history as a reminder of permanent moral truths.

---

[23] And, as so often, behind the English, the classical trope. Here Ovid's *iam serges iacet Troia fuit* [Fields of corn now wave where Troy once stood.] John Dyer, *Grongar Hill*, 1726.

More than fifty years after Dyer, William Cowper, in his best-known poem, *The Task* (1784), had popularized a similar, but much more ominous image of real change that was to gain added – even prophetic – resonance with the advent of the French Revolution:

> Many, whose sequester'd lot
> Forbids their interference, looking on,
> Anticipate perforce some dire event;
> And, seeing the old castle of the state,
> That promis'd once more firmness, so assail'd,
> That all its tempest-beaten turrets shake,
> Stand motionless expectants of its fall.[24]

Here, if anywhere, in 'the old castle of the state', is the central metaphor of substitution for tradition in eighteenth-century political thought. For a country like England the comparison had special resonance. Unlike France, England had always been an architecturally conservative country, not merely in the sense that new fashions (almost always from the Continent) spread more slowly and were often modified by vernacular and traditional ways of working as they were absorbed, but also in the reluctance of landowners who were 'modernizing' their country houses and estates to pull down the existing buildings and start afresh. Whereas the glory of the great French chateaux of the seventeenth and eighteenth centuries was their architectural homogeneity, the distinctive quality of the English great houses was a historical variety that revealed the age and ancestry of the house – and, of course, by extension, its owner. Thus country houses like Penshurst or Knowle, as well as even the main royal residence of the period, Hampton Court, still retained their mediaeval great halls alongside the sixteenth-, seventeenth-, and eighteenth-century additions.[25] Then, as now, English people grew up surrounded by a visible sense of their own past as expressed in their buildings.

Architectural metaphors, therefore, were at one level simple enough for even the least educated to understand, while appealing equally to those capable of appreciating the history they represented. On the one hand, they offered in a visible and concrete form the highly abstract idea of the state as a human artifact. On the other hand, they drew on associations with a parallel sequence of organic imagery, implying that great historic

---

[24] William Cowper, *The Task*, Bk v, in *Poems* (R & W.A. Bartow, 1818), Vol. ii, p. 142.
[25] The classic discussion of this is in Mark Girouard, *Life in the English Country House* (Yale University Press, 1978), but see also Gervase Jackson-Stops, *An English Arcadia 1600–1990: Designs for Gardens and Garden Buildings in the Care of the National Trust* (National Trust, 1992).

buildings were things that had grown 'naturally' over the course of centuries and represented more than the rational planning of any one architect. Conversely, the undeniable fact that many of those historic buildings were dilapidated or in a poor state of repair was seized upon by those who were more impressed by the corruptions of the present than by the past glories of antiquity.

Hardly surprisingly, the image makes a frequent appearance in Burke:

The science of constructing a commonwealth, or renovating it, or reforming it, is, like every other science, not to be taught a priori . . . it is with infinite caution that any man ought to venture upon pulling down an edifice which has answered in any tolerable degree for ages the common purposes of society, or on building it up again, without having models and patterns of approved utility before his eyes.[26]

Further on, discussing the new local government structure of France, he combines architectural with organic metaphors by means of reference to landscape gardening – not unmindful, one suspects, of the long sequence of such horticultural metaphors for politics in Shakespeare: *Richard II*, for example, or the specific application of the image to 'our fertile France' in Burgundy's speech in Act v of *Henry V.* Burke combines his Shakespearean allusions (if such they be) with a clear reference to the well-known difference between the regular geometry of French landscape gardening exemplified, for instance, by Le Nôtre at Versailles, and the studied irregularity of the English style of 'Capability' Brown, Humphry Repton, or Richard Payne Knight, supposedly conforming to the irregularity of nature itself, which had become increasingly fashionable all over Europe – including even France. For Burke, the present revolutionaries 'are in no way embarrassed with an endeavour to accommodate the new building to an old one, either in the walls or on the foundations . . . The French builders, clearing away as mere rubble whatever they found . . . like their ornamental gardeners, form . . . everything to an exact level.'[27]

Other conservative writers were quick to adopt Burke's imagery. By 1793 Hannah More, the religious tract writer and tireless anti-Jacobin, was already making skilful use of the possibilities of architecture as a symbol of stability and order in a dramatic dialogue.

Jack. I'll tell thee a story. When Sir John married, my Lady, who is a little fantastical, and likes to do everything like the French, begged him to pull down yonder fine old castle, and build it up in her frippery way. No, says Sir John; what

---

[26] Edmund Burke, *Reflections on the French Revolution* (Dent, 1940), p. 90.
[27] Ibid., pp. 255–6.

shall I pull down this noble building, raised by the wisdom of my brave ancestors; which outstood the civil wars, and only underwent a little needful repair at
the Revolution; and which all my neighbours come to take a pattern by – shall I
pull it all down, I say, only because there may be a dark closet or an inconvenient
room or two in it? My lady mumpt and grumbled; but the castle was let stand,
and a glorious building it is, though there may be a trifling fault or two, and tho'
a few decays may want stopping; so now and then they mend a little thing, and
they'll go on mending, I dare say, as they have leisure, to the end of the chapter, if
they are let alone. But no pull-me-down works.[28]

The reference to 'repair at the Revolution' (i.e. the Glorious Revolution
of 1688), the 'neighbours'' desire to imitate it, and so on, make it clear that
this is not merely a narrative defending ad hoc development as against
demolition and reconstruction, but an *allegorical* one to be read directly in
relation to contemporary politics.

Even as late as the 1860s this was a motif still popular enough to be
played with by Charles Kingsley in *The Water Babies* (1863). Hartover
House is Hannah Moore's political house with knobs on:

Hartover had been built at ninety different times, and in nineteen different styles,
and looked as if somebody had built a whole street of houses of every imagi-
nable shape, and then stirred them together with a spoon. For the attics were
Anglo-Saxon.
The third-floor Norman.
The second Cinque-cento.
The first-floor Elizabethan.
The right wing Pure Doric.
The centre Early English, with a huge portico copied from the Parthenon.
The left wing pure Boetian, which the country folk admired most
of all, because it was just like the new barracks in the town, only three times
as big.
The grand staircase was copied from the catacombs at Rome.
The back staircase from the Tajmahal at Agra. This was built by Sir John's
great-great-great-uncle, who won, in Lord Clive's Indian Wars, plenty of money,
plenty of wounds, and no more taste than his betters.
The cellars were copied from the caves of Elephanta.
The offices from the Pavilion at Brighton.

And the rest from nothing in heaven, or earth, or under the earth. So that
Hartover House was a great puzzle to antiquarians, and a thorough Naboth's
vineyard to critics, and architects, and all persons who like meddling with
other men's business, and spending other men's money. So they were all

[28] Hannah Moore, *Village Politics. Addressed to all the Mechanics, Journeymen, and Day Labourers, in Great Britain*, by Will Chip, a country carpenter (1793), pp. 8–9.

setting upon poor Sir John, year after year, and trying to talk him into spending a hundred thousand pounds or so, in building, to please them but not himself. But he always put them off, like a canny North-countryman as he was. One wanted him to build a gothic house, but he said he was no Goth; and another to build an Elizabethan, but he said he lived under good Queen Victoria, and not good Queen Bess; and another was bold enough to tell him that his house was ugly, but he said he lived inside it, and not outside; and another, that there was no unity in it, but he said that was just why he liked the old place. For he liked to see how each Sir John, and Sir Hugh, and Sir Ralph, and Sir Randal, had left his mark upon the place, each after his own taste; and he had no more notion of disturbing his ancestors' work than of disturbing their graves. For now the house looked like a real live house, that had a history, and had grown and grown as the world grew; and that it was only an upstart fellow who did not know who his own grandfather was, who would change it for some spick and span new Gothic or Elizabethan thing, which looked as if it had been all spawned in a night, as mushrooms are. From which you may collect (if you have wit enough) that Sir John was a very sound-headed, sound-hearted squire, and just the man to keep the country side in order, and show good sport with his hounds.[29]

This is, of course, parody. But it is very affectionate parody. Kingsley was a founder-member of the Christian Socialists, and *The Water Babies* is ostensibly a fable about the oppression of the poor – Tom, the chimney-sweep, the (magical) Irish Woman, defenceless sea-creatures – but Kingsley is at heart a rural conservative, with no desire to upset the social order. Tom will in the end be restored to the land, and become a 'great man of science, and plan railroads, and steam-engines, and electric telegraphs, and rifled guns'[30] – all technologies to improve the existing order. He will not, we note, become a social reformer, a parson, or Prime Minister – or take up any other profession which might (improbably) seek to change society. In other words, even in writing the book that was in the end to abolish boy chimney sweeps, Kingsley pitches for an idea of society that (unlike the older idea of 'tradition') is gradualist, historical, sentimental, and inclusive to the degree that nothing from the past need really be discarded.

But it was not to be expected that conservative propaganda was going to be allowed a free run with this extraordinarily effective and flexible metaphor. It was almost inevitable, for instance, that Hone, who had

[29] Charles Kingsley, *The Water Babies: A Fairy Tale for a Land Baby*, ill. Linley Sambourne (Macmillan, 1885), pp. 23–5.
[30] Ibid., p. 367.

already made a name for himself by the early years of the century as a brilliant radical satirist with parodies, among other things, of the Litany, the Lord's Prayer,[31] and the Catechism, would sooner or later take up what had by now become the central image of reaction. In 1819 he published *The Political House that Jack Built* – a clever combination of the conservative architectural motif with the children's nursery rhyme. The 'Dedication' to 'Dr Slop' (the slovenly doctor who delivers Tristram Shandy in Sterne's satirical novel of that name) describes the potential readers of this 'juvenile publication' as a 'nursery of children six feet high'. Hone's illustrator, who was soon to become a personal friend, was a talented young cartoonist called George Cruikshank.[32]

For his motto, Hone took the quotation already cited from Cowper's *The Task*, with its idealized pictures of a peaceful and civilized rural life, isolated from war and the corruption of outside life by the reassuring solidity of the 'old castle of the state'. Following the repetitive and cumulative structure of the original nursery rhyme, each verse has its own illustration to provide an ironic commentary on the words – which, if read in isolation could seem entirely harmless. Perhaps a sign of caution from Hone, who had been tried for treason only two years earlier, the visual/rhetorical device offers a brilliant counterpoint. Thus the opening stanza reads:

THIS IS

THE WEALTH

That lay

In the House that Jack Built

But Cruikshank's illustration shows not money, but symbols of the ancient liberties of the English people: Magna Carta, Habeas Corpus, and, no less significantly, in view of the attack on the Church to follow, a large book that looks suspiciously like the Bible – in short, the same 'priceless possessions' that Burke had described by a similar fiscal metaphor as constituting the legacy handed down from past generations.

---

[31] This was the MP's prayer: 'Our Lord, who art in the Treasury, whatsoever be thy name, thy power be prolonged, thy will be done throughout the empire, as it is in each session. Give us our usual sops, and forgive us our occasional absences on division; as we promise not to forgive them that divide against thee. Turn us not out of our places; but keep us in the House of Commons, the Land of Pensions and Plenty; and deliver us from the people. Amen.' See F.W. Hackwood, *William Hone: His Life and Times* (T.F. Unwin, 1912); J. Ann Hone, *For the Cause of Truth: Radicalism in London 1796–1821* (Oxford University Press, 1982); 'William Hone', *Historical Studies*, October 1974.

[32] William Hone, *The Political House that Jack Built* (printed by and for William Hone, 1819).

The next repeat runs:

> THESE ARE
> **THE VERMIN**
> That plunder the Wealth,
> That lay in the House
> That Jack Built

The illustration is not of rats, but the professions: the law, the church, the army, and so on. The following repeat has a picture of a printing-press:

> THIS IS
> **THE THING**
> that in spite of new Acts,
> And attempts to restrain it,
> by Soldiers or Tax,
> Will poison the Vermin,
> That plunder the Wealth,
> That lay in the House
> That Jack Built.

The succeeding repeats offer a mercilessly detailed description of each of the 'vermin' in turn, culminating in a caricature of the Prince Regent himself:

> This is **THE MAN** – all shaven and shorn,
> All cover'd with Orders – and all forlorn:
> **THE DANDY OF SIXTY**
> who bows with a grace,
> And has taste in wigs, collars,
> cuirasses and lace;
> Who, to tricksters and fools,
> leaves the State and its treasure,
> And, when Britain's in tears,
> sails about at his pleasure:
> Who spurn'd from his presence
> the Friends of his youth,
> And now has not one
> who will tell him the truth.

The charge is not that he is corrupt nor foolish, but that (being both) he is in the end to be pitied for having no real friends, must make this Painite lampoon in its own way one of the most devastating ever written – even of Prinny, that most inviting of targets. Moreover, the repetitive and cumulative nursery-rhyme structure means that these lines are repeated over and over again in the ritual incantation as the other bizarre inhabitants and associates of the 'House' (in political circles, of course, the abbreviation for the two Houses of Parliament) are duly paraded for inspection and mockery.

The Political House was an enormous success. It went through fifty-four editions and inspired a host of imitations, not to mention loyalist counter-parodies. So powerful indeed was the political message that serious attempts were made to wrest control of the architectural metaphor back from Hone and the radicals, as attested by such titles as *A Parody on the Political House that Jack Built* by one M. Adams (1820) – printed, interestingly enough, by Joseph Johnson, the radical publisher who had been an inmate of a circle that had included Paine, Blake, Godwin, Mary Wollstonecraft, and the Shelleys – *The Real Constitutional House that Jack Built* (1820) and *The Loyalists House that Jack Built*. Once appropriated, however, the idea of the state as architecture lent itself too easily to metaphors of decay and dilapidation for the opposition to lose its grip of it.

It was, for instance, at precisely this time that Thomas Love Peacock (1785–1866) began work on his satirical romance of ancient Wales, *The Misfortunes of Elphin*, which was to appear almost a decade later in 1829. Though too suspicious of politicians to count as a radical himself, Peacock was a close friend of Shelley, who favoured libertarian non-violent revolution, and had a keen eye for the absurdities of the conservative attempts to block reform. Having just married a Welsh-speaking wife, Peacock began researches into Welsh history and folklore, where, he rapidly discovered, the architectural metaphor for tradition had new and rich possibilities.

The Misfortunes is set in a semi-mythical Wales in the sixth century – a land as rich in treasure as it was in the bards to celebrate it. The greatest source of its prosperity is a fertile low-lying plain to the west of the Cambrian Mountains, now wholly covered by the waters of Cardigan Bay. Even at that time, Peacock tells us, much of this land was actually *below* sea-level, but the waters of the Irish Sea were kept at bay by an enormous sea-wall, running from north to south across the entrance to the bay:

Watchtowers were erected along the embankment, and watchmen were appointed to guard against the first approaches of damage or decay. The whole of these towers, and their companies of guards, were subordinated to a central castle, which commanded the sea-port already mentioned, and wherein dwelt Prince Seithenyn ap Seithyn Saidi, who held the office of Arglwyd Gorwarchiedwad yr Argae Brebinawal, which signifies in English, Lord High Commissioner of Royal Embankment; and he executed it as a personage so denominated might be expected to do; he drank the profits, and left the embankment to his deputies, who left it to their assistants, who left it to itself. [33]

The energetic and reform-minded Prince Elphin is sent to remonstrate with Seithenyn on the state of the embankment. The latter, as usual, is drinking with his friends. His argument for reverencing the wall on account of its age and the fact that it was created by their ancestors goes, of course, straight back to Burke:

'Prince Seithenyn,' said Elphin, 'I have visited you on a subject of deep moment. Reports have been brought to me, that the embankment, which has been so long intrusted to your care, is in a state of dangerous decay.'

'Decay,' said Seithenyn, 'is one thing, and danger is another. Every thing that is old must decay. That the embankment is old, I am free to confess; that it is somewhat rotten in parts, I will not altogether deny; that it is any the worse for that, I do most sturdily gainsay. It does its business well: it works well: it keeps out water from the land, and it lets in the wine upon the High Commission of Embankment. Cupbearer, fill. Our ancestors were wiser than we: they built it in their wisdom; and, if we should be so rash as to try to mend it, we should only mar it.'

'The stonework,' said Teithrin, 'is sapped and mined: the piles are rotten, broken and dislocated: the floodgates and sluices are leaky and creaky.'

'That is the beauty of it,' said Seithenyn. 'Some parts of it are rotten, and some parts of it are sound.'

'It is well,' said Elphin, 'that some parts are sound: it were better that all were so.'

'So I have heard some people say before,' said Seithenyn; 'perverse people, blind to venerable antiquity: that very unamiable sort of people, who are in the habit of indulging their reason. But I say, the parts that are rotten give elasticity to those that are sound: they give them elasticity, elasticity, elasticity. If it were all sound, it would break by its own obstinate stiffness: the soundness is checked by the rottenness, and the stiffness is balanced by the elasticity. There is nothing so dangerous as innovation. See the waves in the equinoctial storms, dashing and clashing, roaring and pouring, spattering and battering, rattling and battling against it. I would not be so presumptuous as to say, I could build any thing that would stand against them half an hour; and here is this immortal old work, which God forbid the finger of modern mason should bring into jeopardy, this immortal work has stood for centuries, and it will stand for centuries more, if we let it alone. It is well: it works well: let well alone. Cupbearer, fill. It was half rotten when I was born, and that is a conclusive reason why it should be three parts rotten when I die.'[34]

---

[33] *The Misfortunes of Elphin*, *The Novels of Thomas Love Peacock*, ed. David Garnett (Hart-Davis, 1948), p. 555.
[34] Ibid.

As we know from his other writings, Peacock was no lover of politicians, economists and paper money, and it is perfectly possible that the 'bank' in 'embankment' is a further satiric pun on the financial corruptions of the unreformed pre-1832 parliament. But much more to the point Peacock has very cleverly here introduced a new element into his satire. Though the architecture of the previous century was often magnificent, the eighteenth-century record on building *maintenance* had been strikingly poor. Hallowed ancient buildings – including Litchfield Cathedral and even the Houses of Parliament themselves – were found to be in ruinous state and on the verge of collapse. Though Burke had compared the state to a venerable building, he nowhere had suggested that it might need repair, restoration, or even adaptation to meet altered social or climatic conditions. But buildings are not merely works of art, in the end they must be functional as well – even if that function is ritualistic and traditional. Architecture is not independent of context and circumstance. Burke's building and gardens had been carefully non-specific; Cowper's ancient castle, whose 'tempest-beaten' turrets were shaking, was by implication ruined, and even specifically in danger of collapse. Finally, and most ominously, Peacock suggests that the sea-level itself might be changing.

'And after all,' said Seithenyn, 'the worst that could happen would be the overflow of a spring tide, for that was the worst that happened before the embankment was thought of; and, if the high water should come in, as it did before, the low water would go out, as it did before. We should be no deeper in it than our ancestors were, and we could mend as easily as they could make.'

'The level of the sea,' said Teithrin, 'is materially altered.'

'The level of the sea!' exclaimed Seithenyn. 'Who ever heard of such a thing as altering the level of the sea? Alter the level of that bowl of wine before you, in which, as I sit here, I see a very ugly reflection of your very goodlooking face. Alter the level of that: drink up the reflection: let me see the face without the reflection, and leave the sea to level itself.' [35]

Shortly afterwards a combination of high winds and spring tides breach the wall, and the sea pours through. Prince Seithenyn, insisting to the end that the cause must be a conspiracy of enemies rather than the rising of the sea, attempts to hold back the flood by brandishing his sword and drunkenly shouting defiance until he is drowned. In the ensuing inundation the greater part of the ancient lowland Wales disappears for ever under the sea, and the remnant of dispirited survivors flee to the mountains that are all that is left today of the once-prosperous kingdom.

[35] Ibid. pp. 560–2.

If, in Peacock's fable, it is elemental forces of external change that finally overwhelm the bastions of the constitution, for Thomas Carlyle, the fate of government and constitution alike is decided by the Paris mob. Carlyle's *French Revolution* was published in 1837, after a second French Revolution in 1830 had, yet again, been decided by mob violence. For him the conflict between the irresistible tides of human history and the immovable architecture of government, constitution, and authority, were symbolized by the siege and fall of the Bastille. Metaphors for the Paris mob swing wildly between the raging of ocean waters and fires of destruction – both biblical images of the wrath of God. The Bastille itself, in this account, has neither the Burkean stability of ancient law and constitution, nor the tottering instability of Seithenyn's embankment, but, rather, the labyrinthine mysteries of Piranesian dungeons, the gothic vaults of the Castle of Otranto, or the Palace of Gormenghast: vast, ancient, brooding and irrational.

To describe this Siege of the Bastille (thought to be one of the most important in History) perhaps transcends the talent of mortals. Could one but, after infinite reading, get to understand so much as the plan of the building! But there is open Esplanade, at the end of the Rue Saint-Antoine; there are such Forecourts, *Cour Avance, Cour de l'Orme*, arched Gateway (where Louis Tournay now fights); then new drawbridges, dormant-bridges, rampart-bastions, the grim Eight Towers; a labyrinthic Mass, high-frowning there, of all ages from twenty years to four hundred and twenty; – beleaguered, in this its last hour, as we have said, by mere Chaos come again! Ordinance of all calibres, throats of all capacities; men of all plans, every man his own engineer: seldom since the war of Pygmies and Cranes was there seen so anomalous a thing. Half-pay Elie is home for a suit of regimentals; no one would heed him in coloured clothes: half-pay Hulin is haranguing Guardes Françaises in the Place de Grève. Frantic Patriots pick up the grapeshots; bear them, still hot (or seemingly so), to the Hôtel-de-Ville: Paris, you perceive, is to be burnt! Flesselles is 'pale to the very lips,' for the roar of the multitude grows deep. Paris wholly has got to the acme of its frenzy; whirled, all ways, by panic madness. At every street-barricade, there whirls simmering a minor whirlpool, – strengthening the barricade, since God knows what is coming; and all minor whirlpools play distractedly into that Grand Fire-Mahlstrom which is lashing round the Bastille.[36]

Though irony is never absent from Carlyle's tumultuous and convoluted style, there is little that is satiric in this portrait of the Bastille as symbol of everything in the *ancien régime* that must be torn down. On the other hand, Carlyle is no radical. There is no love either for the mob, which, though an elemental destructive force, is indiscriminate in its victims and

[36] Thomas Carlyle, *The French Revolution*, 2 vols. (Macmillan, 1900), Vol. I, pp. 189–90.

de-stabilizing to the whole society. Not least of Carlyle's ironies is that Burke's original metaphor of the French razing to the ground the whole edifice of the state and constitution almost certainly refers *en passant* to the destruction of the Bastille in July 1789. Here Carlyle has, in effect, taken the very ground of Burke's image and tried to demonstrate both its true horror and inexorable inevitability.

As might be expected, 'tradition' is not a word that is used often by Carlyle, and when it is, it sums up all that is wrong with the *ancien régime*. It represents 'those decadent ages in which no Ideal either grows or blossoms'.

When Belief and Loyalty have passed away, and only the cant false echo of them remains; and all Solemnity has become Pagentry; and the creed of persons in authority has become one of two things: an Imbecility or a Machiavelism . . . Hapless ages: wherein, if ever in any, it is an unhappiness to be born. To be born, and to learn only, by every tradition and example, that God's Universe is Belial's and a Lie; and 'the Supreme Quack' the hierarch of men![37]

Tradition is embodied by the Bastille; it is Kafka's Castle – the tyranny of the irrational and the unconscious become politics expressed in stone and mortar. Small wonder that the period was experimenting with other ideas, other metaphors, to describe the handing on and development of the wisdom of the past.

Such is one strand, at least, of even conservative thought at the beginning of Victoria's reign – at the very time, according to Hobsbawm, that we begin to find what he calls 'invented traditions'. The questions that must now be asked is not what traditions were now to be invented, but what had happened to the whole idea of tradition by the 1830s, and, indeed, why was there any desire or need at all to *re-invent* what had become for so many patently an embarrassment and an anachronism?

---

[37] Ibid., p. 12.

CHAPTER 5

Inventing Christian culture: Volney, Chateaubriand and the French Revolution

VOLNEY: RUINING THE CHRISTIAN TRADITION

If, in the second half of the eighteenth century, France had become a home of the Enlightenment, it was also home to some of the most prescriptive intellectual rigidities of the age. The political inflexibility of the *ancien régime* was matched by an equal inflexibility in the rules of neo-classical aesthetics not to mention Catholic doctrine. Indeed, it had been Leibniz's friend and correspondent, the Frenchman, Cardinal Bossuet, who had become famous – or notorious – for having produced the most sweeping statement of tradition ever devised by the Catholic Church: if it was new, it was heresy. Full stop. Small wonder, perhaps, that France was also to become home to the Revolution.

For Bossuet there was nothing problematic about tradition – at least of the Catholic variety. In 1688 he had spelled it out with his famous axiom, *Semper Eadem* – always the same. It was, for him, the knockout blow against the Protestants. Variation or change in the teaching of the Church *must* be a sign of error – a point on which he was confident that no Christian could disagree, and remain a Christian. In Owen Chadwick's phrase, the tradition of faith was 'an inexhaustible treasure deposited in a bank, so that all may draw from it'.[1] Centred on the Vincentian canon, it was neither more nor less than that which had always been believed in every place, in every century, by all Christian men and women.

In September 1791, 103 years later, the former aristocrat Constantin-François Chasseboeuf de Volney, now citizen secretary to the Revolutionary French National Assembly, formally presented it with a short monograph entitled *Les Ruines, ou méditation sur les révolutions des empires*. The enigmatic title gave little clue to his real thesis, which purported to describe in the form of a mythological vision the

---

[1] See Owen Chadwick, *From Bossuet to Newman*, 2nd edn (Cambridge University Press, 1987), p. 1.

historical origins of religion, and in particular the origins and evolution of Christianity. According to Volney, not merely all Indo-European and Semitic religion but even astrology as well could be traced back to a common origin in ancient Egypt at least 17,000 years ago.[2] All modern forms of supernatural and revealed religion were, he claimed, in reality nothing more than the misplaced products of primitive nature-worship, time, and the accidents of historical diffusion. Thus the gods of Egypt had been appropriated by the Aryans into their own pantheon before being eventually reduced to a single deity in Persia in the sixth century BCE. This new syncretistic monotheism had in turn been adopted by the Israelites when released from the Babylonian captivity by the Persians, transmitted to the Christians, and thence eventually to the Bedouin tribesmen of the Arabian desert: 'Jews, Christians, Mahometans, howsoever lofty may be your pretensions, you are in your spiritual and immaterial system, only the blundering followers of Zoroaster.'[3]

In keeping with the uniformitarian assumptions of the Enlightenment, miracles were attributed to the power of imagination, the gods to their origins in the forces of nature and the regulation of human society to the operation of natural law and self-love.[4] Volney supported this argument by a dazzling and curious display of erudition ranging from Hindu cosmology to the esoteric doctrines of the Essenes.[5] That, together with its strongly revolutionary and anti-clerical context, was sufficient to account for the book's immediate popularity both inside and outside France. The first English translation was published in 1792 by Joseph Johnson, the radical publisher and friend, among others, of Blake, Godwin, and Paine – though Volney himself is known to have expressed some doubts about its mildness of tone. At least two other translations had appeared by the end of the 1790s, and it was still being reprinted (in its mildest version) by freethinking and radical groups in Britain and the USA as late as the 1890s.

Even by modern scholarly standards, Volney was well-equipped for the demolition-job that he had undertaken. By 1781 he had gained an international academic reputation by publishing an examination of Herodotus' chronology. His next book, *Voyage en Syrie et en Egypte* (1793) had confirmed his status as an Orientalist and earned him a decoration from Catherine the Great. To prepare for his expedition to the Near East he had spent some time in a Coptic monastery and learned Arabic. Like Herodotus, his first subject, he had been overwhelmed by his first-hand experience of the

---

[2] *The Ruins: Or a Survey of the Revolutions of Empires* (Peter Eckler, 1890), pp. 120–1.
[3] Ibid., p. 98.　　[4] Ibid., pp. 22–6; 117–21.　　[5] Ibid., pp. 96–102; 105–6.

historical *difference* of past cultures from his own culture and society. From the first pages of the *Ruins* it is clear that there is a connection in his mind between the ruins of countless Near-Eastern civilizations lost in the desert and those of the (metaphorically) still-smouldering Bastille nearer home. 'Who knows,' says his anonymous traveller: 'Who knows but that here- after some traveller like myself will sit down upon the banks of the Seine, the Thames, or the Zuyder See . . . who knows but that he will sit down solitary amid silent ruins, and weep a people inurned, and their greatness changed into an empty name?'[6] It was an image that was to haunt the his- torically minded nineteenth century, from Macaulay's vision of some New Zealander of the future standing on Ludgate Hill contemplating the ruins of St Paul's, to the pessimism of Kipling's *Recessional* where 'all our pomp of yesterday' is 'one with Nineveh and Tyre'.

For the modern reader, the *Ruins* may seem an oddly puzzling and oblique work – its narrative form often making it seem less like a schol- arly argument than a gothic novel. After a brief allegory of the events of the French Revolution now under way, Volney proceeds to demolish that worst remnant of ancient superstition, now known as the Catholic Church, by a series of extended allegories – of which the opening, with its dramatic invocation of the ruins of time as the leveller of tyrants, provides the key metaphor and indeed the emotional register for what follows. The mix- ture of anecdote and philosophical disquisition, so far from illuminating its subject with any cold light of reason, however, is allegorical, dramatic, and, in its own strange way, even mythological. Indeed, this 'gothick', or mystical quality to Volney's writing often makes it seem less like a demoli- tion of all existing religions than a prelude to a new one based on what he calls the Law of Nature.

In the opening chapters, the narrator, enveloped in romantic melancholy before the ruins of Palmyra, is suddenly confronted by a phantom – whom the first-person narrator proceeds to address in fateful terms as the 'Genius of tombs and ruins', and is thereafter known simply as 'the Genius'. The question asked of this mysterious Genius is at once simple and all- embracing: 'By what secret causes do empires rise and fall; from what sources spring the prosperity and misfortunes of nations; on what princi- ples can the peace of society, and the happiness of man be established?'[7] Not surprisingly, the Catholic Church does not play a large part in the answer – and, no less unsurprisingly for those who have read so far, nor does tradition. Like his fellow *philosophes* of the Enlightenment – not to

---

[6] Ibid., p. 8.   [7] Ibid., p. 13.

mention Lowth or Burke in England – for Volney, tradition is archaic, primitive, and essentially untrustworthy:

> Should it be asked at what epoch this system took its birth, we shall answer on the testimony of the monuments of astronomy itself, that its principles appear with certainty to have been established about seventeen thousand years ago. And if it be asked to what people it is to be attributed, we shall answer that the same monuments, supported by unanimous traditions, attribute it to the first tribes of Egypt; and when reason finds in that country all the circumstances which could lead to such a system; when it finds there is a zone of sky, bordering on the tropic, equally free from the rains of the equator and the fogs of the North; . . . it conceives that the inhabitant of the Nile, addicted to agriculture from the nature of his soil, to geometry from the annual necessity of measuring his lands, to commerce from the facility of communications, to astronomy from the state of his sky... must have been the first to pass from the savage to the social state.[8]

Here 'reason' can verify what ancient (and unanimous) traditions attest. But what happened in ancient Egypt can serve not merely as a model for the origins of civilization in general and organized religion in particular but, no less significantly, as a model for how 'tradition' itself is created and handed down:

> There happened early on the borders of the Nile, what has since been repeated in every country; as soon as a new system was formed its novelty excited quarrels and schisms; then, gaining credit by persecution itself, sometimes it effaced antecedent ideas, sometimes it modified and incorporated them; then, by the intervention of political revolutions, the aggregation of states and the mixture of nations confused all opinions; and the filiation of ideas being lost, theology fell into a chaos, and became a mere logograph of old traditions no longer understood.[9]

This is not, of course, *quite* like MacIntyre's 'existential crises', but the notion that tradition is what is left when a religion has ceased to be observed or understood – that tradition is, as it were, *fossilized* religion– differentiates it subtly from the idea of 'custom' which, for Volney, has the much more straightforward and polemically neutral meaning of 'how things were done' at a particular time or place.[10] Because it contains material no longer understood, tradition, unlike custom, can be ambiguous and even positively misleading – as one polemical footnote makes only too clear: '*Resurgere*, to rise a second time, cannot signify to return to life, but in a metamorphical sense; but we continually make mistakes of this kind resulting from the ambiguous meaning of the words made use of in ancient

[8] Ibid., pp. 120–1.   [9] Ibid., p. 149.
[10] See, among other places, references to 'custom' and 'customs' on pp. 48, 64, and 137–8.

tradition.[11] Indeed, this idea of tradition as providing the fossils from which a forensic study of religion might re-construct the living forms of the past is all-pervasive in the *Ruins* – perhaps as befits an age when fossils were first being debated as a geological phenomenon. [12] The romantic settings in the dusk; the sense of age and cultural remoteness of the vanished glories of the oasis city of Palmyra; the 'religious thoughtfulness' of the narrator who has, in the ancient custom of Near-Eastern prophets, retired into the desert to meditate; all combine to give the *Ruins* a prophetic and even mystical rather than a rationalistic flavour. Volney does not deny religion; he relativizes and historicizes it. So far from being sent out from the darkness of superstition into the cool light of Reason, readers of the *Ruins* were, it is implied, about to be initiated into the ineffable mysteries of a new age of the Spirit – giving Volney a quite different kind of appeal from other rationalist writers of the period, such as Voltaire. Whether or not there is in the well-documented influence of the *Illuminati* of Avignon the shadowy vestige of the Joachimite idea of the 'third age', the so-called 'Age of the Spirit', seems still a matter of scholarly debate, but its presence is well-enough attested in other contemporary anti-religious writers from Lessing to Marx for there to be nothing inherently improbable in the idea.[13] In this sense Volney forms a bridge between the dry scepticism of Enlightenment historiography and the more inward psychological questioning of the meaning of religion by the next generation of critics, such as Feuerbach and Schleiermacher. Comte's subsequent attempt to turn Volney's key to all mythologies into a positivist religion of humanity is, as George Eliot saw, less a perversion than a logical extension of qualities implicit not only in his argument itself, but also in the rhetoric of its presentation.[14]

Thus the expectation of a coming Messiah is linked not merely historically with the Zoroastrian monotheism of the Persian Empire, which the exiled Jews had encountered through the Babylonian Captivity, but also seen in its psychological context:

Events having realized the first part of these predictions, the ruin of Jerusalem, the people adhered to the second with a firmness of belief in proportion to their misfortunes; and the afflicted Jews expected, with the impatience of want and

[11] Ibid., p. 159n.
[12] See, for instance, Stephen Jay Gould, *The Lying Stones of Marrakech* (Jonathan Cape, 2000), especially sections I, and II; and Martin J.S. Rudwick, *The Meaning of Fossils: Episodes in the History of Paleontology* (University of Chicago Press, 1976).
[13] See Marjorie Reeves and Warwick Gould, *Joachim of Fiore and the Myth of the Eternal Evangel in the Nineteenth Century* (Clarendon Press, 1987).
[14] See T.R. Wright, *The Religion of Humanity: The Impact of Comtean Positivism on Victorian Britain* (Cambridge University Press, 1986).

desire, this victorious king and deliverer, who was to come and save the nation of Moses, and restore the empire of David.

On the other hand, the sacred and mythological traditions of preceding times had spread through all Asia a dogma perfectly analogous.[15]

Popular report became an established fact: the imaginary being was realized; and all the circumstances of mythological tradition, being assembled around this phantom, produced a regular history, of which it was no longer permitted to doubt.

These mythological traditions recounted that, in the beginning, a woman and a man had by their fall introduced sin and misery into the world . . . These traditions related that the woman had decoyed and seduced the man.[16]

Finally, these traditions went so far as to mention even his astrological and mythological names, and inform us that he was called sometimes Chris, that is to say, preserver, and from that, ye Indians, you have made your god Chrish-en or Chrish-na; and, ye Greek and Western Christians, your Chris-tos, son of Mary, is the same; sometimes he is called Yes, by the union of three letters, which by their numerical value from the number 608, once of the solar periods.[17]

'Tradition' is thus both a guide and a deceiver. It does indeed tell us much about what people of the past believed, but only to caution us at the same time against a naïve acceptance of that belief. For Volney, it holds little or nothing of the re-invention or selection from the past so implicitly central to the idea of the past as a living, organic, or constructive force, and has everything to do with being led astray. Only in the light of modernity can we read the implications of tradition in ways in which its originators could have had little idea.

In a later work, called *The Law of Nature* (1793), usually thereafter published together with the *Ruins*, we get a further glimpse into how this meaning of 'tradition' (originally, we recall, a Latin legal term) relates to Volney's definition of 'law': 'The word *law*, (i.e. the French *loi* from the Latin *lex, lectio*) taken literally, signifies *lecture*, because originally, ordinances and regulations preferably to all others, were made to the people, in order that they might observe them.'[18] This is a slightly over-literal translation of the French *lecture*, which also carries the connotation of 'reading'. The idea of reading aloud from a set text is also a key image of the *Ruins*, where the mysterious Genius 'reads' both literally and metaphorically from the works of the past.

One does not need to be much of a deconstructionist to find here an indication of the way in which Volney's idea of law involves a 'reading' (or,

<hr>

[15] *Ruins*, p. 154.   [16] Ibid., p. 157.   [17] Ibid., pp. 159–60.
[18] *The Law of Nature*, in *Ruins* p. 1 (separately paginated).

perhaps, even a re-reading) of the 'book of nature' which from mediaeval times had been held to offer an alternative and complementary source of knowledge of God to that provided by the Bible. For Volney, a reading of the laws of Nature provides a much surer route to the understanding of the universe than the garbled and fossilized traditions of antiquity. Thus a proper understanding of Nature leads humanity towards universal justice, peace, and benevolence.[19] We also learn that such an understanding points not towards atheism, but to the existence (however shadowy) of 'a supreme agent, a universal and identical mover' thus illustrating 'that the law of nature is sufficient to raise us to the knowledge of God'.[20]

Not surprisingly, the natural theology behind such vague Deism was hardly strong enough to absolve Volney from the general charge of atheism. Moreover, his 'supreme agent' was close enough to an idea of absolute reason for him to be used by the French Theophilanthropists in the early 1790s as part of their attempt to promote a cultic worship of a goddess of Reason. From the first publication of the *Ruins* in England there was a series of pamphlets attempting to refute his arguments, and his assumed atheism. When, after a period in prison during the Reign of Terror, Volney managed to make his way to America, he was denounced by another immigrant and victim of religious persecution, the Unitarian Joseph Priestley, who, in a splendidly undiscriminating racialist catch-all insult, called him 'an atheist, an ignoramus, a Chinaman, and a Hottentot'.[21]

CHATEAUBRIAND: APPROPRIATING THE GENIUS

Perhaps the most remarkable result of this attempt to undermine the Catholic tradition, however, was the response it was to provoke from another French aristocrat, exiled in England: François René Auguste de Chateaubriand. Even the title of his book, *Le Génie du Christianisme (The Genius of Christianity)*, is a recognizable reference to Volney, whose narrator had been guided through the history of Near-Eastern religions by the mysterious phantom always respectfully addressed as 'Genius' – a word whose primary meaning, in French as in English, was the tutelary spirit of a person, place, or, by extension, idea. The 'Genius' of Christianity, it is implied, is more than a match for any vague spirit of syncretistic Deism dreamed up by some revolutionary opportunist. Published in 1802, by 1804

---

[19] *The Law of Nature*, in *Ruins*, p. 6 (separately paginated).
[20] Ibid., pp. 6-7.
[21] E. L. de Montluzin, *The Anti-Jacobins, 1798–1800* (St Martin's Press, 1988), pp. 155–6.

it had gone through seven editions and had been translated into German, Italian, and Russian. Considering that Chateaubriand himself spoke good English, and had visited both America and England during his exile, it is a mark of England's linguistic as well as intellectual isolation at this period that the first English translation – rather strangely entitled *The Beauties of Christianity* – only followed in 1813. Though it is often seen as first and foremost a Catholic royalist response to the republican Deism of Volney's *Ruins*, the most lasting effect of Chateaubriand's counter-blast was to change for ever the terms of the debate about the nature and meaning of tradition.

As was not infrequently the case in this period of confused loyalties and sudden political reversals, the two writers' careers, and even their eventual views, were less far apart than might appear at first glance. Some ten years younger than Volney, Chateaubriand had been a liberal-minded officer in the army of the *ancien régime*, and had made his way to America two years before him and so escaped the Reign of Terror. While in America Volney had been well received by Washington himself – an honour that Chateaubriand also claimed, though the evidence actually suggests that the American President had, in fact, been unable to meet him.[22] Both returned to France after Napoleon came to power and accepted posts and honours while remaining critical of the authoritarianism of the new Empire. Chateaubriand at first tried to ingratiate himself with Napoleon,[23] and served briefly in a number of diplomatic posts under him; in 1811 Napoleon even offered him a place in the *Académie* – an offer then indefinitely postponed because of his growing criticism of the regime. An ardent royalist, Chateaubriand accepted a ministerial post under the restored Charles XVIII, and was later ambassador to Berlin and then London, but he grew increasingly disenchanted with post-Revolutionary politics altogether and withdrew once more into private life.

Volney became a senator in 1799, a commander of the *Légion d'honneur* in 1804, and continued with scholarly work on ancient history and Oriental languages. After 1815 he was able to make his peace with the restored Bourbon monarchy and took his seat (metaphorically, if not literally) side-by-side with Chateaubriand as a fellow-member of the House of Peers.

[22] The evidence for Chateaubriand's meeting with Washington rests solely on his own *Mémoires d'outre-tombe* (1849–50) and may belong more to what might be kindly called the rhetorical category of invented conversations with great figures rather than to historical fact. See Richard Switzer, *Chateaubriand* (Twayne, 1971), p. 22.
[23] See his sycophantic *Epître dédicatoire au premier consul Bonaparte* to the 1803 edition of *Le Génie du Christianisme*.

The crucial difference between them lay neither in their politics nor their scholarship, but in their religion. Until almost the age of thirty Chateaubriand had held no particular religious convictions, but at the death of his mother and sister, in 1797, he experienced a conversion that was to last the rest of his life: 'Those two voices coming up from the grave, and that death which had now become the interpreter of death, struck me with peculiar force. I became a Christian. I did not yield to any great supernatural light: my conviction came from the heart. I wept, and I believed.'[24] If, as some critics have argued,[25] there was more than a touch of political opportunism in this conversion, this unashamed emotionalism is also a key to Chateaubriand's strategy in the *Genius of Christianity*.

Indeed the main thrust of Chateaubriand's argument is aimed not at the facts of history at all, but at changing the reader's entire perspective on the past. The very attributes of traditional religion which Volney had seen as its weakest points for attack were seized upon by Chateaubriand and extolled as its most essential qualities. Christianity's irrationality and emotion, its ancient mythology, its capacity to inspire the most childish and naïve devotion, not to mention its capacity for development, were all now adduced as proof of its imaginative and psychological depth – its unique capacity to satisfy the whole person, in contrast to what was portrayed as the shallow intellectualism of the Enlightenment sceptics. 'It was,' wrote Chateaubriand, 'necessary to summon all the charms of the imagination, and all the interests of the heart, to the assistance of that religion against which they had been set in array.' His thesis was original, bold, and comprehensive. It was nothing less than to prove that:

the Christian religion, of all the religions that ever existed, is the most humane, the most favourable to liberty and to the arts and sciences; that the modern world is indebted to it for every improvement, from agriculture to the abstract sciences – from the hospitals for the reception of the unfortunate to the temples reared by the Michael Angelos and embellished by the Raphaels . . . that nothing is more divine than its morality – nothing more lovely and more sublime than its tenets, its doctrine, and its worship; that it encourages genius, corrects the taste, develops the virtuous passions, imparts energy to the ideas, presents noble images to the writer, and perfect models to the artist; that there is no disgrace in being believers with Newton and Bossuet, with Pascal and Racine.[26]

---

[24] Chateaubriand, *The Genius of Christianity*, trs. Charles White (J.B. Lippincott, 1856), p. 27.
[25] Notably Pierre Barbéris, *A la recherche d'une écriture: Chateaubriand* (Maison Mame, 1974).
[26] *Genius of Christianity*, pp. 48–9.

We should neither be satisfied with mere intellectual conviction, nor even to admire Christianity its manifold achievements; this is above all a religion to be *loved*. Here Volney, Voltaire, and their fellow *philosophes* have totally misunderstood what religion is about. Chateaubriand's position is the precursor – if not the provable source – of Coleridge's famous dictum in *Aids to Reflection*:

Hence, I more than fear, the prevailing taste for Books of Natural Theology, Physico-Theology, Demonstrations of God from Nature, Evidences of Christianity, &c., &c. *Evidences* of Christianity! I am weary of the Word. Make a man feel the *want* of it; rouse him, if you can, to the self-knowledge of his *need* of it; and you may safely trust it to its own Evidence.[27]

What is at stake for Chateaubriand is the very nature and function of human tradition itself. 'Sublime in the antiquity of its recollections, which go back to the creation of the world, ineffable in its mysteries, adorable in its sacraments, interesting in its history, celestial in its morality, rich and attractive in its ceremonial, it is fraught with every species of beauty.'[28] The richness of the past, with its arts, literature, philosophy, and science is all, even down to the pagan world of antiquity, if properly understood, the domain of Christianity as the presiding 'genius' of the universe – in the new and emotive romantic sense of that word.

Whereas for Volney, traditions were not so much a source of truth as threads guiding us through a labyrinth of past confusions, for Chateaubriand they were central to the human experience of history. As for Lowth or Burke, traditions might well have roots in something primitive, oral, and mythological, but they were nevertheless – or indeed, *because* of that – the vehicle of the most profound truth. They embodied a collective wisdom that could reach further and deeper than the most sophisticated rationality. In Jungian terms one might describe them in terms almost of a collective unconscious. One such, for instance, was the very story that Volney had cited as an example of syncretistic mythology: the story of the Fall:

A universal tradition teaches us that man was created in a more perfect state than that in which he at present exists, and that there has been a fall. This tradition is confirmed by the opinion of philosophers in every age and country, who have never been able to reconcile their ideas on the subject of moral man, without supposing a primitive state of perfection, from which human nature afterward fell by its own fault.[29]

---

[27] Samuel Taylor Coleridge, *Aids to Reflection*, p. 348.
[28] *Genius of Christianity*, p. 50.   [29] Ibid., p. 61.

There are truths which no one calls in question, though it is impossible to furnish any direct proofs of them. The rebellion and fall of Lucifer, the creation of the world, the primeval happiness and transgression of man, belong to the number of these truths. It is not to be supposed that an absurd falsehood could have become a universal tradition.[30]

Tradition may well be the product of a distant and essentially unverifiable past, but it is also, it seems, where history meets the psyche – but with none of the reductionist overtones of Volney. Despite the fact that Volney's work had tacitly incorporated much of the German Higher Criticism of the preceding fifty years, Chateaubriand appears at one level supremely indifferent to questions of scientific evidence, or historical documentation.[31] Though he makes it clear that he is well aware of Lowth's work on the sacred poetry of the Hebrews, and much indebted to it,[32] it is clear that he sees Lowth more as a literary guide than as a historical critic. Similarly, for Chateaubriand, Genesis is not so much 'history' as first and foremost 'the original of the representations met with in popular traditions'[33] – an idea that seems to reflect Herder even more than Lowth.[34] What seems to matter is not so much the literal truth, as the psychological truth embodied in ancient myth – which, in turn, can even be used to create a new version of natural religion.

The fall, then, being attested by general tradition, and by the transmission or generation of evil, both moral and physical, and, on the other hand, the ends for which man was designed being now as perfect as before his disobedience, notwithstanding his own degeneracy, it follows that a redemption, or any expedient whatever to enable man to fulfil those ends, is a natural consequence of the state into which human nature has fallen.[35]

'Tradition', once it is understood in this light, is in its own way a guarantor of truth – not, perhaps, verifiable scientific truth, which proceeds deductively, but 'truth' in the inductive artistic sense in which a novel or poem

---

[30] Ibid., p. 107.
[31] See, for instance, his quixotic commitment to defend the chronology of Genesis. Recent scientific discoveries are pressed into service selectively – remains of 'Indian elephants' [presumably mammoths?] found in Siberia proved the comprehensiveness as well as the truth of the Deluge – but, even in 1802, it was difficult to ignore the mounting scientific evidence that the earth was considerably older than the 5000 years or so produced by a literal adherence to the biblical dating. Chateaubriand's answer anticipates the thesis of Philip Gosse's notorious *Omphalos* by more than fifty years: 'God might have created, and doubtless did create, the world with all the marks of antiquity and completeness which it now exhibits.' Ibid., p. 136.
[32] 'The deep and various learning of Bishop Lowth, and his elegant and refined taste, give him the strong claims to the praise here attributed to his work on the sacred poetry of the Hebrews.' Ibid., note 1, p. 349.
[33] Ibid., p. 110.   [34] See Ch. 6 below.   [35] *Genius of Christianity*, p. 62.

might be more 'true to life' than any specific narrative from a newspaper. It offered, as it were, an artistic verisimilitude.

Indeed, the analogy with poetry, or with literature in general, is more than mere metaphor. 'Voltaire,' writes Chateaubriand, 'somewhere asserts that we possess a most wretched *copy* of the different popular traditions respecting the origin of the world, and the physical elements which compose it.'[36] That word 'copy' – in the French, *copie* – carries not so much the English meaning of 'imitation', but of 'reproduction', or 'transcript', in the sense of making a book, producing a new copy. As a student of Lowth, Chateaubriand is only too well aware of the dangers of progressive deterioration in the transmission of a text through repeated copying – not to mention Lowth's own metaphor of waters growing steadily more polluted the further they are from the original spring. But unlike Lowth, as we have seen, Chateaubriand seems to see 'tradition' (a word he actually capitalizes for emphasis in the original French) more in the nature of an ongoing work of art, constantly renewing itself as it is handed down. For him, unlike Voltaire, there is no comparison between the original muddy spring and the majestic river of Christianity. 'Did he prefer, then, the cosmogony of the Egyptians, the great winged egg of the Theban priests?'[37]

Such a view of tradition allows Chateaubriand openly to appropriate the past in a way that MacIntyre might find completely familiar. For Chateaubriand, just as the Old Testament only finds its true fulfilment in the New, so earlier pre-Christian pagan religions only find their true fulfilment and explanation in Christianity. The argument is a familiar one, from at least mediaeval times, but it can rarely have been presented with such *panache* and verve as here. Thus, though he is careful not to suggest that the mythologies of other, earlier religions, are the *source* of later Christian doctrines, they point towards them. His examples include ideas concerning the future life and the immortality of the soul. Many of these, Chateaubriand is happy to admit, are in truth taken from older religions and philosophies, but in their Christian form they are no longer selective or culture specific: 'The heaven and hell of the Christians are not devised after the manners of any particular people, but founded on the general ideas that are adapted to all nations and to all classes of society.'[38] Unlike the classical Elysium, for instance, the Christian Heaven admits children,

---

[36] 'Voltaire avance quelque part que nous avons la plus mauvaise copie de toutes les TRADITIONS sur l'origine du monde . . .' *Le Génie du christianisme* (1802; Gabriel Roux, 1855), p. 107.
[37] *Genius of Christianity*, p. 107.   [38] Ibid., pp. 203–4.

slaves, and 'the lower classes of men'; unlike the Norse Valhalla, Christians do not specify either the weather or social activities. Moreover, unlike the mystery religions on which it has no doubt drawn, Christianity has no esoteric secrets: 'What the brightest geniuses of Greece discovered by a last effort of reason is now publicly taught in every church; and the labourer, for a few pence, may purchase, in the catechism of his children, the most sublime secrets of the ancient sects.'[39]

But Chateaubriand's appropriation of pagan mythological traditions does not stop there. Even such post-biblical and distinctively Christian doctrines as that of the Trinity, can, he claims, be found in earlier philosophies. The Trinity was, it seems, known to the Egyptians, alluded to by Plato, and familiar in Tibet and the East Indies.[40] But greater antiquity does not imply greater wisdom. Though the biblical (or Mosaic) cosmogony has much in common with those of Zoroaster, Plato, the ancient Chinese, or the Scandinavians, it is nevertheless vastly superior to them.[41]

Once again, we note, the present is in firm control of the past. The vastness of the epistemological crisis of the French Revolution has driven Chateaubriand to appropriate not just a narrow section of antiquity, but, in effect, a no less vast sweep of world history to support a Catholic and fideistic present. His real originality, however, lies in his appropriation of romantic aesthetic theory to give his idea of tradition the organic and self-renewing qualities of a work of art.

This becomes increasing clear in Part II of *The Genius of Christianity*, entitled 'The Poetic of Christianity'. This brings us much closer to the central appropriative thesis of the *Genius*, which is to show how far Christianity has outgrown the pagan world in its capacity to inspire the arts – especially poetry. From the start there are only two possible con-tenders for the bardic bay-leaf crown: 'A poetic voice issues from the ruins which cover Greece and Idumaea, and cries afar to the traveller "There are but two brilliant names and recollections in history – those of the Israelites and of the ancient Greeks."'[42] After what has gone before, it comes as no surprise to learn that whatever may be the beauties of Homer and his fellow Greeks they are occluded by the grandeur and sublimity of the Bible. It is, however, interesting to discover that Chateaubriand is, once again, here following 'the deep and various learning of Bishop Lowth, and his elegant and refined taste' in 'his work on the sacred poetry

[39] Ibid., p. 204.   [40] Ibid., pp. 54–5.   [41] Ibid., pp. 107–10.   [42] Ibid., p. 210.

of the Hebrews'.[43] In comparison with the Christian moderns, moreover, the ancients fare no better, even in the one area where they might be expected to excel: 'whatever may be the genius of Homer and the majesty of his gods, his *marvellous* and all his grandeur are nevertheless eclipsed by the *marvellous* of Christianity'.[44]

But Chateaubriand is less concerned with simple comparisons than with developing a critical theory which would account for the superiority of the Christian moderns – and here his argument becomes much more subtle.

Christianity is, if we may so express it, a double religion. Its teaching has reference to the nature of intellectual being, and also to our own nature: it makes the mysteries of the Divinity and the mysteries of the human heart go hand-in-hand; and, by removing the veil that conceals the true God, it also exhibits man just as he is.

Such a religion must necessarily be more favourable to the delineation of *characters* than another which dives not into the secret of the passions. The fairer half of poetry, the dramatic, received no assistance from polytheism, for morals were separated from mythology.[45]

Once again, the aesthetic tradition of the ancients *needed* Christianity for its completion. The French word *caractère* carries here a connotation not easily conveyed by its English counterpart. Not merely does it suggest 'character' in the novelistic sense, but also a person's social role: such as that of a father, brother, daughter, and so on. Chateaubriand's point is that the modern inner sense of individuality, even self-consciousness, is enhanced by the individual's consciousness of their outer, moral, function within society. This is a point with which Jane Austen could scarcely disagree. But Chateaubriand is also one of the first critics to articulate what has now become something of a critical commonplace: that whereas eighteenth-century and neo-classical criticism laid great stress on the generality and uniformity of human experience, romanticism tended to stress its particularity and individuality.

Moreover, he is no less conscious of the moral and social dimensions of that new sense of individuality. With its new appreciation of individual moral responsibility, 'Christianity . . . has increased the resources of drama, whether in the epic or on the stage'.[46] Pagan antiquity, he claims, had little interest in an after-life, and classical tragedy ended with death. In contrast, in a play like Racine's *Phèdre* the tragic tension is increased by the fact that as a Christian wife Phèdre is also jeopardizing her immortal soul.

---

[43] Ibid., p. 349.   [44] Ibid., p. 330.   [45] Ibid., p. 232.   [46] Ibid., p. 299.

Thus Chateaubriand's idea of tradition as a dynamic and developing stream breaks not merely with Bossuet's idea of a totally static deposit of faith, but also *presupposes* a corresponding development of doctrine. Finally, it assumes that development of doctrine goes hand-in-hand with aesthetic development. But, of course, like all development, the processes of the past can best be understood looking back from the vantage-point of the present.

This allows Chateaubriand to claim another privilege essential to his strategy. He has all along insisted that Christianity forms a complete and coherent philosophical and social system, and that the nature of Christian society is not directly dependent upon the actual beliefs of particular individuals within it. This is important in two ways. Firstly, it allows for the doctrine of Original Sin.[47] In any Christian society there will always be, he maintains, a profound gap between its ideals and its actual practices. Given the fallen state of humanity, such a gap is only to be expected, and the failure of its practitioners, lay or clerical, to live up to their aspirations serves to stress the importance of those ideals rather than invalidating them. Secondly, it enables him to appropriate within his scheme sceptics and infidels who would personally be opposed to any classification as 'Christian'.

His prime example of this is the arch-sceptic, Voltaire, who was actively opposed not merely to the Church, but to Christianity *per se*. To this Chateaubriand has two answers. The first consists of a series of deft historical put-downs: 'This great man had the misfortune to pass his life amid a circle of scholars of moderate abilities, who, always ready to applaud, were incapable of apprising him of his errors.'[48] Or again: 'We have no doubt that Voltaire, had he been religious, would have excelled in history. He wants nothing but seriousness . . .'[49] The second argument is a much more powerful one that has gained increasing currency in the twentieth century. Whether he likes it or not, Voltaire must be seen among the ranks of the Christian poets because he had grown up within a Christian tradition, that is, in a society whose values had been formed by the Bible and generations of Christian teaching. In so far as Voltaire criticized the Church, in particular, or society, in general, on moral grounds, he was acting in the tradition of a long line of Christian social and moral reformers. To see just how different a non-Christian society might be, we have only to look at the pagan classical societies whose values were as alien to us as their

[47] Ibid., p. 60.   [48] Ibid., p. 228.   [49] Ibid., p. 431.

customs were abominable.[50] To some extent this is a matter of the cultural shift noted above. A world where the love of Paris and Helen, or the wrath of Achilles, is the work of gods rather than an internalized sense of human character is one whose values are of action rather than thought, sentiment, or moral choice. An integrated and morally responsible individual in the new Romantic sense belongs essentially to the *psychology* of a biblically based society. But in addition to this psychological revolution there has also been a real revolution in values with the coming of Christianity.

Christianity has changed the relations of the passions, by changing the basis of vice and virtue . . . Among the ancients, for example, humility was considered as meanness and pride as magnanimity [sic: French = *grandeur*]; among Christians, on the contrary, pride is the first of vices and humility the chief of virtues.[51]

The Christian tradition is a one-way stream. It is impossible, even for those who, like Voltaire, rejected the metaphysical foundations of contemporary Christian belief, to return to earlier pagan values. The stern neo-classicism of the early years of the Revolution, with its admiration for Brutus, who condemned his sons to death, was more an affectation than a moral stance – the reality was simply not an option for humanity at the beginning of the nineteenth century. Similarly, for Voltaire, who criticized the God of the Old Testament on moral grounds, it would have been unthinkable to return to the gladiators and beasts of the Colosseum.

This is not to say, of course, that Chateaubriand's view of history itself is necessarily one of progress. For one deeply opposed to the Revolution and scarcely more impressed with Napoleon, that would have been an improbable position in 1802. What he does believe is that, in contrast with either the pagan historians of antiquity or the infidel historians of the present, the Christian tradition provides a theoretical framework for the explanation of all human history. But, of course, as so often in the past, what he claims as the eternal truths of the Christian tradition are qualities that were in fact radically new in his time. In place of the doctrinal and liturgical stasis assumed by Bossuet, Chateaubriand invokes a process whereby faint intimations and stirrings in the pagan world were slowly augmented, developed and honed into the Christian era; where the precepts of Natural Religion were progressively reinforced by Revelation; and where traditions assume the self-development and autonomy of works of art. Perhaps even more radical to contemporary Catholic sensibilities – if not to Protestant ones – this bold re-casting of 1,800 years of Christian tradition is advanced

<hr>

[50] Ibid., p. 668.   [51] Ibid., p. 269.

not by a member of the clergy, but by a *layman* – an amateur without formal theological training, who had neither remit nor authority to speak on behalf of his Church.

Finally, there is in this whole argument another quite distinctive and original strand that immediately distinguishes it from earlier religious polemics – if not from earlier religious experience. We miss the whole point of Chateaubriand's thesis if we read it primarily as an argument addressed to the intellect. To read Christianity as a nexus of ideas, however subtle and profound, is to miss both its hold on individuals and the kind of society it produces. As so often, there is a nuance in the original French not easy for the English (or German) translator to capture. It was left to Friedrich Engels later to observe (with some surprise) how the French word *religion* is less connected with the sense of going to church as with conviction or feeling.[52] Here Chateaubriand anticipates by more than a century a point of what we would now call 'sociology', but which then had no name. But, as Burke had already seen, and Coleridge was shortly to see, the point is nonetheless central. Consciously or unconsciously following Coleridge, Owen Chadwick observes that:

> The word God is not a word which could be replaced by the phrase 'that opinion' or 'that philosophy'. We could not say that some Victorian radical or dissenter, a Clough or a Francis Newman, changed from being Christian to not a Christian as a man ceased to follow Plato and followed Aristotle. We have to probe what difference is made, not merely what different language is used. Whatever Christianity is, it contains a way of life.[53]

In part this explains why, for Chateaubriand, Voltaire could not so easily detach himself from the society which had produced him, but it also explains why a sociologist such as Talcott Parsons could paraphrase Durkheim's approach to society by inverting the old axiom that religion is a social phenomenon – suggesting that society might be viewed as a religious phenomenon.[54] The real strength of Christian tradition lies in its *emotional* and its imaginative ties. For Chateaubriand, the divine meaning of history is not something to be considered by the intellect alone, but something that demands the integration and self-conscious participation of the whole personality of the individual – and, beyond that, the relationship of the individual to society. This, for him, was what true history was about.

---

[52] Owen Chadwick, *The Secularization of the European Mind in the Nineteenth Century* (Cambridge University Press, 1975; Canto edn, 1990), p. 75.

[53] Ibid., p. 13.

[54] Talcott Parsons, *The Structure of Social Action*, 2nd edn (Free Press, 1961), p. 427.

In contrast, pagan historians were mere chroniclers; Voltaire and his ilk mere speculators. Christianity does not just provide a theoretical framework for the understanding of history, important as that is, it also provides warmth and feeling in our approach to the past, a sense of its grandeur and pathos.[55] Over and over again Chateaubriand returns to this theme of the psychological wholeness of Christianity in contrast with the fragmented nature of Enlightenment philosophy or pagan antiquity. Hence his attribution of 'genius' not to an exceptional individual, as the word had hitherto been used by figures like Volney, but to the slow unfolding of the Holy Spirit through human history. If (in some ways strangely like his contemporary, Hegel) he insists that the comprehensiveness of his system, and its metaphysical grounding in the absolute, prevents historical relativism, and allows a privileged hermeneutical viewpoint, it is because he is convinced that only Christianity can offer such a totally integrated vision. That for him, in the last resort, is the real meaning of tradition.

[55]　Ibid., pp. 428–32.

CHAPTER 6

Herder, Schleiermacher, Novalis and Schlegel: the idea of a Christian Europe

HERDER AND THE SPIRIT OF TRADITION

It would be both easy – and wrong – to assume that Romanticism automatically stood for an overthrow of previous tradition. In her now classic work, *Romantics, Rebels and Revolutionaries*, Marilyn Butler has argued that the popular cliché of Romanticism as an intrinsic form of rebellion is based on only a few second-generation examples – perhaps most notably that of Shelley.[1] In reality, she claims, revolutionary thought was more closely associated with neo-classical ideas and art forms – epitomized in the heroic paintings of Jacques-Louis David, such as 'The Oath of the Horatii'.

For the first two decades of the nineteenth century, German Romanticism remained Catholic and counter-revolutionary. In both France and England during these decades it was the classical or antique style that was commonly linked with republicanism. When the Gothic or mediaeval or avowedly Romantic taste began to gain ground in England after the peace came in 1815, it was at first identified with the *anciens régimes* which had triumphed over France, and with their extreme political conservatism.[2]

There is certainly a great deal of evidence for this reactionary view of Romanticism. Butler might well have added, for instance, the case of Johann Nikolas Böhl von Faber, a German scholar and resident of Cadiz, whose 1814 adaptation of the criticism of A.W. Schlegel as the basis of an extreme conservative, Catholic, and monarchist programme was to dominate Spanish debates arguably until the end of the century.[3] Similarly, it is true that popular British opinion in the early nineteenth century saw

---

[1] This view, of course, flies in the face of the belief, almost universal throughout the nineteenth century, that 'romanticism' was *essentially* revolutionary in sympathy. See, for instance, David Perkins, *Is Literary History Possible?* (Johns Hopkins University Press, 1992), pp. 88–101 passim.
[2] Marilyn Butler, *Romantics, Rebels and Revolutionaries: English Literature and its Background 1760–1830* (Oxford University Press, 1981), p. 5.
[3] See Richard Cardwell, 'Introduction to Spanish Romanticism', *An Anthology of European Romanticism*, ed. Stephen Prickett (Argumentum, 2009).

France as the natural home of religious infidelity and political radicalism, while Germany, especially Prussia, Britain's continental ally against
Napoleon, was commonly seen as its opposite – a bastion of conservative
religious and social thought. But, like most national stereotyping, not
merely is this, too, over-simplistic, it ignores the fact that though France
had created the Revolution in politics, there is a sense in which the *idea* of
revolution was created and sustained by Germany long after the event on its
western borders had passed into history. There, as nowhere else, the idea of
revolution was discussed, generalized and philosophized.[4] Despite sporadic
peasant revolts in Saxony and Silesia, and the annexation of the Rhineland
to France, by popular petition, the political impact of the Revolution in
Germany was relatively slight at the time. The lack of political unity or any
common social issues between the 300 or so German states, meant that
from the first the French Revolution was experienced more as a state of
mind than as a political option. Though there was vigorous censorship in
some states, including Austria, this did little to inhibit the intellectual vigour of German cultural life which supported the publication of more books
and periodicals at this period than anywhere else in Europe.[5]

Above all, Butler ignores the fact that though many of the Catholic
states were fiercely conservative and counter-revolutionary *all* the first-
generation German Romantics were themselves either Protestant or from
a Protestant culture. This is not to suggest, however, that Protestants were
necessarily less conservative in their instincts than Catholics. To give but
one example: in 1809, after shattering defeats by Napoleon, Wilhelm von
Humboldt was given the task of creating the new University of Berlin
by the Prussian King, Friedrich Wilhelm III. One of his basic principles
was to separate theology from the humanities, to free the Faculty of Arts
(*Philosophische Facultät*) from the dead hand of the (Lutheran) scholastic theology then practised in most German universities.[6] It is said that
when F.A. Wolf, the founder of classical philology, had tried to enter the
University of Göttingen in 1777 as a 'student of philology', the pro-rector
had laughed at him and informed him that if he wanted (God forbid!)
to become a schoolmaster, he should enrol in the Faculty of Theology.[7]

---

[4] See Ehrhard Bahr and Thomas P. Saine (eds.), *The Internalized Revolution: German Reactions to the French Revolution, 1789–1989* (Garland, 1992).
[5] R.R. Palmer, *The World of the French Revolution* (Allen & Unwin, 1971), p. 233.
[6] See Stephen Prickett, *Words and the Word: Language, Poetics and Biblical Interpretation* (Cambridge University Press, 1986), p. 1.
[7] See Mark Pattison, 'F.A. Wolf' in *Essays*, 2 vols. ed. Henry Nettleship, Vol. 1 (Oxford University Press, 1889), p. 343.

It is hardly surprising that Humboldt should have sought to promote the new spirit of *Wissenschaft* that inspired his conception of what a university should be away from such assumptions of 'theology'. In this he was only echoing the views of so many reformers of the German university system, such as Fichte, Schelling, Schleiermacher, and Steffens, all in their own ways associated with the new Jena Romanticism.[8] Nevertheless, for whatever cause – perhaps because the Lutheran Church, despite its Erastian tendencies, lacked the centralized controls of Catholicism – it was from the Protestant culture that the new 'revolutionary' Romantic ideas – however anti-clerical – were to emerge.

The centre of early German Romanticism, Jena, was a Lutheran university town. Herder was a popular Lutheran preacher; Schleiermacher was not a Lutheran, but, even more independently, an ordained Calvinist minister; and Friedrich von Hardenberg (Novalis) was brought up under the influence of the Moravians. Of the others in this group of what one might call 'lapsed' or 'post-Lutherans' – the 'cultured unbelievers' of Schleiermacher's *Speeches* – only Friedrich Schlegel (as we shall see) was to turn to Catholicism later in life. For all of these at the time of the French Revolution, the metaphor of revolution came to imply not so much a political agenda as a radical and dramatic transformation of ideas. As such it was to become a commonplace in German writing – and its continuing influence can be seen on such figures as Marx and Nietzsche even half a century later. For Fichte, Schelling, and Hegel, all at least intermittent members of the group of young self-consciously styled 'Romantics' in Jena, it was to constitute a key metaphor. The group centred on the Schlegel brothers, August and Friedrich, together with Caroline Michaelis (daughter of J.D. Michaelis, the Lutheran theologian and editor of Lowth), August's mistress (later to marry Schelling), and Dorothea Mendelssohn (who was later to marry Friedrich). They were initially drawn to the university at Jena not by its Lutheran ethos so much as by the proximity of Herder and Goethe at Weimar.

Untypical of his successors as he was in many ways, in this respect at least, Johann Gottfried Herder (1744–1803) was an accurate predictor of what was to follow. He was not merely a Protestant, but a theologian and clergyman by training and practice – and, indeed, partly through Goethe's

---

[8] See Michael J. Hofstetter, *The Romantic Idea of a University: England and Germany, 1770–1850* (Palgrave, 2001), and F.W.J. von Schelling, *On University Studies*, trs. E.S. Morgan (Ohio University Press, 1966). For the writings of Fichte, Humboldt, Schleiermacher, and Steffens, see E. Anrich (ed.), *Die Idee der deutschen Universität: die fünf Grundschriften aus der Zeit ihrer Neubegründung durch klassischen Idealismus und romantischen Realismus* (WGB, 1960).

influence, from 1776, General Superintendent of the Lutheran clergy in Weimar. What makes him fundamentally different, however, from the Jena Romantics was his passionate belief in the meaning and power of tradition. This was not so much a belief in the tradition of the Church in any remotely Catholic sense, as a belief in the strength of national cultures as organic beings with their own distinctive languages, personalities, and memories. The analogy with individuals was pressed to the point of claiming that national cultures possessed the phases of youth, maturity, and decline. In this sense tradition was the memory and inherited wisdom of a culture.

But Herder's ideas did not start with cultures but with something even more basic – language itself. Until quite late in the eighteenth century, there had been little speculation on the question of the origins of language because it had been axiomatic that language had been God's gift to Adam, as he named the beasts (Genesis 2.20).[9] Because of this theological 'block' on further investigation it was only slowly that this so-called 'correspondence' theory of language began to be questioned from observation, first by Vico in Italy, and then by Herder, Humboldt and others, in Germany, and by Condillac and Rousseau in France.[10] But Herder, in his influential Berlin Academy Prize Essay, 'On the Origin of Language' (1772), was careful explicitly to distance himself both from his more conservative contemporary, Johann Peter Süssmilch, who still advanced the traditional view that language was the divine and miraculous gift of God, and from the more radical French views of Condillac and Rousseau that it had evolved from the noises of animals. Though Herder, in fact, follows Condillac quite closely in many places, his real interest is in the *psychological* origins of language as a vehicle not so much for communication as for thought.[11] The distinguishing quality of human language is that it creates the possibility of a continuous internal dialogue with memory, and through memory to the collective memory of the linguistic group – the tribe, or culture.

---

[9] See Prickett, *Words and the Word*, pp. 50–4.
[10] See Hans Georg Gadamer, 'Man and Language' (1966), *Philosophical Hermeneutics*, trs. and ed. David E. Linge (University of California Press, 1976), p. 60. Giambattista Vico, *The New Science* (1744), trs. Thomas Goddard Bergin and Max Harrold Frisch (Cornell University Press, 1968); Johann Gottfried Herder, 'Essay on the Origin of Language' (1772), *Herder on Social and Political Culture*, trs. and ed. F.M. Barnard (Cambridge University Press, 1969); Wilhelm von Humboldt, *On Language* (1836), trs. Peter Heath, intro. Hans Aarsleff (Cambridge University Press, 1988).
[11] Hans Aarsleff, 'The Tradition of Condillac: The Problem of the Origin of Language in the Eighteenth Century and the Debate in the Berlin Academy before Herder', *Locke to Saussure: Essays on the Study of Language and Intellectual History* (University of Minnesota Press, 1982), pp. 146–99.

Whereas most Enlightenment thinkers had still followed the earlier assumption of a high degree of correspondence between one language and another, for proto-Romantics like Herder, language expresses the distinctive experience of a particular people, and thus each language will embody its own unique way of seeing the world. To think and speak in words is to 'swim in an inherited stream of images' in which we come to consciousness and accept on trust.[12] It follows that even the senses themselves are culturally variable: 'The North American,' wrote Herder, 'can trace his enemy by the smell . . . the shy Arab hears far in his silent desert . . . The shepherd beholds nature with different eyes from those of the fisherman.'[13]

This mixture of what would now be called anthropology, history, and linguistics may be characteristic of the age, but this should not detract from the sheer originality of Herder's ideas and his subsequent influence on other thinkers – which has been far greater and more varied than is usually realized.[14] Though his thought is very much of a piece, it is in one of his principal theological works, *The Spirit of Hebrew Poetry* (1782–3), that he expounds most fully his views on tradition. In contrast with the

---

[12] See Isaiah Berlin, 'Herder and the Enlightenment', *Vico and Herder: Two Studies in the History of Ideas* (Hogarth Press, 1976), p. 168.

[13] Cited by Marshall Sahlins, *How 'Natives' Think: About Captain Cook, for Example* (University of Chicago Press, 1995), extract in the *Times Literary Supplement*, 2 June 1995, p. 13.

[14] See, for instance, Michael Forster:

Hegel's philosophy turns out to be an elaborate systematic development of Herderian ideas (especially concerning God, the mind, and history); so too does Schleiermacher's (concerning God, the mind, interpretation, translation, and art); Nietzsche is deeply influenced by Herder (concerning the mind, history, and values); so too is Dilthey (in his theory of the human sciences); even J.S. Mill has important debts to Herder (in political philosophy); and beyond philosophy, Goethe was transformed from being merely a clever but conventional poet into a great artist largely through the early impact on him of Herder's ideas.

Indeed, Herder can claim to have virtually established whole disciplines which we now take for granted. For example, it was mainly Herder (not, as is often claimed, Hamann) who established fundamental ideas about an intimate dependence of thought on language which underpin modern philosophy of language. It was Herder who, through the same ideas, his broad empirical approach to languages, his recognition of deep variations in language and thought across historical periods and cultures, and in other ways, inspired W. von Humboldt to found modern linguistics. It was Herder who developed modern hermeneutics, or interpretation-theory, in a form that would subsequently be taken over by Schleiermacher and then more systematically formulated by Schleiermacher's pupil Böckh. It was Herder who, in doing so, also established the methodological foundations of nineteenth-century German classical scholarship (which rested on the Schleiermacher–Böckh methodology), and hence of modern classical scholarship generally. It was arguably Herder who did more than anyone else to establish the general conception and the interpretive methodology of our modern discipline of anthropology. Finally, Herder also made vital contributions to the progress of modern biblical scholarship.

Michael Forster, 'Johann Gottfried von Herder', *The Stanford Encyclopedia of Philosophy* (Winter 2001 edn), ed. Edward N. Zalta, http://plato.stanford.edu/archives/win2001/entries/herder/.

other German Romantic works examined in this chapter, he uses the word 'tradition' frequently in the text – indeed, one might describe the idea of Hebrew tradition as being key to the whole essay.

The argument is presented in a Socratic dialogue between the sceptic Alciphron and his friend the more aesthetically-inclined Euthyphron. As in his essay 'On the Origin of Language', Herder seems at first sight to be steering a careful course between biblical literalism and the new Higher Criticism, but it gradually becomes clear that by making the ancient Hebrews his prime example of a nation being formed by its language, he is pursuing a larger goal, that of demonstrating his theory as part of the workings of a divine providence.

That he [Moses] recorded his laws ... that he chose a particular tribe of men, who, relieved from other employments, must devote themselves to reading, copying, and carrying into effect his laws and regulations; that he excluded all symbols, figures, and hieroglyphics, and employed writing, alphabetick writing, as well for the ornament of the priests, and thereby secured the advantage of it, for his people; that he probably collected the ancient histories and traditions of his race, and prefixed them to his history, as sacred relicks of antiquity, even as the basis of his law, of his doctrines, and of the claim of Israel to the land of Canaan; is proof, that he devised his plans, or intended to do so, for making a barbarian people, at least in part, and in the fundamental laws of their organizations, into a literary people.[15]

As Herder himself was quick to acknowledge in his text, there is in this argument a strong debt to Lowth – not just in technical detail, but in that reference to the Hebrews as 'a literary people', a broad *aesthetic* respect for poetry that trumps older typological ways of thinking.

What would be the use of the sublimest poetry in the world, if it were but an opiate for the soul, or a veil for the eyes, to prevent our knowing the real forms of things, and the true course of events. But how, think, shall we best pursue the inquiry? Have we not these notions, and this representation of divine providence, resulted from the influence of particular traditions and events? They have at least remained closely connected with these ancient events, and, in their later application even, reference is always had to these. Shall we not then trace the stream from its fountain?[16]

Tradition, in short, may be vague, even inaccurate in some points – Herder several times expresses himself agnostic about precise details – but

---

[15] Johann Gottfried Herder, *The Spirit of Hebrew Poetry*, trs. James Marsh, 2 vols. Edward Smith, 1833, facsimile. edn (Aleph, 1971). Vol. II, p. 277.
[16] Ibid., Vol. I, (Dialogue 8), p. 192.

it nevertheless keeps us 'closely connected with these ancient events' in a way that the scholarly scepticism of the Higher Criticism cannot, and never will. The reference to tracing the stream to the fountain is, of course, an explicit reference to Lowth's image of water becoming increasingly polluted as it flows further and further from its source.

Even more precise is Herder's comparison between 'fable' and 'tradition'. In the story of Adam naming the animals (Genesis 2.20) Herder sees what J.R.R. Tolkien would later call the 'coincidence of myth and history'.[17] 'The divinity has here exhibited before us, as it were, in a sportive representation, a continual Aesopick fable. Nor has any poetical tradition of Paradise forgotten, moreover, to represent man here in conversation with the brutes.'[18] That 'fable' here does not mean a poetic untruth is made clear only a few pages later in the same dialogue where Euthyphron explains that 'it is of the essence of a fable, that it be a consistent whole, and that what is represented in fact be represented in a manner picturable to the sense'.[19] The story of the Garden of Eden, he concludes, does not match up to this criterion, but is shot through with logical inconsistencies. 'Your fable,' he says with dangerous generosity to Alciphron (who has just been criticizing the narrative himself) 'needs a defender'. 'I leave that to you,' says Alciphron, falling at once into the trap that has been set for him. Euthyphron calmly replies: 'That I cannot become, so long as it must be considered a fable. But suppose it to be a tradition, a narrative of an instructive history, the facts of which actually took place with the parents of the human race, and every thing follows naturally.'[20] History, everywhere, is the child of oral tradition, but (please note) some traditions are more equal than others.

The history of Paradise, of our first parents, and of the subsequent patriarchs, of the flood, of the tower of Babel, &c. appear obviously in the character of family and national traditions, and so it continues downwards to the history of the Jewish patriarchs. Tradition has formed into a sacred narrative, a sort of fibula morata, where in every line the favour of Jehovah to their fathers beams forth as the origin, from which they derive the glory of their race, their right to Canaan, and the prerogative which they claim before the nations, which inhabited it. What among other races bears the marvellous character of heroick and extravagant traditions, is here of divine and patriarchal authority, confirmed by genealogical registers and monuments, and exhibiting such simplicity of ornament, that the artificial forms of poetry are unsuitable to it. Among all nations history

---

[17] See C.S. Lewis, *Surprised by Joy, The Shape of my Early Life* (Fontana, 1955), p. 169.
[18] Herder, *Spirit of Hebrew Poetry*, Vol. 1 (Dialogue 6), p. 128.
[19] Ibid., p. 137. [20] Ibid.

has grown out of tradition, and among the Hebrews it has remained even down to the period of the kings, in regard to the style, almost always traditionary in its character.[21]

At least to his own satisfaction, Herder has bridged the gap between fable and history. God has, we recall, forged the Hebrews into a *literary* people, and written history is not a mere recording of events, but a creative narrative, illustrating divine providence through ancient traditions.

ADDRESSING THE CULTURED DESPISERS

With the publication of their journal, the *Athenaeum*, during the years 1798–1800, the group of German Romantics gathered at Jena under the influence of Goethe and Herder at Weimar, briefly acquired a powerful intellectual and critical momentum. Among those drawn into this circle of critical and philosophic talent were two others who, because they lived some distance from Jena, maintained their contacts more by correspondence than by presence. One was Schleiermacher, who was based in Berlin; the other was the young aristocrat, von Hardenberg. Though he had earlier studied in Jena, by 1797 Hardenberg was working in Freiburg, and later as an inspector of mines in Saxony. Both were unusual in this group of 'revolutionary' free-thinkers in that they were committed Christians. Surprisingly, though they were to have a major influence on one another, they had never actually met before Hardenberg's death in 1801.

Though the word 'Romantic' was to give its name to a Europe-wide movement in all forms of the arts, it originated specifically with this group who chose it – loose and vague as it was – to suggest both a backward glance at the world of old romances, and, at the same time, something so new as to require for it a quite new word. Friedrich Schlegel's famous 'definition' of romantic poetry in their 'house' journal, the *Athenaeum*, conveys much of this flavour of paradox:

Romantic poetry is progressive, universal poetry. Its aim isn't merely to unite all the separate species of poetry and put poetry in touch with philosophy and rhetoric. It tries to and should mix and fuse poetry and prose, inspiration and criticism, the poetry of art and the poetry of nature; and make poetry lively and sociable, and life and society poetical; . . . It embraces everything that is purely poetic, from the greatest systems of art, containing within themselves still further systems, to the sigh, the kiss that the poeticising child breathes forth in artless song . . . It alone can become, like the epic, a mirror of the whole circumambient

---

[21]　Ibid., Vol. ii, p. 17.

age . . . It is capable of the highest and most variegated refinement, not only from within outwards, but also from without inwards; capable in that it organises – for everything that seeks a wholeness in its effects – the parts along similar lines, so that it opens up a perspective upon an infinitely increasing classicism . . . Other kinds of poetry are finished and are now capable of being fully analysed. The romantic kind of poetry is still in the state of becoming; that, in fact, is its real essence: that it should forever be becoming and never be perfected. It can be exhausted by no theory and only a divinatory criticism would dare to try and characterise its ideal. It alone is infinite, just as it alone is free; and it recognises as its first commandment that the will of the poet can tolerate no law above itself. The romantic kind of poetry is the only one that is more than a kind, that is, as it were, poetry itself: for in a certain sense all poetry is or should be romantic. (Fragment 116)[22]

Despite the fact that the German word for the novel is *Roman* – and Schlegel had himself written one, *Lucinde*, in 1799 – the stress on poetry rather than prose in this passage reflects (among other things) the low status of the German novel at this period. When the first part of Goethe's novel *Wilhelm Meister* appeared in 1795, Schlegel had reviewed it ecstatically as 'poetry – high pure poetry'.[23] But even given the all-embracing aesthetic status of 'poetry', which, in its role as *the* central and defining art-form of the age, could be elevated from verse on the page into an overarching synaesthesia, what is interesting about this passage is that the 'Romanticism' described here is not so much a thing as an Aristotelian *entelechy* – a *process* of becoming. Though the word 'tradition' is itself as noticeably absent from Schlegel's vocabulary as from any Enlightenment *philosophe*, what he is evidently struggling to define – even while admitting the paradox inherent in the attempt – is a new idea of aesthetic tradition in which the past is constantly incorporated and referred to in the creation of the present. Only in this way could the existential crisis of the French invasion of Germany and the impact of the new republican ideas be contained and absorbed. Here was a potential way of re-shaping the past to which he would return by a very different route less than a decade later.

After the Schlegel brothers themselves, the third most important contributor to the *Athenaeum* fragments was Schleiermacher. Though resident in Berlin, not Jena, he was in close touch with his friends there, and on the morning of his birthday, 21 November 1797, a group of his Jena friends,

---

[22] Friedrich Schlegel, *Philosophical Fragments*, trs. Peter Firchow (University of Minnesota Press, 1991).
[23] Friedrich Schlegel, 'On Goethe's Meister' (1798), *German Aesthetic and Literary Criticism*, ed. Kathleen Wheeler (Cambridge University Press, 1984), p. 64.

including Friedrich Schlegel, burst into his Berlin flat where he was working to hold a surprise party, during which they repeatedly urged him to
justify to them his position as a Christian by writing a book.[24] To encour-
age him, Schlegel announced that he would move in with him for the next
eighteen months. Though it was to be some time before Schleiermacher
took up the challenge, in August 1798, there was never any doubt in his
mind – or in theirs – that this was to be a *Kampfschrift*, a 'fighting book',
that was directly to address his hitherto enigmatic relationship with his
avant-garde Romantic friends in Jena.

The result, *On Religion: Speeches to its Cultured Despisers*, appeared in
1799. The title was an open enough code: the 'cultured despisers' were,
of course, the Schlegels and the other members of the Jena circle. In his
book he develops and expands the philosophical and theological position
hinted at in the fragments both he and Schlegel had contributed to the
Athenaeum:

> Religion's essence is neither thinking nor acting, but intuition and feeling. It
> wishes to intuit the Universe . . . Thus religion is opposed to these two in every-
> thing that makes up its essence and in everything that characterises its effects.
> Metaphysics and morals see in the whole universe only humanity as the centre of
> all relatedness, as the condition of all being and the cause of all becoming; reli-
> gion wishes to see the infinite, its imprint and its manifestation, in humanity no
> less than in all other individual and finite forms . . . Religion shows itself to you
> as the necessary and indispensable third next to those two, as their natural coun-
> terpart, not slighter in worth and splendour than what you wish of them.[25]

Even bearing in mind that this was written for a particular group of
friends, rather than the public at large (and later editions, in 1806 and 1821,
were to soften and to some extent disguise the radical nature of this argument) what we have here is theologically very uncompromising indeed.
In spite of the fact that the words 'God' and 'divinity' appear in the text
with some frequency (56 and 36 times respectively), religion, as he tells us
explicitly in the Second Speech, does not depend on there being a God
at all.[26] Indeed, 'belief in God depends on the direction of the imagination' which is 'the highest and most original element in us . . . it is your
imagination that creates the world for you, and . . . you can have no God
without the world . . . In religion, therefore, the idea of God does not rank

---

[24] Jack Fortsman, *A Romantic Triangle: Schleiermacher and Early German Romanticism* (Scholars
Press, 1977), pp. 65–6.
[25] Friedrich Schleiermacher, *On Religion: Speeches to its Cultured Despisers* (1799), trs. Richard
Crouter (Cambridge University Press, 1998), p. 102.
[26] Ibid., pp. 65 and 136.

as high as you think.' Religion is not so much a matter either of knowledge (which is what Schleiermacher means here by 'metaphysics'), or action (or 'morals'), but primarily a matter of what he calls 'intuition'. Unlike either metaphysics or morals, intuition seems to consist of 'pure receptivity'. For Schleiermacher in 1799, religious self-awareness begins with the familiar romantic dialectic between what was conceived of as a spontaneous act of individual intuition and the more objective action of the universe upon us. Our personal awareness begins with what he calls an 'intuition of the infinite [*Anschauung des Unendlichen*]'.

Though one might construct a model of socialization in which the individual is conditioned by the traditions or customs of his or her society to intuit in certain particular ways, rather than others, there is no evidence to suggest that this is what Schleiermacher has in mind. 'Intuition' is for him an intensely individualistic and personal process. Indeed, it constitutes the very first stirrings of individuation. Tradition, therefore, plays no part whatsoever in either the growing sense of self or in the religious awareness that according to Schleiermacher accompanies it. Religion is not merely individualistic in expression, it actually further individuates its practitioner.

What one commonly calls belief, accepting what another person has done, wanting to ponder and empathize with what someone else has thought and felt, is a hard and unworthy service, and instead of being the highest in religion, as one supposes, it is exactly what must be renounced by those who would penetrate into its sanctuary. To want to have and retain belief in this sense proves that one is incapable of religion; to require this kind of faith from others shows that one does not understand it.[27]

The idea of tradition, as knowledge, religious experience or discipline, handed down from one generation to the next, is thus for Schleiermacher not merely irreligious to its core, it is also misguided because fundamentally *impossible*. Though we can certainly affect the thought of others, Schleiermacher believed (at this stage at least) that we cannot in the end make them react – in the sense of feeling or intuition – as we would wish. The third chapter is significantly entitled 'On *Selbstbildung*'. This idea of 'self-construction' or 'self-cultivation' is a term for which there is no easy English equivalent – perhaps the American idea of 're-inventing' the self might be the closest. It was made popular in Schleiermacher's circle through Goethe's *Wilhelm Meister*, often described as the first *Bildungsroman*, or novel of personal development. Richard Crouter, whose

---

[27] Ibid., p. 134.

1988 translation is used here, renders Schleiermacher's title as: 'On Self-Formation for Religion'. The stress is firmly on the process of internalized self-discovery and construction. 'Everything that, like religion, is supposed to be a continuum of the human mind lies far beyond the realm of teaching and inculcating.'[28] And again: 'show me someone in whom you have inculcated or implanted the power of judgement, the spirit of observation, aesthetic feeling or morality and I shall then pledge myself also to teach religion'.[29] This is the ultimate evangelical Protestant world where the individual encounters God in the loneliness of the heart, and where neither custom, nor tradition, nor, indeed, any organized religion or church has more than a peripheral part to play.

NOTHING NEW IS ANY USE . . .

For Friedrich von Hardenberg – not yet until after his death in 1801 the 'Novalis' of the romantic legend[30] – this was both a stimulus and a challenge. His response, written in October 1799, was an enigmatic and ironic piece which remained unpublished until 1826, *Christendom or Europe. A Fragment.* The title sets the ambiguous tone of what follows by two terms that can be read either as parallel, or in contrast. Whether, and to what extent, 'Christendom' can be equated with 'Europe', and what he means by both is left for the reader to decide. The debt to Schleiermacher is acknowledged with equal irony:

I want to conduct you to a brother [i.e. Schleiermacher] who will talk with you so that your hearts rejoice . . . This brother is the heartbeat of the new age, whoever has felt his presence does not doubt any more that it will come, and he too steps out from the crowd with sweet pride in being a contemporary to join the new band of disciples. He has made a new veil for the Holy Virgin which caresses her body, betraying the heavenly shape of her limbs, yet covering her more chastely than any other. The veil is for the Virgin what the spirit is for the body, her indispensable instrument whose folds are the letters of her sweet Annunciation; the infinite play of the folds is a music of numbers, for language is too wooden and too impudent for the Virgin, her lips open only to sing.[31]

The Greek *apokalypsis* – or apocalypse – is, of course, literally an 'unveiling'. The German word, *Schleier*, means 'veil', so that 'Schleiermacher' – literally

---

[28] Ibid., p. 144.   [29] Ibid., p. 145.
[30] See William Arctander O'Brien, *Novalis: Signs of Revolution* (Duke University Press, 1995), p.4.
[31] Novalis, 'Christendom or Europe', *Novalis: Philosophical Writings*, trs. and ed. Margaret Stoljar (State University of New York Press, 1997), pp. 148–9.

the 'veil-maker' – whose veil will be swept aside at the Apocalypse, is meanwhile the one who at once conceals and reveals the body of the Virgin in
such a way as to make her even more erotically desirable. Yet, as Kevin
Mills says in a somewhat different context, 'despite the fact that unveiling is the founding trope of the Apocalypse . . . the Apocalypse is not an
uncovering, but an obscure text in need of deciphering'.[32] Certainly, there
is little unveiling here. For Hardenberg, Schleiermacher has described the
'spirit' of Christianity in such a way as to make its 'body' infinitely more
desirable – but even that word is mischievously ambiguous. As a good
minister of the reformed Protestant Church, Schleiermacher, needless to
say, does not discuss the Virgin at all in his *On Religion*. He does not
even discuss the Church very much. So just what is this 'Virgin'? What is
this new desirability? *Agape* or *Eros*? Moreover, what was Hardenberg, the
product of a Moravian pietistic upbringing, with no visible attachment to
Catholicism, doing with such apparently overblown and rather unctuous
Catholic imagery?

These were questions that were to baffle his friends and immediate circle almost as much as his modern readers. The tone of ironic praise for
mediaeval Catholicism, so overdone as to question and undermine itself,
is present right from the opening of the essay, which is at once like, and
totally unlike Chateaubriand:

There once were beautiful, splendid times when Europe was a Christian land,
when *one* Christendom dwelt in this continent, shaped by human hand; *one*
great common interest bound together the most distant provinces of this broad
religious empire. Although he did not have extensive secular possessions, *one*
supreme ruler guided and united the great political powers. A numerous guild
which everyone could join ranked immediately below the ruler and carried out
his wishes, eagerly striving to secure his beneficent might. Each member of this
society was honoured on all sides, and whenever the common people sought from
him consolation or help, protection or advice, being glad in exchange to provide richly for his diverse needs, each also found protection, esteem, and a hearing from the more mighty ones, while all cared for these chosen men, who were
armed with wondrous powers like children of heaven, and whose presence and
favour spread many blessings.[33]

Here is a world where, in contrast to Schleiermacher's individualistic spirituality, tradition, in a form as extreme as Bossuet's, should reign supreme.
But the point about the universality of the mediaeval Catholic world is

---

[32] Kevin Mills, *Approaching Apocalypse: Unveiling Revelation in Victorian Writing* (Bucknell
University Press, 2007), p. 97.
[33] 'Christendom or Europe', p. 137.

made with so little historical qualification that it is impossible for the reader to react without suspecting irony – an irony, moreover, clearer to many of his contemporaries than in translation today.[34] In fact what reads at first sight like a eulogy for an idealized and vanished mediaeval-ism turns out to be a mythic history of European civilization, conceived not so much in historical terms as an ironic debate about ideas. 'With the Reformation,' adds Hardenberg, 'it was all up with Christendom.'[35] From thenceforth the history of European Christendom must be conceived as a dialectic between two antithetical but essential forces, each holding only a partial truth, that can only be resolved in a new synthesis:

Both parties have great, essential claims, and must press them, driven by the spirit of the world and of humanity. Both are ineradicable powers of the human heart: on the one hand reverence for antiquity, devotion to human custom, love of the monuments of our forefathers and the glorious old state family, and joy in obedience; on the other hand the delightful feeling of freedom, the uncondi-tional expectation of mighty spheres of influence, pleasure in the new and young, untrammelled contact with all fellow members of the state, pride in the universal validity of the human joy in personal rights and in the property of the whole, and a vigorous sense of citizenship. Let no power hope to destroy the other, all conquests mean nothing here, for the innermost capital of each empire does not lie behind fortified walls and cannot be stormed.[36]

Though he nowhere uses the word 'tradition' here, phrases like 'reverence for antiquity' and 'devotion to human custom' encapsulate much of its mean-ing and force. But for Hardenberg, in a post-Reformation Europe, one side of the dialectic cannot exist without the other – just as for Coleridge the conservative and the progressive aspects of the state could not properly exist except in relation to one another as parts of a single whole.[37] Thus the world of mediaeval faith was opposed by the Lutheran reliance on the word of God in the Bible – a reliance that was eventually to become a fetish until it, in its turn, was challenged by critical biblical scholarship, and the growing separation of knowledge and faith during the eighteenth century:

the more the clerical element of European humanity approached the period of triumphant scholarship, the more the scholars gained ground, and knowledge and faith moved into more decisive opposition. The reason for the general stagna-tion was sought in the faith, and it was hoped to alleviate this through the perva-sive effect of knowledge. Everywhere the holy message suffered under manifold persecutions of the style it had hitherto displayed, its mature personality. The product of the modern way of thinking was called philosophy, and it was held

---

[34] A point most strongly argued by Wilfred Malsch. See O'Brien, *Novalis*, p. 231.
[35] 'Christendom or Europe', p. 142.   [36] Ibid., p. 150.   [37] See below, pp. 203–4.

to embrace everything that was opposed to the old way, principally therefore every objection to religion. What was at first personal hatred of the Catholic faith gradually turned into hatred of the Bible, of the Christian faith and finally even of religion.[38]

What had been lost with Protestantism was the sense of community and wholeness that had underpinned all the particular traditions of the Church. After his *Fichte Studies* of 1796, when he had attempted to come to grips with the ideas of his mentor Johann Gottlieb Fichte, Hardenberg had become increasingly dismissive of what he felt to be the failure of contemporary philosophy to cope with the essentially *fictional* – or narrative nature – of all human descriptions of reality. 'Fichte's I,' he noted, 'is a Robinson – a scientific fiction – to facilitate the presentation and development of the *Science of Knowledge*.'[39] This 'Robinson' is, of course, a reference to Defoe's *Robinson Crusoe* – perhaps the best-known novel of the whole eighteenth century. Crusoe was the ultimate individualist, who managed to create his own world on a desert island from the fragments of civilization rescued from his shipwreck. As Rousseau had noted, he was the archetypal capitalist man – the final expression of an atomistic view of society. It would not have escaped Hardenberg's notice that Schleiermacher's religious individual was a 'Robinson' in precisely the same 'philosophic' sense.

But the critique of the 'philosophy' practised by his Romantic friends did not stop simply at an atomistic view of the individual. What Hardenberg sees as leading ultimately to a hatred of the Bible, the Christian faith, and even of religion itself is caused by a logical extension of the same fallacy. In the end, all three cannot exist in isolation, but depend upon a sense of community, and, even more important, a sense of history. We are not just creations of our own *Selbstbildung* – we are historical creatures, coming to consciousness within a particular society at a particular time and place. A description of 'religion' that excludes the richness of the art, tradition, and spirituality of the past is too anaemic and thin to survive for long.

For a moment it had seemed to Hardenberg that the French Revolution was to be the synthesis, and provide nothing less than the dawn of a new spiritual age, but once again he ironically undermines his own eulogy:

One enthusiasm was generously left for the poor human race and made indispensable as a touchstone for the highest education for every practitioner of it. It was enthusiasm for this splendid, magnificent philosophy and in particular for its

---

[38] 'Christendom or Europe', p. 144.
[39] *Fichte Studies*, III, 445, cited in O'Brien, *Novalis*, p. 107.

priests and mystagogues. France was fortunate enough to become the birthplace and the seat of this new faith, that was stuck together out of nothing but know-ledge. However much poetry was decried in this new church, there were still some poets in it who continued to make use of the old ornaments and the old candles for effect, but in doing so risked setting the new world alight with old fire.[40]

It was not to be so much the sterile ideology of the French Revolution as what the Revolution had done to *all* ideologies that was significant. The very failure of its ideology meant that everything was up for grabs. As Hardenberg was to write in his last major work, *Heinrich von Ofterdingen*: 'During every period of transition higher spiritual powers appear to want to break through as in a sort of interregnum.'[41] In *Christendom or Europe* he was more explicit:

That the time of [religion's] resurrection has come, and that just those incidents that seemed to be directed against its enlivening and threatened to complete its demise have now become the most favourable signs of its regeneration, can no longer remain a matter of doubt for any historical mind. True anarchy is the ele-ment within which religion is born. From the destruction of everything positive it lifts its glorious head as the founder of new world . . . The spirit of God moves across the waters and across the ebbing waves a heavenly island can be seen for the first time as the dwelling place of the new man, as the river of eternal life.[42]

Behind the dialectical – and even sometimes apocalyptic – rhetoric of such passages was a desire to re-position Schleiermacher's *On Religion* within a historical context that would both explain its evident strengths, and – Hardenberg seems to fear – its less obvious weaknesses. *Christendom or Europe* is neither a theological treatise nor a historical one. Rather, it attempts to create a narrative through which he could make sense of the Revolutionary times he and his friends inhabited. It was born from two parents. One, as we have seen, was Schleiermacher's *On Religion*, with its philosophic individualism. The other was the sense of failure and disappointment in the Revolution after the rise of Napoleon. Deeply disappointed over the failure of Romantic theory to account for historical developments, Hardenberg tried to reformulate the 'poetical' logic of his-tory as an allegory for the individual's spiritual or poetic growth to redeem what O'Brien has called 'the intransigent actualities of contemporary poli-tics'.[43] Nowhere in this essay does he use the word 'tradition', yet in one sense the whole essay swirls around this missing term – as does another

[40] 'Christendom or Europe', p. 144.
[41] Novalis, *Henry von Ofterdingen*, trs. Palmer Hilty (Ungar, 1964), p. 25.
[42] 'Christendom or Europe', pp. 145–6.
[43] O'Brien, *Novalis*, p. 272.

piece, *The Novices of Sais*, whose title harks back to the Egyptian priests in Plato's *Timaeus*, where our quest for the Greek meaning of tradition began. But, with typical inversion, whereas Plato's were old priests, receptacles and exponents of tradition, these are the *novices* – innocents approaching and encountering the world without limits or preconceptions.

Perhaps partly because of that, the essay was, in practical terms, a fail-ure. Dorothea Schlegel had disliked it from the first – not least because she disliked Hardenberg personally anyway. Not surprisingly, Schleiermacher suspected it of Catholic sympathies, and consulted Goethe, who agreed with him that it should be rejected for publication in the *Athenaeum*. When it was finally published over quarter of a century later, in 1826, not merely the political scene, but Hardenberg's own reputation, had under-gone a transformation.

Apart from some fragments in the *Athenaeum* which he had called *Blüthenstaub* ('Pollen') Hardenberg had published little in his short life-time, and he had always been dependent on the Schlegel brothers for access to print.[44] As W.A. O'Brien has convincingly argued, the myth of 'Novalis' – a pen-name he had only used four times – was begun only a year after his death, when, in 1802, Ludwig Tieck and August Schlegel published a two-volume edition of *Novalis Schriften*. It is these carefully scripted and edited *Writings* which were the origin of the Romantic poet 'Novalis' to whom we must now refer. Though Tieck, who wrote the intro-ductory preface, is correctly described as a 'friend' of Novalis, he had in fact only known him during the last two years of his life – and he had never even met Sophie von Kuhn, Hardenberg's young fiancée, who had died in 1797, and was to figure so prominently in the Romantic myth as the love of Novalis's life. Between 1802 and 1846, when a third volume was added – and equally carefully edited – by Eduard von Bülow, the story of Novalis, the brilliant young poet who had died tragically young was assiduously cultivated at the expense both of the development of his ideas, and, indeed, much of their content – such as his sympathy for the French Revolution. Even the frontispiece of this 1846 edition was pressed into service – O'Brien describes how a family portrait by Gareis which showed a young man of 'flashing intelligence, candid, open, playful' was engraved by Eichens as 'a dreamy adolescent, sickly sweet, boring and bored to death: the ideal frontispiece'.[45]

Nevertheless, ideas move in strange and unpredictable ways. If Schlegel and Tieck had produced a Novalis partly of their own invention, the terms

[44] Ibid., p. 130.   [45] Ibid., pp. 2–26 passim.

of the debate between Schleiermacher and Hardenberg were not entirely lost to sight. Here, for instance, is part of the first chapter of Schlegel's *Lectures on Dramatic Art and Literature* of 1808 – which appeared in an English translation in 1815.

Religion is the root of all human existence. Were it possible for man to renounce all religion, including that which is unconscious, independent of the will he would become a mere surface without any independent substance. When this centre is disturbed, the whole system of the mental faculties and feelings takes a new shape.

And this is what has actually taken place in modern Europe through the introduction of Christianity. This sublime and beneficent religion has regenerated the ancient world from its state of exhaustion and debasement; it is the guiding principle in the history of modern nations, and even at this day, when many suppose they have shaken off its authority, they still find themselves much more influenced by it in their views of human affairs than they themselves are aware.[46]

When ideas circulate in conversation among a group of friends it is not always possible even for them to know afterwards exactly where a particular notion began. By 1808, moreover, Chateaubriand's *Le Génie du christianisme*, with its spirited defence of the Catholic Church was also well known. But there is little evidence to suggest that either of the Schlegel brothers had any interest in religion prior to Schleiermacher's *On Religion*. On the contrary, they were the specific 'cultured despisers' to whom his arguments were addressed. The idea of an 'unconscious religion' 'independent of the will' was, of course, central to Schleiermacher's argument for the grounding of religion in human psychology and beyond that in sense-perception itself. Far from being common currency, moreover, such a conception was as novel to the general theological world of the 1790s as it was to Schleiermacher's friends. Schleiermacher at this time was also planning a history of the English settlement of Australia, and had read David Collins's 'Remarks on the Manners and Customs of the Natives of New South Wales'. Collins here remarks that 'It has been asserted by an eminent divine that no country has yet been discovered where no trace of religion was not to be found [sic]. From every observation and enquiry that could be made among these people, they appear to be an exception to this opinion.'[47] It seems likely that Schleiermacher was deliberately framing

---

[46] August Wilhelm Schlegel, *A Course of Lectures on Dramatic Art and Literature*, trs. John Black (1815), revised J.W. Morrison (Bohn, 1846), Lecture 1, p. 24.
[47] David Collins, *An Account of the English Colony of New South Wales*, 2nd edn (printed by A. Strahan for T. Cadell and W. Davies, 1804), p. 354. This 'eminent divine' was in fact Hugh

his definition of religion to include what he had been told – rightly or wrongly – about the Aborigines.

But if this remarkable passage begins with Schleiermacher, it moves rapidly through Hardenberg's more collective and historical view of Europe as Christendom, to conclude with something that looks strangely like Chateaubriand's insistence that Voltaire, whether he liked it or not, was inescapably a part, and even a representative, of a Christian culture.

Parallels between poetry and religion were common among the Jena Romantics, and in the pages of the *Athenaeum*, though many originated with either Schleiermacher or Hardenberg.[48] The following passage, for instance, which was well enough known to Coleridge for him to copy it almost verbatim, adheres uncannily to Hardenberg's attempt to subsume the religious into the aesthetic by following the progress of 'the spirit of poetry' in terms hitherto more usually reserved for the progress of the Holy Spirit.[49]

Hence it is evident that the spirit of poetry, which, though imperishable, migrates, as it were, through different bodies, must, so often as it is newly born in the human race, mould to itself, out of the nutrimental substance of an altered age, a body of different conformation. The forms vary with the direction taken by the

Blair, whom, by coincidence. Schleiermacher had already translated into German. The passage from Blair reads:

Cast your eyes over the whole earth. Explore the most remote quarters of the east or the west. You may discover tribes of men without policy, or laws, or cities, or any of the arts of life: But no where will you find them without some form of religion. In every region you behold the prostrate worshipper, the temple, the altar, and the offering. Wherever men have existed, they have been sensible that some acknowledgement was due, on their part, to the Sovereign of the world. If, in their rudest and most ignorant state, this obligation has been felt, what additional force must it acquire by the improvement of human knowledge, but especially by the great discoveries of the Christian revelation? Whatever, either from reverence or from gratitude, can excite men to the worship of God, is by this revelation placed in such a light, as one should think were sufficient to overawe the most thoughtless, and to melt the most obdurate mind.

Hugh Blair, *Sermons*, 2 vols. (Anderson, 1824), Vol. 1, p. 3. See Stephen Prickett, 'Coleridge, Schlegel and Schleiermacher: England, Germany (and Australia) in 1798', *1798: The Year of the Lyrical Ballads*, ed. Richard Cronin (Macmillan, 1998), pp. 170–84.

[48] See, for example, *Athenaeum* Fragment 350:

No poetry, no reality. Just as there is, despite all the senses, no external world without imagination, so too there is no spiritual world without feeling, no matter how much sense there is. Whoever only has sense can perceive no human being, but only what is human: all things disclose themselves to the magic wand of feeling alone. It fixes people and seizes them; like the eye, it looks on without being conscious of its own mathematical operation.

Friedrich Schlegel, *Philosophical Fragments*, trs. Firchow, p. 71.

[49] For further discussion of this, see Kirstin Pfefferkorn, *Novalis: A Romantic's Theory of Language and Poetry* (Yale University Press, 1988), pp. 3ff.

poetical sense; and when we give to the new kinds of poetry the old names, and judge of them according to the ideas conveyed by these names, the application which we make of the authority of classical antiquity is altogether unjustifiable.[50]

Though the word 'tradition' is, as usual, never mentioned, this is in effect one of the first descriptions of what would become a critical commonplace of 'poetic tradition' in the nineteenth century in both Germany and Britain. Here, for instance, is Coleridge in his 1817 *Lectures on Shakespeare*, less concerned with either nomenclature or the authority of classical antiquity, but with the organic and unfolding nature of an aesthetic tradition:

few there have been among critics, who have followed with the eye of the imagination the imperishable, yet ever-wandering, spirit of poetry through its various metempsychoses, and correspondent metamorphoses; – or who have rejoiced in the light of clear perception at beholding with each new birth, with each rare avatar, the human race frame to itself a new body, by assimilating materials of nourishment out of its new circumstances, and work for itself new organs of power appropriate to the new sphere of its motion and activity.[51]

There is a corollary to this stress on organic progression: a sense of history. If religion and poetry have both evolved by slow accretion and development from age to age, then a sense of history is an indispensable aid to understanding the present. Blithely ignoring some of the greatest Baroque cities and the finest Rococo Churches in Europe, Mme de Staël's wildly popular, *On Germany* (1810–13) – the book that, more than any other, brought Romanticism to the attention of the world – focusses solely upon Germany as a land of primeval pine-forests and ruined castles.[52]

Gothic monuments are the only remarkable buildings in Germany. These recall the age of chivalry, which has left its traces in almost every city and public museum. The Northerners, conquerors of the world, seem to have left memories of themselves in leaving Germany, and the whole countryside looks like the dwelling place of a great people, long gone.[53]

August Schlegel had been living with Mme de Staël as her secretary and confidant off and on since 1804, and the echoes of Novalis are, again, unlikely to be accidental. Perhaps even more startling is her claim that

---

[50] A.W. Schlegel, *Lectures on Dramatic Art*, Lecture 22, p. 340.
[51] *Shakespeare Criticism*, ed. T.M. Raysor, 2nd edn, 2 vols. (Everyman, 1960), Vol, I, p. 174.
[52] John Claiborne Isbell, *The Birth of European Romanticism: Truth and Propaganda in Staël's 'De l'Allemagne' 1810–1813* (Cambridge University Press, 1994).
[53] Germaine de Staël, *On Germany* (1813), *Selected Writings of Germaine de Staël* (Ch.I, Sec.I), trs. and intro. Vivian Folkenflik (Columbia University Press, 1987), p. 293.

we enjoy a cultural and spiritual continuity with this 'Romantic' world of the past that is denied us with the classical – again, despite the entire neo-classical trappings of eighteenth-century Europe.

Ancient Greek and Roman poetry is purer as art; modern poetry makes us shed more tears. It is not a question of judging between classical and Romantic poetry, however, but of deciding whether to imitate one or be inspired by the other. For moderns, ancient literature is a transplanted literature. Romantic or chivalrous literature is native to us, and our own religions and institutions have made it blossom . . .

. . . Romantic literature is the only literature still capable of being brought to perfection. Rooted in our own soil, it is the only one that can still grow and find new life. It expresses our religion; it recalls our history. Its origin is ancient but not antique.

Classical poetry must pass through the memories of paganism before it can reach us: Germanic poetry is the Christian era of the arts. Such poetry uses our own personal impressions to move us: the genius inspiring it speaks straight to our hearts.[54]

There are, of course, echoes of Chateaubriand as well as Herder and Novalis, not to mention both Schlegels here, as de Staël weaves her own brand of Romanticism from strands taken from all around her in France and Germany. The 'Romantic' is at once a source of religion and of art – in short, the true source of what de Staël, the Swiss–Frenchwoman with a Swedish name, is happily prepared to think of as 'our' European identity.

Novalis was to have no less significant influence on the other Schlegel brother, Friedrich. For obvious reasons, *Christendom or Europe* was understood by many as a polemical defence of Catholicism, and this belief was reinforced when, in 1808, both Friedrich Schlegel and his wife, Dorothea, who had hitherto been seen as 'progressive' thinkers, were themselves received into the Catholic Church. That it was Friedrich, who had originally challenged Schleiermacher to write his personal defence of religion, who now moved towards what was perceived to be Novalis's counter-position was the more extraordinary. This was hardly an arbitrary choice – the movement towards Catholicism had begun at least as early as 1803. What influence Novalis had had on this decision is open to question, but Friedrich had certainly played a part in his brother's and Tieck's 'invention' of Novalis – in so doing creating not so much a tradition as a *narrative* from an existential crisis.

---

[54] Ibid., p. 301.

From the very beginning of the new century, the emerging European Romantic idea of tradition, whether in Germany or France, was at once religious *and* aesthetic – creating a new symbiosis quite different from the old Catholic idea that art was the handmaid of religion. This new vision was, moreover, dynamic and historical. Religion, like art, had to reflect the changing social and intellectual world of which it was inescapably a part. Bossuet's belief in an unchanging universal truth could itself now be historicized as part of the narrative of the development of doctrine. Like all history, it was a selective narrative. But whatever the various versions, they had one thing in common: the past was different from, and at least arguably superior to, the present. Dorothea Schlegel's words in a letter to a friend about her conversion are telling. 'If only because it is so ancient, I prefer Catholicism. Nothing new is of any use.'[55]

[55] Hans Eichner, *Friedrich Schlegel* (Twayne, 1970), p. 106.

CHAPTER 7

Translating Herder: the idea of Protestant Romanticism

HERDER IN ENGLISH

Given the relatively tiny number of British who knew German at the end of the eighteenth and the beginning of the nineteenth centuries, Herder's influence on the English-speaking world was surprisingly pervasive. As we have seen, he was one of the very few non-Catholic writers in the eighteenth century not merely to defend the value of 'tradition', but to use the word freely and favourably in his writing.

As one might expect, Coleridge had been one of the first to show an interest in Herder. As early as 1799 we find him writing to his brother-in-law, Robert Southey, asking for a copy of Herder's *Ideen*,[1] and two years later discussing with him Herder's views on the Resurrection.[2] Whatever his sources – and he was also attempting to borrow a copy of the *Ideen* from a friend, William Taylor, at more or less the same time – Coleridge's habit of scribbling extensively in all books that he read (including those borrowed from friends) make it unusually easy to trace his reading. The collected *Marginalia* reveals an extensive reading of Herder, especially of his theological works, by the early 1830s.[3]

Something of Herder's general reputation in the 1820s is revealed by another of the few English who could read German at this period, Thomas De Quincey, who casually compares Herder and Coleridge in an essay of 1823 with the implication that his readers are likely to know both at least by reputation.[4] Though De Quincey was not above trying to impress readers

---

[1] 30 September 1799. *Letters of Samuel Taylor Coleridge*, 6 vols., ed. E.R. Griggs (Clarendon Press, 1956), Vol. I, p. 535.

[2] As expressed in Herder's *Von der Auferstehung, als Glauben, Geschichte und Lehre*, ibid., Vol. II., pp. 861–2.

[3] *The Collected Works of Samuel Taylor Coleridge, Marginalia*, 5 vols., ed. George Whalley (Routledge/Princeton University Press, 1984), Vol. II, pp. 1048–88.

[4] The article was published in January 1823, although it is mysteriously dated 24 December 1824. 'Letters to a Young Man whose Education has been Neglected', *Collected Writings of Thomas De Quincey*, 14 vols., ed. David Masson (A&C Black, 1897), Vol. X, p. 12.

with his knowledge of the German scene (he also throws out names of many deeply obscure German 'authorities'), the reference to Herder, like his references to the Schlegel brothers, implies at least some expectation that his readers would be reasonably familiar at least with Herder's name.[5] Similarly we know from notebook entries that Thomas Carlyle was reading Herder in the early 1820s when he was also at work on his massive translation of Goethe's *Wilhelm Meister*.[6] Felicia Hemans (1793–1835), one of the most popular poets of the day, was also reading Herder in German at much the same time – referring approvingly to his translations of El Cid (*Der Cid, nach spanischen Romanzen besungen*) in a note to her *Siege of Valencia*, published in 1823,[7] and *Stimmen der Volker in Liedern* again in *The Forest Sanctuary* (1825).[8]

For those outside the relatively elite circle of those who could read German, a whole chapter of Mme de Staël's best-seller, *On Germany* (which had been published in London in 1813 both in French and English), was devoted to a eulogistic introduction to Herder and his ideas. Meanwhile a steady stream of English translations of Herder's work (some of dubious quality) had been appearing from 1790 onwards, so that by the early 1830s there were perhaps a dozen or so available – some complete, some consisting of selections or extracts, sometimes with obscure titles.[9]

Herder's most important early translator by far is T. O. Churchill, whose translation of Herder's *Ideen* as, *Outlines of a Philosophy of the History of Man*, was published in 1800, and was popular enough to be followed by a second edition in 1803. Given his importance in disseminating the ideas of a leading continental philosopher, little is known about Churchill, beyond

---

[5] His own knowledge is not above question. At one point he seems to confuse Friedrich Schlegel with his brother, August. Ibid., p. 41.

[6] In 1823, he copied into his notebook two passages from Herder – one on sleep and death from *Zerstreute Blätter*, and the other from the fifth book of the *Ideen*. It seems clear that such jottings were only the tip of the iceberg of Carlyle's reading of Herder. See Hill Shine, 'Carlyle's Early Writings and Herder's *Ideen*: The Concept of History', *Booker Memorial Studies*, ed. Hill Shine (University of North Carolina Press, 1950), pp. 3–33; René Wellek, 'Carlyle and the Philosophy of History', *Confrontations: Studies in the Intellectual Relations Between Germany, England, and the United States During the Nineteenth Century* (Princeton University Press, 1965), p. 89; and Chris R. Vanden Bossche, *Carlyle and the Search for Authority* (Ohio State University Press, 1991).

[7] 'Herder's translation of these romances are remarkable for their spirit and scrupulous fidelity.' Felicia Hemans, *The Siege of Valencia: A Dramatic Poem* (Murray, 1823), p. 266, n.5. Given the difference in male and female systems of education at this period, where boys were likely to have studied the classics, and girls more likely to be given modern languages, it is not surprising that many of the German readers in Britain were women.

[8] Felicia Hemans, *The Forest Sanctuary and Other Poems* (Murray, 1825), p. 106.

[9] Bayard Quincy Morgan, *A Critical Bibliography of German Literature in Translation 1481–1927*, 2nd rev. edn (Scarecrow Press, 1965).

the fact that he seems also to have been a clergyman.[10] Biographical notes on him in the *Modern Language Review* of 1947 indicate that other than Semons he was also the author of a *Life of Nelson* (1808) and an English Grammar (1823), but apart from that, and a letter to *The Gentleman's Magazine* in 1827, he seems to have no other publications – at least under that name.[11] He is not listed as the graduate of any university, nor do any contemporaries refer to him, although, since his translations were put out by the radical publisher Joseph Johnson (1738–1809), it is also possible that he was a member of the liberal circle that included Mrs Barbauld, William Blake, Maria Edgeworth, William Godwin, Henry Fuseli, Horne Tooke, and Mary Wollstonecraft – this being, perhaps, the only circle in London at that time where German, and contemporary German ideas, were known and widely discussed, and which was highly receptive to Herder's thought. But, if so, it is strange that none of them ever mentions someone who had undertaken so major a translation. Whether or not Churchill was also behind an anonymous translation of the first part of Herder's *The Spirit of Hebrew Poetry*, published in 1801 with the rather strange title of *Oriental Dialogues*,[12] or, indeed, a subsequent anonymous translation of the *Treatise on the Origin of Language* (1827) is equally unclear.

JAMES MARSH AND *THE SPIRIT OF HEBREW POETRY*

The first full English translation of *The Spirit of Hebrew Poetry* was not published until 1833, fifty years after it had appeared in Germany (1782–3), and eighty years after the original Latin publication of Lowth's *Sacred Poetry of the Hebrews* (1753). The translator was James Marsh (1794–1842), a New England Congregationalist minister, who had been first Professor of Philosophy and then President of the University of Vermont (1826–33). Often associated with Emersonian Transcendentalism, from which in fact he tried to distance himself, Marsh was a key figure in the introduction of Coleridge's philosophy to American readers, producing editions of *Aids to Reflection, The Friend,* and *The Statesman's Manual*.[13]

---

[10] His name comes up again as an author of sermons. See the database to English Pulpit Project, ed. Robert Ellison, Keith Francis and Bob Tennant (still under construction 2008).

[11] A. Gilles, 'T.O. Churchill, Translator: a Note', *Modern Language Review*, 42 (1947), p. 491.

[12] Johann Gottfried Herder, *Oriental Dialogues: containing the conversations of Eugenius and Alciphron on the spirit and beauties of the sacred poetry of the Hebrews* (printed by A. Strachan for T. Cadell jun. and W. Davies, 1801).

[13] See Anthony J. Harding, 'James Marsh as Editor of Coleridge', *Reading Coleridge: Approaches and Applications*, ed. Walter B. Crawford (Cornell University Press, 1979).

For the Transcendentalists, Herder had been a key inspirational figure. In the earliest history of the movement, Octavius Brooks Frothingham (1822–85) describes Herder as one of the 'illuminated minds' behind the movement. His father, the Unitarian minister, Nathaniel Langdon Frothingham (1793–1870) had translated Herder's *Brief, das Studium der Theologie Betreffend* in 1820–1. Another associate, George Ripley (1802–80), published a laudatory review of Marsh's translation in the *Christian Examiner* of May 1835. Central to this cult of Herder was *The Spirit of Hebrew Poetry* itself – and, explicitly, its relation to the idea of tradition. Octavius Frothingham comments:

Herder was one of the illuminated minds; though not profound a disciple, he had felt the influence of Kant, and was cordially in sympathy with the men who were trying to break the spell of form and tradition. With Lessing more especially, Herder's 'Spirit of Hebrew Poetry', of which a translation by Dr. James Marsh was published in 1833, found its way to New England and helped confirm the disposition to seek the springs of inspiration in the human mind, whence all poetry proceeded. The writer of the book, by applying to Hebrew poetry the rules of critical appreciation by which all poetic creations are judged, abolished so far the distinction between the sacred and the secular, and transferred to the credit of human genius the products commonly ascribed to divine. In the persons of all great bards of Israel all bards were glorified; the soul's creative power was recognized, and with it the heart of the transcendental faith.[14]

In fact, this view of Herder (and Marsh) tells us probably as much about Frothingham's interpretation of the Transcendentalists as it does about Herder himself. Moreover, as we shall see in relation to Herder's idea of biblical aesthetic tradition, the Herder whom Frothingham encountered through Marsh's translation was himself as much a construct of New England in the 1830s as of Germany in the 1780s.

From the first, Marsh read Herder through Coleridgean spectacles, and consequently through Lowthian ones as well. The tone of the translation is immediately set in his Preface, where he not merely compares Herder to Lowth, suggesting, somewhat surprisingly to modern readers, that Herder is too much influenced by the German Higher Criticism, but then proceeds to summarize Herder's arguments in words taken almost

---

[14] Octavius Brooks Frothingham, *Transcendentalism in New England* (1876; reprinted Harper Brothers, 1959), pp. 47–8, n.5. For this I am indebted to Ernest A. Menze, 'The Reception and Influence of Herder's *On the Spirit of Hebrew Poetry* in North America: Preliminary Observations', in Daniel Weidner (ed.), *Urpoesie und Morgenland. J.G. Herders 'Vom Geist der Ebräischen Poesie'* (Kadmos Verlag, 2008).

verbatim from Lowth. To understand Hebrew poetry, Marsh explains, the reader:

> must not only be acquainted with the facts of their history [the Hebrews or any foreign people], the modes of life, and the circumstances of every kind, by which their habits of thought and feeling were moulded, as a mass of antiquarian lore, but must learn to place himself entirely in their *point of view*, and see all these particulars in the relation to each other, and to the observer, which they would then assume. When he has done this, he will be prepared to understand why they thought, and felt, and wrote as they did; and if he have the feeling and inspiration of the poet, he will sympathize with their emotions, and the living spirit of their poetry will be kindled up in his own imagination.[15]

Comparison with the original passage of Lowth reveals almost no changes of substance,[16] but what amounts to a significant shift in viewpoint – perhaps befitting a professor of philosophy struggling to assimilate the eighteenth-century German critical historical revolution, while specifically keeping at bay more disturbing elements of the German Higher Criticism. Thus thinking and feeling as an ancient Hebrew now involves also assimilating 'a mass of antiquarian lore' – the addition of such distancing phrases suggesting that the mental effort to bridge the gap to modernity had increased appreciably over the previous seventy years.

Moreover, the places where Herder differs significantly from Lowth in understanding such 'antiquarian lore' are likely to be a cause of censure, rather than praise:

> That he [Herder] has always apprehended in their true sense the early conceptions of the Hebrews is not to be supposed, nor would any one probably undertake to defend all his views, even of important matters, connected with the early traditions of the race. The biblical representations of Paradise, of the garden of Eden, of the temptation and fall of Adam, of the Cherubim, of the deluge, and of what Herder denominates mythological representations generally, have ever furnished

---

[15] Johann Gottfried von Herder, *The Spirit of Hebrew Poetry*, 2 vols, trs. James Marsh (Edward Smith, 1833); facsimile edn (Aleph, 1971), Vol. 1, p. 5.

[16] He who would perceive the peculiar and interior elegancies of the Hebrew poetry, must imagine himself exactly situated as the persons for whom it was written, or even as the writers themselves; he is to feel them as a Hebrew . . . nor is it enough to be acquainted with the language of this people, their manners, discipline, rites and ceremonies; we must even investigate their inmost sentiments, the manner and connexion of their thoughts; in one word, we must see all things with their eyes, estimate all things by their opinion: we must endeavour as much as possible to read Hebrew as the Hebrews would have read it.

Robert Lowth, *Lectures on the Sacred Poetry of the Hebrews*, 2 vols., trs. G. Gregory, 1787, Vol. 1, pp. 113, 114.

an ample field of speculation, in which every critick feels at liberty to form his own opinions, and for the most part to interpret by his own rules.[17]

Modern readers of Herder are often puzzled by his attitude to what are here called 'mythological representations', in that as we have already seen he often seems curiously literalist in his approach to Old Testament material – particularly from Genesis – that the higher critics such as Eichhorn, Lessing, or Reimarus, had already dismissed as myth, fantasy, or even priest-craft. What is interesting here is that Marsh skilfully evades direct confrontation with the Higher Criticism by suggesting that the interpretation of such passages has always been a matter of personal taste. This is, to say the least, disingenuous: the fact that critics from Catholics like Alexander Geddes to extreme Deists like Tom Paine had questioned or ridiculed such passages did not mean that they were open territory for every personal speculation.[18]

What is even more interesting is the role played by that innocent-seeming word 'traditions' in this evasion. At first sight it appears no different from Coleridge's or any common eighteenth-century English usage. It stands for oral, and therefore probably unreliably transmitted sources. But closer examination raises some curious problems. Hasn't Marsh's whole purpose in this delicately phrased editorial been to damp down speculation over stories concerning the Garden of Eden, the Fall, or the Deluge, not to suggest their inherent unreliability?

Later uses of the word may clarify Marsh's dilemma, if not his intentions. Here is his translation of Herder's own 'Author's Preface' to *The Spirit of Hebrew Poetry*:

With these, it [Herder's work] must contain also, especially, the traditions of the patriarchs, which, as among all nations, so peculiarly among this people, were the source from which were derived all the peculiarities of their modes of thinking, consequently also the genius of their poetry. To set forth these, and unfold them correctly, was here so much the more necessary, since most traditions of this kind have themselves more or less of poetical colouring, and what is worse, are often misapprehended.[19]

Here Marsh, though posing as no more than a faithful translator, is in fact subtly manipulating his text. The word *Tradition* exists in German, stems from the same Latin root, has and had much the same meaning as in English – and is used by Herder at some points in his text. But this is *not*

---

[17] James Marsh, Preface to Herder, *Spirit of Hebrew Poetry*, trs. Marsh, p. 7.
[18] Alexander Geddes, *The Holy Bible faithfully translated from corrected Texts of the Originals, with various Readings, explanatory Notes and critical Remarks*, 2 vols., Vol. I, 1792; Vol. II, 1797. See also R.C. Fuller, Alexander Geddes (Almond Press, 1983).
[19] *Spirit of Hebrew Poetry*, p. 17.

the word that Herder commonly uses when discussing 'traditions of this kind' – such as the ideas of Paradise or Babel in Genesis.[20] The word he uses most frequently is *Sage* – as in the English 'saga' or, more straightforwardly, 'legend'. If Marsh had consistently translated *Sage* as 'legend' instead of 'tradition' in these, and similar passages, the whole flavour of his translation would have been very different. Whatever the connotations of 'tradition' in suggesting inherent unreliability and doubtful veracity, 'legend' would have been far stronger. Whether for conscious tactical motives, or for more deep-seated and unconscious ones, Marsh's choice of words was to make Herder *more* conservative and closer to biblical literalism than he might otherwise have appeared. The consequences were to be far-reaching.

While not denying the oral and folk origins of what we must more correctly translate as 'traditional legends', Herder spells out his national and linguistic ideas by inverting the common associations of folk mythology. Rather than being essentially unreliable, traditional legends are, instead, the source of the poetic genius of the race. It is unintelligent literalists who have 'misapprehended' the nature of poetry, and of its traditional roots in the folk culture, and therefore totally failed to understand the language of mythology. So far from being a source of unreliable fact, mythology is the source of ineffable sublimity.

Thus, for Herder, the essential continuity of the Old and New Testaments is not merely (to a Christian) theological, it is also 'enlightening' in a Coleridgean sense, and above all, poetic – and failure to understand this is a not merely a failure of faith but of scholarly scriptural interpretation:

In the Old Testament we find as an aid to this, a rich interchange of history, of figurative representations, of characters, and of scenery, and we see in it the many coloured dawn, the beautiful going forth of the sun in his milder radiance. In the New Testament it stands in the highest heavens, and in meridian splendour, and every one knows which period of the day to the natural eye of sense imparts most life and strength.[21]

Seen in this way modern questions of biblical historicity were beside the point. By looking for what is not there, critics were failing to see the glories that *were* there under their noses.

Among the Hebrews, history itself is properly poetry, that is the transmission of narratives, which are related in the present tense, and here too we may discover

---

[20] Here I must record my gratitude to Daniel Weidner, and discussions with him resulting from the Berlin Herder Symposium in January 2006.
[21] *Spirit of Hebrew Poetry*, p. 22.

an advantage derived from the indefiniteness or fluctuation, of the tenses, especially in producing conviction, and rendering what is described, related or announced, more clearly and vividly present to the senses. Is not this in a high degree poetical?[22]

Marsh's dilemma seems as obvious as it was intractable. If what he chooses to call 'tradition' could be dismissed as the kind of territory where 'every critick feels at liberty to form his own opinions' (p. 7) then it is difficult *also* to argue that it is nothing less than the source of the poetic genius of the race. Nor does Marsh's final disclaimer clarify the position beyond passing the buck:

after making due allowances . . . it will still be felt that the work contains some things irreconcilable with just views, nor would I be understood as subscribing to all the sentiments, which I am herewith exhibiting to the publick.

If it be asked, why do I then exhibit opinions, which I deem erroneous, I can only say, that others, as well as myself, and those in whose judgement I place the highest confidence, have thought it extremely desirable, all things considered, that the work be given to the publick, and my views of duty to my author, as a faithful translator, did not permit me to misrepresent his opinions in any thing of importance.[23]

The endless commas and sub-clauses of that tortuous sentence give the same message in starker terms: in other words, 'don't blame me'. Yet one doubts if one reader in a thousand (assuming the volume to have had so many readers) would have seen that what distinguished Herder, indeed, what makes this volume unique in the English-speaking world of the 1830s, is not what Marsh calls 'the free spirit of Biblical criticism, as exhibited . . . by Eichhorn and other contemporary German writers', but what amounts to a new and revolutionary use of the idea of tradition itself. Yet in a very real sense, it is Marsh, the very man who is apparently trying to wriggle out of committing himself to Herder's viewpoint, who has gone a long way to creating that new sense.

This is a point that needs to be made with some care. At first sight there seems little in this use of the word tradition to distinguish it from other eighteenth-century writers like Lowth or Coleridge, Schleiermacher or Novalis, and much that would seem to set it in opposition to the discreetly demonized Eichhorn. Herder's argument is presented in Part 1 by means of a Socratic dialogue between the sceptic Alciphron and his friend the more aesthetically inclined Euthyphron. In Dialogue 6, for

---

[22] Ibid., p. 37.   [23] Ibid., p. 8.

instance, which is clearly the one that gave Marsh so much unease in the passage quoted earlier, Alciphron, while accepting the idea of the Fall as a theological or poetic myth, questions the reality of any such historical event. I note in italics the occasions where 'tradition' is a translation of *Sage*.

Had Paradise ever a real existence, or is the whole a poetical tradition [*Sage*]? Moses clearly represents it as a wide extended and to him unknown fairy land. He places it, too, precisely in those remote regions, where fable has placed everything marvellous, including in its wide compass Colchis and Cashmire with their golden streams, the Phasis and the Oxus, as well as the regions of the Indus and the Euphrates. In this broad land, to which he gives the name of Eden, or the land of delight, he represents God as planting a garden. Where, then, in a country so extensive was the garden situated? Where are the marvellous trees, which grew in it – the tree of life and the tree of knowledge? Have these ever come to maturity? Where are they now, and where stood the Cherubim? All this, I confess, has to me, the appearance of a fable.

To which Euthyphron, Herder's mouthpiece, replies:

So it should have; and the purpose, which we are now seeking to accomplish, is to distinguish between fable and truth, that is, between historical fact and the dress in which its is clothed. You have remarked correctly, that Moses, or the tradition [*Sage*] copied by him, gives the situation of Paradise only within very wide and vague limits, and that the region in which it is placed, is just that fable-land, in which the nations of antiquity placed their finest pictures of all that is visionary and enchanted – the golden fleece, the golden apples, the plant of immortality, &c. . . . But do not all these later marvels show, that there must have been some more simple tradition [*Sage*], and some real fact in primeval history, in which they had their origin? There must have been some cause for the singular fact, that the traditions [*Sagen*] of the whole world chance to point towards one and the same region. The human race, which, so far as history and the progress if cultivation enables us to judge, has been gradually spread over the earth, must some where have had a beginning; and where more probably – whether we look at history, or the formation of the earth's surface – than in those very regions, to which these traditions direct us? . . . Moreover the very indefiniteness, which you speak of in Moses' account of the situation of Paradise, is an evidence of its truth. He would give no more than tradition [*Sage*] had furnished . . . But it is not our business at present to trace historical truth. We may therefore leave this tradition [*Tradition als eine Sage*] in its original vagueness, and consider only to what poetical representation it has given rise.[24]

---

[24] Ibid., pp. 124–5; Johann Gottfried Herder, *Vom Geist der Ebräischen Poesie* (F.A. Berthes, 1890), pp. 143–4.

In the light of that final sentence where, in the original, Herder actually offers *Tradition* and *Sage* ('tradition or legend') as apparent synonyms,[25] one can, I think, guess why Marsh, the Coleridgean, and Emersonian Transcendentalist, might have wished *both* to steer his translation away from the inherently ambiguous *Sage*, the 'traditional legend', in the direction of strengthening the positive content of ancient wisdom *and*, as someone all too aware of the prejudices of his readership, to distance himself altogether from this dialogue.

But however tendentious the English translation, even in the original German, Euthyphron, the self-proclaimed defender of biblical truth, has seemingly sold the pass to his debating opponent at the outset. Eden, the serpent, and the Cherubim may indeed be just the poetical fictions that Eichhorn had surmised, and traditions may similarly be the leaky and imprecise vessels of knowledge that the Enlightenment critics had always supposed them to be, but they are nonetheless unrivalled sources of truth and poetic wisdom. In other words, Marsh, by giving extra emphasis to a quality already present in Herder, is re-introducing a very old, and, to us by this stage, very familiar quality of the tradition debate into his argument. He is not describing tradition as it would have been understood by Bossuet or any other Roman Catholic expositor of the period. Though this may read like Chateaubriand's defence of the Bible from 1802, or even Paine's much more radical *Age of Reason*, by attributing it to Herder, Marsh can, in effect, pre-date both by nearly quarter of a century. This idea of tradition does not consist of the accretion of commentary and extra-canonical assumptions central to the imperial claims of the Vatican. Nor is it the essentially unreliable process of oral transmission treated with such contempt by most contemporary eighteenth-century writers. Neither Burke nor Paine would have recognized it. The claim that traditions (at least of the Bible) provide a guide both to lost truths – now almost certainly inaccessible to other kinds of investigation – *and*, even more significantly, to the unique sublimity of the poetic traditions of the Hebrews, is a reading-back of Herder's own aesthetics into the ancient world. Faced with a contemporary epistemological crisis in MacIntyre's sense, Marsh has, like Cassiodorus before him, sought to re-create from the strands of the past (in this case Herder's fifty-year-old text) a rope that will lead him

---

[25] It is interesting, incidentally, to see that the first French translation (1845) uses '*un dire*' (italicized) meaning simply 'account' or 'assertion' for the German *Sage* earlier in the paragraph, but follows the same approach as Marsh by eliminating the alternative terms, and simply putting '*tradition*' in that final sentence. A. de Carlowitz, *Historie de la Poésie des Hebreux* (Didier, 1845), p. 115.

both towards a greater understanding of history, and provide a guide for perceiving the present.

There is, of course, a chicken-and-egg quality central to this whole argument. We only come to understand who the ancient Hebrews were by understanding the language and the poetry which formed them, but, naturally, the language and poetry of the Hebrews was in no small measure the result of their unique experiences. Not surprisingly from these premises, the idea of 'history' itself feels the gravitational pull of this idea of tradition. Anticipating – as the German Romantics so often did – arguments that were to be re-presented as original in the twentieth century,[26] Herder sees history as not so much a record of past events as an interpretative narrative of those events, written (like all interpretative narratives) from a particular perspective or viewpoint. There is no such thing as disembodied perception. Just as the French would interpret the wars of the eighteenth century in a different way from the Austrians, the English, or the Prussians, it is natural and entirely proper that the same set of events will be viewed by the Hebrews in one way and, for instance, by the ancient Egyptians in quite another.

In claiming this, Herder, of course, had his own political axe to grind. As we have seen in the previous chapter, his concept of 'cultures' (in the plural) was in deliberate opposition to the French, and, to a lesser extent at this stage, the English,[27] who felt that 'civilization' was one and indivisible (and probably best represented by themselves). 'Civilization', as the word came to be used in France from the 1750s, stood for an ideal order of human society, involving the arts, learning, and manners. In this sense it was used strictly in the singular; only with vanished societies of the past could one speak of 'civilizations'. The connotations, justifying both colonial expansion and European linguistic hegemony, were of the evident superiority of *la civilisation française*. French was the *lingua franca* throughout Europe: it was the language of diplomacy, of aristocrats and of the royal courts of many states in Germany and even Tsarist Russia. The new meaning of the word, though naturally not with its innate French bias, was then taken up in England.[28]

---

[26] See Andrew Bowie, *From Romanticism to Critical Theory: The Philosophy of German Literary Theory* (Routledge, 1997).

[27] The first example of this use of the word in the *Oxford English Dictionary* is Boswell's record of Johnson, in 1772, *refusing* to incorporate it in the fourth edition of his Dictionary.

[28] Almost a century later, Dean Church, in his 1868 lectures on 'The Gifts of Civilization', insists that the word has an essentially moral as well as technical connotation, covering 'all that man does, all that he discovers, all that he becomes, to fit himself most suitably for the life in which he finds

In contrast, 'culture' (*Kultur*), as used by Herder and his fellow Romantics in defiance of the generalized and global pretensions of the Anglo-French idea of 'civilization', was specific, local, and plural, describing not an ideal order of human society in general, but the distinctive modes of existence of different societies. Defending a national *Kultur* both against the rationalism of the *philosophes* and a Francophile Prussian court, Herder urged that different ways of life were valuable in themselves, and not to be seen as stages of development towards a common goal. Unlike 'civilization', which could be transferred between more advanced and less advanced peoples – preferably by a beneficent imperialism – culture was what truly identified and differentiated a people. Culture came in kinds, not in degrees; in the plural, not the singular. Nor could there be any uncultured peoples, as there were uncivilized ones. 'Only a real misanthrope,' Herder once ironically remarked, 'could regard European culture as the universal condition of our species.' Each people had its own appropriate kind of happiness based on the cultural legacy of their ancestral tradition, transmitted in the distinctive concepts of their language, and adapted to their specific life conditions. It is through this tradition, endowed also with the morality of the community and the emotions of the family, that experience is organized, since people do not simply discover the world, they are taught it. Moreover, they experience their world not merely in terms of ideas but values. We cannot speak of reasoning correctly on objective properties known through unmediated sensory perceptions. Seeing is also a function of hearing, and judgement, and in the economy of thought – what Herder once spoke of as 'the family or kinship mode of thought' – reason is invested with feeling and bound to imagination.

One can see both why Marsh finds Herder so important, and also why he is careful to distance himself from some of the implications of some of his ideas, even while he subtly modifies others. What is being suggested in the *Spirit of Hebrew Poetry* is nothing less than a new way of reading the past – and any new way of imagining the past will naturally affect the way in which a society thinks about its own time, and how it has reached the present moment. Tradition has, for Herder, become an act of historical imagination. But, as we suggested in the last chapter, there is nothing oral

himself here'. While the gifts and benefits of Christian civilization, manifestly outweigh those of pagan Rome, the same word nevertheless applies equally to both. By Church's time it had acquired much of its impetus from the way it could be used to differentiate the superior state of the colonizing power from the inferior state of the colonized. For him, India was still in 'a low state of civilization' while Egypt, China, and Japan, though 'singularly ingenious' and 'industrious' have not yet reached a 'high' stage. R.W. Church, *Gifts of Civilization*, new edn (Macmillan, 1880), p. 152.

or 'primitive' about the imagined past offered by biblical tradition. If it is certainly not the extension of dogma still insisted upon by Rome, neither is it the conventional Protestant source of antiquated and unreliable fictions. It is, on the contrary, a sophisticated literary and aesthetic form. If God had formed the ancient Hebrews into a literary people, it is because that is how tradition speaks to the modern world.

Two things follow from this – and both were reflected in other new ideas that were making headway across Europe at the turn of the century. The first is the new idea of the 'aesthetic'. First recorded in English in 1798, with the meaning 'received by the senses', the *Oxford English Dictionary* comments acerbically that the word was 'misapplied in German by Baumgarten, and so used in England since 1830'. In fact, of course, the revolutionary use of the word to mean 'pertaining to the beautiful' by Alexander Gottlieb Baumgarten is itself far too narrow to catch the way in which by the end of the century it had come to stand for something much closer to 'pertaining to the theory – or theories – of art'.[29] In his Third Critique, the *Critique of Judgement* (1790), Kant had attempted to bridge the gap between his two earlier Critiques, of what he called 'pure' and 'practical Reason', by means of reflective or aesthetic judgement – the power by which (for instance) we distinguish between the sublime and the beautiful.[30] For Kant, these qualities were reflected alike in nature and art, but subsequent philosophers, following Schiller in *The Aesthetic Education of Man* (1794), tended to see art rather than nature as central to the construction of the human world. For Hegel the Kantian priorities were explicitly reversed: beauty in art actually has higher status than natural beauty.[31]

Where Kant's influence remained undiminished, however, was in the belief that poetry was somehow the most representative form of this new and very powerful idea of the aesthetic:

Of all the arts poetry (which owes its origins almost entirely to genius and will least be guided by precept or example) maintains the first rank. It expands the mind by setting the imagination at liberty and by offering, within the limits of a given concept, amid the unbounded variety of possible forms accordant therewith, that which unites the presentment of this concept with a wealth of thought to which no verbal expression is completely adequate, and so rising aesthetically to ideas.[32]

---

[29] See Andrew Bowie, *Aesthetics and Subjectivity: From Kant to Nietzsche* (Manchester University Press, 1990).

[30] See, for instance, Hazard Adams, *Philosophy of the Literary Symbolic* (Florida State University Press, 1983), Ch. 2.

[31] Bowie, *Aesthetics and Subjectivity*, p. 133.

[32] Immanuel Kant, *Critique of Judgement*, trs. J.H. Bernard (Hafner, 1951), pp. 170–1.

For Friedrich Schlegel there was a further attribute of the aesthetic that
was of prime importance: it was essentially *mythological*:

we hear so often that the masses should have a sensuous religion. Not only the masses
but also the philosopher needs monotheism of reason of the heart, polytheism of
imagination and of art . . . we must have a new mythology, but this mythology must
be in the service of the Ideas, it must become a mythology of *reason*.

Before we make the Ideas aesthetic i.e. mythological, they are of no interest to
the people and on the other hand before mythology is reasonable the philosopher
must be ashamed of it. Thus enlightened and unenlightened must finally shake
hands, mythology must become philosophical and the people reasonable, and
philosophy must become mythological in order to make the philosophers sensuous. Then eternal unity will reign among us. Never the despairing gaze, never the
blind trembling of the people before its wise men and priests. Only then can we
expect the *same* development of all powers, of the individual as well as all individuals. No power will then be suppressed any more, then general freedom and
equality of spirits will reign! – A higher spirit sent from heaven must found this
new religion among us, it will be the last, greatest work of mankind.[33]

How much of this huge (and in some ways overbearing) superstructure of
ideas was actually implicit in Herder's *Spirit of Hebrew Poetry* must remain
a matter of debate – especially since its publication is more or less contemporaneous with Kant's First Critique, and pre-dates the Third, not to mention the work of Schiller and the other German Romantics. What is very
clear is that his concept of the tradition of Hebrew poetry had opened the
way to some of the central tenets of Romanticism, and, crucially, helped
to create a 'user-friendly' and receptive climate for the later applications
of it by Kant, Hegel, the Schlegels, and so on. It was to change radically the whole subsequent theory of literature and the arts. Hegel's assertion that 'in our time' the theory of art is much more important than any
actual examples of its practice' was only a re-iteration of one of the fundamental tenets of the Jena group.[34] Two twentieth-century French historical critics, Philippe Lacoue-Labarthe and Jean-Luc Nancy, in their book,
The Literary Absolute: The Theory of Literature in German Romanticism,
attribute to Herder, Kant, Hegel, and their successors the whole modern idea of 'literature' as writing charged with an aesthetic value over and
above its ostensible subject.[35]

---

[33] Friedrich Schlegel, cited in Bowie, *Aesthetics and Subjectivity*, pp. 265–6 (Bowie's translation).
[34] G.W.F. Hegel, *Ästhetik*, ed. Friedrich Bassenge, Weimar 1965, Vol. 1, p. 20, cited in Bowie, *Aesthetics and Subjectivity*, p. 135.
[35] Philippe Lacoue-Labarthe and Jean-Luc Nancy, *The Literary Absolute: The Theory of Literature in German Romanticism*, trs. Philip Barnard and Cheryl Lester (State University of New York Press, 1988), p. xiv.

Because it establishes a period in literature and in art, before it comes to represent a sensibility or style (whose 'return' is regularly announced), romanticism is first of all a *theory*. And the *invention* of literature. More precisely, it constitutes the inaugural moment of literature as *production of its own theory* – and of theory that thinks itself as literature. With this gesture, it opens the critical age to which we still belong.[36]

Indeed, one of the features that rapidly became common to Romanticism right across Europe at this period is this new concept of 'Literature'. The *Oxford English Dictionary* lists this value-added variant as the third, and most modern, meaning of the word ('of very recent emergence in both France and England'), defining it as 'writing which has a claim to consideration on the ground of beauty of form or emotional effect'. Certainly the idea of what constituted 'literature' was fiercely debated. De Quincey, ever the *enfant terrible*, dismisses the conventional Johnsonian idea of poetry giving knowledge through pleasure as nonsense. Citing Wordsworth, he insists that: 'The true antithesis to knowledge, in this case, is not *pleasure*, but *power*. All that is literature seeks to communicate power; all that is not literature, to communicate knowledge.'[37]

In Germany the idea of literature was to take on an even higher status than in Britain and France since it could be seen as in some sense *the* mediator of reality. Indeed, it was possible for extreme Kantians to hold that poetic or literary descriptions, as aesthetic constructs, were actually *more* real than direct sense-data, which, in the last resort, have no access at all to things-in-themselves. The distinctive addition made by the Schlegels and their circle, however, is that it was, or should be, impossible to distinguish between such a theory of literature and its actual practice. This produces in much of the Romantic writing of the period a kind of theoretical synaesthesia which links poetry, the novel, philosophy, and frequently theology as well. Friedrich Schlegel, in *Athenaeum* Fragment 304, for example, writes:

Philosophy . . . is the result of two conflicting forces – of poetry and practice. Where these interpenetrate completely and fuse into one, there philosophy comes into being; and when philosophy disintegrates, it becomes mythology or else returns to life. The most sublime philosophy, some few surmise, may once again turn to poetry.[38]

---

[36] Ibid., pp. xxi–xxii.
[37] De Quincey, 'Letters to a Young Man', Vol. x, pp. 47–8.
[38] Friedrich Schlegel, *Philosophical Fragments*, trs. Peter Firchow (University of Minnesota Press, 1991).

According to this view, it is art, rather than our perceptions of the world around us, that gives access to a reality that is in part our own creation.

This post-Kantian orthodoxy was expanded by Julius Hare, as avowed an admirer of Coleridge and Schleiermacher as Marsh himself, to include the way in which poetry (or poesie in its broader archaic English sense) affects our construction of nature:

> The commentator guides and lights us to the altar erected by the author, although it is at the flame upon that altar that he must have kindled his torch. And what are Art and Science, if not a running commentary on Nature? what are poets and philosophers but torch-bearers leading us toward the innermost chambers of God's holy temples, the sensuous and the spiritual world? Books, as Dryden has aptly termed them, are spectacles to read nature. Homer and Aristotle, Shakespeare and Bacon, are the priests who preach and expound the mysteries of the universe: they teach us to decypher and syllable the characters wherewith it is inscribed. Do you not, since you have read Wordsworth, feel a fresh and more thoughtful delight whenever you hear a cuckoo, whenever you see a daisy, whenever you play with a child? Have not Thucydides and Dante assisted you in discovering the tides of feeling and the currents of passion by which events are borne along in the ocean of Time? Can you not discern something more in man, now that you look on him with eyes purged and unsealed by gazing upon Shakespeare and Goethe? From these terrestrial and celestial globes we learn the configuration of the earth and the heavens.[39]

The second word to have entered the European lexicon at roughly the same period was 'hermeneutics' – defined by the *Oxford English Dictionary* 'as the art or science of interpretation, especially of scripture'. Though commonly associated in its modern form with Schleiermacher, the word itself goes back to Sigmund Jacob Baumgarten (brother of Alexander Gottlieb) in the mid-eighteenth century,[40] and beyond that to the idea of the *hermeneutica sacra* of the seventeenth. Schleiermacher's hermeneutics stressed both the interpretative gulf between early texts and the modern reader (especially in the case of biblical writings) as well as the subjectivity and open-ended quality of such interpretations.

Between the time of Herder's original publication in 1782–3 and Marsh's translation in the 1830s, much of this philosophic and hermeneutic background was common not merely to the English Romanticism of Coleridge and Hare, but to the New England Transcendentalists, including, of course, Marsh himself, who was steeped in both the German and English

---

[39] *Guesses at Truth by Two Brothers* [Julius and Augustus Hare], first edn, 2 vols., 1827, p. 80.
[40] Here again I am indebted to Daniel Weidner. For an extensive account of the evolution of modern hermeneutics see Kurt Mueller-Vollmer (ed.), *The Hermeneutics Reader* (Blackwell, 1986).

sources of these ideas. The implications for any reading of Herder were significant – and, in retrospect, perhaps a little surprising.

As we have seen, Marsh was being more than a little disingenuous when he suggests that what he calls Herder's 'mythological representations' are, as it were, an optional extra, for which he, the translator, cannot be held responsible, and which may safely be ignored by readers who wish to do so. Not merely had Marsh had every reason for knowing perfectly well that Herder's aesthetics were very much of a piece, but Marsh's translation from a different age and culture, clarifying an ambiguity it was still possible to leave unresolved in the Germany of the 1780s, has been both selective and covertly polemical. The stories of the Garden of Eden cannot be read as literal truth, and can only be understood as part of a wider mythological pattern of the Hebrew historical imagination. They are works of art – in much the same way as the mediaeval poem, *The Pearl*, Dante's *Divine Comedy* or Milton's *Paradise Lost* must be read as works of art. Such literalist phrases as Eichhorn's 'pious fictions' do not begin to describe what is going on.[41] But, by translating Herder, while playing down and distancing himself from the hermeneutical implications of some of Herder's arguments, Marsh was able to keep his fellow Transcendentalists up to date on German theology and aesthetics, while at the same time keeping on board many New England readers for whom biblical literalism was not so much a conscious article of belief, as an unquestioned basis of their faith. Behind this ostensible agenda, however, is what seems to be the much more radical one of transforming and re-habilitating the word tradition itself.

Certainly Marsh brought back the idea of tradition into mainstream Protestant thought in the English-speaking world. The intervening fifty years between Herder's original German publication and Marsh's translation had clarified and developed many of the ideas that were only embryonic in the 1780s, illustrating with peculiar clarity the basic hermeneutic principle that any writing can only be understood within the social and historical matrix from which it came. In the interval, the Higher Criticism had developed enormously. The French Revolution had polarized European thinking. Kant and Hegel, Schleiermacher and the Schlegels, Volney and Chateaubriand, Coleridge and Hare, had all

---

[41] Much more sympathetic is Daniel Weidner's reading of Herder: 'The 'poetic' is not a given, imposed upon the Bible from the outside; it is constituted in the course of reading . . . it goes beyond the horizon of his contemporaries: unlike even historical criticism, he does not try to prove that the text is historically accurate. He cares about the force, the performative moment of the text.' 'Secularization, Scripture, and the Theory of Reading: J.G. Herder and the Old Testament', *New German Critique: An Interdisciplinary Journal of German Studies*, No. 94 (Winter 2005), p. 185.

contributed to the revolution in European ideas. No longer either the handmaid of Rome, or an obsolete and unreliable historical source, for those at least who understood something of Romantic philosophy, the idea of tradition could now be seen as central to biblical hermeneutics and aesthetics alike – and indeed was so seen by an increasing number of theologians, writers, and artists.

THE CRITICAL HERITAGE

To change the context of an idea is to change the idea itself. Marsh's 1833 translation of Herder appeared in an English-speaking world that was not merely very different philosophically and culturally from that of Germany in the 1780s, but also in terms of criticism – which had developed very differently in the two languages. In the English-speaking world, literary criticism, philosophy, and theology had not yet made their modern retreat into watertight academic boxes.[42] Unlike today, literature, and its associated aesthetic criticism, was still seen as having direct philosophical and theological implications. For the leading critics of the period, such as Arnold, Carlyle, Dallas, De Quincey, Keble, or Ruskin (to name but a few) the idea that the proper field of criticism was solely literature would have seemed as extraordinary as it would to many of the leading poets and novelists – the Brownings, George Eliot, or Tennyson, for instance. Equally significantly, it was still widely assumed that history, philosophy, theology – and even science – were suitable and appropriate areas for informed critical enquiry. Arnold wrote volumes of poetry and criticism (using, and even developing, ethnological and racial scientific theories in the latter)[43], as well as three books of theology. Both Robert and Elizabeth Barrett Browning tackled contemporary theological and social questions in their poetry. Tennyson agonized over both theology and (Lamarckian) evolution in *In Memoriam* (1859). E.S. Dallas's *The Gay Science* (1866), an attempt to ground criticism not in literary texts but in psychology, is based on a fully fledged theory of the unconscious a generation before Freud or Jung. But it is in the work of someone like George Henry Lewes (1817–78), George Eliot's partner of many years, that one can find expression of the full spread of possibilities

---

[42] For fuller discussions of this point see Stephen Prickett, *Words and the Word: Language, Poetics and Biblical Interpretation* (Cambridge University Press, 1986), Ch. 5, and *Narrative, Religion and Science: Fundamentalism versus Irony 1700–1999* (Cambridge University Press, 2002), Ch. 5.

[43] See, for instance, Frederick E. Faverty, *Matthew Arnold the Ethnologist* (Northwestern University Press, 1951).

in the era.[44] In addition to two novels, and numerous essays on drama and on British and Continental writers, he produced *A Biographical History of Philosophy* (1845–6), as well as volumes on *Spanish Drama* (1846), *Comte's Philosophy of the Sciences* (1853), *The Life and Works of Goethe* (1855), *Sea-side Studies at Ilfracombe, Tenby, the Scilly Isles, and Jersey* (1858), *The Physiology of Common Life* (1859), *Studies in Animal Life* (1862), *Aristotle, A Chapter from the History of Science* (1864), and *Actors and Acting* (1875). Moreover, though, by the 1860s, scientists were increasingly successful in distancing their specialist work from what they saw as uninformed lay criticism – or even, as in the case of the Darwin debate, deliberate obscurantism[45] – Lewes's scientific work cannot be dismissed as mere journalism. It was the fruit of genuine research, and at least one of his ideas – what is now called the doctrine of the functional indifference of the nerves – has stood the test of time.[46]

Perhaps most significant of all for Herder's reception in the 1830s, however, was a new sense of history. For a generation that had experienced the traumas of the French Revolution, it was no longer possible to assume that things were very much as they always had been. Recent European history had made the irony of Gibbon's Enlightenment epigram that history was little more than the record of the 'crimes, follies, and misfortunes of mankind' begin to look very threadbare. The underlying assumption of Thomas Gray's hugely popular *Elegy in a Country Churchyard* (1750), that the life of a contemporary ploughman in the Buckinghamshire village of Stoke Poges was essentially similar to that of the peasantry in the first century *Campagna* around Rome (as described in Lucretius' *De Rerum Natura*), was no longer even remotely tenable. History could never again merely be a record of events against a background of stasis, but from henceforth had to be a study of change itself. The translation of Niebuhr's massive *History of Rome* by Julius Hare and Connop Thirlwall in 1827 has (in retrospect) sometimes been seen as a watershed in British historiography but, in truth, it would be no less accurate to see it as a 'sign of the times' – itself a phrase taken up by Carlyle. Though not as thoroughgoing as the principles of so-called 'scientific' history, later to be pioneered by his younger contemporary Leopold von Ranke (1795–1886), Barthold Georg Niebuhr (1776–1831)

---

[44] For fuller illustration of this polymathic aspect of Lewes, see Rosemary Ashton, *G.H. Lewes: A Life* (Clarendon Press, 1992).

[45] See for instance, the objectives of T.H. Huxley and the 'X Club'. See Adrian Desmond and James Moore, *Darwin* (Michael Joseph, 1991).

[46] An idea subsequently confirmed independently by Wilhelm Wundt, *Grundzüge der Physiologische Psychologie*, 2nd edn, 1880, p. 321.

was the first modern historian to attempt to go beyond the accretions of myth and tradition handed down by the Latin authors themselves, and to search for documentary evidence. Where that was impossible, he looked for explanations in areas not necessarily always obvious to contemporary observers, such as institutions, laws, class, culture, and even race. Carlyle's own titles, from his 'Signs of the Times' (1829), to *Past and Present* (1843), hammer home the message of flux and transformation – a theme also central to his monumental history of *The French Revolution* (1837) itself, which explored change not so much as process as apocalypse.

Not all this new emphasis on historical change was progressive. In many cases what had been a romantic and wildly unscholarly interest in an imagined gothick Middle Ages became transposed into an idealization of the past in comparison with what was seen as the grime and materialism of the present. Augustus Welby Pugin's *Contrasts* (1836) delivers its message of catastrophic moral and aesthetic decline by a series of prints contrasting an idealized Catholic mediaeval England with the civic decay induced by industrialism and the harshness of the new Poor Law. Carlyle's pre-Reformation Abbot Samson in *Past and Present* is a peaceful but heroic figure, who stands in marked contrast to the degeneracy of modern leaders. What he called 'the condition of England question' was to dominate much of Carlyle's writing on contemporary Britain. Similarly, Disraeli's *Sybil* (1845) swiftly gives the reader a contrast between the honest communal labour for the common good by the monks of old, and a dissolute modern aristocracy ('a Venetian oligarchy') whose family fortunes were based on the theft of monastic lands at the Reformation.

As the century wore on this theme of social and cultural change, and of the progress, or the commercial or aesthetic degeneracy of the times, becomes ever stronger. It was one that was to dominate much of Ruskin's artistic and social criticism – and is even clearly implicit in the titles of such novels as Trollope's *The Way We Live Now* (1875). The worship of mediaevalism, which had included a return to gothic architecture for everything from railway stations to the newly rebuilt Houses of Parliament – even such things as statues of Queen Victoria and Prince Albert in thirteenth-century dress (in Albert's case, a full suit of armour) – was to reach its final apotheosis in Kenelm Digby's five-volume introduction to the mysteries of chivalry, *The Broad Stone of Honour* (1876–7). It was, in short, a world in which the idea and meaning of tradition was becoming an ever-more important question.

CHAPTER 8

Keble and the Anglican tradition

THE PROBLEM OF CATHOLIC EMANCIPATION

In the England of 1833 – the year of Marsh's translation of Herder – the renewed sense of history was focussed above all on one specific theme: Catholicism. Catholic Emancipation – formally introduced by the Catholic Relief Act of 1829 – had given Irish Catholics the right to vote for the first time, resulting, also for the first time since 1688, in a substantial body of Irish Catholics in the newly elected reform Parliament of 1832. The implications of this for the Anglican Church did not take long to sink in. The (Protestant) Church of Ireland, a part of the Anglican communion, and a key instrument in the Protestant ascendancy, had never in numerical terms been more than a tiny minority of the Irish population. Now, not merely had its hitherto secure political dominance in Ireland disappeared, but the composition of the British Parliament itself had been radically changed. While membership of the House of Commons had been, nominally at least,[1] limited to Anglicans, and excluded all dissenters – Catholic and Protestant alike – it was just possible to maintain that Parliament was not merely the supreme law-giving body, but also the supreme governing body of the Established Church – a fiction made slightly more plausible by the presence of the Bench of Bishops in the House of Lords. Now the introduction of some sixty Irish Catholic MPs, many of whom were deeply resentful of the privileges previously exercised by the Protestants, had demolished the last shreds of this notion's credibility.

In 1833 the Church of England was, in effect, a department of government. It was technically subject to the will of a Parliament, which, if not

---

[1] As so often, English practice had come to differ from the clear letter of the law. The common custom of 'occasional conformity' meant that if a Member of Parliament, or indeed any holder of civic office, was seen to be at an act of worship in an Anglican church one Sunday in the year, he would be deemed to be a member of the Established Church, even if it was well known that he attended somewhere else (or even nowhere else) for the remaining fifty-one Sundays.

exactly democratically elected, was now catholic enough (with a small 'c') to include both non-conformists and a substantial number of the Irish variety with the large 'C'. Previously, from the Reformation in 1534 until the new Liberal reforming government of 1832, ecclesiastical disputes had been settled by Courts set up on an ad hoc basis by the Sovereign, exercising the Royal Supremacy instituted by Henry VIII. Appeals from the Archbishop's Courts went to the Crown in Chancery, which, in turn, appointed a Court of Delegates which (in matters which did not 'touch the King') was supreme. In 1832, however, this royal prerogative was taken from the Crown and passed to a Judicial Committee of the Privy Council, of which only the Lord Chancellor himself was obliged to be a member of the Anglican Church.[2]

If the obvious problems inherent in this arrangement (which Keble had prophesied in 1833) were to come to a crisis in 1850 in the intricacies of the Gorham Case, it was more immediately evident in 1832 that the new Whig Government, with the support of the newly elected Irish MPs, was prepared to use its majority to sweep away other privileges of the Church of Ireland. Ten out of twenty-two Irish bishoprics were abolished, and proposals were made for the removal of the tithing system by which an impoverished Irish Catholic peasantry had been made to contribute some £750,000 (perhaps £1.5 billion in today's terms) a year towards the Protestant Church's upkeep.[3]

Where many saw in this only natural justice, others, like Francis Newman, John Henry's brother, saw it rather as final proof 'that the Anglican Church was the creature of the State'.[4] In this crisis of identity, John Keble's Oxford Assize Sermon of 14 July 1833, 'National Apostacy', oblique as it may seem to modern readers, was seen by many as a rallying call:

The point really to be so considered is, whether, according to the coolest estimate, the fashionable liberality of this generation be not ascribable, in great measure, to the same temper which led the Jews voluntarily to set about degrading themselves

---

[2] See H.P. Liddon's Preface to Keble's *Difficulties in the Relations between Church and State* (1850) (Parker, 1877), pp. v–vi.
[3] These reforms, together with the disestablishment of the Church of Ireland, would wait for another thirty years to be completed. See Geoffrey Faber, *Oxford Apostles* (Faber and Faber, 1933), p. 352. For these and other facts and statistics I have relied not merely on Faber, but on Georgina Battiscombe's *John Keble: A Study of Limitations* (Constable, 1963), and David Newsome's, *The Parting of Friends* (John Murray, 1966). See also Stephen Prickett, *Romanticism and Religion: The Tradition of Coleridge and Wordsworth in the Victorian Church* (Cambridge University Press, 1976).
[4] Francis William Newman, *Contributions Chiefly to the Early History of the Late Cardinal Newman, with Comments by his Brother, F.W. Newman* (Kegan Paul, Trench, Trübner & co., 1891), p. 35

to a level with the idolatrous Gentiles? And, if it be true any where, that such enactments are forced on the Legislature by public opinion, is APOSTACY too hard a word to describe the temper of that nation?[5]

By the time it was published, only eight days later, on 22 July, the proposed changes to the Church of Ireland had become law, and Keble was already able to point to the first of the dire consequences he had foretold:

Since the following pages were prepared for the press, the calamity, in anticipation of which they were written, has actually overtaken this portion of the Church of GOD. The legislature of England and Ireland (the members of which are not even bound to profess belief in the Atonement,) this body has virtually usurped the commission of those whom our SAVIOUR entrusted with at least one voice in making ecclesiastical laws, on matters wholly or partly spiritual.[6]

For those 'high-church' Tories who had never been happy with the 1688 settlement, with its assumption that the descendants of the Elector of Hanover, who ruled not by Divine Right, but only by the will of Parliament, could also be the Head of the Church of England and Defender of the Faith, the changes instigated by the Whig reform Parliament raised questions at the very heart of the relationship of Church and State. 'What answer,' asked Keble, 'can we make henceforth to the partisans of the Bishop of Rome, when they taunt us with being a mere Parliamentary Church?'[7] What, now, was the Church of England? Did a body claimed by its enemies to be merely the convenient vehicle for Henry VIII's divorces, and the enrichment of a grasping Tudor nouveau-aristocracy, have any real historical legitimacy as a Protestant Episcopal Church? What were its antecedents? How, in other words, did its tradition relate to history?

For those like Keble, and his Oxford associates, Richard Hurrell Froude, H.P. Liddon, John Henry Newman, or Edward Bouverie Pusey, these were vital questions on which the future of their Church depended, and it was to answer precisely these questions that the Oxford Series, 'Tracts for the Times' (1833–41), together with a more substantial historical series, 'The Library of the Fathers' (begun in 1835), were created. Explicitly designed to remind Anglicans of their catholic inheritance from the early church, the Tracts were intended as a defence against the excesses of Reformation Protestantism and contemporary evangelical neglect for the traditions of

---

[5] John Keble: *National Apostacy, A Sermon Preached in St Mary's, Oxford, before his Majesty's Judges of Assize, Sunday July 14, 1833* (Parker, 1833), p. 16.
[6] Ibid., 'Advertisement', p. iii.   [7] Ibid., p. iv.

the institutional Church.[8] Though both enterprises were couched in the language of the Vincentian Canon,[9] claiming to be about the very central doctrines of the historic Church – what all Christians at all times everywhere had believed – one aspect of this, at least, was very untraditional: Newman and his associates supported their claims on a solid basis of detailed historical scholarship. In another sense, however, their work was deeply traditional: in a time of epistemological crisis they were, like all their predecessors in search of tradition, reading back into the past their own concerns, thus implicitly denigrating the pre-Nicene Church, and finding in mediaeval Catholicism the seeds of a new synthesis on which the Anglican settlement might be based.

What was less immediately noticed in the these years of ecclesiastical and legal turmoil of the 1830s and 1840s was that the idea of 'tradition' was itself again coming under radical examination. Though it seems an obvious point, it is worth noting the inexorable progression by which what was initially an essentially legal dispute moved into a debate over the nature of the Church itself. The idea of tradition, which had begun largely as an assumption of the Apostolic Episcopal succession, rapidly involved not merely the Tracts themselves (with their own internal dynamic that was to lead many to Rome before Newman's eventual reception – or, in contemporary jargon, 'perversion' – in 1845), but the interpretation of Church history implicit in such projects as the 'Lives of the English Saints', and the aesthetics of worship. All three elements of this tradition – Apostolic succession, Church history, and aesthetics – were widely caricatured and misunderstood, then as now. It is easy, for instance, to mock the author of the 'Life of St Neot', who concluded, with an honesty even more commendable than his piety, 'and that is all, and, indeed, rather more than all that is known about the life of the blessed St Neot'; or the 'smells and bells' of ritualists – which were nearly as much despised by Keble and Newman as by their evangelical critics. Yet there was behind such ecclesiastical kitsch a genuine thirst for historical truth about the Church that had been missing for generations – and which was, in the end, to affect the Catholic Church as much as its Protestant rival.[10]

For the so-called 'Tractarians' the question of the meaning of 'tradition' was now clearly vital. Yet it presented problems so large that it is clear that

---

[8] For an extended account of Catholic–Protestant relations in nineteenth-century England, see Michael Wheeler, *The Old Enemies: Catholic and Protestant in Nineteenth-Century English Culture* (Cambridge University Press, 2006).

[9] Following the formula of Vincent of Lerins: *Quod semper, quod ubique, quod ab omnibus.*

[10] See Prickett, *Romanticism and Religion.*

few of them understood immediately what a minefield they had encountered. Keble himself had made no direct appeal to tradition in his 1833
sermon. On the one hand was the Roman, post-Tridentine, meaning: that
tradition had been laid down by the teaching of the Catholic Church, and
that its truth was guaranteed by that teaching. In other words: traditions
in the plural, and tradition in the singular, were indistinguishable from the
rest of the Church's teaching, and could not therefore be separated from
the deposit of faith as a whole. In 1833, at least, none of the Tractarians
was prepared to go this far – not least because to do so was immediately to
admit the illegitimacy of the Anglican *via media*, the so-called distinctive
'middle way' between the Roman Catholics and the Bible-based Protestant
non-conformist sects. These rejected Bishops, the Apostolic succession,
and the idea of tradition altogether, and sought to model themselves
upon their (unmediated) idea of the early New Testament Church. Yet,
without that dogmatic connotation of 'tradition', what else was there in
the English inheritance but the idea of the essentially unreliable verbally
transmitted source that we have traced through the preceding chapters?
Bishop Phillpotts, the formidable 'Henry of Exeter', was one of the few
High Churchmen to see some of these problems in advance. In his 1839
Charge to his diocesan clergy he gives a very nuanced defence of tradition,
challenging those who would denigrate it, while carefully distancing himself from the extremes of Tractarianism.[11]

For the Tractarians' opponents, on the other hand, the perceived unreliability of tradition did not, of course, present a problem – indeed, for
them it exposed the essential weakness of the position of Roman Catholics
and Tractarians alike. As early as 1819, Edward Hawkins, a Fellow, and
later to be Provost, of Oriel College, had staked out his position in his
Dissertation upon the Use and Importance of Unauthoritative Tradition.[12]
Tradition, though not valueless, is taken throughout with its now-familiar
eighteenth-century connotations of primitiveness and historical unreliability. This is a point he returned to in a sermon of 1830. 'We [unlike the
Romish Church], acknowledge the Scriptures as the only rule of faith, and
appeal to no uncertain traditions in proof of Christian doctrines.'[13]

---

[11] Henry Phillpots (Bishop of Exeter), *Charge to the Clergy of the Diocese of Exeter*, for August,
September, and October, 1839 (John Murray, 1839), pp. 73–7.

[12] Edward Hawkins, *A Dissertation upon the Use and Importance of Unauthoritative Tradition as an
Introduction to the Christian Doctrines; Including the Substance of A Sermon Preached before the
University of Oxford*, May 31, 1818 (W. Baxter for J. Parker, 1818).

[13] Edward Hawkins, *Christianity not the Religion either of the Bible only, or of the Church*: A Sermon
Preached at Maldon, July 28, 1830, at the Primary Visitation of Charles James Blomfield, Bishop
of London (Parker, 1830), p. 15.

In 1838, Hawkins came out against the whole notion of ecclesiastical tradition in even stronger terms:

On observing how common it is for men of all countries and names, whether Christians, Jews, or Mahometans, to receive the religion of their fathers, I have again and again asked myself, whether I too was not a slave? whether I too was not blindly walking in the path of tradition, and yielding myself as passively as others to an hereditary faith?[14]

By 1842, no doubt as the result of almost a decade of polemical struggle with the Tractarians, this metaphor of a false trail had hardened still further into the actual suggestion of 'false report'.

It is no act of Christian faith to believe a point of Ecclesiastical History which cannot be proved. How many are there in England who have heard the traditionary rumour of an objection to the Succession of Bishops in this Reformed Church, who know not, and cannot know, any thing of its refutation. And what if, many centuries later, the tradition of the objection should outlive the historical evidence by which it is disproved?[15]

Reading Keble or Newman in the early 1830s there would seem to be little disagreement between them, their eighteenth-century forerunners, or their ecclesiastical opponents over what they meant by the word 'tradition' itself. It still signified an essentially oral sequence of transmission, with no real proof of veracity. But though Herder had clearly made no impression on Oxford at this time, it is important to remember that Keble and Newman, the two most important religious thinkers of the 1830s and 1840s, were also both poets. Keble was already famous as the author of *The Christian Year* (the best-selling poetry book of the century) well before the Assize Sermon of 1833, and any account of his thought that fails to stress the importance of both *Tract Eighty Nine*, and the *Lectures on Poetry*, misunderstands the degree to which the tradition of the Church had always been for Keble as much an aesthetic as a legal or theological one. Newman, the author of such popular poems as 'Lead Kindly Light', and, later, 'Praise to the Holiest in the Height', from the longer poem, *The Dream of Gerontius*, was no less aesthetically inclined. Both had been heavily influenced by their romantic predecessors, especially Coleridge and Wordsworth, and had inherited from them an idea of the Church which was essentially poetic.[16] Religion and aesthetics

---

[14] Edward Hawkins, *The Duty of Private Judgement*, A Sermon Preached before the University of Oxford, Nov. 11, 1838 (J.H. Parker, 1838), p. 29.
[15] Edward Hawkins, *The Apostolical Succession*, A Sermon Preached in the Chapel of Lambeth Palace, Sunday, February 27, 1842 (B. Fellowes/J.H. Parker, 1842), p. 15.
[16] See Prickett, *Romanticism and Religion*, Chs. 4 and 7.

met not merely in forms of worship, but also in the belief that the unity of the Church itself was best understood by means of aesthetic analogies.

'It would be hard to believe,' declares Keble in the *Lectures on Poetry*, that poetry and theology 'would have proved such true allies unless there was a hidden tie of kinship between them.'[17] 'Poetry ... supplies a rich wealth of similes whereby a pious mind may supply and remedy, in some sort, its powerlessness of speech.'[18] It is the proper medium or vehicle of religious experience because it does not make direct statements (which the limitations of human language would render impossible) but through its symbols, which express the hidden inwardness of religion: 'In short, Poetry lends Religion her wealth of symbols and similes: Religion restores these again to Poetry, clothed with so splendid a radiance that they appear to be no longer merely symbols, but to partake (I might almost say) of the nature of sacraments.'[19] The echoes of Coleridge's description of symbols in the appendix to *The Statesman's Manual* – published less than twenty years before – are obvious.[20] So, indeed, is Newman's gloss on this idea written now not as a Tractarian, but as a Catholic:

It is sometimes asked whether poets are not more commonly found external to the Church than among her children; and it would not surprise us to find the question answered in the affirmative. Poetry is the refuge of those who have not the Catholic Church to flee to and repose upon, for the Church herself is the most sacred and august of poets. Poetry, as Mr Keble lays it down in his University Lectures on the subject, is a method of relieving the overburdened mind: it is a channel through which emotion finds expression, and that a safe regulated expression. Now what is the Catholic Church, viewed in her human aspect, but a discipline of the affections and passions?[21]

---

[17] John Keble, *Lectures on Poetry*, trs. E. K. Francis, 2 vols. (Oxford University Press, 1912), Vol. II, pp. 479–80.

[18] Ibid., Vol. II, p. 581.   [19] Ibid., Vol. II, p. 480.

[20] For Coleridge, the narratives of the Bible are:

the living educts of the imagination; of that reconciling and mediatory power, which incorporating the Reason in images of the Sense, and organising (as it were) the flux of the Senses, by the permanence and self-circling energies of the Reason, gives birth to a system of symbols, harmonious in themselves, and consubstantial with the truths, of which they are the *conductors* ... Hence ... the sacred book is worthily intitled *the* WORD OF GOD.

Similarly, the poetic symbol

is characterised by a translucence of the special in the Individual, or of the General in the Especial, or of the Universal in the General. Above all by the translucence of the Eternal in and through the Temporal. It always partakes of the Reality which it renders intelligible; and while it enunciates the whole, abides itself as a living part in that Unity, of which it is the representative.

S.T. Coleridge, 'The Statesman's Manual', *Lay Sermons*, ed. R.J. White (Routledge, 1972), pp. 28–30.

[21] J.H. Newman, 'Keble', *Essays, Critical and Historical*, 9th edn, 2 Vols. (Longman, 1890), Vol. II, p. 442.

Small wonder that Bishop Blomfield in his *Charge to the Clergy of the Diocese of London* in 1846 should have inveighed as much against those – especially apparently women – who 'seem to have been misled by the treacherous light of a poetical mysticism, following the guidance, not of their reason but of imagination', as against those who (he alleged) had remained in the Anglican Church with the express purpose of making converts to Rome.[22]

But given such similar premises, and such similar ecclesiastical opposition, despite the small matter of which Church was the more truly 'poetic', one might imagine that Keble and Newman would hold fundamentally similar views on the nature and meaning of tradition, and its role in the life of the Church. Yet it did not prove to be so. From this common Oxford poetic matrix were to emerge in the end two absolutely opposed interpretations of how aesthetic and ecclesiastical traditions were to be understood.

KEBLE AND THE IDEA OF TRADITION

Between 1833 and 1837 it is clear that Keble's views on the nature of tradition had in fact undergone rapid (though subsequently unacknowledged) change and development. If he had begun to think of tradition in 1833 very much in the eighteenth-century sense of unreliable hearsay, we can trace the subsequent evolution of his thinking through one of the most original pieces of critical writing of the period: his *Lectures on Poetry: De Poeticae vi Medica*, published in 1844, but written between 1832 and 1841 when he was Oxford Professor of Poetry, and more or less at the same time, therefore, as he was developing his theological ideas on tradition.

Though, as we have said, Keble was initially cautious about tradition, using the word in contexts of classical mythology rather than verifiable history, he moves increasingly towards the view that it is, potentially at least, a useful source of extra-textual information. Keble had never been as inherently sceptical as Newman, and in the early 1830s many would have assumed his view of tradition was even closer to that of Rome than his friend. But in the *Lectures on Poetry* any belief in the value of tradition comes across more as intelligent scholarship than as blind obedience. Simply because there is no external pressure to believe in the truth of an

---

[22] Charles James Blomfield (Bishop of London), *Charge to the Clergy of the Diocese of London*, 2nd edn (B. Fellowes, 1846), pp. 20; 15.

aesthetic idea, a Herderian valuation of tradition as an expression of folk wisdom becomes easier to accept. Thus, he writes, 'it has long since been a traditional canon of criticism that the more sculptors show of poetic conception, the more warmly they are applauded; and that, certainly, sculptures are far closer akin to Poetry than paintings are'.[23]

For Keble tradition is, therefore, neither more nor less than the unwritten or extra-textual sources from any period – sometimes blatantly mythological, but more often a deposit of information whose veracity should be trusted unless there is clear evidence to the contrary. On the Greek dramatists, for instance, he comments that:

Assuredly, Euripides seems to have willingly sacrificed, not only polished phrase, but even the signs of a lofty spirit, rather than admit the least swerving from the simple and unvarnished truth of things; and to such a degree, that one may perhaps not unfairly say as to the whole body and range of his poetry, what, as tradition goes, he himself urged in extenuation of the quality of his characters: namely, that he had painted them as in deed and truth they are; Sophocles as they ought to be.[24]

But perhaps most interesting is Keble's appreciation of Virgil's respect for the existing Roman traditions concerning the underworld:

And we know there is no topic more fitted to test such reverent modesty than the problem of divine retribution and the last great dread place of doom of all; so much, then, the more worthy of honour is Virgil, who with a religious self-restraint has superadded nothing of his own to the traditional beliefs concerning this dread place of doom, but has simply touched with his poetic power the conceptions commonly handed down.[25]

Somewhere along the line, one feels, Dante's Virgil has so appropriated the original Latin poet that Keble seems to be admiring Virgil as a vehicle of Christian tradition rather than pagan learning.

But in matters of religion, what is 'handed down' has a much greater compulsion. In an 1836 sermon he returns to what he sees as the original Latin meaning of 'tradition' as a deposit, or inheritance, to be passed on from generation to generation. This statement was evidently important enough – and popular enough – to be later re-issued first with an extensive 'Postscript' of supporting notes and evidence, and finally with his *Tract 78* on the Vincentian Canon. 'Tradition,' he argues here, constitutes nothing more nor less than the deposit of faith entrusted by the disciples to the next generation of their followers. This is the reference to the 'charge' of

---

[23] Keble, *Lectures on Poetry*, Vol. I, p. 42.   [24] Ibid., Vol. II, p. 237.   [25] Ibid., Vol. II, p. 463.

doctrine referred to in the First Epistle of Timothy (1 Tim. 1.3; 6.14.20), Keble writes:

Upon the whole, we may assume with some confidence that the good thing left in Timothy's charge, thus absolutely to be kept at all events, was the treasure of apostolical doctrines and church rules: the rules and doctrines which made up the charter of CHRIST's kingdom. [26]

Separated out from later ecclesiastical accretions and the abuses of Romanism, this deposit is complete and perfect in itself. This 'deposit in question is spoken of, not as an incomplete thing on its progress towards perfection, but as something so wholly sufficient, so unexceptionally accurate, as to require nothing but fidelity in its transmitters'. [27] It is, he argues, the peculiar privilege of the Protestant Episcopal Churches – and the Anglican Church in particular – to have been entrusted with the original charge: [28]

Thus the reverence of the Latin Church for tradition, being applied unscrupulously, and without the necessary check from Scripture, to opinions and practices of a date comparatively recent, has led a large portion of Christendom to disuse and contempt, not of Scripture only, but of that real and sure tradition, which they might and ought to have religiously depended upon. [29]

There can, he insists, be no alterations, developments, or modifications to this charge, and he warns, specifically, against 'the fatal error of treating theology like any human science, as a subject in which every succeeding age might be expected to advance on the former'. [30]

St Paul, writing to the Thessalonians, discourages every intrusion of speculative doctrine . . . And then he proceeds, 'Wherefore, brethren, stand fast, and hold the traditions which ye have been taught, whether by word or our epistle.' . . . Observe, again, the phraseology of the Apostle, how it is formed throughout upon the supposition that in the substance of the faith there is no such thing as improvement, discovery, evolution of new truths; none of those processes, which are the pride of human reason and knowledge, find any place here.' [31]

In religion there was no such thing as progress – only a constant danger of falling away, through human pride and ignorance, from the full and

---

[26] John Keble, 'Primitive Tradition Recognised in Holy Scripture'. A Sermon preached in the Cathedral Church of Winchester, at the Visitation of the Worshipful and Reverend William Dealtry D.D. Chancellor of the Diocese, September 27, 1836, p. 20.

[27] Ibid., p. 23.

[28] A view widely repeated: see also William Dealtry (Chancellor of the diocese of Winchester), *On the Importance of Caution in the Use of Certain Familiar Words*. A Charge delivered in the autumn of 1843 at the Visitation in Hampshire (Hatchard, 1843), p. 41. I owe this reference to Dr Bob Tennant.

[29] Keble, 'Primitive Tradition Recognised in Holy Scripture', p. 45.

[30] Ibid., p. 48.   [31] Ibid., pp. 47–8.

sufficient truths entrusted by Christ and the Apostles to his Church. It was a belief that he carried into every part of his teaching. 'Don't be original', he would solemnly admonish his bemused students at Oxford.[32]

Not content with taking his idea of tradition back to the original Latin root of the word in the idea of a deposit, however, Keble also links it with the accompanying legal analogy:

> If any one ask, how we ascertain them [the primitive, unwritten system of the Church]; we answer, by application of the well-known rule, Quod semper, quod ubique, quod ab omnibus: Antiquity, Universality, Catholicity: tests similar to those which jurists are used to apply to the common or unwritten laws of the realm. If a maxim or custom can be traced back to a time whereof the memory of man runneth not to the contrary; if it pervade all the different courts, established in different provinces for the administration of justice; and, thirdly, if it be generally acknowledged in such sort, that contrary decisions have been disallowed and held invalid: then, whatever the exceptions to it may be, it is presumed to be part and parcel of our common law. On principles exactly analogous, the Church practices and rules above mentioned, and several others, ought, we contend, apart from all Scripture evidence, to be received as traditionary or common law ecclesiastical. They who contend that the very notion of such tradition is a mere dream and extravagance: who plead against it the uncertainty of history, the loss or probable corruption of records, the exceptions, deviations, interruptions which have occurred through the temporary prevalence of tyranny, heresy, or schism; must, if they would be consistent, deny the validity of the most important portion of the laws of this, and of most other old countries.[33]

This conception of law as totally unchanging system might have had the support of the great eighteenth-century Oxford legal authority, Sir William Blackstone (1723–80) who had argued in his *Commentaries on the Laws of England* (1765–9) a similar case – and, indeed, Blackstone may well have been in Keble's mind. Nevertheless, to argue for such legal stasis – even in common law – during the Whig ministry of the reformed House of Commons in the 1830s, and at a period of some of the greatest legal changes in English history, required an extraordinarily narrow and rigid cast of mind – and this, by all accounts, Keble certainly had.

He could not bear to associate with those who disagreed with him in any way. J.A. Froude, brother of the Tractarian, Richard Hurrell Froude, observed that 'If you did not agree with him, there was something morally wrong with you.' For Tom Mozley, Newman's brother-in-law, 'There was no getting on with Keble, without entire agreement,

---

[32] See Prickett, *Romanticism and Religion*, p. 93.
[33] Keble, 'Primitive Tradition Recognised in Holy Scripture', p. 32.

that is submission. . . . He very soon lost his temper in discussion.'[34] His erstwhile friend, Thomas Arnold, was banned from Keble's house after a theological argument, though his son, Matthew Arnold, the poet, whose theological questionings were far more radical than his father's, was still invited because he was Keble's godson, and therefore had to be admitted, whatever his views.[35]

Perhaps the paradox between Keble's undoubted originality and rigid conservatism is most clearly evident neither in his ecclesiology, nor his poetics, but in his attitude to educational reform: where tradition and history had to find expression in social policy. On 12 June 1839, it was his role, as Professor of Poetry, to give the Crewian Oration at the Oxford Commemoration ceremony at which William Wordsworth was presented for an honorary degree. The account of this occasion is given by Keble's first biographer, J.T. Coleridge:

> The Oration commences with pointing out a close analogy between the Church and the University as institutions, and after tracing this out in several particulars, notices a supposed and very important failure of the analogy in respect to the poorer classes, to whom the gates of the latter are not practically open, nor instruction afforded. This failure the orator then proceeds to explain and neutralize so far as he is able.[36]

This passage, concluding with Keble's graceful tribute to Wordsworth himself as the poet of the poor, and its tumultuous reception, has become one of the most famous accounts of Keble's attitude not merely towards poverty, but in particular towards the virtual exclusion of the poor from higher education in general and Oxford in particular. Its ambiguity has been read as symptomatic of an ambivalence towards education and social privilege that was endemic in the Oxford Movement right from its beginnings.

Examination of the original manuscript of Keble's speech, however, tells a very different story.[37] In the first place it is clear that J.T. Coleridge himself must have been the source of all previous references to this speech.

---

[34] Thomas Mozley, *Reminiscences, Chiefly of Oriel College and the Oxford Movement*, 3 vols. (Longman, 1882), Vol. 1, p. 220.

[35] Faber, *Oxford Apostles*, p. 97. The frequency of Matthew's subsequent visits to the Keble household is not recorded.

[36] J.T. Coleridge, *Memoir of the Rev. John Keble* (Parker, 1869), p. 248.

[37] The speech was never published. All we have are Keble's own lecture notes – written in his private Latin shorthand. I am deeply indebted to the late Paul Jeffries-Powell of Glasgow University's Department of Humanity who produced from these notes a readable Latin text, and an English translation.

Though in passing he refers to Dr Wordsworth's printing of 'it in the original' this seems only to refer to the paragraph directly concerned with
William Wordsworth. For the rest we are apparently reliant either on
Coleridge's own recollections of the occasion twenty-six years later, or on
notes he had made at the time. Either way, his summary of its contents was
selective to the point of being totally misleading. Keble had indeed noted
that Oxford was in no sense open to the poor, but so far from proceeding
to 'explain and neutralize' this failure, as Coleridge suggests, he had gone
on to say something very much more pertinent:

First, I pray you, recall and re-imagine what was the shape and figure of academic
things, at the time when we began to enjoy a firm succession of records. There
were more than thirty thousand Clerks: some attended to learning here, some
wandered all over England, in such a condition of life, for the most part, that
the phrase became proverbial: Oxford means poor; while meantime aristocratic
youths despised and detested all pursuits except soldiering.

Poverty, for Keble, was never an accidental quality of Oxford in its early
days. Citing page after page of evidence, he argues that poverty, and its
concomitant, unworldliness, was actually an ideal of the founding patrons
of the various colleges: as it were, part of the platonic idea of Oxford. Here
he is on the foundation of his own college:

And I have a superstitious dread of leaving out at this point the name of the founder of Oriel; who of his piety made sure that this eloquent rule was sworn to,
that none should be received into his number 'except the decent, the chaste, the
lowly, and the needy'. No need for more: almost everybody bears witness that it
was for the sake of the poor that they had these houses founded; right up to the
time when the ceremonies of religion, and the whole spirit of literature and politics was changed, and the custom gradually grew up of allowing access to the
Academy for the talented rich.

Once again, ecclesiology is paramount: the mediaeval idea of a university, centring on poverty and learning, had been fatally undermined by
the materialism of the Reformation. Nonetheless, Keble's role-call of poverty, godliness, and good learning does not stop at the sixteenth century.
Samuel Johnson, who 'was not so far removed from true piety and ancient
faith', stands as a shining witness that even in the eighteenth century the
old ideals had not been quite extinguished.

Significantly, there is no discernable attempt in J.T. Coleridge's terms
to 'neutralize' the failure of nineteenth-century Oxford to open its doors
to the poor. Immediately after the enconium on Wordsworth somewhat

floridly translated and quoted by Coleridge, Keble returns to his main theme of the true calling of the University:

So he who would pay his debt of gratitude, let him to the best of his ability defend that part especially of our discipline which is contained in a worthy and thrifty mode of life; let nothing profuse, nothing immoderate, nothing voluptuary be readily allowed to cross this threshold, within which dwell the poor; and in the tutelage of the poor are honoured the testaments of the dead.

That Alfred Doolittle might have been somewhat sceptical of this sentimentalized portrait of the 'deserving poor' is beside the point. As the following paragraphs make clear, Keble is not just paying lip-service to a lost ideal. Contained within the rhetoric of his peroration is a perfectly practical programme to realize this dream.

Therefore we will call such people back as best we can, and devote ourselves to ensuring that since the waters have been, as it were, divided, our Academy may share its blessings with the commonality and the tribe of the needy. I would wish there to go forth from this place men who shall lead colonies, so to speak, (planted) on every shore of our (native) Britain, nay, and of her provinces. Let the Academy join itself more closely with the views of those who, at this very moment, have by divine inspiration (for I shall speak boldly) formed the plan of propagating in each town not only elementary schools or places to learn a profitable trade, leaving aside the lecture-rooms of a wordy and empty philosophy, and creating those schools which nurture servants and children worthy of Holy Church.

At this very moment, I say, there have gone forth from the bosom of this Academy – and may they succeed and prosper – distinguished architects of this policy; and I pray that our Lord may favour their enterprise, and that he may bring it about, day by day, that this dear and kindly mother of ours may reflect the (true) image of his Church.

For Keble the time had come. Through poets like Wordsworth, the hated Reform Bill of 1832–3, and the whole process of early nineteenth-century social agitation that was yet to culminate in Chartism, the poor, like a new Israel, have been led out of bondage to the shores of the Red Sea. There could be no return to the old order. The social transformation that had begun six years earlier must be met not by stubborn resistance, but by constructive change. In particular, the university must reform itself. There should be set up a system of scholarships to allow scholars from any class of society to attend it. In short, Oxford must be re-invigorated academically from top to bottom. But for Keble the idea of 're-forming' meant quite literally a return to the past – the pre-Reformation Oxford. As Keble has already made clear, admitting the poor with a desire to learn has an inevitable concomitant: excluding the idle rich, the nouveau-aristocrats, and descendants of the Tudor profiteers who made fortunes from the dissolution of the monasteries, and had no real desire for either the disciplines or the piety of the old learning.

Moreover, it is clear from that metaphor of 'colonies' that the Latin *Academia* is not simply to be translated by the word 'University' let alone by implication, 'Oxford University'. What he seems to mean by 'colonies' is nothing short of a nation-wide system of provincial universities, presumably on the lines of newly founded Durham University, and King's College, London, which will make the ideal of Godliness and good learning available to all who really wanted it sufficiently to take the path of academic poverty. Even more interesting, perhaps, is the hint that Oxford might stand at the apex of such a national system – providing, in effect, what might nowadays be described as a 'graduate school'. He does not, of course, mention Cambridge – presumably already too far gone down the paths of secularism and the physical sciences to be within the scope of his proposal.

A marginal note to the manuscript in Keble's handwriting, possibly of later date,[38] clarifies the reference to the 'distinguished architects of this policy' who are named as 'Mr Acland, Mr Mathieson, Mr Wood and others'. Thomas Dyke Acland, was the son of a reforming and philanthropic West-Country MP, a graduate of Christ Church, who had been a Fellow of All Souls from 1831 to 1939. His plans for such a national educational system reaching out from his university were to lead to the establishment of the Oxford Local Examinations syndicate in the 1850s. Gilbert Farquhar Graeme Mathieson had left Oxford without a degree, but after working for a while in the opium trade (which he abandoned on moral grounds) he went on to become private secretary to the Chancellor of the Exchequer and finally Secretary to the Mint. With Acland and Wood he played a central role in the re-invigoration of the National Society for the Education of the Poor – the main educational arm of the Anglican Church. Samuel Wood, the brother of the Earl of Halifax, had been a pupil of both Keble and Newman at Oriel, and continued to work closely with them, as with Acland and Mathieson, to promote Church schools.[39]

---

[38] But, if so, it is probably before 1843, when Wood died.
[39] Here, and in the next paragraphs I am much indebted to James Pereiro's article, 'Tractarians and National Education (1838–1843)', *Victorian Churches and Churchmen*, ed. Sheridan Gilley (Boydell and Brewesr, 2005), pp. 249–78.

Much of the detail of what Keble is advocating reflects the thinking of this group. But his visionary ideas for the reformation of Oxford reach far beyond them. The years leading up to 1839 had produced a ferment of new educational ideas, and in April 1839, only two months before Keble's speech, the Whig Government under Lord John Russell had set up a Parliamentary Commission on Education which had both Acland and Gladstone among its members, and which was still sitting at the time of Keble's speech. Both were to incur great unpopularity with non-conformists and the more radical secularizers by their (successful) rear-guard action to delay the findings of the Commission so that the Church could set up its own system of national education in advance of the government reforms – whose purpose had been to take education out of what it saw as potentially divisive sectarian control.[40]

Since it was in Latin, and could hardly have been meant as a popular rallying call, Keble's Oration was clearly intended to give a force and direction to the social conscience of his university, and of the Oxford Movement, that the former never, and the latter hardly ever achieved. The intention was clearly to support the efforts of Acland and his associates to extend the influence and ethos of Oxford to a much wider circle: and, going beyond their immediate and practically limited objectives, to give a vision of plain living and high thinking that for Keble was essential to the original conception of what a university should be – the direct equivalent for Oxford of the recovery of first principles that he wished to see in the Church. No matter that it was not immediately achievable; neither was his goal of a re-generated Church. One day indeed, in God's good time, there might flourish a Church of England, true to its ancient principles, and co-extensive with a national system of university education, also true to its ancient statutes, and bringing the benefits of university education, as Keble understood it, to all serious-minded scholars. In the meantime, the Oration was on record in much the same way as the Assize Sermon of 1833: a prophetic call for reform and a return to primitive purity. It provided a programme that, with hindsight, suddenly begins to draw together what might otherwise seem to be scattered, uncoordinated, and spasmodic attempts to improve not just primary, but secondary and university education on a national basis. Nathaniel Woodard's systematic attempt from 1847 onwards to found church schools in every region of the country may have been a personal

---

[40] See Bishop Blomfield's 1846 *Charge*, pp. 45–8.

crusade, but it was also no more than Keble's ambitious programme had already laid down.

What went wrong? Why, if this were so, did the Oration fail to ignite his peers in the way the 1833 Sermon had? Why was it later so carefully edited as to make it lose all its revolutionary thrust? The short answer is almost certainly Newman. It was, by coincidence, the very next morning after that Commemoration, 13 June 1839, that Newman began reading about the Monophysites: 'It was during this course of this reading,' he tells us in the *Apologia*, 'that for the first time a doubt came upon me of the tenableness of Anglicanism.'[41] The rest, as they say, is history . . . Writing to Bishop Selwyn in December 1845, just after Newman's defection to Rome, Charles Marriott, sub-Dean of Oriel, commented: 'There has been much talk of extending Education in Oxford. Had it been eighteen months ago, I could have raised money to found a college on strict principles. Now, people are so shaken that I do not think anything can be effected.'

But history is not the story of inevitabilities. Another, quite fortuitous, tragedy had also distracted the energies of the Movement: less than three weeks before that Commemoration of 1839, on 26 May, Pusey's wife had died, and with her much of his personal energy and vitality. With both Pusey and Newman otherwise occupied, Keble's call to reform Oxford and the education system it represented scarcely stood a chance. Samuel Wood died tragically young in 1843. The crisis into which Newman was to plunge the Oxford Movement was to last for the whole of the 1840s, and the Movement that was finally to emerge as the High Church of the 1850s was, in some ways, a very different creature. Not merely had it lost Newman, its most charismatic leader, it had also lost Manning – perhaps the only one of the Tractarians to have any real understanding of, or sympathy for the working-classes. Pusey was by then a shadow of his former self. Moreover, the world of the 1850s was also itself a very different place. Any faint chance there might have been of creating a reformed Anglican Oxford in 1839 was finally dispelled by the Royal Commission of 1851 that was effectively to secularize the institution and to hand control of it from the clergy to a new generation of career dons who were totally to transform it within a generation.

How practical, in any case, was this idea of a university? What kind of institution would Keble and his fellow-Tractarians actually have produced

---

[41] John Henry Newman, *Apologia pro Vita Sua*, ed. M.J. Svalgic, Oxford University Press, 1967, p. 108.

if they had been able to realize their vision? The first thing to note is that despite the ostensible appeal to return to the Middle Ages, this was, like all appeals to tradition, a tactical reading of a disputed past for contemporary purposes. There is something unmistakably Victorian about the implicit social engineering behind this concept of a seamless and comprehensive national system from primary school to graduate school whose only criterion of entry was need – and a desire to learn. Keble says little about curriculum beyond indicating the study of theology and philosophy, but even from those references it is not unreasonable to assume that what we have here is, in effect, a first draft of the nexus of ideas that were to be given final articulate form in Newman's 1852 lectures on a new University of Dublin, eventually to be published as *The Idea of a University*. But from Keble's *Lectures on Poetry*, published only five years after the Crewian Oration, in 1844, it is also a fair assumption that his curriculum would also have included one other very important element – the study of poetry. If on the one hand this recapitulates the education of Plato's philosopher kings outlined in *The Republic*, those same lectures make it clear that this was no empty gesture towards the classical tradition. Keble's poetic canon had included not merely the English classics – Milton, Shakespeare, Spencer, and so on – but living poets, such as Wordsworth, himself, whom he was honouring in this address. Perhaps even more surprisingly, it also included Byron and Shelley – notorious atheists, whose sexual antics had titillated the readers of a British press then, as now, always happy to relay scandal. There is no evidence that Keble shared any of Newman's interest in contemporary science.

More important than speculations on the curriculum, however, is what Keble does not say about his reformed Oxford. First, it is ruthlessly sectarian. This is a point he would have hotly disputed, because for him the National Church could not, by definition, be sectarian. It was the other religious groups, Protestant and Catholic alike, who were 'non-conformist' and sectarian because they had rejected the broad cover of the National Church. The repeal of the Tests Acts, which had hitherto excluded non-conformists from Oxford and Cambridge, only came in the wake of the Royal Commission of 1851 – and was fiercely resisted by the Tractarians. Secondly, and associated with this, there is little evidence that Keble had ever understood the value of freedom of speech and open intellectual debate. We have already mentioned his intolerance of dissent – either at a personal or an ecclesiastical level.

What we have here, in other words, is yet another striking example of Keble's attitude to tradition – on the one hand radical and contemporary, and, on the other, bound rigidly to a particular conception of the past. Behind the call for reform is a desire to re-create an education which, like the deposit of faith entrusted by Timothy to his Church, was a fixed 'deposit', an educational 'charge' to be handed on to future generations. Yet even if there could be no change in the teaching of theology, which unlike other academic studies could not evolve, it is far from clear whether Keble was really thinking of a return to the mediaeval *Trivium* and *Quadrivium* for which Oxford had once been famous.[42] However much he might have been drawn to such a past, his love of romantic poetry pulled in a quite different direction. The fact that he was lecturing on Byron and Shelley in Latin, and even, for good measure, translating Burns's 'My love is like a red, red rose' into Theocritan Greek tells us all.

What Keble (along with many of his Oxford contemporaries, it must be said) never recognized was the degree to which the England of the 1830s was already a highly pluralistic society, where expectations of religious or philosophic conformity could never be assumed – and, in the wake of the 1832 Reform Bill, were totally unrealistic politically. Whether a non-sectarian Christian university which actively engaged with all the doubts, antagonisms, and complexities of the surrounding society would ever have been possible is, of course, still an open question.[43]

In view of this, the fate of Keble's address at the hands of J.T. Coleridge in 1868 takes on a different significance. Coleridge's *Memoir* is the first of a whole series of works that display the old unreformed Oxford in a golden haze of nostalgia. Its purpose is not to show a lost moment of opportunity, but to eulogize a vanished era. Money was already being raised to build the Oxford College that was to bear Keble's name. In a sense, Coleridge's book was less a biography than a hagiography – a fund-raiser for the memorial to a saint, not a plea for allowing the working-class into Oxford. By switching the focus of the address specifically to Wordsworth, Keble's biographer is able to make it seem that it was primarily the tribute of one poet to his master. Wordsworth's death in 1850 was yet another finality sealing off the present from that vanished past. The statement that Keble 'explains and neutralises' the 'supposed failure' of Oxford to admit

---

[42] The *Trivium* (Grammar, Logic, and Rhetoric), is the thirteenth-century ancestor of what would now be considered the 'liberal arts'; the *Quadrivium* (Arithmetic, Astronomy, Geometry, and Music) was intended to be the foundation for the study of philosophy and theology.

[43] The attempt by Baylor University, in Waco, Texas, in the twenty-first century, to create a 'Christian University' as a diverse research institution rather than the 'Christian' liberal arts College already common in the USA, is an interesting experiment which, on present showing, must be judged a failure.

the poorer classes is part of the process of gilding a past whose importance is already more symbolic than actual. In so doing, of course, he is, consciously or unconsciously, re-writing the history of the Movement and making his hero less worldly, less socially aware, less prophetic than in fact he turns out to have been. It also prevents us from seeing what just might have been a serious proposal for one of the boldest social and educational experiments of the last 300 years. Finally, of course, it represents yet another example of re-inventing a tradition.

CHAPTER 9

Newman and the development of tradition

HAMPDEN'S INSENSIBLE PROGRESSION

So much has lately been said and written on the subject of Tradition, that it might seem almost superfluous to have selected it for peculiar notice from this Chair. But the very fact of the increased and marked attention which questions relating to Tradition have attracted among us lately, renders it more imperative on me... that I should... bring before your consideration what appears to me to be the true doctrine of our Church on this most important subject.[1]

Renn Dickson Hampden (1793–1868) was perhaps the most controversial Regius Professor of Divinity ever to have held that office at Oxford. After his Bampton Lectures of 1832, which were accused of Arianism,[2] his name was anathema to the Tractarians. At the centre of the dispute were two conflicting ideas of tradition. Hampden wished to separate early, pre-Nicene, theology from what he saw as scholastic additions by the later Church, and, stress the 'primitive truth' of the earlier doctrine. For Newman and his fellow-Tractarians, however, it rapidly became clear that, in the words of his brother, Francis Newman, 'the scholastic *additions* were the most valuable part, namely, that which he oddly called *tradition*'.[3] Hampden's use of the word, in contrast, followed the standard eighteenth-century view that tradition was a verbally transmitted and essentially unreliable source of information. Like many who held such views, he was quick to cite earlier authorities – in what was in itself rapidly evolving into a substantial interpretive tradition.[4]

---

[1] R.D. Hampden [Regius Professor of Divinity, University of Oxford], *A Lecture on Tradition*, Read at the Divinity School, Thursday March 7, 1839, 5th edn (B. Fellows, 1842), p. 3.

[2] A fourth-century heresy that held that the Son was not co-eternal with the Father.

[3] F.W. Newman, *Contributions Chiefly to the Early History of the Late Cardinal Newman, with Comments by his Brother, F.W. Newman* (Kegan Paul, Trench, Trübner & co., 1891), p. 83.

[4] See, for instance, Hampden's use of John Davison (1777–1834: Fellow of Oriel, 1800):

For all that is commonly asserted of those primary revelations concerning the mystery of our Redemption, as having been given to the First Ages, and conveyed down, in succession, to the

Hampden, however, produces one innovation in his 1839 *Lecture on Tradition* that, in retrospect, may have been highly significant. He was by no means the first to argue for the progressive nature of Christianity – the Old Testament had always been read as leading towards the New, and Newman had been doing nothing new in his 1836 essay on 'Apostolical Tradition' by highlighting such arguably post-biblical doctrines as the Trinity.[5] But most authorities also agreed that the New Testament revelation was complete as it stood.[6] Hampden, however, allows his imagery to suggest more than his doctrine. We get the first clue to this in his deployment of what, as we have seen, was already a commonly used image of tradition: that of a stream or river. At first sight, the references seem unremarkable. Thus tradition is constantly flowing: 'in the stream of Tradition, as in the successions of Time itself, there may be no pause. . . '. In this sense it becomes a metaphor for the unfolding of revelation, from 'the passing, ever-flowing Tradition of the truth. . . '. But what emerges, perhaps more clearly than ever before, is a temporalizing of truth: that the 'truth' to, say, the nineteenth century, is perhaps more rich, more complex than the truth as revealed to the early Church. One can understand how such a suggestion of progressive development of understanding might well lend itself to accusations of Arianism from Tractarian opponents such as Keble. But, as we shall see, it was an idea that, once uttered, rapidly found itself a place in the psyche of the period.

Also significant is Hampden's sense that the meaning of 'tradition' now, more than ever, required careful definition as a prelude to the kind of debate already tearing Oxford apart. He writes:

Following Ages of the Ancient Church, is an admission, that great truths, beyond the record of Holy Writ, truths of pure and authoritative revelation, were entrusted to that extraneous channel of conveyance; and that there existed a *second*, a *collateral Canon*, of Unwritten Doctrine. An admission that seems not more derogatory to the Scripture, than inconsistent with the main maxim of our Protestant Belief. Before the rise of the Written Scripture, Tradition, of necessity, was the record of Faith. But since those primary revelations, not now extant in Holy Writ, are said to have been transmitted to the Following Ages for their instruction, after the Mosaic Scripture was given, there would still be the flaw and opprobrium of an Unwritten Faith in the Ancient Church of Israel; and that which we disclaim for our own Church we ought not to impute to theirs. So long as we pretend, that they divided their faith between Scripture and Tradition, we give the Romanist the Mosaic Church on his side.

John Davison, *Inquiry into the Origin and Intent of Primitive Sacrifice* (1825), *Lecture on Tradition*, p. 7.
[5] See below, p. 172.
[6] See, for instance, John Howson's 1841 Norrisian Prize Essay: 'if there be any law which may be called universal in all that we see around us and within us, it is the law of *continuous progression* . . . Are we to be surprised if we discover a similar law in the Revelation of the Deity? . . . We must not press this consideration too far. Christianity is now perfect and no longer to be regarded as a field for progressive discovery.' John Saul Howson, *Both in the Old and New Testaments Eternal Life is Offered to Mankind through Jesus Christ Only* (Cambridge University Press, 1842), p. 18.

This then would be the primary sense of the term: and it would evidently apply in this sense to any matter whatever, – to institutions, and rites, and ceremonies, as well as to doctrines, – to the volumes of Scripture itself, as well as to the personal oral teaching of the Apostles. The sacred writers of the New Testament would naturally use the term in this extended sense, as it would be suggested to them by the very nature of Judaism, a religion embodied in visible institutions, and rites, and ceremonies transmitted from age to age. The next stage of its meaning involves the notion of succession: and here a most material difference in the use of the term is introduced. For here it applies more properly to unwritten doctrines and institutions. For the Scriptures, being once delivered, are a standing fixed document; and cannot be said to be *perpetuated* by being delivered down. They are perpetuated by their simple existence from the first, and subsequent preservation; and not by virtue of their *transmission* from hand to hand. But oral teachings, and institutions, and rites, vanish with the utterance and the use, and exist only as they are constantly revived and perpetuated by repetition from time to time. This sense, then, the term Tradition would acquire, when, in the lapse of time, the first preachers and teachers of the Gospel had disappeared from the world, and others carried on the delivery of what had been received from them. But the term being now more appropriate to oral teachings and institutions, though not perhaps at once restricted to these, would, in another stage, become the representative of a body of doctrines and rites so transmitted; and Tradition would soon be used in contradistinction to Scripture, in like manner as from the original use of Doctrine to denote *teaching*, we now apply the term to denote *the matter taught*. And hence, last of all, the transition was easy from Tradition, now considered as a distinct class of things belonging to Religion, to Traditions in the plural, to denote the several particulars falling under this head.[7]

In other words, Hampden argues, the existence of a body of oral teaching would naturally move by a kind of insensible – and, indeed, because over many generations, *invisible* – progression from the *act* of teaching, to the *content* of that teaching, and, in an equally insensible progression, that reified content would itself become a counter-weight to written doctrine.

Hampden was (among other things) one of the most able Greek scholars of his generation, and there is little doubt that behind this argument is an awareness of the change in the meaning of the Greek *paradosis* from Platonic oral debate to an ever-increasing reliance on written sources.[8] But, be that as it may, even though the ostensible thrust of his whole argument was towards the standard eighteenth-century Protestant position of discrediting oral tradition as a source of doctrinal deviance and confusion,[9] his actual arguments – and in particular his sense of developing revelation – were, I believe, to have a significant impact on some of

[7] *Lecture on Tradition*, pp. 78–81.   [8] See Introduction, p. 10.   [9] *Lecture on Tradition*, p. 74.

those who had studied his arguments in the greatest detail – his opponents. Of these, undoubtedly the most significant would turn out to be John Henry Newman.

NEWMAN AND THE DYNAMIC OF DOCTRINE

Though Newman, like Keble and Pusey, was clearly inclined to give much greater weight to the evidence of historical tradition in the Church, it is interesting that to begin with, as we have seen, none of them used the word itself in a significantly different sense either from each other, or from the general usage of the period. A hymn of Newman's, written in December 1832, describes, in phrases almost identical to Keble's 'deposit of faith', how the 'Prophets' of the early Church:

> fenc'd the rich bequest He made,
> And sacred hands have safe convey'd
> Their charge from age to age.[10]

Much of Newman's lengthy defence of the 'Apostolical Tradition' in an essay in the *British Critic* of 1836 is devoted to arguing the probability of the historical correctness of traditions emanating from New Testament times.[11] The Divinity of Christ and its logical extension in the Doctrine of the Trinity, he points out, neither of which his opponents like Hampden or Hawkins would be prepared to deny, cannot be explicitly supported by the words of scripture, but rest on the traditions of the early Church, and were only incorporated into the Nicene Creed in the fourth century. He also makes the point that the bishops at Nicea, who were virtually unanimous in holding that this was, and always had been, the belief of the entire historic Church, were otherwise riven with factions, and could agree on little else. Though an effective debating point, this was, of course, a potentially dangerous argument: as his sceptical brother at once saw, if the other beliefs of the first three centuries are mostly discounted because they cannot be made to support later (post-Tridentine) Catholic doctrine, then claiming to be the true inheritor of 'tradition' becomes very problematic. Indeed, Francis Newman's claim is that his brother's basic concern was to justify the re-definition of tradition by the Council of Trent by finding a way of discounting the early Church altogether:[12]

[10] F.W. Newman, *Early History of the Late Cardinal Newman*, p. 56.
[11] John Henry Newman, 'Apostolical Tradition', *Essays Critical and Historical*, 9th edn, 2 vols. (Longman, Green & Co., 1890), Vol. 1 (first published in the *British Critic*, July 1836).
[12] F.W. Newman, *Early History of the Late Cardinal Newman*, p. 71.

My brother has worried me with *Tradition*, and now, by cutting away the first three centuries, he leaves no *Tradition* at all, but only the sectarian broils of fierce fanatics who fought with more or less aid from the unbaptized Constantine . . . I since make sure that in his book on Development he has earned praise for 'subtlety' by defending what to my blunt mind is monstrous: but to deny that he cuts himself off from Tradition is impossible.[13]

What is interesting about J.H. Newman's presentation of this argument, therefore, is the way in which he avoids invoking faith or authority, and supports his case by historical detail, arguing always for overwhelming probability rather than on dogmatic certainty based on the authority of the Church. When this essay was re-published after Newman converted to Catholicism in 1845, he added a footnote explaining that the doctrine of the essay was 'consonant with what I should write upon its subject now'.[14]

A year later than the article on 'Apostolical Tradition', in *Lectures on the Prophetical Office of the Church* (1837), Newman tackles another elephant in a rather crowded room: the political dimension of the debate. To argue in favour of ecclesiastical tradition is not merely to lean towards Rome, but, implicitly, to challenge the political settlement of the 1688 'Glorious Revolution' – of which the contemporary Anglican Church was a part.

These reflections would serve to justify inquiries far beyond the scope of the following Lectures, such, I mean, as bear upon our political and ecclesiastical state; whereas those which will here come into consideration have more reference to religious teaching than to action, – to the Church's influence on her members, one by one, rather than to her right of moving them as a whole. But the distinct portions of the general subject so affect each other, that such points as Church authority, Tradition, the Rule of Faith, and the like, cannot be treated without seeming to entrench upon political principles, consecrated by the associations of the Revolution. It has ever required an apology, since that event, to speak the language of our divines before it; and such an apology is not found in the circumstances of the day, in which all notions, moral and religious, are so unsettled, that every positive truth must be a gain.[15]

But if politics exert a dangerous gravitational pull in theology, they also offer a surprisingly useful commonsense secular analogy:

At this very time a great part of the law of the land is administered under the sanction of such a Tradition; it is not contained in any formal or authoritative code, it depends on custom or precedent. There is no explicit written law, for instance,

---

[13] Ibid., p. 51.   [14] 'Apostolical Tradition', p. 137.
[15] John Henry Newman, *Lectures on the Prophetical Office of the Church, Viewed Relatively to Romanism and Popular Protestantism* (J.G. & F. Rivington, 1837), p. 15. For much of what follows on this work I am greatly indebted to the researches of Dana White.

simply declaring murder to be a capital offence; unless indeed we have recourse to the divine command in the ninth chapter of the book of Genesis. Murderers are hanged by *custom*. Such as this is the Tradition of the Church; Tradition is uniform custom. When the Romanists say they adhere to Tradition, they mean that they believe and act as Christians have always believed and acted; they go by the custom, as judges and juries do. And then they go on to allege that there is this important difference between their custom and all other customs in the world; that the tradition of the law, at least in its details, though it has lasted for centuries upon centuries, any how had a beginning in human appointments; whereas theirs, though it has a beginning too, yet, when traced back, has none short of the Apostles of Christ, and is in consequence of divine not of human authority, – is true and intrinsically binding as well as expedient.[16]

This definition of tradition as 'uniform custom' follows Keble's sermon of the previous year to suggest the connections between tradition and custom we discussed in Chapter 1. The reminder that the law is also a form of tradition is similarly important. Not merely does it take us back to the roots of the word itself, but, as we saw in Chapter 2, it skirts the corollary, that though the law is indeed a tradition, handed on from one generation to the next, it is also in a process of continual evolution – an ordered process for the regulation of change. Though legal 'tradition' is not graced with a capital letter, like the 'Tradition' of the Church, this application of the word is an explicit reminder that there were already in existence traditions for which the normal current connotations of unreliability, hearsay, or folk tales were totally inadequate. It was, moreover, this – almost subversive – idea that tradition could be understood not so much as an inflexible code of belief, but as *a way of embracing change* that was to be central to Newman's next major work, the *Essay on the Development of Christian Doctrine*. This was written in the hiatus between the Anglican world he had just left and the Roman Catholic one not yet entered, and published on the eve of his reception into the Catholic Church in 1845.

Here, however, in his still-Protestant 1837 *Lectures*, Newman revives the image of a river flowing down the years, as a kind of collective unconscious, flowing through the mind and imagination of the Church:

If we ask, why it is that these professed Traditions were not reduced to writing, it is answered that the Christian doctrine, as it has proceeded from the mouth of the Apostles, is too varied and too minute in its details to allow of it. . . . And thus they would account for the indeterminateness on the one hand, yet on the other the accuracy and availableness of their existing Tradition or unwritten Creed. It is latent, but it lives. It is silent, like the rapids of a river, before the rocks

[16] Ibid., pp. 39–40.

intercept it. It is the Church's unconscious habit of opinion and feeling; which she reflects upon, masters, and expresses, according to the emergency. We see then the mistake of asking for a complete collection of the Roman Traditions; as well might we ask for a collection of a man's tastes and opinions on a given subject. Tradition in its fullness is necessarily unwritten; it is the mode in which a society has felt or acted during a certain period, and it cannot be circumscribed any more than a man's countenance and manner can be conveyed to strangers in any set of propositions.

Such are the Traditions to which the Romanists appeal, whether viewed as latent in the Church's teaching, or as passing into writing and being fixed in the decrees of the Councils or amid the works of the ancient Fathers. [17]

What is interesting about this argument is that it makes much more explicit something that has been latent throughout Newman's defence of tradition: that the word is, itself, a metaphor for something so complex, yet real, that it can only be described by a series of other metaphors.

In the 1845 *Essay on the Development of Christian Doctrine* Newman elaborates on this complexity in the image of the river of tradition, used so effectively (though not originated) by Lowth, and taken up by Coleridge, and again by Hampden:

It is indeed sometimes said that the stream is clearest near the spring. Whatever use may fairly be made of this image, it does not apply to the history of a philosophy or belief, which on the contrary is more equable, and purer, and stronger, when its bed has become deep, and broad, and full. It necessarily rises out of an existing state of things, and for a time savours of the soil. Its vital element needs disengaging from what is foreign and temporary, and is employed in efforts after freedom which become more vigorous and hopeful as its years increase. Its beginnings are no measure of its capabilities, nor of its scope. At first no one knows what it is, or what it is worth. It remains perhaps for a time quiescent; it tries, as it were, its limbs, and proves the ground under it, and feels its way. From time to time it makes essays which fail, and are in consequence abandoned. It seems in suspense which way to go; it wavers, and at length strikes out in one definite direction. In time it enters upon strange territory; points of controversy alter their bearing; parties rise and fall around it; dangers and hopes appear in new relations; and old principles reappear under new forms. It changes with them in order to remain the same. In a higher world it is otherwise, but here below to live is to change, and to be perfect is to have changed often.[18]

The geographical sub-text to this extended metaphor reminds us of Newman's own early studies in mineralogy and chemistry, and his

---

[17] Ibid., pp. 40–1.
[18] John Henry Newman, *Essay on the Development of Christian Doctrine* (1845), 6th edn, reprinted with Foreword by Ian Ker (University of Notre Dame Press, 1989), Ch. 1, Section 1, Part 7, p. 40.

enthusiasm for Buckland's lectures on geology.[19] But here the image of a flowing river is developed far beyond the embryonic metaphor of the 1837 *Lectures on the Prophetical Office of the Church*.

Though there is – of course – no mention of Hampden's 1839 *Lecture on Tradition*, it is remarkable how much the *Essay on Development* is also dominated by the idea of an insensible progression. Here, the word he uses for it is 'tradition' – elsewhere he uses the word 'development', or even simply 'life'. Insensible as its movement may be on a human time-scale, the tradition of the Church is likened to the unstoppable powers of a river in geologic time, flowing this way and that, and eventually finding its way through every barrier. But if a mighty river wears down its bed and selects its course over periods too long for human life to observe, something analogous happens in the life of a single person. Not for nothing do we use the metaphor of the 'course' of one's life. As in much of his writing, this metaphor may be seen in terms of his attempt to find a satisfactory theoretical account of a phenomenon for which his reading of philosophy had left him inadequately tutored and whose practical importance he had discovered first in his own life. Like Paul and Augustine before him, the author of 'Lead kindly light' came increasingly to feel an overall path and flow to his life that was guided by forces beyond his control.

So much, indeed, that this as an idea can be seen to lie at the heart of all Newman's thinking – whether on literature, education, theology, or philosophy. Over and over again, at level after level, we find him returning to the question of what differentiates genuine organic life with an internal dynamic and momentum of its own from a mere mechanical ordering or arrangement. The 'life' of a work of literature, for instance, the relation of its parts to the whole, and the development of character and action so revealed is a touchstone of an author's literary powers. Similarly, the development of the individual lies at the centre of Newman's notion of what constitutes a university. In theology the idea of development – most famous, of course, in his book of that name – is in fact present throughout his thinking: it underlies for instance his 'Biglietto' speech in Rome,[20] with its critique of liberalism, as much as it does his early Anglican work on the *Lives of the Fathers*. Perhaps most notably of all, it is central to the concept of the 'illative sense', the central topic of his last major work, *An Essay in Aid of a Grammar of Assent*, with its power of moving the human mind from partial theoretical evidence to practical certainty.

---

[19] See, for instance, Geoffrey Faber, *Oxford Apostles* (Faber and Faber, 1933), pp. 60–1.
[20] So called because it was given at the award of his cardinal's hat.

The *Grammar* was published in 1870 – he often told friends that it had taken him nearly twenty years to write it. In fact, it had taken him much longer. As can be seen from the extracts from 'Apostolical Tradition' and *Lectures on the Prophetical Office of the Church* above, the same themes, the same images, the same questions are already present in his mind in the mid-1830s. Here, for instance, is his discussion of tradition in the *Grammar*, not in terms of Apostolic succession, but in those of its legal status. Almost every word could well have come from his 1836 defence of Anglicanism:

On the other hand, Mr. Clinton lays down the general rule, 'We may acknowledge as real persons, all those whom there is no reason for rejecting. The presumption is in favour of the early tradition, if no argument can be brought to overthrow it.' Thus he lodges the *onus probandi* with those who impugn the received accounts; but Mr. Grote and Sir George Lewis throw it upon those who defend them. 'Historical evidence', says the latter, 'is founded on the testimony of credible witnesses.' And again, 'It is perpetually assumed in practice, that historical evidence is different in its nature from other sorts of evidence. This laxity seems to be justified by the doctrine of taking the best evidence which can be obtained. The object of [my] inquiry will be to apply to the early Roman history the same rules of evidence which are applied by common consent to modern history.' Far less severe is the judgment of Colonel Mure: 'Where no positive historical proof is affirmable, the balance of historical probability must reduce itself very much to a reasonable indulgence to the weight of national conviction, and a deference to the testimony of the earliest native authorities.' 'Reasonable indulgence' to popular belief, 'deference' to ancient tradition, are principles of writing history abhorrent to the judicial temper of Sir George Lewis. He considers the words 'reasonable indulgence' to be 'ambiguous', and observes that 'the very point which cannot be taken for granted, and in which writers differ, is, as to the extent to which contemporary attestation may be presumed without direct and positive proof, . . . the extent to which the existence of a popular belief concerning a supposed matter of fact authorizes the inference that it grew out of authentic testimony'. And Mr. Grote observes to the same effect: 'The word *tradition* is an equivocal word, and begs the whole question. It is tacitly understood to imply a tale descriptive of some real matter of fact, taking rise at the time when the fact happened, originally accurate, but corrupted by oral transmission.' And Lewis, who quotes the passage, adds, 'This *tacit understanding* is the key-stone of the whole argument'.[21]

Newman has lost none of his Humean scepticism as to the historical value of testimony as it has been transmitted over countless generations. In legal

---

[21] John Henry Newman, *An Essay in Aid of A Grammar of Assent*, ed. I.T. Ker (Clarendon Press, 1985), p. 236. The italics, ellipsis, and the word "my" in brackets are as found in the text.

terms the most one can say is that the concept is ambiguous. Religious certainty, if it is to be found at all, must come from another quarter.

For Newman, in the *Grammar of Assent*, it comes not from dogma, nor from Paleyan 'proofs' of God, but rather from the slow accumulation of 'probabilities'. This idea of tradition, as he develops it for the rest of his life, constitutes his most effective answer to the question of how the believer might ground his faith. If the sense of 'recognition', as in a face, also has echoes of the Platonic recognition of truth, it is also a description of the way in which the human psyche works. Indeed, by the time we come to the *Grammar*, in what one might call its 'illative' form it has come to resemble much more a Kierkegaardian leap by which the co-ordinated totality of the human personality is able, through the process of what he calls 'real' assent, to reach existentially towards levels of experience quite inaccessible to the merely 'notional' propositions of reason or dogma alone. In the best tradition of Christian theology what began as an observed phenomenon of contingent weakness ends by becoming the cornerstone of the whole edifice of faith.

This also helps to explain what to many observers, then and later, seemed a peculiar arrogance in the labyrinthine process of Newman's conversion to Rome. After the publication of the notorious *Tract Ninety*, in February 1841, in which he demonstrated, at least to his own satisfaction, how every one of the Thirty-Nine Articles could be interpreted in a manner fully consonant with Catholicism, it was obvious to everyone except apparently Newman himself that his Anglican days were over. For those of his followers who still hesitated, the Bishop of Oxford's formal condemnation of the Tract in his *Charge* of May 1842 provided final proof that the *via media* of the Church of England was closed to them. Almost all had joined the Roman Catholic Church before Newman broke his silence. It was not until September 1843 that he preached his last sermon as an Anglican at Littlemore, and it was more than two years later, on 9 October 1845, that he was finally received as a Catholic by the providentially itinerant Dominic Barberi – the extraordinary Italian priest who, in response to a vision, and against the wishes of his superiors, had been drawn to England for such a time as this.

Four years is a long time in anyone's life. Other Victorians were to convert to Rome and leave again within the same period. Newman's view of the Anglican and Roman Churches did not substantially alter between 1841 and 1845. What then caused the delay? The fact that we know that during the latter part of that period, from March 1844 to September 1845, he was at work on the *Essay on Development* serves to account for his occupation during that time, as well as his reasons for taking the final step to Rome, but that first, historically based, apologia for his actions could as equally well have been written after his reception as a Catholic as before. The explanation he himself later offered, and which has been accepted by most sympathetic biographers since, is that he needed time for his heart to catch up with his head. Though he was by 1841 intellectually convinced of the validity of the claims of Rome, he still *felt* an Anglican. Only when he could feel himself to be emotionally a Catholic – only when he could give real rather than notional assent to its claims upon him was he prepared to act. If, as I suggest we have every reason to do, we accept this explanation for Newman's extraordinary delay at this crucial stage of his life at its face value, we should also accept as the corollary a much more personal interpretation than is usually given to the *Essay on Development*.

So far from being unmistakable evidence for heresy (as, we recall, Bossuet had argued) changes in doctrine, rightly understood, are, Newman argues, powerful evidence for the 'organic life' of Christian belief. What he calls the 'idea' of Christianity is not received passively by its adherents, 'but it becomes an active principle within them, leading them to an ever-new contemplation of itself, to an application of it in various directions, and a propagation of it on every side'.[22] It displays the common characteristic of all living organisms: it flows onward in a continual process of growth and change. The true test of Catholicity is not just which Church is most like the supposed primitive form, but also which Church has demonstrated the greatest powers of organic development. Not surprisingly, most of the debate about Newman's idea of development, then and since, has centred on the obvious religious conflict from which the book arose. Thus the seven tests by which we may distinguish 'genuine development' from its opposite, decay or 'corruption', are rightly seen as a way of distinguishing between the changes inherent in contemporary Catholicism and those visible in Protestantism. As Owen Chadwick has pointed out in his book, *From Bossuet to Newman*, the argument, though impressive, is nevertheless finally a circular one.[23] How are we to know which are organic changes? Those that appear in Catholicism. But there is another aspect to Newman's argument whose polemical purpose is rather less clear: an argument for complexity rather than simplicity.

At first this is presented modestly enough. 'The more claim an idea has to be considered living,' he notes, 'the more various will be its aspects; and

[22] *Essay on the Development* p. 36.
[23] Owen Chadwick, *From Bossuet to Newman*, 2nd edn (Cambridge University Press, 1987), Ch. 8.

the more social and political its nature, the more complicated and subtle will be its issues, and the longer and more eventful will be its course.'[24] This is especially true of something with such ancient and complex traditions as Christianity. No one aspect of it can be 'allowed to exclude or obscure another; . . . Christianity is dogmatical, devotional, practical all at once; it is esoteric and exoteric; it is indulgent and strict; it is light and dark; it is love and it is fear'.[25] Though this is a powerful celebration of the many strands that go to make up the Catholic tradition through the ages it is, as some of his critics noted at the time, not at first sight particularly relevant to the main thrust of his argument. Indeed, in some ways it actually makes his case marginally more difficult to demonstrate, since it prevents him at the outset from identifying a palpably Catholic 'leading idea' or core to Christianity by reference to which the truth or corruption of all the other accretions might be judged. Newman, however, has another final test up his sleeve much more dramatic and searching than the search for 'logical sequence' or 'chronic vigour' by which one might know particular doctrines or practices. We do not pick and choose our beliefs testing them one by one for their historic continuity, we accept or reject the Catholic Church *as a whole* – taking its many and varied parts on trust as we do so. And how do we know the Catholic Church itself? We know that the mighty river before which we stand is one and the same as the tiny rivulet which began its course in the far-off mountains. We can trace its long and often meandering course from the distant past until now. There can be no doubt in our minds when we encounter the true Church:

There is a religious communion claiming a divine commission, and holding all other bodies around it heretical or infidel; it is a well-organized, well disciplined body; it is a sort of secret society, binding together its members by influences and by engagements which it is difficult for strangers to ascertain. It is spread over the known world; it may be weak or insignificant locally, but it is strong on the whole from its continuity; it may be smaller than all other religious bodies together, but it is larger than each separately. It is a natural enemy to governments external to itself; it is intolerant and engrossing, and tends to a new modelling of society; it breaks laws, it divides families. It is a gross superstition: it is charged with the foulest crimes; it is despised by the intellect of the day; it is frightful to the imagination of many. And there is but one communion such.[26]

The passage is one of the most rhetorically splendid in Newman's entire output, but Newman's literary rhetoric always serves an end. It is as

---

[24] *Essay on Development*, p. 56.   [25] Ibid., p. 36.   [26] Ibid., p. 208.

though his attempt to focus with minute verbal precision on something as indefinable yet persistent as total identity that survives the alteration of every constituent part also calls forth new powers of verbal expression. Thus here, anyone, pagan or Protestant, who stubs his toe against this rock, knows what he has encountered. 'Place this description before Pliny or Julian; place it before Frederick the Second or Guizot . . . Each knows at once, without asking a question, who is meant by it.'[27]

The tactical leap from Pliny to Guizot makes the point: they see not the same organism, or the same river – how could they after that passage of time? – but they *recognize* it, as it were, by the direction of its flow, or the same stubborn expression on the face of the nineteen-hundred-year-old institution as was on the face of the unruly infant disrupter of the Roman Empire. It is this notion of the intangible unity of the whole that makes sense of his idea of tradition, unifying the disparate parts and providing direction and meaning to the inevitable processes of change.

This is not, of course, how Newman's Anglican opponents were to see it. In October of 1846 the Bishop of London, C.J. Blomfield, devoted the central part of the *Charge* to his diocesan clergy to discussing Newman. Though he criticizes Newman's preference for development over Scripture as being totally unacceptable to any true Christian, he is more interested in contextualizing Newman than denouncing him. For him, the *Essay on Development* represents the final admission of defeat of the post-Tridentine Catholic idea of tradition. When the champions of Rome:

long ago defeated upon Scriptural grounds, are also driven from tradition itself, by the plain unequivocal evidence of primitive antiquity against them. . . they proceed to undermine the very foundations of the Christian faith itself, by advancing the theory of 'development', or rather, I should say, by expanding into a formal system a principle incidentally put forth centuries ago by more than one writer of the Roman communion, that the primitive Church was ignorant of some things, and dissembled others, which were afterwards discovered and asserted, when Christianity was fully established.[28]

Having abandoned Bossuet's inflexible stand on tradition, Newman, Blomfield suggests – with what degree of irony one can only guess – has appropriated the most extreme form of German liberalism: 'It is manifest that this theory involves in itself the radical principle of infidelity. The disciples of Moëhler and Newman are in a state of hopeful training for

---

[27] Ibid.
[28] Charles James Blomfield (Bishop of London), *Charge to the Clergy of the Diocese of London*, 2nd edn (B. Fellowes, 1846), p. 26.

the school of Strauss.'[29] But some such manoeuvre was always going to be necessary if the idea of tradition were ever to be rescued from its post-Tridentine deep freeze. 'Indeed,' he continues:

I strongly suspect, that the advancing of this theory is an attempt, on the part of subtle, but not thoroughly satisfied, advocates of Romanism, to emancipate that Church from the self-imposed fetters of the Trent decrees; but how that is to be effected without satisfying . . . infallibility, I am unable to conjecture.[30]

The fact remained, Blomfield concludes, that these were impossible gyrations – the Roman position on tradition was not merely impossible, it could now, more than ever, clearly be *seen* to be impossible:

He, who maintains the theory of development, as it has been maintained of late, is unavoidably implicated, as a heretic, in the anathema of the council of Trent, which condemns all those who teach that any one of the traditions, received by the Church, has not been handed down, and preserved in continued succession, through the holy Apostles, from Christ himself.[31]

Blomfield's was not, of course, the only contemporary refutation of Newman's essay.[32] But, unlike the more plodding point-by-point critics of Newman's arguments, Blomfield has seen two very important things. The first is that the *Essay on Development* represents the death-knell of the Catholic attempt to defend the idea of tradition as totally inflexible and unchanging. The second is that the idea of development is somehow central to what drives Newman.

Both these were probably truer than Blomfield could recognize. As I have argued at length elsewhere,[33] Newman, like Wordsworth, is always trying to tell us his own story. It is no accident that the *Essay on the Development of Christian Doctrine* emerges from that four-year hiatus of 1841–5 which constituted the greatest crisis of Newman's life, and that in presenting its 'hypothesis to account for a difficulty' it specifically endows the Church with all the subtlety and complexity of a human psyche. Some changes to the individual are beneficial – even necessary, if they allow adjustment to new circumstances – others are retrograde and even damaging to the health of the whole. Implicit in the whole argument of the *Essay* is the unspoken question of the sub-text: is Newman the Roman Catholic more or less John Henry Newman than was the Anglican fellow

---

[29] Ibid., p. 27.   [30] Ibid., p. 29.   [31] Ibid., p. 28.
[32] Blomfield recommends Dr O'Sullivan's *Theory of Developments Applied and Tested*, and the tracts of J. Endell Taylor, and Mr Brogden.
[33] See Stephen Prickett, *Romanticism and Religion: The Tradition of Coleridge and Wordsworth in the Victorian Church* (Cambridge University Press, 1976), p. 174.

of Oriel College, Oxford? Is there a living organic development from one to the other? It was only when he felt able to answer *that* question in the affirmative that he felt able to take the final step. I believe we fail to understand the full thrust of the *Essay* unless we see it as, in effect, the first draft of Newman's great and lifelong apologia that was in the end to include nearly all his written output.

Certainly we quickly get a very clear answer to that question in institutional terms once Newman had finally taken the plunge. The delicately ironic title of the *Lectures on Certain Difficulties Felt by Anglicans in Submitting to the Catholic Church* (1850) conceals what is perhaps his most devastating attack on his old communion in terms of that final test of the overall life of the organism. And it is not merely any organism. This time the anthropomorphic nature of the metaphor (if metaphor it still is) which was implicit in the *Essay on Development* of five years earlier is now made fully explicit. Images of sap or new shoots are discarded in favour of those of mummification. For Newman, the Church of England above all lacks that basic condition of intelligent life: self-consciousness: 'As a thing without a soul, it does not contemplate itself, define its intrinsic constitution, or ascertain its position. It has no traditions; it cannot be said to think; it does not know what it holds and what it does not; it is not even conscious of its own existence.'[34] It requires no great shift of focus to read all of the above as a negative statement of Newman's own vision of what individual consciousness *does* entail. For Newman now the true analogy of the Church is not a grain of mustardseed, nor yet a vine, but a sentient human being – and preferably one who had been educated at Oxford through the controversies of the 1820s and 1830s, and had held a fellowship at Oriel. But even as Newman begins to elaborate his metaphor there occurs a typically Romantic shift of perspective. Just as Wordsworth, in his Preface to the *Lyrical Ballads*, had answered his own question, What is a Poem?, by defining the nature of a poet, so Newman answers his own question, What is the Church?, by shifting from anthropomorphic imagery of the institution to the mind of the individual who is doing the imagining:

Thus it is that students of the Fathers, antiquarians, and poets, begin by assuming that the body to which they belong is that of which they read in time past, and then proceed to decorate it with that majesty and beauty of which history tells, or which their genius creates . . . But at length, either the force of circumstance or some unexpected accident dissipates it; and, as in fairy tales, the magic

[34] John Henry Newman, *Lectures on Certain Difficulties felt by Anglicans in Submitting to the Catholic Church*, 2nd. edn (1850), p. 7.

castle vanishes when the spell is broken, and nothing is seen but the wild heath, the barren rock, and the forlorn sheep-walk: so it is with us as regards the Church of England, when we look in amazement on that which we thought so unearthly, and find so common-place or worthless.[35]

The description of the enquirers as 'students of the Fathers, antiquarians, and poets', leaves us in little doubt as to who these deluded romantic figures are. Nor is the origin of this extended conceit in any way concealed. Those left 'alone and palely loitering' by la belle Dame sans merci, thinly disguised as the Church of England, are Keble, Pusey, and the remnants of the Oxford Movement. Anglicanism is in reality less a Church than a stage in the growth of the individual's religious imagination, offering to those not yet ready for the real thing a simulacrum whose ultimate function is to awaken a longing in the soul for what it ultimately cannot satisfy – and so lead to the only Church that can meet these hitherto disappointed expectations. Keats's letters were not yet known to the general public, but it is hard to think that Newman did not have in mind here his dictum that 'The Imagination may be compared to Adam's dream: he awoke, and found it true.'

This is confirmed by Newman's charge that what pass for traditions in the Anglican Church are but inventions. The movement of 1833 was not a return to the Church's roots, but the creation of a pastiche.

The want of congeniality which now exists between the sentiments and ways, the moral life of the Anglican communion, and the principles, doctrines, traditions of Catholicism – I speak of this in order to prove something done and over long ago, in order to show that the movement of 1833 was from the first engaged in propagating an unreality.[36]

For Newman, of course, this argument is implicit in everything that has gone before. If the principles, doctrines, and traditions of Catholicism are true, then those of Anglicanism – in so far as they differ from those of the Catholic Church – *must* be false. They differ from those of the living Church in the same way as a lake, or tank of water, differs from the living waters of a river. Like Hobsbawm, Newman believed that there are 'genuine' traditions and 'invented' traditions. But the difference between them is not so much the date of their creation – the Anglicans, after all, looked back to Apostolic times as much as the Catholics – as the evidence for continuous organic life versus its febrile imitations. Newman here comes very close to admitting what is one of the underlying theses of this book – that

[35] Ibid., pp. 6–7.   [36] Ibid., p. 41.

all traditions constitute selective readings of the past, and their truth or falsehood depend on external criteria rooted in the needs of the present.

But here a new element has crept in. How are we, finally, to distinguish between the living body and the vain enchantments of simulacra? Beyond the application of rule-of-thumb tests, the final answer appears to be by means of the imagination. This is the reason for the apparent circularity of the argument of the *Essay*. It is only after our imaginations have intuitively grasped the whole picture that such tests will serve to convince us. Moreover it is the imagination, the very power that first led us to seek the Church in the wrong place, that will, eventually, also leave us dissatisfied with the insubstantiality of the false forms and guide us towards the one place where truth will be found. Those who know C.S. Lewis's early autobiographical allegory, *The Pilgrim's Regress*, will recognize here a surprising similarity between the conversion experiences of two very different kinds of Oxford men. It is perhaps the less surprising when we recall that the common link here is that particular English Romantic view of the imagination as the power that not merely responds to sense impressions, but actively shapes our apprehension of the world, not just in terms of sense-data, but also in our intellectual and spiritual existences. Once again, the stress lies on the wholeness of the individual person in contrast to those systems or ways of thinking that would fragment our experience and so, in the end, deny our humanity. As Newman writes in the *Grammar of Assent*: 'It is to the living mind that we must look for the means of using correctly principles of whatever kind.'[37] And again:

We are what we are, and we use, not trust our faculties. To debate about trusting in a case like this, is parallel to the confusion implied in wishing I had a choice if I would be created or no, or speculating what I should be like, if I were born of other parents . . . We are as little able to accept or reject our mental constitution as our being . . . We do not confront or bargain with ourselves.[38]

Whether individually or ecclesiastically we must start from where we are – and we must be guided by what we are. Such a movement from the institution to the individual foreshadows the spirit behind the *Apologia Pro Vita Sua* – even if the actual occasion of its writing was still in the future and unforeseeable. Yet once we have seen how strong, for Newman, was the strength of the analogy between the body corporate and body personal it is not hard to see how the ideas of tradition and development are as much the activating principle behind Newman's spiritual autobiography as they

---

[37] *A Grammar of Assent*, p. 232.   [38] Ibid., p. 46.

were in the *Essay on Development*. What Charles Kingsley had done, in effect, with his 1864 pamphlet, *What then does Dr Newman Mean?* with its accusation that the Catholic Church (and by implication, Newman himself) tolerated lying, was to challenge the whole of Newman's personal development to date. Once again it is a matter of the expression on the face. Was Newman the Catholic – a largely forgotten figure in the early 1860s – more fully John Henry Newman than the Protestant of twenty years before, or was he in some sense a shrunken, warped, in some way even a diminished figure? Was the development that had followed his journey to Rome a true unfolding of latent powers that had not found an outlet in his previous existence, or was he in some way perverted and contaminated by the principles of his new spiritual environment? Ironically, in what we have seen to be the terms set by the *Essay on Development*, Kingsley's challenge amounted to nothing less than a charge of 'corruption', or in other words what in an institution rather than an individual would amount to 'Protestantism'. It is small wonder that Newman reacted so vehemently – and, rather than by rebutting the specific charges, by telling the story of his own life. Only in that way, by seeing the picture as a whole, could he put the specific points into context. 'There is', wrote Newman in the *Grammar of Assent*, 'no ultimate test of truth besides the testimony borne to truth by the mind itself.' Man's 'progress is a living growth, not a mechanism.'[39]

The *Grammar* is, indeed, the culminating work of Newman's theory of development – by which, with hindsight, we can understand better the significance of the two earlier works, where, first on the macrocosmic, and then on the microcosmic scale, he had attempted to explore the difference between a living tradition and a sterile mechanism. What in the *Essay on Development* he had perceived primarily as a historical mode of growth, and in the *Apologia* had been linked with personal integrity, by 1870 he had come to see also as a fundamental law of the mind's operation. For Newman the human psyche was neither logical nor a-logical, but possessed of powers that made it rather 'super-logical' – capable of reaching beyond the powers of reason and proof to conclusions that we nevertheless act upon as certainties. At first sight this looks like a now-familiar form of German idealism, but in fact Newman's argument here stems directly from a bold inversion of Locke, and seems to owe almost nothing to Herder, Kant, or to Kant's repudiated followers such as Fichte or Jacobi. Whereas the Kantian

---

[39] Ibid., p. 226.

'reason' applies only to a limited range of innate ideas, the whole point of Newman's account of what he calls the 'illative sense' is that it applies equally to the entire range of mundane sense-experience.

Religious assent is not therefore a peculiar and isolated phenomenon of human experience – of 'believing where we cannot prove', as Newman's contemporary, Tennyson, seems to be implying in *In Memoriam* – but only the extreme end of a spectrum that begins in simple sense-perception, and includes in its scope all our normal intercourse with the external world. Newman had read Hume as a teenager, and had been lastingly impressed by his so-called 'scepticism' – the demonstration of that yawning gulf between probabilities so strong that we stake every aspect of our lives upon them, and real 'proof'. It is this very Humean scepticism, based in turn upon logical extensions of Locke, that Newman now turns so effectively in the service of faith to produce a Copernican revolution of his own. Certainty, Newman argues:

is the culmination of probabilities, independent of each other, arising out of the nature and circumstances of the particular case which is under review; probabilities too fine to avail separately, too subtle and circuitous to be convertible into syllogisms, too numerous and various for such conversion, even were they convertible. As a man's portrait differs from a sketch of him, in having, not merely a continuous outline, but all its details filled in, and shades and colours laid on and harmonized together, such is the multiform and intricate process of ratiocination, necessary for our reaching him as a concrete fact, compared with the rude operation of syllogistic logic.[40]

Newman is drawing here, as so often, on Joseph Butler, but he adds to Butler's force of probability the common Romantic assertion of the active and assimilating nature of our mental powers. So far from being the *tabula rasa* assumed by Locke, the human mind has the capacity to step beyond evidence and create for itself wholes that are greater than the constituent parts. It is so much an accepted characteristic of our normal behaviour, moreover, that it occurs at an unconscious level in every act of sense-perception, and even when it occurs at a conscious level we scarcely notice what it is that we are doing. 'Such a living *organon* is a personal gift,' writes Newman, 'and not a mere method of calculus.' Thus, even in everyday affairs, certitude is not so much a state of mind as 'an *action* more subtle and more comprehensive than the mere appreciation of a syllogistic logic'.[41] It 'is not a passive impression made upon the mind from without by argumentative compulsion, but . . . an *active* recognition of propositions as true'.[42]

---

[40] Ibid., p. 187.   [41] Ibid., p. 205.   [42] Ibid., p. 223.

This, the central argument of the *Grammar of Assent*, is probably Newman's most powerful contribution to philosophical theology. It is not the case that religious faith demands a peculiar kind of existential leap, but rather that it represents the most extreme, and therefore the most clearly visible example of a process that is constantly going on in every part of our lives without our normally being aware of it. The stress now is no longer on the truth or falsehood of specific propositions, but on the wholeness of human experience. We do not perceive in terms of propositions; our schemata come from the life of the whole personality, and, beyond that, from the no less organic life of the cultural, linguistic, and finally spiritual community in which we live, and move, and have our being.

It is this organic continuity between the culture and the individual, of course, that provides Newman with the link between the macrocosm and the microcosm, between the idea of development in the doctrine of the Church and the personal apologia for his own life. It was also, I suspect, one of the main reasons why he was as frequently misunderstood by his new communion as by his old. There are powerful reasons why one might believe that the *only* way to authenticate something as personal and inward as religious belief must be by an equally personal and inner 'recognition' of its truth, but historically that view has more often been held by Protestant Romantics than by Catholic dogmatists.

Though he was to return over and over again throughout his life to the evils of 'liberalism,' in the sense of putting the judgement of a private individual before the teachings of the Catholic Church, as I once heard Karl Rahner argue, Newman was equally resolute in his insistence that to accept those teachings in the first place inescapably involved a prior act of the individual conscience. This was a point that was not so much anathema as simply incomprehensible to many, both in Rome, and, as we have seen, like Bishop Blomfield in England, who continued to feel – and from their point of view quite correctly – that there was something dangerously liberal even about Newman's critique of liberalism. Whatever metaphor one might choose: a river, an organism, even a human face, for Newman it was the process, the *connection* between beginning and end, more than any single constant attribute, which guaranteed authenticity and through which an emerging and ever-changing truth could be discerned.

Whether this idea could be effectively secularized will be the subject of the next two chapters.

CHAPTER 10

Arnold: taking religion out of religion

PLURALIZING THE PAST

By the middle of the nineteenth century not merely the *idea* of tradition, but the word itself had returned to general circulation in a way that would have been unthinkable a hundred years earlier – allowing it to join that select band of words that have been temporally dropped from, and then subsequently restored to, the English language.[1] Indeed, by this time there were, in effect, at least four overlapping or competing connotations of tradition in circulation. The oldest, and still common idea of an essentially unreliable oral transmission (held, for instance, by F.W. Newman to the end of his long life in 1897) was now under challenge from at least three other competing meanings: from Herder's ideas of creative, aesthetic, and even performative readings of the past; from Keble's opposing notion of a precious and unalterable inheritance; and, finally, from Newman's slowly growing conviction that a developmental conception of tradition might offer a way of understanding the alteration and changes over time of an institution such as the Catholic Church.

Such meanings, even where they contradicted one another, were, clearly, never sealed definitions, and there was – as always – much blurring at the margins. Many who used the word 'tradition' would, no doubt, have been unaware of the degree to which it was contested territory. Others, like the High-Church Christina Rossetti, well aware of the controversy surrounding the word, continued to use it in an almost neutral sense as 'ancient wisdom' but without specific connotations of immutability or doctrinal authority.[2] Newman, who loathed Hampden, and who once described Coleridge as 'exercising a liberty of speculation which no Christian can

---

[1] See Ch. 4 above, p. 71 and 'Epilogue', p. 226.
[2] See, for instance, her commentary on Revelation, *The Face of the Deep* (1892), 6th edn (S.P.C.K, 1911), pp. 136 and 509.

tolerate',[3] was nevertheless fully capable of taking and re-using ideas and metaphors from both. Similarly, if it were not for Newman's repeated excoriation of German criticism, and all that it stood for, one might plausibly imagine that the author of *A Grammar of Assent* had taken much from Marsh's translation of Herder – if not from other available sources. Drawing a parallel with Newman's assertion late in life that he had never read a word of Coleridge (often kindly interpreted as a sign of the old Cardinal's failing memory), some sceptics have continued to suspect more than a little German influence, direct or indirect, in Newman's mature thought. But the very fact that tradition, and all the complex associations that went with it, was so widely invoked, and so fiercely debated, suggests not merely the intellectual flux of the period, but the importance attached to the outcome. It is no exaggeration to say that in a society that was undergoing the most rapid intellectual and social changes ever experienced by any comparable country, the understanding of and feeling for continuity with the past represented by the idea of tradition – or, conversely, the rejection of it – was central to almost every major question of the age.

For G.M. Young (1882–1959) the Victorian age was, above all, an era of loss of Faith:

Somewhere between [1829 and 1899] we must put the decisive secularization of English society and thought, a process the origins and stages of which it would be interesting to have traced for us. Perhaps one might put it thus. The conception of a church transmitting a tradition and interpreting it by authority had no place in the general English mind or imagination. The faith of Protestantism in its various modes was a documentary faith, and the documents were losing their validity. . . . Could the documents, when analysed by the new criticism, and read in the light of the new biology and archaeology, justify the philosophy that in the course of ages had been raised on them, or developed out of them? To a Catholic the question does not present itself quite in this way, but England was Protestant. And to an ever-increasing number the answer was definitely no. They were making the discovery which Ruskin made, that the religion in which they had been brought up was simply not true. To a smaller group the answer was yes, in so far as that philosophy explains the world to me, or explains me to myself. In other words, the only alternatives open to a sincere and thoughtful mind were agnosticism, often a reverent and pious agnosticism, and a religion of personal acceptance. The social atmosphere was on the whole decidedly adverse to belief.[4]

---

[3] From the *British Critic*, April 1839, reprinted by Newman in *Apologia Pro Vita Sua*, ed. M.J. Svalgic (Oxford University Press, 1967), p. 94.
[4] G.M. Young, *Victorian Essays* (Oxford University Press, 1962), pp. 156–7.

For Young, and his late-Victorian generation, the agnosticism of Matthew Arnold, of George Eliot, or of T.H. Huxley was clearly the most important religious trend in their pluralistic society, yet Huxleian 'agnostics' – the word is his coinage – however significant intellectually, were never more than a tiny minority. Figures for church attendance, the circulation of religious novels, magazines and periodicals, and the popular interest in major ecclesiastical debates of the day all tell a rather different story.[5]

Moreover by the mid-nineteenth century, the word 'tradition' had returned to common circulation in such diverse contexts that all we can do is look at a tiny selection of what seem to be significant examples. Beyond the narrow confines of Oxford theology, it is not difficult to find the word being used in more poetic, if no less literally sceptical senses. Poets – whether romantic or not – have always adapted many of their worlds from existing myths and traditions. For the romantics, of whatever variety, truth could be 'created' or re-discovered from fictions. We have already mentioned Felicia Hemans' praise for Herder in her 1823 volume *The Siege of Valencia*. Her own notes to that edition provide a sense both of the ambiguity of tradition as a source of inspiration, and the shifting meaning of the word from the 1820s. In the first she mentions a Spanish 'tradition that the great bell of the cathedral of Saragossa always tolled spontaneously before a king of Spain died',[6] whereas a head-note to the 'Songs of the Cid', three pages later, tells us that: 'The following Ballads are not translations from the Spanish, but are founded upon some of the "wild and wonderful" traditions preserved in the romances of that language, and the ancient poems of the Cid.'[7] In a later volume, *The Forest Sanctuary and Other Poems* (1825), she makes her own sense of the word, and its derivation from Herder, very clear: 'The following pieces may so far be considered a series, as each is intended to be commemorative of some national recollection, popular custom, or tradition. The idea was suggested by Herder's "Stimmen der Volker in Liedern", the execution is however different, as the poems in his collection are chiefly translations.'[8] How far this apparently Herderian idea of tradition had passed into popular consciousness by the late 1820s or early 1830s is obviously problematic. It is always difficult to identify moments of change – especially when one suspects that the shift in meaning of a word or concept may

[5] See Robert Currie, Alan Gilbert and Lee Horsley (eds.), *Churches and Churchgoers: Patterns of Growth in the British Isles since 1700* (Clarendon Press, 1977).
[6] Felicia Hemans, *The Siege of Valencia: A Dramatic Poem* (Murray, 1823), p. 246.
[7] Ibid., p. 249.
[8] Felicia Hemans, *The Forest Sanctuary and Other Poems* (Murray, 1825), p. 106.

be largely unconscious. Words can, and often do, change their meaning apparently arbitrarily in general oral transmission; on other occasions, even where there may be a precise written source for the change, that source may actually have been read by only a few of those influenced by it.[9] Freudian terminology, for instance, passed into common parlance in the twentieth century among many who had never read a word of the Viennese psychoanalyst. Similarly, it is unlikely that Newman's developmental use of the word comes from nowhere. What is clear is that in the field of aesthetics the boundaries always were more flexible and blurred than in the entrenched and conservative reaches of theology.

Herder was, as we have seen, relatively well-known in early nineteenth-century Britain. In addition to the examples mentioned earlier, Coleridge cites him on the perils of authorship in Chapter XI of his *Biographia Literaria* (1816) and, in 1823, De Quincey was quick to cite this reference of Coleridge's.[10] Whether or not De Quincey himself had actually read Herder, he undoubtedly wishes to give the impression that he has, and his own use of the word 'tradition' is completely free from echoes of the Protestant–Catholic controversies otherwise dominating ecclesiastical debates of the period, and is not inconsistent with Herder's. In a surprisingly wide-ranging piece on 'Style' written in 1841, he invokes 'tradition' in a sense that could mean simply unwritten but totally credible gossip, or (following Herder) a story that has wider symbolic connotations:

we know by traditions which they [the scholiasts] have preserved, and we know from Aristotle himself, the immediate successor of the great tragic poets . . . that Aeschylus was notorious to a proverb amongst the very mob for the stateliness, pomp, and towering character of his diction, while Euripides was equally notorious not merely for a diction in a lower key, more household, more natural, less elaborate, but also for cultivating such a diction by study and deliberate preference.[11]

But the same textual enquiries that were revising scholarly opinion of Greek and Roman literature, were also having an even greater impact on the much less neutral area of biblical studies. Others, besides Coleridge, were indulging in a liberty of speculation that certainly no biblical literalist could tolerate.

---

[9] A point Matthew Arnold, for instance, was well aware of. See n.35 below.
[10] Thomas De Quincey, 'Letters to a Young Man whose Education has been Neglected', *Collected Writings of Thomas De Quincey*, 14 vols., ed. David Masson (A & C Black, 1897), Vol. X, pp. 12–13.
[11] Thomas De Quincey, 'Style', Part IV (first published in four parts in *Blackwoods* for July, September, and October 1840, and February 1841) republished ibid., p. 219.

In 1844, the same year as the publication of Keble's *Lectures on Poetry*, another woman poet, Elizabeth Barrett (not yet married to her fellow-poet Robert Browning) published her Miltonic epic, *A Drama of Exile*. In it Lucifer addresses Adam ('my clay-king!') and prophesies:

> Thou wilt not rule by wisdom very long
> The after-generations. Earth, methinks,
> Will disinherit thy philosophy
> For a new doctrine suited to thine heirs,
> And class these present dogmas with the rest
> Of the old-world traditions, Eden fruits
> And Saurian fossils.
>
> [ll. 733–8]

This represents a surprisingly complex cultural cross-over. If the story of the fruit in Eden is no more than an 'old-world tradition' what are we to make of its juxtaposition with the very latest in science – the fossils of extinct dinosaur giants being discovered all over the world, and whose significance was even then being hotly debated? [12] Are both stories equally unreliable, or should this prophecy by Lucifer, the father of lies, be treated as what would now be called 'strategic disinformation'? Does the Devil dislike both religious tradition *and* scientific discovery? Or are we simply to see both religion and science as what Kuhn would call cultural paradigms – that will, in time, be so modified and invisibly smoothed out that we lose all sense of the fierce controversies that lay behind these changes? Perhaps also the Devil is being ironic, in that he is predicting that the truths revealed to Adam will (like knowledge of the creatures of deep time) be disparaged by the know-it-all generations of the future – which suggests, paradoxically, that the Father of Lies was a secret Herderian, who knows that the ancient biblical texts contain a greater truth than any literal meaning.

Though this may be reading too much into one passage, Barrett was never one to use images lightly. What is undoubtedly true is that what can easily look, from a historical perspective, like a period of relative cultural homogeneity compared with our own, was in fact fissured and ruptured by culture wars as ferocious and hard-fought as anything we witness in our own time. What we have already seen in the way of *odium theologicum* in Oxford represents only a fraction of the debates that were raging both within and between various religious sects and groupings within the

---

[12] 'Saurian' = 'lizard'. The term 'dinosaur' had first been proposed by Richard Owen in 1841. See Adrian Desmond, *The Hot-Blooded Dinosaurs* (Blond & Briggs, 1975), p. 15.

United Kingdom.[13] As one might expect from the culture wars of a society still struggling to come to terms with the notion of pluralism, the word 'culture' itself rapidly became a secular synonym for the notion of 'tradition' in religion.

'Pluralism' in the nineteenth century was a relatively new word for a relatively new condition. It was first used in a strictly material sense at this very period in the first half of the century to describe the practice of well-placed clergy drawing salaries from several churches at the same time – often without residing at any of them. It was only in 1887 that it was first applied, presumably as a metaphor from the corruptions of Anglicanism, to the holding of fundamentally different and incompatible ideas – perhaps originally with the implication that like the *rentier* clergy any such mental 'pluralist' would in the end 'reside' in none of them. In practice, however, it quickly came to refer less to individual people than to the kind of society whose inhabitants held widely differing views about themselves and about how that society should operate. As we have seen in Chapter 2, the first such society had been seventeenth-century England, which, unlike any other countries in Europe, had experienced within the span of a single century officially condoned clergy from across the whole spectrum of Christianity, from the Catholic priesthood through to Puritan ministers.[14] Even a disastrous Civil War had failed to produce a viable or enforceable consensus, and over the next hundred years or so, the English had slowly had to come to terms with the fact that there was no going back to any traditional world of common beliefs and aspirations.

As a result, one of the first modern meanings of 'pluralism' to emerge during the nineteenth century referred to the agreed stand-off between once rival Christian Churches – or, just as often in the case of the Church of England, between different ecclesiastic factions. Taking its cue from this, in modern democratic countries, theories of the state, of justice, and of what constitutes the 'good life' in general are essentially pluralistic in outlook – not just in religion, but in every form of social, political, and economic existence. Thus we take it for granted in a modern democratic state that though conservatives and socialists may differ profoundly about

---

[13] The Armstrong Browning Library at Baylor University in Texas has a collection of over 1,400 religious pamphlets (not including the *Tracts for the Times*) written in response to nineteenth-century ecclesiastical controversies.

[14] See Peter Harrison, 'If the time of the appearance of this new interpretative framework was the late seventeenth and early eighteenth centuries, then the place was England.' *'Religion' and the Religions in the English Enlightenment* (Cambridge University Press, 1990), pp. 3; 84.

the means to their political goals, they do so within an agreed political framework.

But perhaps just because they were so obviously causes of tension and conflict, politics and religion were historically in some ways easier to accept as essentially pluralistic than culture itself. Culture, after all, was the glue that held society together – especially once the idea of a common religious community of belief had visibly collapsed in the acrimony of sectarian debates. Whatever might be the differences between Keble and Newman, Gladstone and Manning, they were all at least products of the same Oxford education, had all been socialized into the same educated class – were all members of what Coleridge had called 'the Clerisy': the teachers, preachers, and educators who provided not merely spiritual, but social and cultural leadership both at a local and national level through-out the country.[15] They shared, or believed they shared, a common feeling for what constituted 'English' culture – a word also in need of some unpacking.

For much of the century – as now – the word English stood as much for the language as the country. With a few exceptions, little attention was paid (in England at least) to the corresponding ideas of what might constitute 'Irish', 'Scottish', or 'Welsh' culture. Scotland, with by far the best educational system of any part of the United Kingdom, and home of the 'Scottish Enlightenment' at the turn of the century, had possessed such internationally known intellectual and literary luminaries as Burns, Scott, Mackintosh, Adam Smith, Ferguson, Watt, and a host of others. Though Edinburgh was the centre of a flourishing periodical and publishing industry, and probably had in real terms the strongest local Clerisy and sense of national identity at this period, Scotland was never-theless often content to be described as 'North Britain'.[16] Conversely, the widespread popularity of Burns and Scott among the romantics, and the presence of such figures as Carlyle and MacDonald in the London lit-erary world mid-century, ensured what one might call an ever-present 'Scottish dimension' to any sense of 'English' culture. Yet by the middle of the century many were becoming uneasy about even these apparent cultural certainties of country, class, education – and inherited literary tradition.

---

[15] See Stephen Prickett, 'Coleridge and the Idea of the Clerisy', *Reading Coleridge: Approaches and Appreciations*, ed. Walter. B. Crawford (Cornell University Press, 1979), pp. 252–73.
[16] See, for instance, Henry Cockburn's *Memorials of his Time* (A & C Black, 1856).

HEBREW VERSUS HELLENE: CULTURE,
TRADITION – AND ANARCHY

It is yet another example of the continual back-formation of tradition that a work like Matthew Arnold's *Culture and Anarchy* (1869) should be written to celebrate – or defend – something as recently invented as English literary culture. Arnold's assumed consensus over what constitutes 'culture' is, in effect, an appeal to a tacit common notion of tradition. Invoking 'culture', in this singular sense, we note, runs directly counter to Herder's stress on the multiplicity of human cultures (in the plural) and his belief that no society is without its culture. In contrast, Arnold's idea of a common English cultural tradition belongs to the same nexus of ideas as the Anglo-French notion of 'civilization' in the sense of claiming to provide a single and, by implication, universal, set of values that incorporated the literature and philosophy of the past, represented as a living tradition which shaped the values and conduct of the present. In this form, the idea of 'culture' (national or supra-national), like the idea of 'literature' itself, dates only from the late eighteenth century,[17] but by presenting itself as (among other things) an amalgam of national 'great writers' over the previous 500 years – taken to include such figures as Chaucer, Shakespeare, Milton, and even the recently dead Lake Poets, Coleridge and Wordsworth – it managed not merely to lay claim to represent the best that had been thought and expressed by the collective wisdom of past ages, but also to imply a much greater depth and continuity with those past ages than the history of the idea actually justified. English 'culture', like English literature, was a retrospective ordering of the past – by implication as old as its constituents. In promoting this notion, Matthew Arnold is clearly a key player in creating the modern meaning of the word.

More to our point, Arnold's conception of 'culture' was a direct response, yet again, to the existential crisis presented by the nineteenth-century discovery of living in an incurably pluralist society. It constituted the most thoroughgoing attempt yet made to take the religious connotations of tradition and secularize them as an inheritance not of divine revelation but of a human value-system. What Arnold really wanted was to have his cake and eat it. As A.O.J. Cockshut has acutely commented, Arnold did not want to

---

[17] See, for instance, Philippe Lacoue-Labarthe and Jean-Luc Nancy, *The Literary Absolute, The Theory of Literature in German Romanticism*, trs. Philip Barnard and Cheryl Lester (State University of New York Press, 1988).

abolish the religion he could no longer believe in, but, somehow, adjust or re-tune it to embrace the cultural values he most cherished:

> Arnold possessed a combination of qualities that is not very common. He was intensely conservative, he was intensely practical, and he was sceptical about doctrines and historical events (though not about values). Both the first two qualities drove him to seek for the continuity of religion in an institution; while his scepticism made it necessary for him to give a new, personal meaning to all the beliefs and customs of his chosen institution; the Anglican Church. Moreover, the combination of conservatism and scepticism made him feel that the search for continuity was peculiarly urgent, and the consequences of failure terrible.[18]

Small wonder, perhaps, that Arnold's own definition of 'culture' remains curiously elusive. It embraces the 'study of perfection', it is 'sweetness and light', it even goes beyond religion (with which it is elaborately compared) involving 'a harmonious expansion of all the powers which make the beauty and worth of human nature, and is not consistent with the over-development of any one power at the expense of the rest'.[19]

> It is in making endless additions to itself, in the endless expansion of its powers, in endless growth in wisdom and beauty, that the spirit of the human race finds its ideal. To reach this ideal, culture is an indispensable aid, and that is the true value of culture. Not a having and resting, but a growing and a becoming, is the character of perfection as culture conceives it; and here, too, it coincides with religion.[20]

Yet agree with such high ideals as we may, pinning down this Aristotelian entelechy – this process of unending becoming – is not easy. Indeed, if we were honest, we would probably admit that *Culture and Anarchy* has been promoted, as it were, by seniority rather than talent in debates over the relationship of culture and society. What most readers will have gleaned from it is not any positive defence of culture, or public values, but a vague feeling of unease that with the spread of mass literacy has come a decline in public taste and the decay of what was supposed to be a classical 'high' culture, and that this was to be greatly regretted. This is a point Arnold had already made, almost to the point of laboriousness, in one of his first pieces of prose criticism, the Preface to his *Poems* of 1853.[21]

---

[18] A.O.J. Cockshut, *The Unbelievers: English Agnostic Thought, 1840–1890* (Collins, 1964), pp. 71–2.
[19] 'Culture and Anarchy', *Complete Prose Works of Matthew Arnold*, 11 vols., ed. R.H. Super (University of Michigan Press, 1965), Vol. v, p. 94.
[20] Ibid.
[21] Interestingly, his most extensive modern editor, R.H. Super, includes this Preface in a volume entitled 'On the Classical Tradition' – yet the word 'tradition' itself is notably absent from the writings included. Ibid., Vol. i, 1960.

Mr Luke, in *The New Republic* (1877), W.H. Mallock's brilliant satire of the philosophical movements of the day, captures this Arnoldian spirit of gentle melancholy with wicked perfection:

'Culture', said Mr Luke, 'is the union of two things – fastidious taste and liberal sympathy. These can only be gained by wide reading guided by sweet reason; and, as it were, of a new sense, which at once enables us to discern the Eternal and the absolutely righteous, wherever we find it, whether in an epistle of St Paul's or in a comedy of Menander's. It is true that culture sets aside the larger part of the New Testament as grotesque, barbarous, and immoral; but what remains, purged of its apparent meaning, it discerns to be a treasure beyond all price. And Christianity – such Christianity, I mean, as true taste can accept – culture sees as the guide to the real significance of life, and the explanation,' Mr Luke added with a sigh, 'of that melancholy which in our day is attendant upon all clear sight'.[22]

Mallock was James Anthony Froude's nephew, and had doubtless had more experience than most of Arnoldian melancholy. Yet when we have finished our fun at Arnold's expense (and the game is almost too easy) the fact remains that *Culture and Anarchy* is a historically important work: not because people were necessarily convinced by its controversial arguments, let alone its shadowy remedies, nor, even, because people actually read it at all, but, quite simply, because it is one of those rare works which has significantly modified the English language. As with all such works, it has produced words that are used by people who may never have heard of *Culture and Anarchy*, let alone read it. And for those who have read it, when they have forgotten everything else that Arnold says, what remains are those remarkably evocative key terms. 'Hebrew' and 'Hellene', 'Barbarian', and, above all in colloquial usage, 'Philistine', have passed into the language. We may not know exactly what Arnold meant by culture (we may not even be sure he did) – still less agree with him – but we all know that it involves resisting the Philistines, and that to do so is unequivocally a Good Thing. We can also be sure that whatever else constitutes a Philistine, at the very centre of philistinism is a lack of any sense of history or tradition.

Arnold did not, of course, invent the word 'philistine' as a term of cultural abuse. Its original application, going back at least as far as 1600, is simply as a term for 'the enemy' of whatever hue – often with connotations of drunkenness and debauchery – and was applied to such well-known anti-social elements as bailiffs and literary critics. The *Oxford English Dictionary* records its use by German students in the 1820s to

---

[22] W.H. Mallock, *The New Republic* (Chatto and Windus, 1877), p. 31.

mean specifically those not in the university,[23] but what we now think of as the distinctively Arnoldian meaning of one deficient in taste and liberal culture seems to have been first used in English by Carlyle as early as 1827, possibly following a similar usage by Novalis written in 1797.[24] What is undoubtedly true, however, is that Arnold so effectively appropriated the word for his own purposes in *Culture and Anarchy* that it is his name that has been stamped on it ever since. The term belongs to him.

Or almost so. For the word was, of course, one of two binary pairs: 'Philistine' and 'Barbarian'; 'Hebrew' and 'Hellene'. It is only when we line them up like this that we begin to notice something rather odd about these famous twins. They are, of course, *mismatched*. They represent mixed metaphors. To make any historical or figurative sense they *should* read: 'Hellene' and 'Barbarian'; 'Hebrew' and 'Philistine' – the classical world and the biblical world: Athens and Jerusalem. Logically, as historically, Hellenes should be threatened by Barbarians; Hebrews by Philistines. But in fact they never are. This is precisely the grouping that Arnold steadfastly refuses to make. The more one thinks about it, the odder this becomes. It would not be difficult, for instance, to construct an argument to the effect that Philistines are the enemies of the Hebraic virtues (such as Arnold grudgingly allows them to be) and Barbarians the enemies of the 'sweetness and light' represented by Hellenism. But Arnold, surprisingly, never says this. Barbarians are simply indifferent to culture, whereas Philistines hold a narrow or wrongheaded view of it: 'The people who believe most of our greatness and welfare are proved by our being very rich, and who give most of their lives and thoughts to becoming rich, are just the very people whom we call Philistines.'[25] Though it is possible to characterize Hebrews and Philistines as both being narrow-minded, it makes little or no sense to say the opposite: that Barbarians and Hellenes are both broad-minded; nor does it make any greater sense to see Barbarians as uncultivated Hellenes, or Philistines as uncultivated Hebrews. The *obvious* balancing of Arnold's metaphorical structure is consistently frustrated or ignored.

Even stranger in *Culture and Anarchy* is Arnold's notion of the ideal Hellene. As David Delaura's exhaustive and scholarly study of Arnold's

---

[23] Robert Schumann's *Carnival* (1834–5) closes with a witty march – unexpectedly in 3/4 time – called '*Marche des 'Davidsbundler' contre les Philistins'*. I owe this reference to Amy Vail.

[24] 'We destroy illusion as we destroy diseases – and accordingly illusion is but an inflammation or an expiration of the intellect – the affliction of the fanatic or the Philistine.' Novalis, 'Miscellaneous Writings' (1797), *German Aesthetic and Literary Criticism: The Romantic Ironists and Goethe*, ed. Kathleen Wheeler (Cambridge University Press, 1984), p. 84.

[25] 'Culture and Anarchy', p. 97.

private reading and correspondence during the period he was at work on the book shows, there is no doubt at all that his model Hellene, radiating 'sweetness and light', is none other than John Henry Newman, whose recently published lectures, *On the Scope and Nature of University Education* (1852) and *Lectures on Universities* (1859), had been a major formative influence on Arnold's own ideas of 'culture'.[26]

This choice of Newman as the ideal Hellene must surely give us pause. *Newman?* Consider again Arnold's description of the two personality types: 'the governing idea of Hellenism is *spontaneity of consciousness*; that of Hebraism, *strictness of conscience*'.[27] The problem is that Arnold's idea of what might constitute such 'spontaneity' seems at first sight to be directly contrary to Newman's.

For Arnold such 'spontaneity' was the very opposite of the shallow and second-hand dogmatism that he saw all around him in the religious disputes of the day. In a lecture of 1871 he poured scorn on the view that:

All religions but a man's own are utterly false and vain; the authors of them mere impostors; and the miracles which are said to attend them, fictitious. We forget that this is a game which two can play at; although the believer of each religion always imagines the prodigies which attest his own religion to be fenced by a guard granted to them alone. Yet how much more safe it is, as well as more fruitful, to look for the main confirmation of a religion in its intrinsic correspondence with the urgent wants of human nature, in its profound necessity! Differing religions will be found to have much in common...[28]

This is so suspiciously close to Newman's definition of 'liberalism', however, that it is hard to imagine he does not have Arnold specifically in mind:

Now by Liberalism I mean false liberty of thought, or the exercise of thought upon matters, in which, from the constitution of the human mind, thought cannot be brought to any successful issue, and therefore is out of place. Among such matters are first principles of whatever kind; and of those the most sacred and momentous are especially to be reckoned the truths of Revelation. Liberalism then is the mistake of subjecting to human judgement those revealed doctrines which are in their nature beyond and independent of it, and of claiming to determine on intrinsic grounds the truth and value of propositions which rest for their reception simply on the external authority of the Divine Word.[29]

---

[26] David DeLaura, *Hebrew and Hellene in Victorian England* (University of Texas Press, 1969), pp. 61–80.
[27] Ibid., p. 165.
[28] Arnold, *Complete Prose Works*, ed. Super, Vol. III, p. 258.
[29] J.H. Newman, *Apologia Pro Vita Sua*, ed. C.F. Harrold (Longmans, Green, 1947) p. 261.

Given this fundamental gulf between Newman and Arnold, it seems almost perverse that Arnold should see Newman, who had spent five years agonizing over the claims of the Roman Catholic Church, as his prime example of 'spontaneity of consciousness' as against 'strictness of conscience'. Indeed, it would hardly be an exaggeration to say that after the publication of his *Apologia* in 1864, Newman's was the best publicized conscience of the century.

What is going on here? Why are Hellenes being matched with Philistines rather than Barbarians? and why is Newman – of all people – being put up not as a Hebraist but a Hellene? I would suggest that the answer would seem to lie in their respective attitudes to tradition. Barbarians, by definition, *have* no sense of tradition or history; they are the sports morons, 'the muddied oaf and flannelled fool', or the practical men of the world, who are uninterested in how and why they are who they are. But the Hebraists, those governed by 'strictness of conscience', who should be the natural opposites of Philistines, *do* have a sense of history. The problem for Arnold is that it is *the wrong sense of history.*

Arnold spells out in some detail who these people are. They are to be found, for instance, in unnamed droves in the pages of *The Nonconformist* – not one of Arnold's favourite journals. The named include a Mr Murphy, who despite his name – or perhaps because of it – was a fiercely anti-Catholic lecturer from Birmingham; also guilty, at least by association is the philosopher, Henry Sidgwick; not to mention a gentleman by the name of the Reverend W. Cattle. This clergyman, indeed, seems to have stepped straight from the pages of structuralist anthropology.[30] In a letter to Clough, of 1849, Arnold, while admitting that he is 'more sniffing after a moral atmosphere to respire in than ever before in my life', assumes that honest doubters like himself and Clough are superior to such people as his elder brother Tom, who was about to follow Newman and convert to Rome. He and Clough, he declares, are 'The children of the second birth / Whom the world could not tame;' the rest, those still preoccupied with religion, like J.A. Froude and F.W. Newman, John Henry's brother, are 'mystics and cattle'. Tom Arnold, he adds with a burst of brotherly feeling, is 'not in any sense cattle or even a mystic but he has not a "still considerate mind"'.[31]

What distinguishes these 'children of the second birth', those with 'still considerate minds', from the rest who – to continue Arnold's curious livestock metaphor – remain part of the 'common herd'? How exactly

<hr />

[30] See, for example, Edmund Leach, *Genesis as Myth and other Essays* (Cape, 1969).
[31] DeLaura, *Hebrew and Hellene*, p. 19.

does 'spontaneity of consciousness' demonstrate its superiority over mere 'strictness of conscience'? Part of the answer clearly lies in the fact that, for Arnold, the Rugby and Oxford classicist, the word 'spontaneity' still carried much of its older Latin force of *sua sponte*, 'of his own volition' – a meaning also present in Wordsworth's 'spontaneous overflow of power-ful feelings' in the Preface to the *Lyrical Ballads*. It carried not so much the modern connotations of unreflective instinctive action, but of actions based upon a deliberate and inner-directed personal will and independ-ence of judgement. The possessors of such a consciousness – like Clough and Newman (not to mention Arnold himself) – have resisted the herd-mentality of their fellows, with its ready-made historical judgements, and are prepared to see things (in the words of another Arnoldian cliché) 'as they really are'. Above all, however, these few are the true inheritors of their culture – now not a static collection of pre-fabricated ideas and opin-ions, but a way of seeing the world developmentally, shedding 'sweetness and light' (a phrase borrowed, of course, from Swift) both on the present and its history. This distinction between the two kinds of tradition – two different senses of history – would explain at one go two of the perennial puzzles of *Culture and Anarchy* – the mismatched pairs, and the curious role of Newman as the prime Hellene.

For the actual source of Arnold's binary pairs, we need look no further than Coleridge's *Church and State* (1830), written in the dubious cause of opposing Catholic emancipation, and which was probably his best-known work in the 1840s and 1850s.[32] Here Coleridge builds his case on a series of dialectical oppositions on which, he argues, the 'English' state depends. Thus 'Church' and 'State' are like the two poles of a magnet, the one claiming religious allegiance, the other secular and political. It would be as monstrous a perversion of the proper order of things for the Church to claim political power (as, for instance, the Catholic Church did in the Papal States of Italy) as it would be for the State to claim religious author-ity (as happened in the early days of the French Republic of the 1790s). The 'British Constitution' – an abstract and notional entity which Coleridge invokes with supreme confidence – happily unites secular and religious authority in the Crown, but divides them carefully at an executive level between Westminster and Canterbury, according to their proper sphere of authority. But this initial binary opposition is repeated, once again, *within* each of these powers. The 'State' is thus the product of a further dialectic

---

[32] See Prickett, 'Coleridge and the Idea of the Clerisy'.

between what Coleridge calls the 'permanent' and the 'progressive' forces within the nation. The former is essentially conservative and identified with the landowning interest; the latter with manufacturing – providing, as it were, a schematized basis for the two main political parties of the period, Tory and Whig. That such a theoretical basis for the party conflict of the day had never existed, let alone formed part of any mythical 'Constitution' is beside the point; under the guise of describing Church and State 'according to the [Platonic] idea of each', Coleridge is prescribing his *own* ideal and entirely notional system.[33] Moreover, the real centre of his interest lay not in any theoretical political dialectic, but in the Church.

By 'Church' Coleridge, needless to say, intends specifically the Church of England. The whole thrust of his argument is to show that non-conformity – and especially Catholicism – simply does not accord with the 'idea' of the Church within his scheme. According to this, the Church, like the State, is also composed of a dialectical polarity between what Coleridge calls the 'National Church' on the one hand, and the 'Church of Christ' on the other. The former exists within a particular society at a particular historical moment, and is peculiar to that specific nation; the latter represents the universal Church, embodying the great and eternal truths of the Christian religion. Though these two 'ideas', as he calls them, co-exist in the same body, they are nonetheless entirely separate and distinct:

As the olive tree is said in its growth to fertilize the surrounding soil, to invigorate the roots of the vines in its immediate neighbourhood, and to improve the strength and flavour of the wines; such is the relationship of the Christian and National Church. But as the olive is not the same plant with the vine . . . even so is Christianity . . . no essential part of the being of the National Church, however conducive or even indispensable it may be to its well being. And even so a National Church might exist, and has existed, without . . . the Christian Church.[34]

Since one suspects that the real model for this almost mystical dual nature was the dual nature of Christ, it is perhaps hardly surprising that Coleridge has some difficulty in giving specific examples of a non-Christian National Church that embodies the spiritual values of its particular culture, and resorts to some vague references to the role of the Druids within the 'Celtic nation'. However, by what he calls a 'blessed accident' the National Church in England is officially Christian, and for its members in their dual role he coins the word 'Clerisy' – a term

---

[33] Among the sources of this structure is probably the American Constitution.

[34] S.T. Coleridge, *On the Constitution of the Church and State*, ed. John Colmer, Bollingen Series (Routledge/Princeton University Press, 1976), p. 56.

whose quasi-ecclesiastical overtones exactly capture the status of what he wants to describe. For Coleridge, the Clerisy, or members of the National Church in England, is composed of three intellectual estates: the clergy; teachers in the universities (who, we recall, were still, in 1830, almost exclusively in Cambridge or Oxford, where they had to be ordained); and the teachers in the 'great schools'. This Clerisy, composed of both ordained and lay 'guardians' in an almost platonic sense, is thus not just concentrated in specific centres of education, but is spread across the face of the country, exercising its moral and teaching function in every parish where there was a resident priest. Coleridge, we notice, was among the first to stress that peculiarly British identification of educational excellence with moral value.[35]

Such an appeal to the traditional underpinnings of the 'British Constitution' – however a-historical – was an idea in tune with the times, and *Church and State* enjoyed an influence and reputation that grew, rather than waned, as the specific issue of Catholic emancipation was forgotten. Disraeli was to make use of its political theory both in his 'Young England' novels, and, later, in his more pragmatic attempts to widen the narrow power-base of the Conservative Party to form a coalition of interests capable of providing a natural majority.[36] It was to make a no less profound impact at the other end of the political spectrum. Many readers of John Stuart Mill's seminal essay on Coleridge are unaware that it was written as a review of the second (1839) edition of *Church and State*. Its impact on educational theory was perhaps even more significant. Mark Pattison's evidence to the Royal Commission on Oxford in 1852 defends the existence of what he calls 'a cultivated Clerisy' with the clear assumption that the term and its connotations will be familiar to friend and foe alike.[37] Though I know of no example of his use of the actual term, the idea is also clearly present in the senior Arnold's reforms at Rugby in the 1830s – from whence it passes to A.P. Stanley in his biography of Thomas Arnold, and to Thomas Hughes in *Tom Brown's Schooldays* – the two works which, as John Honey argues, did most to establish the myth of

---

[35] Keble's use of this idea in his Crewian Oration of 1839 is obvious.

[36] A point on which it will be seen that I disagree with Robert [Lord] Blake, in his magisterial biography: *Disraeli* (St Martin's Press, 1967).

[37] 'Report of H.M. Commissioners appointed to enquire into the State, Discipline, Studies, and Revenues of the Universities and Colleges of Oxford', *Parliamentary Papers XXII* [1852], Evidence, p.45. Contrasting lecture and tutorial based systems of education, he told the Commisioners: 'Each system has its own place; they should not be rivals; the one for the mass of the people, the other for a cultivated Clerisy.' See John Sparrow, *Mark Pattison and the Idea of a University* (Cambridge University Press, 1967), p. 93.

Arnold of Rugby.[38] Still later it was to find expression in the ideology of the Christian Socialists, the Christian Social Union, and, through figures like T.H. Green, in the Worker's Educational Association.[39] When John Sterling and Frederick Denison Maurice founded the Cambridge debating society that was later to achieve such a mystique as 'The Apostles' it was rapidly assumed that its privileged membership should see themselves in terms of the Clerisy.[40] Tennyson's *In Memoriam*, written for his friend and fellow Apostle, Arthur Hallam, is framed, for those in the know, in apostolic and clerisical language.

Coleridge's belief in the need for a guiding elite of cultural guardians was rapidly absorbed by Mill and Matthew Arnold.[41] In 'The Bishop and the Philosopher' (1863) Arnold advances one of his most forthright arguments for the need for cultural leadership:

Knowledge and truth, in the full sense of the words, are not attainable by the great mass of the human race at all. The great mass of the human race have to be softened and humanised through their heart and imagination, before any soil can be found in them where knowledge may strike living roots . . . Old moral ideas leaven and humanise the multitude: new intellectual ideas filter slowly down to them from the thinking few, and only when they reach them in this manner do they adjust themselves to their practice without convulsing it.[42]

Nor was there any doubt in the minds of contemporaries as to where these ideas had come from. Here, for instance, is Edward Miall, a prominent non-conformist MP, speaking in 1871:

I wish to say something of the rural parishes of the kingdom. In each of these, we are told, the clergyman, maintained by national endowment, is a living link between the highest and the lowliest of the parishioners – is a cultivated gentleman, located just where there is, if not the greatest need, at any rate the best opportunity, for diffusing both 'sweetness and light' – is the fixed centre in the parish of civilization, of education, of charity, of piety – and I am told that I propose to abolish him and leave the people to fall back into ignorance and Paganism . . . These rural parishes have been in the undisturbed spiritual occupation of the clergy of the Church of England for generations past . . . Well, what on a large scale has been the result? What are the most conspicuous characteristics

---

[38] J.R. de S. Honey, *Tom Brown's Universe: The Development of the Victorian Public School* (Milligan, 1977), pp. 22–30.
[39] See Stephen Prickett, *Romanticism and Religion: The Tradition of Coleridge and Wordsworth in the Victorian Church* (Cambridge University Press, 1976), Ch. 5.
[40] See P.L. Allen, *The Cambridge Apostles* (Cambridge University Press, 1978).
[41] See Ben Knights, *Mind and Society: The Idea of the Clerisy in the Nineteenth Century* (Cambridge University Press, 1977).
[42] *Complete Prose Works*, Vol. III, p. 44.

of our labouring agricultural population? Do they include 'sweetness and light'? Do they include fairly-developed intelligence? Do they include a high state of morality? Do they offer affectionate veneration for religion? Are these the most prominent features by which the character of our agricultural population is distinguished, and in respect of which they bear away the palm from the inmates of towns? And the discouraging and painful answers to these queries – are they not to be found in blue-books, verified as they may be by personal observation?[43]

The references to Coleridge and Arnold are unmistakable.

Though there is no doubt about the origins of Arnold's ideas of the Clerisy, there is little doubt that Coleridge *also* supplied the context in which he developed his binary opposition of 'Hebrew' and 'Hellene'. Coleridge's idea, we recall, had been essentially religious. The activities of the National Church were, for him, constantly under judgement from the highest ideals of the other pole: the Church of Christ. If, as Miall and others had been quick to point out, the actual state of the Church of England did not quite live up to the role Coleridge has assigned to it as part of its essential 'idea', then it stood condemned by its own Christian teachings.

But for Arnold, the reluctant secularizer, this dialectical vision of a Christian culture was itself mere *Aberglaube* – as he explains it in *Literature and Dogma*, a transcendental encrustation of myth and fairy-story around the basic moral truths for which Christianity – properly understood and stripped of all its accretions – really stood.[44] His satirical *alter ego*, Mr Luke, in *The New Republic*, says it all. Thus, suitably demythologized by that tiny minority who can see things as they really are, what is left of the Church of Christ is a narrow moralism: in other words 'Hebraism'. To the Clerisy, on the other hand, belongs the whole rich cultural fabric of national life, with all its heritage and traditions, and for this Arnold appropriates the name 'Hellenism'. That his prime example of this 'Hellenistic' culture, thus implicitly defined, should be Newman is not that surprising. Newman's rigid moral conscience (the subject of the dispute with Kingsley that led to the publication of the *Apologia*) is, from this point of view, immaterial. From a national and cultural standpoint, Newman's real significance is not his Catholicism – something of a regrettable aberration for Arnold – but his visible embodiment of the traditions and cultural heritage of the Clerisy, expressed most notably in *The Idea of a University*. Arnold saw, quite correctly, the underlying Platonism of

---

[43] Cited by Donald Davie, *A Gathered Church: The Literature of the English Dissenting Interest, 1700–1930* (Oxford University Press, 1978), p. 78.
[44] See Prickett, *Romanticism and Religion*, pp. 211–23.

Coleridge's elite of cultural guardians, and that there was in *Church and State* a quite conscious balancing of biblical and classical ideals, of Greek culture with Hebrew spirituality, of Athens and Jerusalem.

Here then, is the *right* sense of history – as well as the explanation of the mismatched binary pairs at the heart of *Culture and Anarchy*. This combination of the literary heritage of England and the Whig interpretation of history would,[45] Arnold believed, provide the guiding cultural tradition that would (or at least *should* – he was not an optimist) replace the myth-encrusted superstitions of Christianity that had hitherto provided the 'noble myth' that Plato saw as essential to the cohesiveness of the just State. The real danger to this national culture came not from the 'Barbarians', who had threatened the ancient Greeks, but the 'Philistines' – those who believed money was the driving force in any society, and either had no cultural sense, or (even worse) the kind of vulgar and opulent taste whose purpose was not cultural but to display conspicuous consumption, and to show how even culture could be purchased if one had sufficient wealth.

To ward off the Philistines, in what Arnold saw as an unprecedented crisis, his only hope seemed to be to enlist the same weapon that the Church had grasped under essentially similar circumstances. If pluralism – in the form of Catholic emancipation, and a wider recognition of the political rights of non-conformists – had been met by a renewed (and, as always, partly created) sense of tradition in the Anglican Church, then perhaps a renewed stress on cultural tradition could stave off the growing cultural pluralism of nineteenth-century Britain. But simply because the word 'tradition' had already been appropriated and fought over in ecclesiastical culture-wars, it could not so easily be reclaimed for secular purposes. Moreover, as we suggested at the beginning of this chapter, only one of the four principal uses of the word available to Arnold carried a clearly secular meaning – and that suggested either antique mythology and/or dubious authority. He was certainly not against using such traditions – in 'The Scholar Gypsy' (1853), for instance, he takes an oral tradition from the Oxfordshire countryside noted by Glanvill in *The Vanity of Dogmatizing* (1661) and ends it with a classical twist.[46] Yet the word itself had been too

---

[45] See Herbert Butterfield, *The Whig Interpretation of History* (G. Bell, 1963).

[46] And a most odd one in the light of *Culture and Anarchy*. Here is the footnote from the *Norton Anthology*:

The trader from Tyre is disconcerted when, peering out through the foliage... that screens his hiding place, he sees noisy intruders entering his harbor. Like the Scholar Gypsy, when similarly intruded upon by noisy extroverts, he resolves to flee and seek a new home. The reference... to the Iberians as 'shy traffickers' . . . is. . . derived from Herodotus' *History* (iv.196). Herodotus describes a distinctive

effectively pre-empted, or, at least, had what one might call distracting overtones.

Moreover, just as problematic for Arnold was the fact that of the various uses suggested earlier, it was not the ideas of unreliability or stasis that appealed to him. The notion of tradition that runs unspoken throughout *Culture and Anarchy* is closest to that of Newman. That is, it is essentially dynamic and developmental – a progressive unfolding of the human spirit. Once again, the prevailing metaphor is that of a flowing river:

> Another hour in man's development began in the fifteenth century, and the main road of his progress then lay for a time through Hellenism. Puritanism was no longer the central current of the world's progress, it was a side stream crossing the central current and checking it. The cross and the check may have been necessary and salutary, but that does not do away with the essential difference between the main stream of man's advance and a cross or side stream. For more than two hundred years the main stream of man's advance has moved towards knowing himself and the world, seeing things as they are, spontaneity of consciousness; the main impulse of a great part, and that the strongest part, of our nation has been towards strictness of conscience. They have made the secondary the principal at the wrong moment, and the principal they have at the wrong moment treated as secondary. [47]

Here, if we needed it, is a fuller explanation of why the Hebraists have the wrong sense of history. Hellenism constitutes the 'main stream' of modern development. It is the 'true' cultural tradition; Hebraism is a mere 'side stream' by comparison. And this is because Hellenism – 'spontaneity of consciousness' – is of its nature progressive and developmental, seeking ever greater knowledge, whether of self or the material world, whereas Hebraism is static or even backward-looking. 'Strictness of conscience', on the other hand, doesn't *have* to show development. Moral values do

---

method of selling goods established by Carthaginian merchants who used to sail through the straits of Gibraltar to trade with the inhabitants of the coast of West Africa. The Carthaginians would leave bales of their merchandise on display along the beaches and, without having seen their prospective customers, would return to their ships. The shy natives would then come down from their inland hiding places and set gold down beside the bales they wished to buy. When the natives withdrew in their turn, the Carthaginians would return to the beach and decide which payments were adequate, a process repeated until agreement was reached... For the solitary Tyrian trader such a procedure, with its avoidance of contact... would have been especially appropriate.

Norton Anthology of English Literature, 4th edn (Norton, 1979), p. 1377. The 'Carthaginans' from Tyre are, of course, the biblical 'Philistines' – here, apparently unable to stand the 'hearty extroverts' of the Greek rowing-club, fleeing to the ends of the known world to find a form of commerce that could be conducted without meeting. Even here, we note, the pairing is unexpected: Hellenes versus Philistines.

[47] 'Culture and Anarchy', p.175.

not change – they merely have to be chipped free, liberated, from the encrustation of centuries of *Aberglaube*. This is, if you like, Newman versus Keble – and Newman, on these criteria, wins hands down.

What Arnold seemingly cannot do in this context is to bring himself to use the word 'tradition'. The reason is the very opposite of Coleridge's reluctance some eighty years before. Whereas for Coleridge the word is virtually obsolete, representing a notion without credibility – without 'voucher' in Paine's terminology – for Arnold the word is too much with us. It is a political and ecclesiastical football, and to use it would be to bring up too many irrelevant associations. Culture must be Hellenistic: appealing to the past while looking to the future. Culture is wider and, as Arnold argued at the beginning of his essay, in a pluralistic society, even more important therefore than religion. Given recent battles in both America and Britain about what exactly constitutes American or British traditional values in societies far more multi-ethnic and multi-religious than Arnold could possibly have envisaged, his questions – as so often – are far more prescient than his answers. What exactly culture *was* in a positive sense for Arnold is, as we have seen, often less clear than its emotional connotations, but Mallock's accusation that it was what was left of religion after the religion has been removed has more than a little snide truth to it.

Newman's *Grammar of Assent* was published in 1870, the year after Arnold's *Culture and Anarchy*, but Newman's idea of an unfolding development of tradition had been clearly marked ever since the *Essay on the Development of Christian Doctrine* in 1845. Secularizing Newman's idea of tradition was never going to be an easy task. It was left to another poet in the twentieth century to complete Arnold's project – T.S. Eliot.

CHAPTER II

Radical tradition: theologizing Eliot

[I]f the only form of tradition, of handing down, consisted in following the ways of the immediate generation before us in a blind or timid adherence to its successes, 'tradition' should be positively discouraged. We have seen many such simple currents lost in the sand; and novelty is better than repetition. Tradition is a matter of much wider significance. It cannot be inherited, and if you want it you must obtain it by great labour. It involves in the first place, the historical sense, which we may call nearly indispensable to anyone who would continue to be a poet beyond his twenty-fifth year; and the historical sense involves a perception, not only of the pastness of the past, but of its presence; the historical sense compels a man to write not merely with his own generation in his bones, but with a feeling that the whole of the literature of Europe from Homer and within it the whole of the literature of his own country has a simultaneous existence and composes a simultaneous order.[1]

Eliot's famous dicta on tradition in his 1919 essay 'Tradition and the Individual Talent' have become so much a part of the furniture of twentieth-century literary criticism that much of their original shock-value has been lost. He obviously considered the central thesis of this essay so important, that he repeated much of it, verbatim, in a 1923 essay with the deliberately Arnoldian title, 'The Function of Criticism':

No poet, no artist of any art, has his complete meaning alone. His significance, his appreciation is the appreciation of his relation to the dead poets and artists. You cannot value him alone; you must set him, for contrast and comparison, among the dead. I mean this as a principle of aesthetic, not merely historical, criticism. The necessity that he shall conform, that he shall cohere, is not one-sided; what happens when a new work of art is created is something that happens simultaneously to all the works of art that preceded it. The existing monuments form an ideal order among themselves, which is modified by the introduction of the new (the really new) work of art among them. The existing order is complete

---

[1] T.S. Eliot, 'Tradition and the Individual Talent', *Selected Essays* (Faber and Faber 1932), p. 14.

before the new work arrives; for order to persist after the supervention of novelty, the whole existing order must be, if ever so slightly, altered; and so the relations, proportions, values of each work of art toward the whole are readjusted; and this is conformity between the old and the new.

... To conform merely would be for the new work not really to conform at all; it would not be new, and would therefore not be a work of art.[2]

So familiar have these passages become to anyone studying the history of twentieth-century criticism, that it is easy to forget that this 1919 essay, Eliot's first published critical work, pre-dates all but a handful of his most controversial poems, including *The Waste Land*. It appeared two years after his first volume of poetry, *Prufrock and Other Observations*, which had attracted only a small amount of (mostly unfriendly) attention.[3] Perhaps even more remarkable is the fact that in November of 1917 he had described 'tradition' as '. . . all the ideas, beliefs, modes of feeling and behaviour which we have not time or inclination to investigate for ourselves [and] take second-hand'.[4] Prompted by that observation, maybe Eliot had himself taken the time to explore his own reactions to the word.

Certainly by the mid-1920s, with the additional publication of *Poems 1920*, *The Waste Land* (1922), and 'The Hollow Men' (1925), the paradox of Eliot's defence of tradition was both much more apparent, and much more challenging. Here was a radically new poetic voice from across the Atlantic, at once jarringly iconoclastic and apparently wilfully pretentious, passing off passages of prose as 'verse', mixing the smell of steak in passageways and the banal seduction of a lonely typist, with references to modernists like Ezra Pound, to (then) obscure French poets such as Jules Laforgue – and the even more obscure Jean Verdenal.

The conventional view of Eliot's progression from the world-weary questionings of the early poems, through his religious conversion of 1927 (celebrated in 'Ash Wednesday' 1930), to the arch-conservative editor of *The Criterion*, the apparent mystic of the *Four Quartets*, and the verse playwright of the 1950s, has long been challenged by those who point to the (retrospectively) obvious religious leanings of 'The Hippopotamus' (1920)

---

[2] Ibid., p. 15.
[3] See Michael Grant (ed.), *T.S. Eliot: The Critical Heritage* (Routledge, 1982), pp. 67–92 and passim.
[4] T.S. Eliot, 'Reflections on Contemporary Poetry', *The Egoist*, November 1917, p. 151. I owe this reference to Jan Gorak.

and 'The Waste Land' itself.[5] But those leanings were certainly not obvious to contemporaries. In a letter of 1928 Virginia Woolf wrote:

I have had a most shameful and distressing interview with dear Tom Eliot, who may be called dead to us all from this day forward. He has become an Anglo-Catholic believer in God and immortality, and goes to church. I was shocked. A corpse would seem to me more credible than he is. I mean there's something obscene in a living person sitting by the fire and believing in God.[6]

Such responses from those who thought themselves close friends are a reminder of just how puzzling and contradictory his career seemed to contemporaries.

However one views this development, it is obviously a remarkable and complex one, of considerable importance to any discussion of twentieth-century ideas of tradition. Yet central to any understanding of Eliot's long and very varied literary career, as poet, critic, and general man of letters, is the fact that it *begins* – rather than concludes – with that essay on tradition. It is, moreover, a theme he returns to repeatedly for the rest of his life. His standpoint is the more remarkable because he pointedly refuses to use the word 'tradition' in its normal and conventional sense. Comparing Andrew Marvell with William Morris, for instance, he writes:

Marvell is no greater personality than William Morris, but he had something much more solid behind him: he had the vast and penetrating influence of Ben Jonson. Jonson never wrote anything purer than Marvell's Horatian Ode; this ode has that same quality of wit which was diffused over the whole Elizabethan product and concentrated in the work of Jonson . . . this wit which pervades the poetry of Marvell is more Latin, more refined than anything that succeeded it.[7]

This is not one of Eliot's best arguments, and his judgement may be questionable on a number of grounds,[8] but what is surely remarkable is that he does *not* use the word 'tradition' to describe that 'vast and penetrating influence' – whether Jonsonian or Latin in origin. Indeed, his earlier statement that 'tradition cannot be inherited' more or less precludes him from employing the word to describe poetic influence in the normal sense.

---

[5] Despite numerous excellent studies of Eliot's life and development, I still find Northrop Frye's little 1963 study in the Oliver and Boyd 'Writers and Critics' series one of the most irreverently stimulating.

[6] Virginia Woolf, letter of 11 February 1928. In Adrian Hastings, *A History of English Christianity 1920–1990* (SCM Press, 1991), p. 236.

[7] 'Andrew Marvell', *Selected Essays*, p. 301.

[8] For example, If Jonson never wrote anything as good as the Horation Ode, why should he somehow get the credit for the qualities of what is admittedly the inferior work?

There is, nevertheless, nothing essentially new in Eliot's basic premise. The idea of poetry as a timeless order goes back at least as far as Coleridge and Shelley[9] – and its theological roots are clear enough beyond that. By the end of the century, however, other links between literary and religious traditions were being developed. W.B. Yeats, who was normally more interested in the occult than any conventional religious practices, was nevertheless at pains to centre his poetic development not merely on a sense of tradition, but on specifically religious tradition. Once again it was invented *backwards*: 'I was unlike others of my generation in one thing only', he writes in his *Autobiographies*:

I am very religious, and deprived by Huxley and Tyndall, whom I detested, of the simple-minded religion of my childhood, I had made a new religion, almost an infallible Church of poetic tradition, of a fardel of stories, and of personages, and of emotions, inseparable from their first expression, passed on from generation to generation by poets and painters with some help from philosophers and theologians. I wished for a world where I could discover this tradition perpetually.[10]

At first sight two things stand out about this. The first is that Yeats, feeling, like Arnold, deprived by science of the conventional religious tradition that could have been accepted unquestioningly by an earlier generation, is impelled to create his own religion more or less from scratch. Like Blake, he is a *bricoleur* of tradition.[11] Like Picasso, only fifteen years his junior, he creates what look at first sight like familiar forms from unfamiliar, even incongruous ingredients – literary bric-à-brac. The second is that *only* a religious tradition ('an infallible Church . . . with some help from philosophers and theologians') can adequately embody the aesthetic tradition that he is actually seeking to fabricate. But a second glance suggests something else as well. Despite the need for community implicit in the idea of tradition, this is essentially a one-off job. A home-made infallible Church – let alone a do-it-yourself aesthetic tradition – is, of course, a contradiction in terms. Yet it is all of a piece with Yeats's restoration of his mediaeval 'tower', Thoor Ballylee, in an idiosyncratic arts-and-crafts style, or, more ambitiously, inventing an 'Ireland' to match the Celtic dreams of one born into the Protestant Ascendency.

---

[9] 'No living poet ever arrived at the fullness of his fame; the jury which sits in judgement upon a poet, belonging as he does to all time, must be composed of his peers: it must be empanelled by time from the selectest of the wise of many generations.' Percy Bysshe Shelley, *A Defence of Poetry*, in *English Romantic Poetry and Prose*, ed. Russell Noyes (Oxford University Press, 1956), p. 1100.

[10] W.B. Yeats, 'The Trembling of the Veil', in *Autobiographies* (1927), pp. 115–16.

[11] The phrase is Jon Mee's. See *Dangerous Enthusiasms: William Blake and the Culture of Radicalism in the 1790s* (Clarendon Press, 1992).

Yeats's literary 'modernism' – the latest and most aesthetic manifestation of Cassiodorus's modernity – is at once historically self-conscious
and individualistic to the point of solipsism. What is equally clear, is that
for anyone approaching Eliot's idea of tradition from a reading of Herder
or Newman, Arnold or Yeats, the tension between commonality and individualism remains essentially unresolved. If Eliot is only following earlier
figures in secularizing and aestheticizing the theological debate of the previous century, the dual conflicts of the individuality of the artist versus the
artistic tradition, and the corresponding clash of innovation and conformity was one that was not going to disappear.

But, for at least one near-contemporary of Eliot and Yeats there was a
more positive side to this personal construction of a tradition. In a 1951
lecture on 'The Argentine Writer and Tradition', Jorge Luis Borges (1899–
1986) disputed the nationalistic notion that Argentine literature either
was, or should be, rooted in *gauchesco* poetry, or some other local equivalent. Writing as an Argentine, he argues:

> I believe that our tradition is the whole of Western culture, and I also believe that
> we have a right to this tradition, a greater right than that which the inhabitants of
> one Western nation or another may have. Here I remember an essay by Thorstein
> Veblen, the North American sociologist, on the intellectual pre-eminence of Jews
> in Western culture. He wonders whether this pre-eminence authorizes us to posit
> an innate Jewish superiority and answers that it does not; he says that Jews are
> prominent in Western culture because they act within that culture and at the
> same time do not feel bound to it by any special devotion; therefore, he says, it
> will always be easier for a Jew than for a non-Jew to make innovations in Western
> culture. We can say the same of the Irish in English culture. Where the Irish
> are concerned, we have no reason to suppose that the profusion of Irish names
> in British literature and philosophy is due to any social pre-eminence, because
> many of these illustrious Irishmen (Shaw, Berkeley, Swift) were the descendents
> of Englishmen, men with no Celtic blood; nevertheless, the fact of feeling them-
> selves to be Irish, to be different, was enough to enable them to make innovations
> in English culture. I believe that Argentines and South Americans in general, are
> in an analogous situation; we can take on all the European subjects, take them on
> without superstition and with an irreverence that can have, and already has had,
> fortunate consequences.[12]

Perhaps the only surprise in Borges's list of pre-eminent Anglo-Irish
writers is the omission of Yeats himself – for here the greatest South
American writer of the mid-century is consciously drawing alike on both

---

[12] Jorge Luis Borges, 'The Argentine Writer and Tradition', *Selected Non-Fictions*, ed. Eliot
Weinburger, trs. Esther Allen, Suzanne Jill Levine, and Eliot Weinburger (Viking, 1999), p. 426.

the collective vision of Eliot and the more homespun one of Yeats to suggest a promise that was to be amply fulfilled in the wave of fresh and innovative Latin American literary talent that was to include Carlos Fuentes, Mario Vargas Llosa, and Gabriel Garcia Márquez.

Yet to miss Borges's implicit reference to Eliot would be to miss the whole thrust of his argument. Whereas Arnold (despite his protestations) seems to have seen 'culture' in much the same light as Keble's 'deposit of faith', Eliot seeks to re-define tradition in terms of constant development and progression, always entering new ground as it encounters the challenges of contemporary society, always surprising and unanticipated, always changing our perspective on the deposit of the past. So far from it being the function of criticism at the present time to identify the true historic path of culture, and to seek to defend and preserve that line, we have, in effect, always to be responsive to 'the really new'. Thus defined, such shadowy reifications as 'the mind of Europe' or 'the poetic tradition', substituted for the divinely inspired deposit so central to the nineteenth-century debate, may look to us like an alternative path to aesthetic secularization.

This is certainly true as far as it goes. Eliot's dynamic re-definition of tradition *is* clearly much more satisfactory than Arnold's attempt to find in 'culture' the civilizing values of a radically pluralized society. Moreover Eliot's version undoubtedly *is* based on a secularized religious ideal. But, especially in the light of his later religious development, we need to look much more carefully at some of the implications of his theory.

The comparison with Arnold is crucial. No twentieth-century literary figure has been more haunted by what Harold Bloom has called the 'anxiety of influence' than Eliot.[13] Simply by attempting to be poet, critic, and, later, theologian, Eliot inevitably invited comparison with his two greatest forebears: Coleridge and Arnold. Both offered models that were at once alluring and (for him) ultimately unsatisfactory. Both are therefore none-too-subtly damned with faint praise in Eliot's criticism. 'Coleridge', he tells us, was a 'ruined man' – though perhaps, he adds, mysteriously, that that was 'his vocation'.[14] Undoubtedly comparison with a man whose early poetry had been first abused, then accepted as a classic, who had ceased writing poetry at a fairly early age, whose inner life had been torn by crises of faith and a failed marriage,[15] and who had

[13] Harold Bloom, *The Anxiety of Influence: A Theory of Poetry* (Oxford University Press, 1975).
[14] T.S. Eliot, 'Wordsworth and Coleridge', *The Use of Poetry and the Use of Criticism* (Faber and Faber, 1933). See also Seamus Perry, 'T.S. Eliot's Coleridge', *Coleridge's Afterlives*, ed. James Vigus and Jane Wright (Palgrave, 2008).
[15] See Lyndall Gordon, *Eliot's New Life* (Oxford, 1988).

attempted to re-establish himself as a critic and theologian in middle-age, was perhaps too close for comfort. He himself, Eliot delicately hinted, was better compared with Dante and Donne – both of whom were safely distanced by time.[16]

But Eliot's attempt to create his own tradition does not obliterate the very clear debt to Coleridge. In his 1811–12 lectures on Shakespeare, Coleridge had re-applied his concept of method, elaborated in his earlier and somewhat intermittent periodical, *The Friend*, to Shakespeare, not so much as an individual writer on his own, but as an example of the flowering of literary tradition.[17] Here he is on Shakespeare – in a passage already cited in connection with August Schlegel above:[18]

few there have been among critics, who have followed with the eye of the imagination the imperishable, yet ever-wandering, spirit of poetry through its various metempsychoses, and correspondent metamorphoses; – or who have rejoiced in the light of clear perception at beholding with each new birth, with each rare avatar, the human race frame to itself a new body, by assimilating materials of nourishment out of its new circumstances, and work for itself new organs of power appropriate to the new sphere of its motion and activity.[19]

This close cross-reference between the inner development of the poet and the outer framework of the tradition within which he worked is important – not merely in the development of Coleridge's own critical theory, but also in the way it shaped the thinking of later critics. Creativity is not just the mark of the great writer, but of the sustaining literary tradition – though Coleridge, for the reasons mentioned, still cannot bring himself to use the word 'tradition' in this sense, but resorts to a Goethe-like image of organic and vegetable growth. Moreover, this is not here, we notice, a pluralistic or fragmented line, but the main stream of developing human consciousness: 'the spirit of poetry'. But 'genius' is singular. Despite superficial appearances of multiplicity and confusion, for Coleridge unity over-rides plurality:

And still mounting the intellectual ladder, he [Shakespeare] had as unequivocally proved the indwelling in his mind of imagination, or the power by which one image or feeling is made to modify many others, and by a sort of *fusion to force*

---

[16] See T.S. Eliot, 'The Metaphysical Poets' (1921), 'Dante' (1929) in *Selected Essays*, and 'What Dante Means to Me' (1950) in *To Criticize the Critic* (Faber and Faber, 1965).

[17] See Stephen Prickett, *Coleridge and Wordsworth: The Poetry of Growth* (Cambridge University Press, 1970), pp. 115–17.

[18] See p. 126. Coleridge's own anxiety of influence is well illustrated by his somewhat overemphatic assertion that he could not possibly have been influenced by August Schlegel in his 'Essay on Plagiarism'. *Shakespeare Criticism*, ed. T.M. Raysor, 2nd edn, 2 vols. (Everyman, 1960), Vol. II, p. 188.

[19] Ibid., Vol. I, p.174.

many into one . . . which, combining many circumstances into one moment of consciousness, tends to produce that ultimate end of human thought and feeling, unity, and thereby the reduction of the spirit to its principle and fountain, who is alone truly one.[20]

This, as Eliot would say, is a principle not merely of aesthetic, but historical criticism. The true critic sees 'with the eye of the imagination' – a continuing process of organic growth, in which each new 'avatar' involves a re-creation of all that has gone before in a form appropriate its time and purpose. The word 'avatar' comes from India – describing the descent of a Hindu deity to the earth in a particular incarnation. Though this constant aesthetic re-creation can be interpreted in an idealist, almost Platonic way (and there are times in *The Friend* when Coleridge, as here in the Shakespeare lectures, seems to be implying some such idea) the general trend of this argument is increasingly concrete and historical.

This is even more marked in the criticism of Coleridge's most immediate disciple, Julius Hare (1795–1855). Hare's aphoristic criticism – with its clear debt to the Schlegels and the *Athenaeum* – reveals a sense not merely of the enormous range and diversity of his own literary heritage, but also of how far that heritage had developed and changed over the years. This shift in perspective is very clear in a lengthy piece devoted to a comparison between ancient and modern poetry:

Goethe in 1800 does not write just as Shakespeare wrote in 1600: but neither would Shakespeare in 1800 have written just as he wrote in 1600. For the frame and aspect of society are different; the world which would act on him, and on which he would have to act, is another world. True poetical genius lives in communion with the world, in a perpetual reciprocation of influences, imbibing feeling and knowledge, and pouring out what it has imbibed in words of power and gladness and wisdom. It is not, at least when highest it is not, as Wordsworth describes Milton to have been 'like a star dwelling apart'. Solitude may comfort weakness, it will not be the home of strength . . . In short, Genius is not an independent and insulated, but a social and continental, or at all events a peninsular power . . . Now without entering into a comparison of Shakespeare's age with our own, one thing at least is evident, that, considered generally and as a nation, we are more bookish than our ancestors . . . While the conflict and tug of passions supplied in Shakespeare's days the chief materials for poetry, in our days it is rather the conflict of principles . . . This appears not only from the

---

[20] Coleridge's Shakespeare lectures are all reconstructed from notes of those present, and therefore differ considerably in detail. Here I have used that of the *Literary Remains*, ed. H.N. Coleridge, 1836, reprinted ed. E. Rhys (Everyman, 1907), p. 39. For a somewhat different version, see also S.T. Coleridge, *Shakespeare Criticism*, ed. Raysor, Vol. I, p. 188.

works of Goethe and others of his countrymen, but from the course taken by our own greatest poets, by Wordsworth, Coleridge, and Landor. They have been rebuked indeed for not writing otherwise: but they have done rightly; for they have obeyed the impulse of their nature, and the voice of their age has been heard speaking through their lips.[21]

If there was any doubt about Coleridge's, Hare's is definitely a progressive, and historical rather than an idealist aesthetic. His strong historical sense is impelled by a thoroughly English pragmatism. The development of human sensibility is indeed closely enmeshed with the particular conditions of time and place, rather than with any abstract Hegelian outworking of the spirit of the age. Wordsworth, Coleridge, and Landor, are not products of the prevailing *Geist*, but of specific and concrete historical and cultural conditions – and none the less great for that.

As we have seen,[22] it was the second generation of romantic critics, Dallas, De Quincey, Hare, Landor and others, who historicized the idea of an aesthetic tradition. Here this is not merely a retrospective explanation of why Goethe in 1800 should differ from Shakespeare in 1600, it lays down the principle of why Goethe *had* to differ. The same work written 200 years later would be, of necessity, a different work simply because of its context – or, in Eliot's words 'it would not be new, and would therefore not be a work of art'.

Yet the comparison between Shakespeare and Goethe is revealing in other ways. For Hare, not merely does each represent the greatest of their respective ages, but the comparison also reminds us that no country (not even England) is a cultural island in itself. Though Coleridge's Shakespeare lectures are rightly seen as a milestone in the British appreciation of Shakespeare, the fact is, of course, that they follow A.W. Schlegel's in Germany. But as Germany has learned to appreciate Shakespeare's genius – and, incidentally, taught the British to do so – so Britain must learn to respond to the genius of Goethe. 'True genius lives in communion with the world' – or, as Eliot was to say 100 years later, in relation to that reformulated collective cultural entity, 'the mind of Europe'.[23]

Though Arnold was not the first to make it, this is again a very Arnoldian point. The literature of the English-speaking peoples, however rich and varied, cannot be understood merely within its own historical terms. It must always be understood in relation to both its classical antecedents and its European context, past and present. With Carlyle's great translation

---

[21] Julius and Augustus Hare, *Guesses at Truth*, 1827, Vol. II, pp. 136–40.
[22] See Ch. 7, above.
[23] See T.S. Eliot, 'Tradition and the Individual Talent', pp. 14–15.

of *Wilhelm Meister* in 1824 Goethe had become as much a part of English literature as Shakespeare had in German literature with A.W. Schlegel's translations. It had always been one of Arnold's lifelong ambitions to make insular English readers aware of the great Continental writers – in *Essays in Criticism*, essays on Marcus Aurelius, and the English romantics rub shoulders with those on Amiel, Maurice and Eugénie de Guérin, Heine, Joubert, Spinoza, and Tolstoy.

But Eliot, like Coleridge and Arnold, is not merely a literary critic. His own choice of mentors – Dante and Donne – however partial and even misleading by themselves, make his ambitions unmistakable. Though he would presumably not have seen himself as a theological critic in 1917,[24] as we have suggested, the trail is in retrospect there to follow. Nor is Eliot alone in feeling that there is an intimate link between theological and literary criticism. Ever since Coleridge, literary criticism has suffered from what I have called elsewhere an 'ache in the missing limb'.[25] In other words, the critical study of secular literature, which arose historically from the study of sacred literature – primarily the Bible – has never really lost the feeling that it is somehow still in the salvation business. This accounts both for some of the stranger statements made by agnostic or atheist critics in the twentieth century, and for the anti-religious fervour of some other critics.

Eliot addresses this phenomenon in his essay 'The Modern Mind', labelling it as a Romantic heresy, and citing – with modified support – the words of Jacques Rivière:

If in the seventeenth century Molière or Racine had been asked why he wrote, no doubt he would have been able to find but one answer; that he wrote for the entertainment of decent people (*pour distraire les honnêtes gens*). It is only with the advent of Romanticism that the literary act came to be conceived as a sort of raid on the absolute and its result a revelation.[26]

He goes on to quote with approval Jacques Maritain's criticism of I.A. Richards's statement that 'poetry is capable of saving us'. 'By showing us where moral truth and the genuine supernatural are situate', writes Maritain, 'religion saves poetry from the absurdity of believing itself destined to transform ethics and life: saves it from overweening arrogance.'[27]

---

[24] The story of his embarrassment meeting his old Harvard tutor, Irving Babbitt, in 1927, and being forced to explain why he had become a Christian suggests the distance he had travelled during the previous decade. See also his essay, 'The Humanism of Irving Babbitt' (1928).

[25] See Stephen Prickett, *Narrative, Religion and Science: Fundamentalism versus Irony, 1700–1999* (Cambridge University Press, 2002), Ch. 5.

[26] T.S. Eliot, *The Use of Poetry and the Use of Criticism* (Faber and Faber, 1933), p. 128.

[27] Ibid., p. 137.

Richards's claim is, of course, an extreme one, but one only has to look at the attempts of Richard Rorty and other postmodernists (including even the theologian Don Cupitt) to deny the existence of objective truth altogether,[28] to see how fierce a contemporary debate this still is – fought with the true mediaeval fervour of *odium theologicum.*[29] Moreover, there is a real irony in the fact that Eliot, even while rejecting Richards's view of poetry, presents himself by implication as being capable of re-uniting the 'dissociated sensibility' of English poetry that he claimed had persisted ever since the seventeenth century, and so restoring the unity of thought and feeling he attributes to Donne and the Metaphysical poets,[30] and before them to Dante. In short, my point is that, in retrospect at least, Eliot's idea of tradition is not merely a theory of literary criticism, but also a not-very-covert *theological* principle.

This has been noted by a number of critics. In the introduction to *The Visionary Company* (1971), Harold Bloom writes:

> To understand fully the link between the Revolution and English Romantic literature, it is perhaps most immediately illuminating to consider the case, not of one of its great poets, but of the critic William Hazlitt.
>
> Like that of all the English Romantic poets, Hazlitt's religious background was in the tradition of Protestant dissent, the kind of non-conformist vision that descended from the Left Wing of England's Puritan movement. There is no more important point to be made about English Romantic poetry than this one, or indeed about English poetry in general, particularly since it is a displaced Protestantism, or a Protestantism astonishingly transformed by different kinds of humanism or naturalism. The poetry of the English Romantics is a kind of religious poetry, and the religion is in the Protestant line, though Calvin or Luther would have been horrified to contemplate it. Indeed, the entire continuity of English poetry that T.S. Eliot and his followers attacked is a radical Protestant or displaced Protestant tradition.[31]

Bloom's aim here is to counter Eliot's version of English literary history by rewriting the story dialectically, historicizing Eliot's conservative Anglo-Catholic tradition into a larger cultural pattern of a radical, endlessly

---

[28] See Prickett, *Narrative, Religion and Science*, pp. 195–217.

[29] *Odium Theologicum*, or intellectual hatred: 'The most savage controversies are those about matters as to which there is no good evidence either way. Persecution is used in theology, not in arithmetic, because in arithmetic there is knowledge, but in theology there is only opinion.' Bertrand Russell, 'An Outline of Intellectual Rubbish' in *Unpopular Essays* (Allen & Unwin, 1950).

[30] See Eliot, 'The Metaphysical Poets' (1921).

[31] Harold Bloom, 'Prometheus Rising: The Backgrounds of Romantic Poetry', *The Visionary Company: A Reading of English Romantic Poetry*, rev. edn (Cornell University Press, 1971), pp. xvii–xix.

protean, Protestantism. For Christopher Strathman, such a reading, for better and for worse, is profoundly American[32] – Emerson or Thoreau, he adds, could easily be substituted for Hazlitt, reminding us that this is precisely the New England Unitarian background from which Eliot himself had emerged. But the argument also reminds us that with Eliot we must always look behind the secular representation for the theological core.

There are, of course, much earlier precedents for this linkage. As we saw in the Introduction, the idea of *paradosis* was, as it were, built into the very foundations of the Christian gospel. What has to be transmitted, or handed over, is not merely a face-to-face encounter – an idea obviously relevant to the eighteenth-century evangelical revival – but something inherently dangerous, and even, possibly, sacrificial. What *paradosis* does not support so well is the notion of a fixed deposit of 'truth', the same yesterday, today, and forever. Eliot's idea that each truly original work of literature 'is something that happens simultaneously to all the works of art that preceded it' suggests a principle much closer to the dynamism of Herder or Newman than it does to that of his fellow high-Anglican, Keble. Though Eliot was famously to describe himself as a 'classicist in literature, royalist in politics, and anglo-catholic in religion',[33] he was not above defining each of these standpoints in ways that might have surprised others grouped under the same banner. Certainly, if we consider the idea of a theological tradition in the light of his idea of a literary tradition what emerges is very interesting indeed.

To begin with, it would touch on the very central tension behind nearly 2,000 years of debate over the nature and function of tradition. 'The existing order' of works of poetry, for Eliot, we recall, 'is complete before the new work arrives; for order to persist after the supervention of novelty, the whole existing order must be, if ever so slightly, altered; and so the relations, proportions, values of each work of art toward the whole are readjusted; and this is conformity between the old and the new.'[34] Does this also apply to theology?

In fact, Christianity has always been tacitly ambivalent about the relationship of new ideas to the original deposit of faith – not least, because that original deposit, and its context, has never been absolutely clear – and this (I would argue) is not a contingent quality of Christianity, but has

---

[32] Christopher Strathman, 'Introduction to American Romanticism', *An Anthology of European Romanticism*, ed. Stephen Prickett and Simon Haines (Argumentum, 2009).

[33] Preface to 1928 essays *For Lancelot Andrewes: Essays on Style and Order* (Faber and Gwyer, 1928), p. ix.

[34] 'Tradition and the Individual Talent', p. 15.

always been an integral, if often unacknowledged, part of its narrative. As Rowan Williams has remarked, 'Christians were people for whom the past had become a problem.'[35] When it finally gained political power, he argues, the Church's previous experiences had left it with 'an agenda, a set of questions about the relation of the *ekklesia* to the changing forms of political life. It left itself, we might say, with a rationale for thinking about history'.[36] One might add that the conditions of its formation – including the appropriation of the Hebrew Scriptures, the Jewish midrash, a sense of both Christian difference from, and continuity with, the world of the Roman Empire – also left it with an agenda with regard to tradition. Are all four gospels, for instance, of equal status, or must we hold (with Roman Catholics) to the primacy of Matthew? Where exactly do the boundaries of the New Testament lie, and what is their relation to the Old Testament (again, not quite the same as the Hebrew Bible)? What is the status of the Council of Nicea, which finally decided the contents of the New Testament? Was it divinely inspired, as John Henry Newman insisted, or, as his brother, Francis Newman among many others had suspected, simply a piece of political manipulation by Constantine? Would we be safer sticking by the Vincentian Canon? As we have seen, the Council of Trent did more to muddy the waters of controversy than clarify them.

Partly as a result of these – and many other debates – theology has usually proceeded by finding the roots of whatever innovation is being debated in scripture, and then claiming any developments as exegesis. But clearly this has notoriously been a two-edged sword: the Devil, we are told, knows how to quote scripture; the Reformation was a battle over biblical interpretation and the deposit of faith – as a Dutch commentator had observed in the middle of the sixteenth century, scripture was a 'nose of wax' that could be moulded to fit any face;[37] even an undoubted historical innovation such as the abolition of slavery was vehemently defended and attacked by both sides with a wealth of scriptural justification. There has always been a sense in which the 'deposit of faith' has been a creation of the time or faction appealing to it.[38] Indeed, what, in retrospect,

---

[35] Rowan Williams, *Why Study the Past? The Quest for the Historical Church* (Eerdmans, 2005), p. 9.
[36] Ibid., p. 48.
[37] Albertus Pighius, *Hierarchiae Ecclesiasticae Assertio* (Cologne, 1538), fo. xxxx, sect. B, trs. Jewel, *Works* (Parker Society, 1841–53), Vol. IV, p. 759. Cited by H.C. Porter, 'The Nose of Wax: Scripture and the Spirit from Erasmus to Milton', *Transactions of the Royal Historical Society*, 5th series, Vol. XIV, 1964, p. 155.
[38] A point well made also by F.W. Newman, *Contributions Chiefly to the Early History of the Late Cardinal Newman, with Comments by His Brother, F.W. Newman* (Kegan Paul, Trench, Trübner & co., 1891), Ch 5.

is so remarkable about Newman's *Essay on the Development of Christian Doctrine* is its unashamed willingness to admit how far the Roman Catholic Church had moved from its New Testament roots, and to centre its defence of Catholicism not on its historic roots, but on the scale of that very movement. It is notable that few Catholic theologians have used this argument since.

Certainly it is clear to anyone with even a slight acquaintance with Church history that however much Christian doctrine has been modified by subsequent debates, what *has* changed radically is the *context* in which those debates have been conducted. In other words, we should perhaps be looking not so much at doctrinal formulations, but what we might call 'the Christian imagination' – and that imagination has been formed and nurtured above all by works of art. This has been a recurring theme throughout this book. What the history of three centuries of debate about tradition has shown is that over and over again it has proved impossible to separate theological notions of tradition from its aesthetic concomitants. Thus Dante's *Divine Comedy* altered forever the climate of feeling – the way in which Christian teaching was felt – eventually even by those who had never read it. This is true whether it is read literally or (as Dante clearly intended his densely polysemous narrative to be read) as a gigantic extended metaphor. The whole expansion of interior space which Chateaubriand saw as the inevitable concomitant of the spread of Christianity has, in itself, transformed the way in which the Bible was read and understood.[39]

Thus for Friedrich Schlegel, for example, the Bible was not merely a theological work, but 'the absolute book':

The new eternal gospel that Lessing prophesied will appear as a bible: but not as a single book in the usual sense. Even what we now call the Bible is actually a system of books. And that is, I might add, no mere arbitrary turn of phrase! Or is there some other word to differentiate the idea of an infinite book from an ordinary one, than Bible, the book per se, the absolute book? And surely there is an eternally essential and even practical difference if a book is merely a means to an end, or an independent work, an individual, a personified idea. It cannot be this without divine inspiration, and here the esoteric concept is itself in agreement with the exoteric one; and, moreover, no idea is isolated, but is what it is only in combination with all other ideas. An example will explain this. All the classical poems of the ancients are coherent, inseparable; they form an organic whole, they constitute, properly viewed, only a single poem, the only one in which poetry

---

[39] See Stephen Prickett, *Origins of Narrative* (Cambridge University Press, 2002), pp. 168–79.

itself appears in perfection. In a similar way, in a perfect literature all books should be only a single book, and in such an eternally developing book, the gospel of humanity and culture will be revealed.[40]

Though Eliot, significantly, rarely refers to German critics, and (to my knowledge) never refers to Schlegel, the idea of the whole of classical literature forming a single organic whole is, nevertheless, one present in what one might call Eliot's intellectual and aesthetic hinterland.

But if Eliot's ostensible description of how each new work of art changes the appreciation of all that has gone before, is not merely descriptive of the history of aesthetics, but also of theology, this in turn changes the way in which we view his own aesthetics. In other words, the curious gravitational relationship between aesthetics and theology of which he was a major interpreter has shown little sign of slackening. Each still responds to the pull of the other in unexpected ways. The biblical texts that form the basis of Handel's *Messiah* (not, incidentally, selected by Handel) are not changed by the existence of the oratorio, but no one who has heard some of the more famous arias can read those texts in quite the same way afterwards.

This is more than saying Christian doctrine has changed and developed over the course of time – which, of course, it certainly has. In the Romantic terms of a Coleridge or a Schlegel, it is an assertion of organic unity between seed and subsequent growth. But, again, it is more than that also: an assertion that the 'seed' is modified by the subsequent development of the organism, as we return to 'where we started, / And know the place for the first time'.[41] This may well be a theological truism, but it is still far from being a theological commonplace. What links the two ends of the chain is a particular idea of tradition – that in which the new, the truly new, changes all that has gone before it to establish, if not a 'new' tradition, then a new version of an existing tradition.

Indeed, in his 1919 essay Eliot is concerned less with the actual history of aesthetic change than with the mechanism by which it appeared to happen. Though one might argue that the body of his later essays does indeed offer a literary history of a kind, and at certain points – such as the theory of the seventeenth-century 'dissociation of sensibility' in his 1921 essay on 'The Metaphysical Poets'[42] – it is quite explicit, there is little

---

[40] Friedrich Schlegel, *Philosophical Fragments*, trs. Peter Firchow (University of Minnesota Press, 1991). *Ideas*, p. 95
[41] T.S. Eliot, 'Little Gidding', section v.
[42] *Selected Essays*, p. 288.

evidence that Eliot himself thought of his essays in this light, and there are enough inconsistencies to make the construction of such a history highly problematic. What is undoubtedly true, as Hare argued, is that just as Goethe, 200 years after Shakespeare, writes differently from the Elizabethan, so Eliot's criticism is different from that of a Johnson or a Wordsworth. What is less obvious, but also implicit in Eliot's theory, is that twentieth-century theologians not merely write differently from, say, sixteenth-century theologians, but would *have* to do so in order to practise their craft. In other words, *no* writer writing after, say, 1830, with as substantial a body of critical or theological essays as Eliot, could avoid creating some kind of assumed literary–historical framework in which to operate. The remarkable thing is not that Eliot attempts to do so, but that by allowing the present to re-interpret the past, he points openly to the process by which tradition, whether literary, theological, or even historical, is constantly at work, re-fashioning and re-creating our understanding of the world in which we find ourselves.

Re-energizing the past

The history of words is often a window into the history of thought. We have already seen David Norton's examples of words in the King James Authorized Version that were current or familiar archaisms in the sixteenth century but which had dropped out of use by the eighteenth century, and were later revived into common speech in the nineteenth century.[1] The point here is not just that, as Norton very convincingly argues, the Authorized Version has acted 'as a kind of uncrowded Noah's ark for vocabulary for perhaps two hundred years',[2] but also that such words, even where not specifically coined for the needs of translation, were restored to us from that ark subtly transformed, and often with added value.

As we have seen in the course of this book, the word 'tradition' has gone through a similar arc of neglect and subsequent re-discovery, though in this case it might be argued that the idea of 'tradition' helped to preserve the Authorized Version rather than vice versa. Similar also, however, was the attempt to find and use other ways of expressing the concept, before re-instating the older term with added value and new meaning. The biggest difference from these other biblical words, however, is the evident popularity of this particular restored and newly historicized one. At the same time as critics and theologians have been engaged in scholarly debate over questions of original deposits versus innovation and creativity, at the vernacular level everyone from politicians to advertising agencies has discovered, colonized, and finally claimed tradition as their ancestral territory – invoking everything from traditional values ('family' ones, naturally) to traditional recipes. What this popular usage has in common with the more scholarly controversies, of course, is that politicians, like commercial bakeries, are selecting a particular lineage that seems to lead to their current position.

---

[1] See Ch. 4 above. David Norton, *History of the Bible as Literature*, 2 vols., (Cambridge University Press, 1993), Vol. II, pp. 80–5.
[2] Ibid., p. 85.

Just as no one is invited to suppose that political appeals to 'traditional social values' involve a return to crossing-sweepers or little match girls dying of cold on the streets, we are expected to forget that 'traditional recipes' from modern commercial bakeries contain chemical preservatives unknown in the period from which they are supposedly drawn – and whose long-term effects may well be equally unknown today.

What, then, accounts for the steady rise in status of the idea of 'tradition' over the past 200 years? Is it simply that in a world of ever-increasing speed of change, and increasingly artificial ingredients (of both the culinary and intellectual variety) people need to cling to something identifiable as a rock of ages, for some assurance of continuity? Is it rather that its many protean meanings allow for almost any interpretation the user chooses? Or are there underlying and enduring themes in common to all its forms?

One common theme we have seen in these pages is that any serious use of the idea of tradition inevitably invites historical comparison. If, as Alasdair MacIntyre and Rowan Williams have both suggested in their own ways, tradition is the pre-occupation of those for whom the past has become a problem, it is also, contrariwise, a source of appeal to those with little or no sense of the past at all. In the former case, it may address existential crises; in the latter, it may provide reassurance that a dimly perceived past does not constitute a threat. If the former worked itself out in such places as the battles over the Reformation, or the nature of the Church of England, the latter is visible in the attempts of commerce and advertising to suggest a cosy, safe (and usually rural) childhood home well outside the actual experience of most of those being appealed to. 'Mother's Pride', after all, turns out to be sliced bread.

More alarmingly, this modern alliance of tradition with the commercial in what Rebecca Mead calls the 'traditionalesque', has led to the creation of a whole new world of tradition-fantasy. She cites the example of the 'Apache wedding prayer', read at weddings by a freelance multi-faith 'wedding minister' called Joyce Gioia for a mere $1,000 fee, where neither bride, groom, nor prayer is actually connected with Apache culture, but was actually invented for a Hollywood movie called 'Broken Arrow'.[3] Whether the arrow in question belonged to Cupid or hostile Indians is left to the reader's imagination.

But for the strenuous minority, like Newman or Eliot, for whom the historical comparison works the other way – to suggest the differentness

[3] Rebecca Mead, *One Perfect Day: The Selling of the American Wedding* (Penguin, 2007). See review in *The Economist*, 26 May 2007, p. 107.

of the present[4] – the invitation to historical comparison is no less cogent. Even Eliot's dictum that tradition 'cannot be inherited', contrarian as it may sound, is nevertheless an assertion of historical comparison. Both are struggling with the wish to reconcile a passionately held sense of the past with the recognition of evident change.

But historical comparisons also assert continuity. What really has to be explained in either case is not so much the similarity of the past to the present, but its essential *dissimilarity* – with the implied need to account for how we got from 'there' to 'here'. For those who wish to deny change, the appeal to tradition is an anodyne reassuring assertion that nothing really has changed; for those who wish to recognize and engage with change, tradition seeks to be not an explanation so much as a template by which development (or degeneration) may be differentiated from the mere random alteration of conditions. We have already cited Williams's version of the hermeneutics of suspicion:

When people set out to prove that nothing has changed, you can normally be sure that something quite serious has. The very fact of feeling you need to show that things are the same implies that there has been an unsettlement of what was once taken for granted. When there is no awareness of things changing, certain questions are not asked; what exists seems obvious, natural. If you have to *prove* that it's natural, you may succeed or you may not, but there has been a sort of loss of innocence. It has become plain that you can no longer take for granted that everyone really knows what is obvious or natural.[5]

More confusingly, what is apparently a statement of one kind of tradition may subsequently be read as quite another. We must presume that Velázquez's *La Tela Real* (see Appendix), was read, at least by his royal patrons, as a re-assuring assertion that nothing *had* changed at the Court of Philip IV. The fact that we find it so easy to read quite another message into the grouping of the foreground figures and the difficulty of finding the king in the middle distance may or may not be evidence that Velázquez had another view of the hunt. What it certainly does provide is evidence that the same material can support radically different ideas of tradition. After all, the New Testament, one of the main centres of the Western tradition, provides the basis for the Roman Catholic tradition and the Eastern Orthodox, as well as for numerous competing Protestant traditions. Nor is Eliot's conception of tradition the only one to be deduced from English poetry.

---

[4] I have chosen this slightly cumbersome term to avoid the word 'difference' so easily subverted by a certain school of critics.
[5] Rowan Williams, *Why Study the Past? The Quest for the Historical Church*, p. 4.

We do know, however, that what we may call the 'Eliot view' has been enormously influential in the twentieth century. For the literary critic, L.C. Knights, for instance, even a writer as unique and original as Shakespeare had to be understood within not merely his socio-economic context but also within that society's sense of what it had inherited from the past. 'I sometimes suspect', he wrote:

that in concentrating on what was peculiar to the age, on categories of thought that can only be reconstructed by an effort of the historical imagination, we are in danger of losing sight of something even more important. May it not be that what was most nourishing of creative achievement in the past was what, in the tradition of the time, is – or should be – most available for us now?[6]

What he means by that phrase the 'tradition of the time' – significantly a singular word, not the plural – is a totality of social, moral, and religious assumptions, rooted in the end in one particular book:

Of the habits helping to constitute the tradition something, clearly, was due to the characteristic features of communities not yet large enough to obscure direct dealing between men with impersonal forms. But social life alone did not make the tradition: it was made by proverbs and preachings, by ballads and plays, by words read and listened to; in Elizabethan England it was made largely by the Bible.[7]

The 'historical imagination' invoked by Knights involves not merely the recognition that early modern European society was founded on biblical stories, ideas, conceptions – and, indeed, misconceptions – that made it, as Coleridge observed, impossible to decide what it owed, or did not owe to that all-important source.[8] For the gently agnostic Knights, it also involved a kind of tacit nostalgia for what Peter Laslett has graphically called *The World We Have Lost*.[9] Even to have become conscious of that earlier tradition is also to realize how far we have moved from it.

---

[6] L.C. Knights, 'Shakespeare's Politics: With Some Reflection on the Nature of Tradition', Annual Shakespeare Lecture of the British Academy, 1957. *Proceedings of the British Academy*, Vol. XLIII. (Oxford University Press, 1957), pp. 115–16.

[7] Ibid., p. 127.

[8] I take up this work with the purpose to read it for the first time as I should any other work, – at least as far as I can or dare. For I neither can, nor dare, throw off a strong and powerful prepossession in its favour – certain as I am that a large part of the light and life, in which and by which I see, love, and embrace the truths and the strengths co-organised into a living body of faith and knowledge ... has been directly or indirectly derived to me from this sacred volume, – and unable to determine what I do not know to its influences.

Confessions of an Inquiring Spirit, ed. H.N. Coleridge, 2nd edn, 1849, p. 9.

[9] Peter Laslett, *The World We Have Lost* (Scribner, 1971).

Yet, as critics ever since the seventeenth century have noticed, Shakespeare himself provides a kind of parallel universe of traditions to that of the Bible.[10] In his book, *Shakespeare's Lives*, the would-be biographer, Samuel Schoenbaum, bemoans the growth of an *Aberglaube* around his subject's life and works paralleling that which had so troubled Arnold around the Bible, writing of 'the vast accretion of legend' that over time had come 'to surround like a nimbus the blurred outlines of the Bard of men's idolatry'.[11] But for the Argentine writer Jorge Luis Borges, in a 1964 lecture on Shakespeare, this *Aberglaube* is not so much a pollution as an extra layer – a midrash containing endless possibilities:

> Shakespeare's work has been progressively enriched by the generations of its readers. Undoubtedly Coleridge, Hazlitt, Goethe, Heine, Bradley, and Hugo have all enriched Shakespeare's work, and it will undoubtedly be read in another way by readers to come. Perhaps this is one possible definition of the work of genius: a book of genius is a book that can be read in a slightly or very different way by each generation. This is what happened with the Bible. Someone has compared the Bible to a musical instrument that has been tuned infinitely. We can read Shakespeare's work, but we do not know how it will be read in a century, or in ten centuries, or even, if universal history continues, in a hundred centuries.[12]

This is at once an obvious but also a deeply subtle observation. It is not that (as some romantics held) Shakespeare must be freed from the grime of centuries of commentary and exegesis for his genius to shine out – in the way that Lowth believed that a stream was purest near its source. Rather that what we now know as 'Shakespeare' is the amalgam of the texts of the plays, the life of the man, *and* the centuries of commentary and criticism that followed. 'Shakespeare' (like any major writer) is thus not a fixed object, but a still-flowing conduit of ideas and emotions, a moving, inexhaustible tradition. If – as has sometimes been claimed – Borges as a proto-postmodernist really wanted to deny the stability of the self, his final purpose was to replace it not with any arbitrary instability, but with the dynamic of the ongoing debate, the universal palimpsest that is literature.

Edward Shils makes a similar point not merely about literature, but about what one might call the 'social imagination' in general:

---

[10] See, for instance, John Sharp (1645–1714), Archbishop of York, who is reported to have said that the Bible and Shakespeare had made him archbishop. Gilbert Burnet, *History of His Own Time* (1725), 4 vols., Vol. III, p. 100.

[11] Samuel Schoenbaum, *Shakespeare's Lives* (Oxford University Press, 1993), p. 41.

[12] Jorge Luis Borges, 'The Enigma of Shakespeare', *Selected Non-Fictions*, ed. Eliot Weinberger (Viking, 1999), p. 473.

Constellations of symbols, clusters of images, are received and modified. They change in the process of transmission as interpretations are made of the tradition presented: they change also while they are in the possession of their recipients. This chain of transmitted variants of a tradition is also called a tradition, as in the 'Platonic Tradition' or the 'Kantian Tradition'. As a temporal chain, a tradition is a sequence of variations on received and transmitted themes. The connectedness of the variations may consist in common themes, in the contiguity of presentation and departure, and in descent from a common origin. [13]

What is unresolved here, of course, is that key question of *change*: what part does disruption play in the construction of tradition? What part is played by the subjectivity of the growing post-romantic inner space?

As one might expect, there are parallels here with other late-twentieth-century debates – that, for instance, about the nature of history itself. In his seminal 1961 book, *What is History?*, E.H. Carr summed up the state of the argument over the preceding sixty years by comparing the assumptions behind Lord Acton's *Cambridge Modern History* (1903–11) with those of Sir George Clark's *New Cambridge Modern History* of 1957. For Acton it was axiomatic that a complete and objective record of the past could be created by scholarship alone. In his instructions to contributors he insisted 'that our Waterloo must be one that satisfies French and English, German and Dutch alike; that nobody can tell, without examining the list of authors where the Bishop of Oxford laid down the pen, and whether Fairbairn or Gasquet, Liebermann or Harrison took it up'.[14] Once such a history had been created, it might stand for all time. Only new information could supersede it. For Clark, writing fifty years later, it was no less obvious that contemporary historians:

expect their work to be superseded again and again. They consider that knowledge of the past has come down through one or more human minds, has been 'processed' by them, and therefore cannot consist of elemental and impersonal atoms which nothing can alter . . . The exploration seems to be endless, and some impatient scholars take refuge in scepticism, or at least in the doctrine that, since all historical judgements involve persons and points of view, one is as good as another and there is no 'objective' historical truth.[15]

'It does not follow', Carr dryly observes, 'that because a mountain appears to take on different shapes from different angles of vision, it has objectively

---

[13] Edward Shils, *Tradition* (University of Chicago Press, 1981), p. 13.

[14] Acton, *Lectures on Modern History* (Macmillan, 1906), p. 318. Cited by E.H. Carr, *What is History?* (Macmillan, 1961), pp. 3–4.

[15] G. Clark, *The New Cambridge Modern History*, Vol. 1 (1957) (Cambridge University Press, 1957), pp. xxiv–xxv. Carr, *What is History?*, pp. 1–2.

either no shape at all or an infinity of shapes.'[16] His own view, however, is, as one would expect, closer to that of Clark than Acton:

The facts are really not at all like fish on the fishmonger's slab. They are like fish swimming about in a vast and sometimes inaccessible ocean; and what the historian catches will depend, partly on chance, but mainly on what part of the ocean he chooses to fish in and what tackle he chooses to use – these two factors being, of course, determined by the kind of fish he wants to catch. By and large, the historian will get the kinds of facts he wants. History means interpretation.[17]

Since Carr wrote, of course, the debate has moved away from the slipperiness of 'facts' to the even more problematic studies of 'intellectual history' and thence to such sub-sections as 'literary history'. If few would deny the possibility of writing history at all, many more might dispute the possibility of intellectual history, and perhaps more still the creation of literary history.[18] Both concern abstractions, at one or more remove from concrete events; both are essentially teleological, explaining the present in terms of the past, through the creation and labelling of historical periods, by classifying, categorizing, and tracing influences.

For David Perkins, for instance, writing in the early 1990s, 'literary history' is a product of particular historical circumstances, and can itself be historicized.

[The] fundamental premises of literary history as a discipline come to us from the romantic movement.[19] Among these are the importance attached to the beginnings or origins, the assumption that a development is the subject of literary history, the understanding of development as continual rather than disjunctive, and the creation of suprapersonal entities as the subjects of this development.[20]

Such 'suprapersonal' figures, ranging from Chateaubriand's 'genius' (echoing and parodying the mysterious 'genius' of Volney's *Ruins*) to MacDonald's 'England'[21] are among many examples of developmental entities we have seen in the course of this discussion. Perkins' assumption that behind such developmental narratives is a naïve belief in the possibility of objectivity, and that this in the end invalidates all such attempts at classification, is no less familiar to us.

---

[16] Ibid., p. 21.   [17] Ibid., p 18.
[18] See, for instance, Richard Whatmore and Brian Young (eds.), *Intellectual History* (Palgrave, 2006).
[19] See Clifford Siskin, *The Historicity of Romantic Discourse* (Oxford University Press, 1988) [original note].
[20] David Perkins, *Is Literary History Possible?* (Johns Hopkins University Press, 1992), p. 86.
[21] As in his anthology, *England's Antiphon* (Macmillan, 1868).

For approximately the first seventy-five years of the nineteenth century, literary history enjoyed popularity and unquestioned prestige. It was characterized, at this time, by three fundamental assumptions: that literary works are formed by their historical context; that change in literature takes place developmentally; and that this change is the unfolding of an idea, principle, or suprapersonal entity. Viewing literary works in relation to their historical context, we can, it was argued, achieve a juster interpretation and a more complete appreciation than is otherwise possible. We can explain features of texts as products and expressions of the social structures, ways of life, beliefs, literary institutions, and so on, of the communities in which they were created. As a synthesis of history and criticism, literary history seemed more powerful, for some purposes, than either discipline separately.[22]

Yet for Perkins to identify literary history with Acton rather than with Clark seems historically wilful. There is, in fact, little evidence that critics like De Quincey or Hare saw their versions of literary history in absolute terms, and even to read Arnold or Dallas in this way would probably seem against the grain to most readers. Nevertheless, what all these debates have in common is a search for ways to explain historical change – whether in terms of raw events, interpretative ideas, or the aesthetics of writing.

But what they do *not* have in common is precisely that Actonian ideal of impartiality. 'Americans use tradition to evade history,' writes Richard E. Nicholls.[23] Without discussing the general truth or falsehood of the accusation, the polemical thrust is clear. Tradition is an ongoing stream; it does not submit easily to being dammed, diverted, or simply denied. In the case of the USA, the narrative of the founding fathers, and the ideal of liberty and exceptionalism, constitutes so powerful a narrative that those who wish to talk of other histories – of broken Indian treaties, slavery or wars of aggression – simply exclude themselves from the popular national tradition invoked by politicians of all political hues while on the stump.

But as those who have read so far will appreciate, it is no part of this book, either, to separate the 'real' from 'invented' traditions supposed by Hobsbawm, let alone to distinguish 'true' from 'false' traditions – as if they may be judged by some objective standard of history. If MacIntyre's argument that traditions are the creation of existential crises is correct – as much of the evidence we have seen here seems to suggest – then the question is not 'is this or that tradition "true"?' but 'how well does this tradition serve the needs for which it was created?' The braid of Cassiodorus is a rope, a sheet-anchor, to give us continuity with the past, and, perhaps, a

[22] Perkins, *Is Literary History Possible?*, pp. 1–2.
[23] Quoted by Michael Anderson in the *Times Literary Supplement*, 25 July 2003, p 5.

hand-rail to guide us into the future, and it is made up of many strands: part historical fact, part historical interpretation, part folk-memory, part even art and aesthetics – think, for instance, of the degree to which not merely 'America', but a sense of 'Irishness', 'Scottishness', or 'Welshness' is made up of poetry, music, folk-legends, and ballads.

And here distinctions do arise. Surveying the decline and eventual revival of the idea of tradition, even over the past 400 years, there is a fundamental difference between attitudes which bind and enslave to the past, and those that liberate, and provide tools for exploring the future. But as we have also seen, no one tradition is consistent in this. Indeed, the history of tradition is one of continual paradox. If Herder was a key figure in re-invigorating Protestant conceptions of tradition, this may have had a more profound effect on the English-speaking world than on the German. Moreover, it was not Keble, leading a resurgent Anglicanism, who was to develop that notion, but Newman, who claimed not to have read a word of Herder, and who, though he came from the same Anglican stock as Keble, consciously tried to place himself in the tradition of Trent and the Counter-Reformation. Furthermore, it was Newman, the vocal opponent of 'liberalism', who was to see tradition in terms of development and change, and Arnold, the arch-liberal and opponent of conservative dogma, who, even while he denounced 'Hebraism' and argued in favour of the 'Hellenistic' spontaneity of consciousness that he saw epitomized in Newman, was to attempt to laager the wagons around a class-bound and prescriptive idea of 'culture'. Finally, it was Eliot, the American poetic *enfant terrible*, provocatively styling himself classicist, royalist, and Anglo-Catholic, who argued that tradition, if it was to be any more than a dead hand, must be not merely in a constant process of radical change, but that each poetic innovation inevitably re-wrote the past as well.

In other words, though the post-romantic re-emergence of the idea of tradition in the nineteenth century was centred on the idea of change in a way that it had not previously been, it was also marked by a greater tension *inside* each tradition between static and dynamic ideas of what the word should convey, than existed *between* the various traditions. As we have seen, there is nothing new about this. The same was true of the Hellenistic and Jewish traditions that Cassiodorus had so valiantly attempted to braid together in the sixth century. But if Cassiodorus had been confident of the strength of those cultural and religious strands of which his braid was woven, no such certainties could be claimed by those who had truly embraced his hated modernity. As he seems to have suspected, modernity was to turn out to be not merely a matter of the temporarily prevailing conditions, but a *permanent* state of temporary conditions – in short, a state of continuous change.

But as the modern emergent idea of tradition presupposes, all change is not necessarily random change. It is no accident that the re-emergence of the idea of tradition at the beginning of the nineteenth century was accompanied by a fundamental and seemingly irreversible change in epistemology itself. Instead of being seen as absolute – and, in some cases, even God-given – knowledge was increasingly seen as contingent, relative, and, above all, time-bound. Whereas Newton seems to have assumed that even though he was only like a boy playing on the sea-shore whilst the great ocean of truth lay all undiscovered before him,[24] at least the pebbles that he had found represented hard and permanent truth; today new advances in astronomy or physics are advanced not as the 'truth' but merely as how things seem in our present state of understanding. In this sense modern knowledge is openly 'ironic' in the correct etymological sense of the word – as representing something that is 'hidden', in much the same way, perhaps, as 'dark matter' is believed to permeate the visible universe and to be by far its largest constituent.[25] This is by no means the only way of distinguishing between pre-Romantic (or Enlightenment) and post-Romantic ways of knowing, but it is certainly one of the most fundamental.

For those, such as Richard Rorty, or Don Cupitt, who have openly embraced the slippery relativism of Post-Modernism, the past is no problem – indeed, there is a sense in which it is so infinitely malleable that it can scarcely be said to exist outside our varied interpretations of it.[26] But in its revived, or re-emergent, state, the nineteenth- and twentieth-century idea of tradition does attempt to address both the key problems of historicism – that is, not just the recognition that the past may differ from the present, but also the question of why this should be so. More subtly, perhaps, it also addresses the inevitable historical question: what makes traditions die? How does a society, a religious or an intellectual movement turn from a 'living tradition' to a state of affairs where we can speak of the 'dead hand of tradition'? The metaphors say it all.

---

[24] 'I do not know what I may appear to the world, but to myself I seem to have been only like a boy playing on the sea-shore, and diverting myself in now and then finding a smoother pebble or a prettier shell than ordinary, whilst the great ocean of truth lay all undiscovered before me.' Sir David Brewster, *Memoirs of the Life, Writings, and Discoveries of Sir Isaac Newton*, 2 vols. (T. Constable, 1855) Vol. ii. ch. 27.

[25] See Stephen Prickett, *Narrative, Religion and Science: Fundamentalism versus Irony, 1700–1999* (Cambridge University Press, 2002).

[26] See Richard Rorty, *Contingency, Irony and Solidarity* (Cambridge University Press, 1989). And my comments in *Narrative, Religion and Science*, pp. 195–207.

This is not a purely academic question. Anyone who looks at the internal debates with the Roman Catholic and Anglican communions over sexuality, or within the American Baptist churches over 'intelligent design', can see how the desire to keep to an authoritative deposit of faith or culture clashes with new pressures, and uncomfortable new forms of evidence and experience. Nor is it confined to religious groupings. Conflicts between critical schools of thought in educational theory, literature, historiography, of psychotherapy, or even of economics show exactly the same structural tensions. In each case the basic internal narrative of the dominating movement finds itself challenged, and either the challenge must be resisted, and the intruding ideas – and those who hold them – must be expelled in the name of orthodoxy, or the new must somehow be accommodated within the existing narrative, which must then also explain that development.

The very existence and repetition of this dynamic surely suggests that the tension we have noted is probably essential for the life of any tradition. An authority or a consensus that stifles argument and debate, whether within a church or a literary movement, usually spells the demise of that movement. Without the new – as Eliot insisted, 'the really new' – the established past rapidly becomes ossified and inflexible. Which brings us to another word that has been always hovering in the wings of this discussion – sometimes as an insult, at other times as high praise: the word 'imagination'. For sixteenth-century Protestant reformers and for Counter-Reformation clerics alike, the idea that imagination might play a part in their traditions would have seemed more like the propaganda of their opponents than a central plank of their own position. Indeed, so long as Enlightenment assumptions of a rational, uniformitarian, and essentially static world-picture predominated, neither ideas of history nor of tradition could gain much traction in the Protestant world.[27] Again, Herder was a key figure in this realization of historical change: 'The whole course of a man's life is change: the different periods in his life are tales of transformation, and the whole species is one continued metamorphosis . . . Thus the history of man is ultimately a theatre of transformation.'[28] That image, 'a theatre of transformation', is significant in that it presents change not merely as an unstoppable reality, but as an *aesthetic* reality. Theatre is a self-consciously

---

[27] The contradiction between a static and anti-historical world picture, and assumptions of the superiority of rational civilization against a barbarous past has often been noted. One historian has even suggested that the transition from the latter to the former state could only be the result of some kind of one-off 'miracle'.

[28] J.G. Herder, *Reflections on the Philosophy of the History of Mankind* (1784–91), ed. Frank E. Manuel (University of Chicago Press, 1968).

created art form. It is neither random nor accidental. Drama is not merely to be *seen* by an audience, but it is specifically *constructed* to be seen. And the 'audience'? We start with the history of an individual, in an image that implies self-conscious imagination, but with the removal of the article in the second sentence we slide from the specific to the general – what starts with a process of self-examination, ends with something that looks more like Lessing's *Education of the Human Race* or Schiller's *Aesthetic Education of Man.*[29]

Indeed, if the post-romantic re-discovery of tradition presupposes a recognition of historical change, it also presupposes an act of imagination on the part of those participating in a tradition. As Owen Barfield has cogently argued, post-romantic tradition can only be an internalized tradition.[30] Indeed, this was, in effect, the 'added value' that made tradition once more a live area of debate.

Yet the moment that the idea of tradition becomes fully internalized, to become not so much something to which the individual must be under pressure to conform, but part of that individual's personal mental furniture, the influence of the imagination is inescapable – as Schleiermacher, Newman, and Williams, in their very different ways, all understood. Indeed, tradition then becomes inescapably an imaginative concept. But in becoming part of each individual's interior space, it also becomes essentially subjective.[31] This is, of course, a point of which Eliot was well aware. The whole thrust of his essays on tradition is designed to rescue 'tradition' from being thought of as a set of rules, correct models, or accepted ways of thinking, and to re-establish it as a mode of internal transformation. For Eliot, Petrarch's break with the scholastic method, and his insistence on a personal internalized dialogue with the great writers of the past, would have been a perfect example of his idea of a literary tradition.[32]

It is hardly surprising, therefore, that the word 'tradition' – and all that it represents in modernity – is not merely ambiguous in the casual language of the media and the market-place, but (as Newman so clearly recognized) is *necessarily* ambiguous. A tradition represents choice. What

---

[29] Gotthold Ephraim Lessing, *The Education of the Human Race* (1778); Friedrich Schiller, *On the Aesthetic Education of Man* (1794).

[30] See, for instance, Owen Barfield, *Worlds Apart* (Wesleyan University Press, 1963); *Saving the Appearances* (Harcourt Brace, 1965); and *Romanticism Comes of Age* (Wesleyan University Press, 1966).

[31] For a description of the growth of interior space, see Charles Taylor, *Sources of the Self: The Making of the Modern Identity* (Cambridge University Press, 1989).

[32] See above, pp. 30–1.

it stands for is not so much a linear descent but an ongoing history of tension and conflict. Nor do easy clichés about 'free speech' or 'open and democratic debate' allow the commentator to evade involvement. The narratives of tradition, whether expressed through fiction, history, music, or philosophy are narratives of engagement, not passive acceptance or disinterested observation. To study any tradition is inevitably to place oneself in relation to it. Just as there is no perspectiveless vision, so there is no omniscient description of what creates and sustains that particular idea of tradition – and that, of course, includes the present account.

Velázquez and the Royal Boar Hunt

In the National Gallery in London is a very large painting by Velázquez entitled *La Tela Real*. As we shall see, this contains a pun in Spanish that the literal English translation, 'The Royal Canvas', fails to convey. The Gallery's own slightly fuller English title is 'Philip IV Hunting Wild Boar'. What this picture shows is something very strange indeed. The catalogue to a recent exhibition describes the picture as follows:

this painting purports to document a moment in the life of the court. Not an everyday incident, but a type of 'boar hunt' that was staged occasionally at great expense and labour on feast days and to honour special guests. Introduced to Spain by Charles V, the sport involved the engagement of wild boar by horsemen in an arena formed of canvas in a forest clearing . . . 'Boarfighting' permitted the king to take the starring role and we see him just left of centre engaging a charging animal, watched by the queen and her guests from the safety of their carriages.[1]

The picture has, as was intended, an iconic significance. Contemporary Spanish treatises on hunting describe the extensive preparations necessary for what amounts less to a hunt in the normal sense than an elaborate Court ritual. Dawson Carr writes:

The elusive boar were first trapped by encircling them with a vast fence of heavy canvas or *tela* strung between trees and supported by stakes. The arena that dominates Velázquez's composition was called the *contratela* or counter-*tela* and was limited in size for the main event. The *tela* itself encompassed a much larger area, up to a league – more than 21/2 miles or 4km – in circumference. Velázquez depicts it branching off behind the *contratela*, seemingly taking in the whole upper part of the composition. In theory, the enormous size allowed for the *tela*'s deployment without sending the boar scurrying. The trapped animals were driven to a smaller holding area for culling and later admission to the *contratela* via a chute. The horsemen in the clearing at upper right are presumably just beginning the long journey and one arm of the pen or the chute can be seen

---

[1] Dawson W. Carr, with Xavier Bray, John H. Elliott, Larry Keith and Javier Portús, *Velázquez* (National Gallery Company / Yale University Press, 2006), p. 200.

branching off at centre. The huge enterprise was obviously costly and limited this kind of hunting to the royal house, hence the name *'Tela Real'*.[2]

Even from an art-history point of view Velázquez's picture, however, is highly unusual. As a Court painter, in his pictures he is normally careful to place the royal subject at a place where the eye is immediately drawn to him – or, less often, her. In contrast, here one actually has to search in the middle distance for the mounted figure of the king, flanked by the just-recognizable figures of the Duke of Olivares, Master of the Horse, and possibly also his two brothers, Carlos and Ferdinand. Dawson Carr comments:

Velázquez departs from tradition by foregrounding behind-the-scenes activity, reversing the expected as was his predeliction. Some people scurry about playing their supportive roles, while others watch the action or rest. This reflects a role reversal at such events because here the grandees toil while courtiers and servants enjoy a period of leisure on the fringes. For Velázquez and his patrons, this would have carried no social significance and the foreground figures would have been read as ingenious use of staffage [painterly props and padding] that gives the scene a greater sense of actuality and makes it possible to show the king in an arena.[3]

This may indeed have 'no social significance' in narrowly art-historical terms. But it is hard to see a royally commissioned picture where one has

Figure: 'Philip IV Hunting Wild Boar (*La Tela Real*)' by Diego Velázquez (NG197) © National Gallery, London.

[2] Ibid., p. 202.   [3] Ibid., pp. 200–2.

to *search* for the king as having no social significance at all in seventeenth-century Spain. Moreover, a detailed inspection of what actually is going on in that foreground 'staffage' suggests that rather more is happening than Carr's description suggests.

In fact *very* few of the foreground characters are actually looking at the royal group. The most prominent group of richly-dressed courtiers in the foreground are deep in conversation facing the viewer, with their backs to the action. Those who are watching (mostly on the left of the canvas) are not watching the king, but another boar on the far left which is being attacked and killed by hounds. This is realistically probable, in that there would have been much more noise (and blood) in that area, than around the king, on the right, who seems to be merely fending off another boar with the point of his lance. His pose, as well as the body-language of the other members of his group, hardly suggests any danger or even drama in the event.

Moreover, though it is difficult to see it in small reproductions, if one looks at those with their backs to us on the right of the mound only a few of those, too, seem to be looking in the direction of the king. From the angles of the hats of the group in shadow, they seem to be looking at the (unidentified) man on the white horse just to the right of centre, who is galloping across the arena towards the royal party. Further to the right of this group are three mounted men in cloaks – gold, blue, and what looks like a very faded purple. From the set of their hats, the men in gold and blue seem also to be watching the man on the white horse. The third man, on the right of the group, in the faded purple cloak, has his head at a slightly different angle – apparently watching the man in the grey cloak with the white lace collar. Sumptuary laws – presumably observed at Court if not elsewhere – not to mention the sheer cost of hand-made lace, would suggest this man in the grey cloak is of higher social status. He is bareheaded, having apparently just doffed his hat, not to the group waving sticks immediately in front of him, but to the lady in the second carriage who, though positioned closest to the king and the wild boar, is not looking in the direction of the hunt at all, but out of the opposite window towards her admirer.

The iconographic meaning of this display, we are told, would be very clear to the audience for which it was intended in 1638. Originally, of course, the leader of the tribe was the one who provided food from hunting, and protection and victory in time of war. Over the course of centuries, this essential function, transferred to the king, had become symbolized through his ceremonial function as chief hunter of the nation. As in many

European countries, what was once publicly expressed in terms of military prowess, must now be demonstrated through the less physically dangerous role of huntsman.[4] From the time of William the Conqueror onwards, English monarchs – like their French and Spanish counterparts – had all made much public display of their roles as expert huntsmen, and large tracts of land were set aside for the exclusive use of the royal hunting parties – with savage punishments for hungry locals who dared to poach the king's deer. In the story of Robin Hood, we recall, his supposed crimes were as much in killing deer in Sherwood Forest as in robbing the rich and giving to the poor. The Habsburgs were no exception to this royal preoccupation with the hunt. The Emperor Maximilian I, claimed that he would have presumed his son – later Charles V – to be a bastard if he had not been a fine hunter. Charles's son, Philip IV, Velázquez's patron, was no less enthusiastic over the sport.

But here the symbolic prey – the unfortunate wild pigs – have been so corralled, trapped, and finally, we are told, 'culled' (particularly, perhaps, the most dangerous ones?) that this ceremony of kingship could not endanger the life or health of the monarch, for whom it is now primarily a chance to display his horsemanship – also, of course, something expected of a royal leader. Though such hunts may have been regular Court events, they were of necessity relatively infrequent. For an age like ours, clothed and wrapped literally by the fruits of the loom – the result of the mass-production of textiles pioneered at the beginning of the industrial revolution – a period where, as in seventeenth-century Spain, textiles were among the most expensive products of civilization, is difficult to imagine. Even this sheer quantity canvas in itself would have been an immense demonstration of conspicuous consumption – as the constant repetition of *tela* in the technical terminology reiterates. Nor should we miss the implied pun on the word: Velázquez's commemoration of the event (whether it is a particular one, or a generic display) is, of course, painted in oils on *tela* – canvas. More remote, but just possible perhaps, in view of the lady in the carriage, is the original Latin meaning of *tela*: a 'web', as in spider's web, which is still present in Spanish, and which, for the close observer of the foreground activity, could easily carry the meaning of a web of intrigue.

---

[4] Though increasingly rare, it was still not unknown in the seventeenth century for major European monarchs to lead their subjects into battle. The last recorded English king to do so was actually in the eighteenth century, when George II led an Anglo-German force (the so-called 'Pragmatic Army') to victory over the French at the Battle of Dettingen in 1743.

Whatever it may have represented for his own age, however, Velázquez's picture represents something quite different to viewers from our own century. For Carr, what is interesting is not so much what is being purportedly represented, but the way in which he departs from that 'tradition' – a word that encompasses both the event itself and the method of recording it in paint on canvas. Here is a display originally intended to manifest the power of the king to provide for his people, show off his virility, and demonstrate his command of martial skills, now being attenuated into a ritual from which chance and danger have largely been eliminated. But whatever it once meant, it has become hollowed-out, and lost practically all meaning. The ordinary people, for whom it must once have been enacted, are not present, even as spectators. The residual audience – dog-handlers, grooms, personal servants of the nobility, courtiers, and even the nobility themselves – are scarcely interested. Indeed, if we notice the details of what is going on in the foreground, it has become an opportunity for flirtation and intrigue. At the same time, this very meaninglessness holds an altogether different story for posterity – providing a perfect image of the decline of Spain and the Hapsburg monarchy, whose wealth from the New World has paradoxically weakened the economy, and encouraged a bigoted, intransigent, and backward-looking political system.

It also provides us with a vivid image of how the idea of 'tradition' can carry many, sometimes conflicting, meanings. On the one hand it describes a ritual supposedly central to the role of the Spanish monarchy. On the other, the descriptions and other paintings we have of it date from the 1630s, around about the same time as Velázquez's painting, and, as we know, the whole ceremony of the *tela* was in fact a 'tradition' no older than the reign of Philip's father, Charles V.[5]

But the real 'meaning' of the tradition, of course, is to be found not in the event itself but in Velázquez's representation of it. Here, in the picture originally displayed in Philip's hunting lodge, the *Torre de la Prada*, is the 'showing', the display of royal finesse, and, finally, the record for posterity – though neither Velázquez nor Philip IV could have foreseen it – carrying the image of Philip as a great hunter (or alternatively a participant in dead rituals) to us in the twenty-first century in the National Gallery in London and in illustrated books around the world. Indeed, it does not even matter if the hunt portrayed ever took place at all. If it is true, as some critics have suggested, that two of the horsemen with the king are his brothers, Carlos

5 See Mateos (1634), Martínez de Espinar (1644), Francisco Collante, *Boar Hunt* (1634), Peter Snayers, *Philip IV Hunting* and *A Court Hunt* (both 1638: Prado, Madrid).

and Ferdinand, then we may have reason to question whether the picture does actually portray a real event. Carlos had died in 1632, four years before the earliest date for the picture, and Ferdinand had left Madrid the same year.[6]

At a different, but intimately related, level, we have Dawson Carr's use of the word 'tradition' not to describe the hunt, nor even its representation, but the artistic medium used: in other words what lies behind Velázquez's painting. Court painters had been around for hundreds of years, and, as we have seen, there had been a series of Spanish royal hunting paintings in the 1630s, serving at once as decoration and propaganda. As E.H. Gombrich has pointed out, all art, consciously or unconsciously, tends to imitate not real life so much as previous works of art.[7] In this sense, Velázquez did not start with a blank canvas. Simply by being employed by the king, and undertaking this particular commission, he has already engaged with certain ideas, conventions, and expectations. As all great innovative artists have done, he has already begun to subvert this artistic tradition, and, like Caravaggio, look at the bystanders to the action rather than the action itself – but such innovations cannot, of course, be understood without reference to that previous tradition.

But if, with the twenty–twenty vision of hindsight, we were to conclude that the social price for the ritual of the royal hunt was perhaps even higher than the exorbitant cost of the miles of *tela* needed to channel the boar into the arena, we need also to remember the positive values of tradition. Before we judge the stifling centralization and absolutism of the seventeenth-century Spanish political system too harshly, we need only to remember the instability which it was struggling to overcome. Spain, after all, is the only country in the world that (in the twentieth century) nearly elected an Anarchist government. To suggest that the subsequent Civil War was actually a war over the nature of tradition would be grossly to oversimplify the particularity of that situation. But revolution and civil war have always been part of the struggle over the understanding of tradition throughout modern European history – and few countries have escaped such conflicts.

---

[6] Carr, *Velázquez*, p. 202.
[7] E.H. Gombrich, *Art and Illusion: A Study in the Psychology of Pictorial Representation*, revised edn (Princeton University Press, 1961).

Bibliography

Aarsleff, Hans, *Locke to Saussure: Essays on the Study of Language and Intellectual History*, University of Minnesota Press, 1982.

Abbott, Edwin A., *Paradosis or 'In the Night in Which He Was(?) Betrayed'*, Adam & Charles Black, 1904.

Acton, Sir John Emerich Edward Dalberg, *Lectures on Modern History*, Macmillan, 1906.

Adams, Hazard, *Philosophy of the Literary Symbolic*, Florida State University Press, 1983.

Allen, P.L., *The Cambridge Apostles*, Cambridge University Press, 1978.

Anrich E., (ed.), *Die Idee der deutschen Universität: die fünf Grundschriften aus der Zeit ihrer Neubegründung durch klassischen Idealismus und romantischen Realismus*, WBG, 1960.

Arnold, Matthew, *Complete Prose Works*, ed. R.H. Super, University of Indiana Press, 1965.

Ashton, Rosemary, *G.H. Lewes: A Life*, Clarendon Press, 1992.

The German Idea: Four English Writers and the Reception of German Thought, Cambridge University Press, 1980.

Aston, Margaret, *England's Iconoclasts*, Oxford University Press, 1988.

Augustine, St, *Confessions*, trs. E. B. Pusey, Everyman, 1907.

Bahr, Ehrhard and Thomas P. Saine (eds.), *The Internalized Revolution: German Reactions to the French Revolution, 1789–1989*, Garland, 1992.

Barbéris, Pierre, *A la recherche d'une écriture: Chateaubriand*, Maison Mame, 1974.

Barfield, Owen, 'The Meaning of Literal', in Basil Cottle and L.C. Knights (eds.), *Metaphor and Symbol*, Butterfield, 1960 (reprinted in *The Rediscovery of Meaning*, Wesleyan University Press, 1977).

Romanticism Comes of Age, Wesleyan University Press, 1966.

Saving the Appearances, Harcourt Brace, 1965.

Worlds Apart, Wesleyan University Press, 1963.

Barrett, Elizabeth Barrett, *A Drama of Exile and Other Poems*, Henry G. Langley, 1845.

Battiscombe, Georgina, *John Keble: A Study of Limitations*, Constable, 1963.

Baumgarten, Alexander Gottlieb, *Aesthetica*, 2 vols., 1750–8.

Bellarmine, Cardinal, *De Controversiis Christianae Fidei, adversus huius temporis haereticos*, Ingolstadt, 3 vols: 1586; 1588; 1593.

Berlin, Isaiah, 'Herder and the Enlightenment', *Vico and Herder: Two Studies in the History of Ideas*, Hogarth Press, 1976.

Berman, Harold J., *Law and Revolution: the Formation of the Western Legal Tradition*, Harvard University Press, 1983.

    Law and Revolution II: The Impact of the Protestant Reformers on the Western Legal Tradition, Belknap Press of the Harvard University Press, 2003.

Bickerman, E.J., *The Jews in the Greek Age*, Harvard University Press, 1988.

Blackstone, Sir William, *Commentaries on the Laws of England* (1765–9).

Blair, Hugh, *Sermons*, 2 vols., Anderson, 1824.

Blake, Robert, *Disraeli*, St Martin's Press, 1967.

Blake, William, *Complete Writings*, ed. Geoffrey Keynes, Oxford University Press, 1966.

Blomfield, Charles James (Bishop of London), *Charge to the Clergy of the Diocese of London*, second edn, B. Fellowes, 1846.

Bloom, Harold, *The Anxiety of Influence: A Theory of Poetry*, Oxford University Press. 1975.

    The Visionary Company: A Reading of English Romantic Poetry (1961), rev. edn, Cornell University Press, 1971.

Borges, Jorge Luis, *Selected Non-Fictions*, ed. Eliot Weinberger, trs. Esther Allen, Suzanne Jill Levine, and Eliot Weinburger, Viking, 1999.

Boswell, James, *Life of Samuel Johnson* (1791).

Bowie, Andrew, *Aesthetics and Subjectivity: From Kant to Nietzsche*, Manchester University Press, 1990.

    From Romanticism to Critical Theory: The Philosophy of German Literary Theory, Routledge, 1997.

Brewster, Sir David, *Memoirs of the Life, Writings, and Discoveries of Sir Isaac Newton*, 2 vols., T. Constable, 1855.

Bruns, Gerald R., 'What is Tradition?', *Hermeneutics Ancient and Modern*, Yale University Press, 1992.

Budick, Sanford, *The Western Theory of Tradition: Terms and Paradigms of the Cultural Sublime*, Yale University Press, 2000.

    and Geoffrey Hartman (eds.), *Midrash and Literature*, New Haven: Yale University Press, 1986.

Bunyan, John, *The Holy War, Made by Shaddai upon Diabolus, for the Regaining of the Metropolis of the World, or, The Losing and Taking Again of the Town of Mansoul*, Printed for Dorman Newman and Benjamin Alsop, 1682.

Burke, Edmund, *A Philosophical Enquiry into our Ideas of the Sublime and the Beautiful* (1757).

    Reflections on the French Revolution, Dent, 1940.

Burnet, Gilbert, *History of His Own Time*, 4 vols., 1725.

Butler, Marilyn, *Romantics, Rebels and Revolutionaries: English Literature and its Background 1760–1830*, Oxford University Press, 1981.

Butterfield, Herbert, *The Whig Interpretation of History*, G. Bell, 1931, reprinted, 1963.

The Cambridge Modern History, planned by Lord Acton, ed. A.W. Ward, G.W. Prothero, and Stamley Leathers, 13 vols., Cambridge University Press, 1903–11.

Cardwell, Richard, 'Introduction to Spanish Romanticism', *An Anthology of European Romanticism*, ed. Stephen Prickett, Argumentum, 2009.

Carlowitz, A. de, *Historie de la Poésie des Hebreux*, Didiers, 1845.

Carlyle, Thomas, *The French Revolution* (1837), 2vols., Macmillan, 1900.

Past and Present, Chapman and Hall, 1843.

'Signs of the Times' (1829), *The Collected Works of Thomas Carlyle*, 16 vols., Vol. III, Chapman and Hall, 1858.

Carr, Dawson W., with Bray, Xavier, Elliott, John H., Keith Larry and Portús, Javier, *Velázquez*, National Gallery Company / Yale University Press, 2006,

Carr, E.H., *What is History?*, Macmillan, 1961.

Cassiodorus, *De orthographia* 143.1–6[1] (PL 70. 1241 D).

An Introduction to Divine and Human Readings by Cassiodorus Senator, intro. and trs. L.W. Jones, Octagon, 1966.

Chadwick, Owen, *From Bossuet to Newman*, second edn, Cambridge University Press, 1987.

The Secularization of the European Mind in the Nineteenth Century, Cambridge University Press, 1975; Canto edn, 1990.

Chateaubriand, *Le Génie du christianisme* (1802), Gabriel Roux, 1855.

The Genius of Christianity, trs. Charles White, J.B. Lippincott, 1856.

Chatwin, Bruce, *The Songlines*, Vintage, 1987.

Chesterton, G.K., *The Ball and the Cross*, Wells Gardner, Darton, 1910.

Church, R.W., *Gifts of Civilization*, new edn, Macmillan, 1880.

Clark, G., *The New Cambridge Modern History*, Cambridge University Press, 1957.

Clark, J.C.D., *English Society 1688–1832*, Cambridge University Press, 1985.

Cockburn, Henry, *Memorials of his Time*, Adam & Charles Black, 1856.

Cockshut, A.O.J., *The Unbelievers: English Agnostic Thought, 1840–1890*, Collins, 1964.

Coleridge, J.T., *Memoir of the Rev. John Keble*, Parker, 1869.

Coleridge, Samuel Taylor, *Aids to Reflection*, ed. James Marsh (1829), Kennikat Press, 1971.

Biographia Literaria, or, Biographical Sketches of my Literary Life and Opinions, ed. James Engell and W. Jackson Bate, Bollingen Series, Routledge, 1983.

Collected Notebooks, 4 vols., ed. Kathleen Coburn, Vol. II: 1804–1808, Routledge, 1962.

The Collected Works of Samuel Taylor Coleridge, Marginalia, 5 vols., ed. George Whalley, Bollingen Series, Routledge/Princeton University Press, 1984.

Confessions of an Inquiring Spirit, ed. H. N. Coleridge, second edn, Pickering, 1849.

The Friend, ed. Barbara E. Rooke, 2 vols., Bollingen Series, Princeton University Press/Routledge, 1969.

Lay Sermons, ed. R.J. White, Bollingen Series, Princeton University Press/ Routledge, 1972.

Lectures 1795 On Politics and Religion, ed. Lewis Patton and Peter Mann, Bollingen Series, Princeton University Press/Routledge, 1971.

Lectures 1818–1819 On the History of Philosophy, ed. J.R. de J. Jackson, Bollingen Series, Princeton University Press/Routledge, 2000.

Letters of Samuel Taylor Coleridge, 6 vols., ed. E.R. Griggs, Clarendon Press, 1956.

Literary Remains, ed. H.N. Coleridge (1836), reprinted (ed. E. Rhys), Everyman, 1907.

On the Constitution of Church and State, ed. John Colmer, Bollingen Series, Princeton University Press/Routledge, 1976.

Shakespeare Criticism, ed. T.M. Raysor, 2nd edn, 2 vols. Everyman, 1960.

Collins, David, *An Account of the English Colony of New South Wales*, 2nd edn, printed for A. Strachan for T. Cadell and W. Davies, 1804.

Cooper, Trevor, *The Journal of William Dowsing*, Boydell & Brewer, 2001.

Cowper, William, *Poems*, 2 vols., R. & W.A. Bartow, 1818.

Currie, Robert, Alan Gilbert and Lee Horsley (eds.), *Churches and Churchgoers: Patterns of Church Growth in the British Isles since 1700*, Clarendon Press, 1977.

Dallas, E.S., *The Gay Science*, Chapman & Hall, 1866.

Davie, Donald, *A Gathered Church: The Literature of the English Dissenting Interest, 1700–1930*, Oxford University Press, 1978.

Davison, John, *Inquiry into the Origin and Intent of Primitive Sacrifice* (1825).

De Quincey, Thomas, 'Letters to a Young Man whose Education has been Neglected', *Collected Writings of Thomas De Quincey*, ed. David Masson, A & C Black, 1897.

De Staël, Germaine, *On Germany* (1813), *Selected Writings of Germaine de Staël*, trs. and introduction by Vivian Folkenflik, Columbia University Press, 1987.

Dealtry, William (Chancellor of the diocese of Winchester), *On the Importance of Caution in the Use of Certain Familiar Words*. (A Charge delivered in the autumn of 1843 at the Visitation in Hampshire), Hatchard, 1843.

DeLaura, David, *Hebrew and Hellene in Victorian England*, University of Texas Press, 1969.

Dennis, John, *The Grounds of Criticism in Poetry* (1704).

Desmond, Adrian and James Moore, *Darwin*, Warner Books, 1992.

Desmond, Adrian, *The Hot-Blooded Dinosaurs*, Blond & Briggs, 1975.

Digby, Kenelm Henry, *The Broad Stone of Honour: Or The True Sense and Practice of Chivalry*, 5 vols., Bernard Quaritch, 1876–7.

Dyer, John, *Grongar Hill*, 1726.

Eagleton, Terry, *Literary Theory: An Introduction*, Blackwell, 1983.

Eichner, Hans, *Friedrich Schlegel*, Twayne, 1970.

Eliot, T.S., *For Lancelot Andrews: Essays on Style and Order*, Faber and Gwyer, 1928.

'Reflections on Contemporary Poetry,' *The Egoist*, November 1917.

Selected Essays, Faber and Faber, 1932.

To Criticize the Critic, Faber and Faber, 1965.

'Wordsworth and Coleridge', *The Use of Poetry and the Use of Criticism*, Faber and Faber, 1933.

Eusebius, *Eusebii Caesariensis Eclogae Propheticae*, ed. T. Gaisford (Oxford, 1842).

Faber, Geoffrey, *Oxford Apostles*, Faber and Faber, 1933.

Faverty, Frederick E., *Matthew Arnold the Ethnologist*, Northwestern University Press, 1951.

Forster, Michael, "Johann Gottfried von Herder", *The Stanford Encyclopedia of Philosophy* (Winter 2001 edn), ed. Edward N. Zalta, http://plato.stanford.edu/archives/win2001/entries/herder/.

Fortsman, Jack, *A Romantic Triangle: Schleiermacher and Early German Romanticism*, Scholars Press, 1977.

Frothingham, Octavius Brooks, *Transcendentalism in New England*, G.P. Putnam's Sons (1876); reprinted Harper Brothers, 1959.

Frye, Northrop, *T.S. Eliot*, 'Writers and Critics' Series, Oliver & Boyd, 1963.

Fuller, R.C., *Alexander Geddes*, Almond Press, 1983.

Gadamer, Hans Georg, 'Man and Language' (1966), *Philosophical Hermeneutics*, trs. and ed. David E. Linge, University of California Press, 1976.

Geddes, Alexander, *The Holy Bible Faithfully Translated from Corrected Texts of the Originals, with various Readings, Explanatory Notes and Critical Remarks*, Vol. I, 1792; Vol. II, 1797.

Geertz, Clifford, *The Interpretation of Cultures*, Basic Books, 1973.

Gilles, A., 'T.O. Churchill, Translator: a Note', *Modern Language Review*, 42 (1947).

Girouard, Mark, *Life in the English Country House*, Yale University Press, 1978.

Gombrich, E.H., *Art and Illusion: A Study in the Psychology of Pictorial Representation*, revised edn, Princeton University Press, 1961.

Gordon, Lyndall, *Eliot's New Life*, Oxford University Press, 1988.

Gould, Stephen Jay, *The Lying Stones of Marrakech*, Jonathan Cape, 2000.

Grant, Michael (ed.), *T.S. Eliot: The Critical Heritage*, Routledge, 1982.

Greene, Thomas, 'Petrarch and the Humanist Hermeneutic', *In the Light of Troy: Imitation and Discovery in Renaissance Poetry*, Yale University Press, 1982.

Gruen, Erich S., 'Cultural Fictions and Cultural Identity', University of California, *Transactions of the American Philological Association*, Vol.123 (1993), pp. 1–14.

Hackwood, Frederick William, *William Hone: His Life and Times*, T.F. Unwin, 1912.

Hampden, R.D., *A Lecture on Tradition*, Read at the Divinity School, Thursday March 7, 1839, fifth edn, B. Fellows, 1842.

Harding, Anthony J., 'James Marsh as Editor of Coleridge', *Reading Coleridge: Approaches and Applications*, ed. Walter B. Crawford, Cornell University Press, 1979.

Hare, Julius, and Augustus Hare, *Guesses at Truth by Two Brothers,* first edn, 2 vols., 1827.

Harrison, Peter, *'Religion' and the Religions of the English Enlightenment,* Cambridge University Press, 1990.

Hart, Kevin, *Samuel Johnson and the Culture of Property,* Cambridge University Press, 1999.

Hartman, Geoffrey, and Sanford Budick (eds.), *Midrash and Literature,* Yale University Press, 1986.

Hastings, Adrian, *A History of English Christianity 1920–1990,* SCM Press, 1991.

Hawkins, Edward, *The Apostolical Succession,* A Sermon Preached in the Chapel of Lambeth Palace, Sunday, February 27, 1842, B. Fellowes, J.H. Parker, 1842.

    Christianity not the Religion either of the Bible only, or of the Church: A Sermon Preached at Maldon, July 28, 1830, at the Primary Visitation of Charles James Blomfield, Bishop of London, Parker, 1830.

    A Dissertation upon the Use and Importance of Unauthoritative Tradition as an Introduction to the Christian Doctrines; Including the Substance of A Sermon Preached before the University of Oxford, 31 May, 1818, W. Baxter for J. Parker, 1818.

    The Duty of Private Judgement, A Sermon Preached before the University of Oxford, Nov. 11, 1838, J.H. Parker, 1838.

Hegel, G.W.F., *Ästhetik,* ed. Friedrich Bassenge, Weimar, 1965.

Hemans, Felicia, *The Forest Sanctuary and Other Poems,* Murray, 1825.

    The Siege of Valencia: A Dramatic Poem, Murray, 1823.

Herder, Johann Gottfried, 'Essay on the Origin of Language' (1772), *Herder on Social and Political Culture,* trs. and ed. F.M. Barnard, Cambridge University Press, 1969.

    Oriental Dialogues: containing the conversations of Eugenius and Alciphron on the spirit and beauties of the sacred poetry of the Hebrews, printed by A. Strahan for T. Cadell jun. and W. Davies, 1801.

    Reflections on the Philosophy of the History of Mankind (1784–91), ed. Frank E. Manuel, University of Chicago Press, 1968.

    The Spirit of Hebrew Poetry (1783), trs. James Marsh, 2 vols., Edward Smith, 1833; facsimile edn, Aleph, 1971.

    Vom Geist der Ebräischen Poesie, F.A. Berthes, 1890.

Hobsbawm, Eric and Terence Ranger (eds.), *The Invention of Tradition,* Cambridge University Press, 1983.

Hofstetter, Michael J., *The Romantic Idea of a University: England and Germany, 1770–1850,* Palgrave, 2001.

Hone, J. Ann, *For the Cause of Truth: Radicalism in London 1796–1821,* Oxford University Press, 1982.

    'William Hone', *Historical Studies,* October 1974.

Hone, William, *The Political House that Jack Built,* printed by and for William Hone, 1819.

Honey, J.R. de S., *Tom Brown's Universe: The Development of the Victorian Public School,* Milligan, 1977.

Howson, John Saul, *Both in the Old and New Testaments Eternal Life is Offered to Mankind through Jesus Christ Only*, Cambridge University Press, 1842.

Hughes Thomas, *Tom Brown's Schooldays*, 1857.

Humboldt, Wilhelm von, *On Language* (1836), trs. Peter Heath, introduction Hans Aarsleff, Cambridge University Press, 1988.

Hurst, André, *Education and the Knowledge Society*, Springer, 2005.

Isbell, John Claiborne, *The Birth of European Romanticism: Truth and Propaganda in Staël's 'De l'Allemagne' 1810–1813*, Cambridge University Press, 1994.

Jackson-Stops, Gervase, *An English Arcadia 1600–1990: Designs for Gardens and Garden Buildings in the Care of the National Trust*, National Trust, 1992.

Jacob, Giles, *An Historical Account of the Lives and Writings of our most Considerable English Poets*, 1720.

Jarrick, John, (ed.), *Sacred Conjectures: The Context and Legacy of Robert Lowth and Jean Astruc*, T&T Clark, 2007.

Jeffrey, David Lyle, *The People of the Book: Christian Identity and Literary Culture*, Eerdmans, 1996.

Jones, Mark, *Fake? The Art of Deception*, University of California Press, 1990.

Josephus, *Antiquities of the Jews*, trs. William Whiston, 4 vols. (Glasgow, 1818).

Kant, Immanuel, *Critique of Judgement* (1790), trs. J.H. Bernard, Hafner, 1951.

Critique of Pure Reason (1781), trs. James Creed Meredith, Oxford University Press, 1952.

Keble, John, *Lectures on Poetry*, trs. E. K. Francis, 2 vols., Oxford University Press, 1912.

National Apostasy, A Sermon Preached in St Mary's, Oxford, before his Majesty's Judges of Assize, Sunday July 14, 1833, Parker, 1833.

'Primitive Tradition Recognised in Holy Scripture'. A Sermon preached in the Cathedral Church of Winchester, at the Visitation of the Worshipful and Reverend William Dealtry D.D., Chancellor of the Diocese, September 27, 1836.

Kierkegaard, Søren, *The Concept of Irony, with Continual Reference to Socrates* (1841), trs. and ed. Howard V. Hong and Edna H. Hong, Princeton University Press, 1989.

Kingsley, Charles, *The Water Babies: A Fairy Tale for a Land Baby*, ill. Linley Sambourne, Macmillan, 1885.

What then does Dr Newman Mean?, 1864.

Knights, Ben, *Mind and Society: The Idea of the Clerisy in the Nineteenth Century*, Cambridge University Press, 1977.

Knights, L.C., 'Shakespeare's Politics: With Some Reflection on the Nature of Tradition', Annual Shakespeare Lecture of the British Academy, 1957, *Proceedings of the British Academy*, Vol. XLIII. Oxford University Press, 1957.

Knowles, David, *Bare Ruined Choirs: The Dissolution of the English Monasteries*, Cambridge University Press, 1976.

Kuhn, Thomas, *The Structure of Scientific Revolutions* (1962) [*International Encyclopedia of Unified Science*, Vol. II, no. 2], University of Chicago Press, 1962.

Kung, Hans, *Does God Exist?*, trs. Edward Quinn, Collins, 1980.

Labbe, Philippe (ed.), *Traditiones sine scripto authoritatis: de Traditionibus quae observantur in Ecclesia, et quanto sint usui,* in *Tridentini Concilii: Canones et Decreta* (Ex Lovaniensi Anni MDLXVII) 1667.

Lacoue-Labarthe, Philippe and Jean-Luc Nancy, *The Literary Absolute: The Theory of Literature in German Romanticism,* trs. Philip Barnard and Cheryl Lester, State University of New York Press, 1988.

Laslett, Peter, *The World We Have Lost,* Scribner, 1971.

Leach, Edmund, *Genesis as Myth and other Essays,* Cape, 1969.

Lessing, G.E., *On the Education of the Human Race,* 1778.

Lewis, C.S., *Pilgrim's Regress: An Allegorical Apology for Christianity, Reason, and Romanticism* (1943), Eerdmans, 1981.

Surprised by Joy, The Shape of my Early Life, Fontana, 1955.

Liddon, H.P., Preface to Keble's *Difficulties in the Relations between Church and State* (1850), Parker, 1877.

Locke, John, *A Letter Concerning Toleration,* in *Treatise of Civil Government and A Letter Concerning Toleration,* ed. Charles L. Sherman, Appleton-Century-Crofts, 1965.

Lowth, Robert, *Isaiah: A New Translation* (1778), reprinted Routledge/Thoemmes Press, 1995.

Lectures on the Sacred Poetry of the Hebrews, trs. G. Gregory, 2 vols, 1787.

Lucretius, *De Praescriptione Haereticorum,* 7.

MacDonald, George, *England's Antiphon,* Macmillan, 1868.

MacIntyre, Alasdair, 'Epistemological Crises, Dramatic Narrative and the Philosophy of Science', *The Monist,* Vol. 60, no. 4, October 1977, pp. 453–72.

Whose Justice? Which Rationality?, University of Notre Dame Press, 1988.

McCalman, Iain, 'Mad Lord George and Madame La Motte: Riot and Sexuality in the Genesis of Burke's "Reflections on the Revolution in France"', *Journal of British Studies,* July 1996, pp. 343–67.

Mallock, W.H., *The New Republic,* Chatto and Windus, 1877.

Manguel, Alberto, *A History of Reading,* HarperCollins, 1996.

Markus, R.A., *The End of Ancient Christianity,* Cambridge University Press, 1990.

Marshall, Donald G., *The Force of Tradition: Response and Resistance in Literature, Religion, and Cultural Studies,* Rowman and Littlefield, 2005.

Maurice, F.D., *The Kingdom of Christ,* fourth edn, Macmillan, 1891.

Mead, Rebecca, *One Perfect Day: The Selling of the American Wedding,* Penguin, 2007.

Mee, Jon, *Dangerous Enthusiasms: William Blake and the Culture of Radicalism in the 1790s,* Clarendon Press, 1992.

Mellor, Anne, and Richard Matlak, *British Literature, 1780–1830,* Harcourt Brace, 1996.

Menze, Ernest A., 'The Reception and Influence of Herder's *On the Spirit of Hebrew Poetry* in North America: Preliminary Observations', in Daniel

Weidner (ed.), *Urpoesie und Morgenland. J.G. Herders 'Vom Geist der Ebräischen Poesie'*, Kadmos Verlag, 2008.

Mill, John Stuart, *Bentham and Coleridge*, ed. F.R. Leavis, Chatto, 1950.

Mills, Kevin, *Approaching Apocalypse: Unveiling Revelation in Victorian Writing*, Bucknell University Press, 2007.

Milton, John, 'Of Reformation and Church Discipline', *Milton's Prose*, ed. Malcolm W. Wallace, Oxford University Press, 1959.

Moffatt, James, *The Thrill of Tradition*, Macmillan, 1944.

Momigliano, A.D., *Alien Wisdom: The Limits of Hellenization*, Cambridge University Press, 1975.

Montanari, Massimo, *Food is Culture*, trs. Albert Sonnenfeld, Columbia University Press, 2004.

Montluzin, E. L. de, *The Anti-Jacobins, 1798–1800*, St Martin's Press, 1988.

Moore, Hannah, *Village Politics. Addressed to all the Mechanics, Journeymen, and Day Labourers, in Great Britain*, by Will Chip, a country carpenter, 1793.

Morgan, Bayard Qunicy, *A Critical Bibliography of German Literature in Translation 1481–1927*, second revised edn, Scarecrow Press, 1965.

Mozley, Thomas, *Reminiscences, Chiefly of Oriel College and the Oxford Movement*, 3 vols., Longman, 1882.

Mueller-Vollmer, Kurt (ed.), *The Hermeneutics Reader*, Blackwell, 1986.

Newman, Francis William, *Contributions Chiefly to the Early History of the Late Cardinal Newman, with Comments by his Brother, F.W. Newman*, Kegan Paul, Trench, Trübner & co., 1891.

Newman, John Henry, *A Letter Addressed to his Grace The Duke of Norfolk on Occasion of Mr. Gladstone's Recent Expostulation*, B.M. Pickering, 1875.

An Essay in Aid of A Grammar of Assent, ed. I.T. Ker, Oxford: Clarendon, 1985.

Apologia pro Vita Sua, ed. M.J. Svalgic, Oxford: Oxford University Press, 1967.

Apologia pro Vita Sua ed. C.F. Harrold, Longmans, Green, 1947.

'Apostolical Tradition', *Essays Critical and Historical*, ninth edn, 1890.

Essay on the Development of Christian Doctrine (1845), reprinted sixth edn, with Foreword by Ian Ker, University of Notre Dame Press, 1989.

'Keble', *Essays, Critical and Historical*, ninth edn, 2 vols., Longman, 1890.

Lectures on the Prophetical Office of the Church, Viewed Relatively to Romanism and Popular Protestantism, J.G. & F. Rivington, 1837.

Lectures on Certain Difficulties felt by Anglicans in Submitting to the Catholic Church, second edn, 1850.

Newsome, David, *The Parting of Friends*, John Murray, 1966.

Niebuhr, Georg Barthold, *History of Rome* (1827), trs. Julius Hare and Connop Thirlwall, Taylor, Walton and Maberly, 1851.

Norton, David, *History of the Bible as Literature*, 2 vols., Cambridge University Press, 1993.

Novalis (Friedrich von Hardenberg), 'Christendom or Europe', *Novalis: Philosophical Writings*, trs. and ed. Margaret Stoljar, State University of New York Press, 1997.

Henry von Ofterdingen, trs. Palmer Hilty, Ungar, 1964.

'Miscellaneous Writings' (1797), *German Aesthetic and Literary Criticism: The Romantic Ironists and Goethe*, ed. Kathleen Wheeler, Cambridge University Press, 1984.

O'Brien, Conor Cruise, Introduction to the Penguin edition of Burke's, *Reflections on the Revolution in France*, Pelican Books, 1968.

O'Brien, William Arctander, *Novalis: Signs of Revolution*, Duke University Press, 1995.

O'Donnell, James, *Cassiodorus*, University of California Press, 1979; www.georgertown.edu/faculty/jod/texts/cassbook/toc.html.

Ong, Walter J., *Orality and Literacy: The Technologising of the Word*, Routledge, 1992.

Paine, Thomas, *The Age of Reason* [1793–1795], *The Theological Works of Tom Paine*, 1827.

    Rights of Man, Writings of Thomas Paine, ed. Moncure Daniel Conway, 4 vols., A.M.S. Press, 1967.

Palmer, R.R., *The World of the French Revolution*, Allen and Unwin, 1971.

Parsons, Talcott, *The Structure of Social Action*, Free Press, 1949, 2nd edn, 1961.

Pattison, Mark, 'F.A. Wolf' in *Essays*, 2 vols., ed. Henry Nettleship, Oxford University Press, 1889.

Peacock, Thomas Love, *The Misfortunes of Elphin*, *The Novels of Thomas Love Peacock*, ed. David Garnett, Hart-Davis, 1948.

Pereiro, James, *'Ethos' and the Oxford Movement: At the Heart of Tractarianism*, Oxford University Press, 2008.

    'Tractarians and National Education (1838–1843)', *Victorian Churches and Churchmen*, ed. Sheridan Gilley, Boydell and Brewer, 2005.

Perkins, David, *Is Literary History Possible?*, Johns Hopkins University Press, 1992.

Perry, Seamus, 'T.S. Eliot's Coleridge', *Coleridge's Afterlives*, ed. James Vigus and Jane Wright, Palgrave, 2008.

Pfefferkorn, Kirstin, *Novalis: A Romantic's Theory of Language and Poetry*, Yale University Press, 1988.

Phillpots, Henry (Bishop of Exeter), *Charge to the Clergy of the Diocese of Exeter*, for August, September, and October, 1839, John Murray, 1839.

Plato, *Timaeus*, 2nd edn, trs. Benjamin Jowett, Clarendon Press, 1875.

Porter, H.C., 'The Nose of Wax: Scripture and the Spirit from Erasmus to Milton', *Transactions of the Royal Historical Society*, fifth series, Vol. 14, 1964.

Price, Richard, *A Discourse on the Love of our Country*, 1789.

Prickett, Stephen, 'Coleridge and the idea of the Clerisy', *Reading Coleridge: Approaches and Appreciations*, ed. Walter B. Crawford, Cornell University Press, 1979.

    Coleridge and Wordsworth: The Poetry of Growth, Cambridge University Press, 1970.

'Coleridge, Schlegel and Schleiermacher: England, Germany (and Australia) in 1798', *1798: The Year of the Lyrical Ballads*, ed. Richard Cronin, Macmillan, 1998.

England and the French Revolution, Macmillan, 1989.

Narrative, Religion and Science: Fundamentalism versus Irony, 1700–1999, Cambridge University Press, 2002.

Origins of Narrative: The Romantic Appropriation of the Bible, Cambridge University Press, 1996.

Reading the Text: Biblical Criticism and Literary Theory, Blackwell, 1991.

Romanticism and Religion: The Tradition of Coleridge and Wordsworth in the Victorian Church, Cambridge University Press, 1976.

Words and the Word: Language, Poetics and Biblical Interpretation, Cambridge University Press, 1986.

Prickett, Stephen, and Robert Carroll, *Introduction to World's Classics Bible*, Oxford University Press, 1997.

Pugin, Augustus Welby Northmore, *Contrasts* (1836), Leicester: Leicester University Press, 1969.

Reeves, Marjorie and Warwick Gould, *Joachim of Fiore and the Myth of the Eternal Evangel in the Nineteenth Century*, Clarendon Press, 1987.

'Report of H.M. Commissioners appointed to enquire into the State, Discipline, Studies, and Revenues of the Universities and Colleges of Oxford', *Parliamentary Papers* XXII [1852].

Rorty, Richard, *Contingency, Irony and Solidarity*, Cambridge University Press, 1989.

Rossetti, Christina, *The Face of the Deep* (1892), sixth edn, S.P.C.K, 1911.

Rudwick, Martin J.S., *The Meaning of Fossils: Episodes in the History of Paleontology*, University of Chicago Press, 1976.

Russell, Bertrand, 'An Outline of Intellectual Rubbish', *Unpopular Essays*, Allen & Unwin, 1950.

Sahlins, Marshall, *How 'Natives' Think: About Captain Cook, For Example*, University of Chicago Press, 1995.

Schelling, F.W.J. von, *On University Studies*, trs. E.S. Morgan, Ohio University Press, 1966.

Schiller, F.C., *On the Aesthetic Education of Man*, 1794.

Schlegel, August Wilhelm, *A Course of Lectures on Dramatic Art and Literature*, trs. John Black (1815), revised by J.W. Morrison, Bohn, 1846.

Schlegel, Friedrich, 'On Goethe's Meister' (1798), *German Aesthetic and Literary Criticism*, ed. Kathleen Wheeler, Cambridge University Press, 1984.

Philosophical Fragments, trs. Peter Firchow, University of Minnesota Press, 1991.

Schleiermacher, Friedrich, *On Religion: Speeches to its Cultured Despisers* (1799), trs. Richard Crouter, Cambridge University Press, 1998.

Schoenbaum, Samuel, *Shakespeare's Lives*, Oxford University Press, 1993.

Shelley, Percy Bysshe, *A Defence of Poetry* (1840), in *English Romantic Poetry and Prose*, ed. Russell Noyes, Oxford University Press, 1956.

Shils, Edward, *Tradition*, University of Chicago Press, 1981.

Shine, Hill, 'Carlyle's Early Writings and Herder's *Ideen*: The Concept of History', *Booker Memorial Studies*, ed. Hill Shine, University of North Carolina Press, 1950.

Siskin, Clifford, *The Historicity of Romantic Discourse*, Oxford University Press, 1988.

Sparrow, John, *Mark Pattison and the Idea of a University*, Cambridge University Press, 1967.

Strathman, Christopher, 'Introduction to American Romanticism', *A Reader in European Romanticism*, ed. Stephen Prickett and Simon Haines (forthcoming).

 Romantic Poetry and the Fragmentary Imperative: Schlegel, Byron, Joyce and Blanchot, State University of New York Press, 2006.

Switzer, Richard, *Chateaubriand*, Twayne, 1971.

Taylor, Charles, *Sources of the Self: The Making of the Modern Identity*, Cambridge University Press, 1989.

Tennant, Bob, 'John Tillotson and the Voice of Anglicanism', *Religion in the Age of Reason: A Transatlantic Study of the Long Eighteenth Century*, ed. Kathryn Duncan, AMS Press, 2007.

Trapp, Joseph, *Lectures on Poetry*, trs. William Bowyes, 1742.

Tyrell, George, *Through Scylla and Charybdis*, Longman, 1907.

Vanden Bossche, Chris R., *Carlyle and the Search for Authority*, Ohio State University Press, 1991.

Vico, Giambattista, *The New Science* (1744), trs. Thomas Goddard Bergin and Max Harrold Frisch, Cornell University Press, 1968.

Vigus, James, and Jane Wright (eds.), *Coleridge's Afterlives*, Palgrave, 2008.

Volney, C.F.C. de, *The Ruins: or a Survey of the Revolutions of Empires*, Peter Eckler, 1890.

Wadsworth, Michael, 'Making and Interpreting Scripture', *Ways of Reading the Bible*, ed. Michael Wadsworth, Harvester Press, 1981.

Walsh, P.G., 'Epilogue' to G.J. Kenney (ed.), *The Cambridge History of Classical Literature*, Vol. II, part 5: *The Later Principate*, Cambridge University Press, 1982.

Warburton, William, *The Divine Legation of Moses Demonstrated*, 4 vols. reprinted from the 4th edn, 1765, Garland, 1978.

Watson, Richard, *An Apology for the Bible in a Series of Letters Addressed to Thomas Paine by R. Watson, D.D., F.R.S.*, Hilliard and Brown, 1828.

Watson, William, *A sparing discoverie of our English Jesuits*, 1601.

Watts, Isaac, 'Preface' to *Horae Lyricae*, 1709.

Weidner, Daniel, 'Secularization, Scripture, and the Theory of Reading: J.G. Herder and the Old Testament', *New German Critique: An Interdisciplinary Journal of German Studies*, No. 94, Winter 2005.

 (ed.), *Urpoesie und Morgenland: J.G. Herders 'Vom Geist der Ebräischen Poesie'*, Kadmos Verlag, 2008.

Wellek, René, 'Carlyle and the Philosophy of History', *Confrontations: Studies in the Intellectual Relations Between Germany, England, and the United States During the Nineteenth Century*, Princeton University Press, 1965.

Wesley, John, *Letter to Conyers Middleton occasioned by his late 'Free Enquiry'*, 1748–9.

Whatmore, Richard and Brian Young (eds.), *Intellectual History*, Palgrave, 2006.

Wheeler, Michael, *The Old Enemies: Catholic and Protestant in Nineteenth-Century English Culture*, Cambridge University Press, 2006.

Williams, Rowan, *Why Study the Past? The Quest for the Historical Church*, Eerdmans, 2005.

Wordsworth William, *Prose Works*, ed. W.J.B. Owen and J.W. Smyser, 2 vols., Clarendon Press, 1974.

Wright, T.R., *The Religion of Humanity: The Impact of Comtean Positivism on Victorian Britain*, Cambridge University Press, 1986.

Yeats, W.B., 'The Trembling of the Veil,' in *Autobiographies*, Macmillan, 1927.

Young, G.M., *Victorian Essays*, Oxford University Press, 1962.

Index